High-Speed Computation

NATO ASI Series

Advanced Science Institutes Series

A series presenting the results of activities sponsored by the NATO Science Committee, which aims at the dissemination of advanced scientific and technological knowledge, with a view to strengthening links between scientific communities.

The Series is published by an international board of publishers in conjunction with the NATO Scientific Affairs Division

A Life Sciences	Plenum Publishing Corporation
B Physics	London and New York
C Mathematical and Physical Sciences	D. Reidel Publishing Company Dordrecht, Boston and Lancaster
D Behavioural and Social Sciences **E Applied Sciences**	Martinus Nijhoff Publishers Boston, The Hague, Dordrecht and Lancaster
F Computer and Systems Sciences **G Ecological Sciences**	Springer-Verlag Berlin Heidelberg New York Tokyo

High-Speed Computation

Edited by

Janusz S. Kowalik

Boeing Computer Services, Advanced Technology Applications Division,
Artificial Intelligence Center, P.O. Box 24346, Seattle, WA 98124, USA

Springer-Verlag Berlin Heidelberg New York Tokyo 1984
Published in cooperation with NATO Scientific Affairs Division

Proceedings of the NATO Advanced Research Workshop on High-Speed Computation held at Jülich, Federal Republic of Germany, June 20–22, 1983

ISBN 3-540-12885-9 Springer-Verlag Berlin Heidelberg New York Tokyo
ISBN 0-387-12885-9 Springer-Verlag New York Heidelberg Berlin Tokyo

Library of Congress Cataloging Publication Data.
Main entry under title: High-speed computation. (NATO ASI series. Series F, Computer and systems sciences ; vol. 7)
„Proceedings of the NATO Advanced Research Workshop on High-Speed Computation, held at Jülich, Federal Republic of Germany, June 20–22, 1983"-- T.p. verso. „Published in cooperation with NATO Scientific Affairs Division." 1. Parallel processing (Electronic computers)--Congresses. 2. Electronic digital computers--Congresses. 3. Multiprocessors--Congresses. I. Kowalik, Janusz S. II. North American Treaty Organization. Scientific Affairs Division. III. NATO Advanced Research Workshop on High-Speed Computation (1983 : Jülich, Germany) IV. Series: NATO ASI Series. Series F, Computer and systems sciences ; no. 7. QA76.6.H534 1984 001.64 84–1349
ISBN 0-387-12885-9 (U.S.)

© Springer-Verlag Berlin Heidelberg 1984
Printed in Germany

Printing: Beltz Offsetdruck, Hemsbach; Bookbinding: J. Schäffer OHG, Grünstadt
2145/3140-543210

Preface

This volume contains twenty-seven papers presented at the NATO sponsored Advanced Research Workshop on "High-Speed Computation," held in Julich, Federal Republic of Germany, from June 20 to June 22, 1983. The purpose of the Workshop was to bring together practitioners and theoreticians of parallel computation to discuss the current situation and potential of applied parallel computing. We define parallel computation to include algorithms, software and hardware for parallel or pipeline machines with central control, as well as, multiprocessors with distributed control.

Parallel computation plays important roles in many areas of science and engineering but is most often required in the execution of large-scale simulation and design problems. High-speed processors enable the scientist or the engineer to treat complexity in models that is not otherwise tractable, and study phenomena that cannot be studied under laboratory conditions. Hence the greatest value of high-speed computers lies in their ability to handle larger sets of computationally tractable problems and gain new insights or understanding.

Evidence of the interest in the area of high-speed computation abounds. For example, some 40 companies now manufacture some kind of array processor to aid in numerical computation. Floating Point Systems alone has sold several thousand such systems to date. The workshop emphasized the larger computers, of course, but there are many of these as well. Within the past few years, extensive work on such large machines has been reported by Burroughs, Control Data, Cray Research, Denelcor, Fujitsu, Hitachi, IBM, ICL, Lawrence Livermore National Laboratory, and Univac. In fact, some of these companies have had several supercomputers under development or study. There are also national projects under way in France and Japan to produce high-speed computers. At this moment, Control Data and Cray Research alone probably have sold or taken orders for over 50 such systems, at an average cost of some $10 million each.

Evidence that there are practical difficulties in this area is also easy to obtain. While the Cray-1 and Cyber 205 both are capable of delivering over 100 megaflops on certain computations, on most Fortran compiled jobs they are more likely to deliver about 10 to 20 megaflops. The reasons for this inefficiency are manifold, including poor hardware designs, poor compiler designs, poor choices of algorithms, or the nonexistence of good parallel algorithms for some problems.

While the current term "high-speed computation" generally refers to a computation performed by a large-scale, number crunching processor, this type of processor is only one important tool in the future of computing. Several significant efforts have been initiated to develop computer systems that would support artificial intelligence applications. One of these projects is the Japanese national project to develop knowledge information processing systems which include inference machines, knowledge base machines and intelligent man-machine interface machines. This project is briefly described in paper 1.5 by Professor Tohru Moto-oka.

All participants are indebted to NATO and the U.S. Army for the generous financial support that made the Advanced Workshop possible. We wish to express our thanks to Kernforschungsanlage for hosting the Workshop and their willing assistance and attention during and after the meeting.

Individuals who deserve special thanks include those who served with me on the Organizing Committee, namely: Billy L. Buzbee, Wolfgang Handler, Roger W. Hockney, Friedel Hossfeld, David J. Kuck, George A. Michael and Dennis Parkinson. Our thanks are also due to the following members of the Local Organizing Committee: H. Beyer, J.-Fr. Hake, B. Krahl-Urban, W. Oed and P. Weidner, and to the meeting secretary, Helga Bongartz.

My secretary, Judy Frigon, has been extremely helpful in all phases of the Workshop preparations and activities.

Boeing Computer Services,   Janusz S. Kowalik
Bellevue,
November, 1983

Contents

Part 2. Performance and Capabilities
of Computer Systems

Part 3. Algorithms and Applications

OPENING ADDRESS

Opening Address
R. Theenhaus, Board of Directors
Kernforschungsanlage Jülich GmbH

Ladies and gentlemen, distinguished guests,

It is a special pleasure and honour for me to welcome you in the name of the Jülich
Nuclear Research Centre's Board of Directors to the Advanced Research Workshop on
High-Speed Computation, which is being jointly organized by the NATO Scientific
Affairs Division and the Jülich Nuclear Research Centre. I would like to extend a
warm welcome to those guests who have come here to us in Jülich from other parts of
Europe and also from overseas. I would like to particularly welcome Dr. Stanislav Ulam,
who will be our banquet speaker, and I am especially gratified that Prof. Kenneth
Wilson, winner of the 1982 Nobel Prize for Physics, can be with us and will present
a keynote lecture tomorrow.

First of all, ladies und gentlemen, I would like to say a few words about the KFA:
The KFA was established about 25 years ago and today is supported and financed by
the Federal Goverment and the Federal State of North Rhine-Westphalia. It has over
4,000 employees and a wide-ranging research programme. About half its work is to be
found in the field of basic research, the other half being application-oriented research and development, particularly in the energy sector. In high-temperature energy
technology, we are especially concerned with questions of the second grid, high temperature reactor plant designs and developments, the fuel cycle, long distance energy
transport, general reactor and waste disposal technology and, last but not least, with
non-nuclear energy research. A centre such as the KFA must of course look into the
distant future and to this end in the field of future fossil fuels we are working on
the exploration and exploitation of fossil fuels, the environmental effects of fossil
fuels and bioconversion. Nuclear fusion, which takes up about 10 % of our research
activities, is still in the field of basic research and fundamental development, however, on the other hand also involves large technical experiments. The central feature
of this work is a medium-sized TOKAMAK experiment, TEXTOR, with which we are investigating plasma-wall interaction.

The basic research carried out here at Jülich ranges from research and technology for
health and the environment, as well as substance characteristics and materials research,
and basic nuclear research to the spallation neutron source. These main fields in basic
research thus subsume environmental research, medical research and technology, neuro-
biological research, solid state physics, surface and vacuum research, nuclear physics,
radio and nuclear chemistry. There is really no need for me to emphasize here that

NATO ASI Series, Vol. F7
High-Speed Computation. Edited by J. S. Kowalik
© Springer-Verlag Berlin Heidelberg 1984

interdisciplinary research plays a significant role.

Let me also mention at this point that the idea has been raised in our country of constructing a large spallation neutron source which should then be sited here at Jülich. Preliminary work has already been started here at Jülich for the construction of this novel neutron source which will then stimulate many fields, both in basic research as well as in applied research and development.

Right from the very beginning, computers have played an important role in the KFA. The KFA already installed the IBM 1401 for batch operation about 20 years ago. There were two IBM machines here in 1971, a 370 for batch operation and a 360 for time sharing. Three large IBM machines have been in operation here since 1980. The present status is that we have installed two IBM 3033 machines and an IBM 3081, an AP 190 array processor and about 200 mini and supermini computers for experiments and process control, which are partly linked to each other in a local network. I am not disclosing any secrets when I tell you that a Cray X-MP is on the way and that it will be operative at the end of this year. This will be the first Cray X-MP installation in Europe.

The Federal Republic of Germany is undoubtedly one of the great industrialized countries with a long tradition and history in science, technology and engineering. However, since our country is short of natural resources an industry with prospects for the future of course depends on scientific and technical know-how, on innovation and progress. It is all the more surprising that in comparison with the USA and even Japan we are behind in computer technology, computer design and manufacturing, which can no longer be ignored. A clear sign that we have recognized this deficiency and are attempting to compensate it, at least in the field of supercomputing, is perhaps the fact that in 1983 seven supercomputers will have been installed in the Federal Republic of Germany. By the end of 1983 three machines will be in research centres (1 Cray X-MP, 2 Cray-1), 3 in universities (Bochum, Karlsruhe, Stuttgart), namely two Cyber 205 and one CRAY-1, and also in the industrial sector 1 - 2 machines will also probably be installed this year.

Computational science, which has been developing in the past decade, can really only now become a genuine science by means of the new supercomputers. I certainly do not need to emphasize the significance of this new science here, but you will perhaps permit me to mention a few subject headings representative of the range of application: climate, weather, atmosphere, flow mechanics, turbulence, plasma physics, statistical mechanics, solid state research, lattice gauge theory, molecular and atomic physics, nuclear engineering, energy technology, large-scale technical systems, biochemistry, ecosystems, global models, social systems, economics, microelectronic circuit technology (design, test, performance).

Many people still do not realize that this significance will not only be in the field of basic research and science but that computational science will also open up a broad application mix in the industrial sector.

The analysis and treatment of complex systems, which will greatly increase in importance, requires high performance computer systems and high speed computation.

We are therefore especially gratified that this NATO Advanced Workshop on High-Speed Computation is taking place here at Jülich with a very impressive workshop programme. System designers from manufacturers, universities and research centres on the one hand, and computer users, such as mathematicians, physicists, engineers and others, on the other hand will engage in an intensive exchange of information for three days in order to evaluate recent progress in the field, to define the state of the art as well as limitations to progress and to extrapolate future developments and needs.

I would just like to mention that most important research centres are represented, as well as the universities, all supercomputer companies are present, and Japan is presenting the fifth generation computer project. An overwhelmingly high concentration of distinguished experts in the field of supercomputers and high-speed computation are gathered together here, as far as I am informed, for the first time at an event of this kind, at least in Europe.

The hardware for the further development of general purpose large-scale computers in the next few years has undoubtedly not yet been fully developed, there is still progress in it. Nevertheless, I am convinced that real evolution - not to say revolution - will take place in the field of supercomputers by means of further developing the computer structures, exploiting VLSI technology and the intelligent development of corresponding algorithms and, generally speaking, by developing intelligent handling techniques with these supercomputers. For this reason close cooperation between the system designers (hardware and software), the manufacturers and users will become even more important. Only in this way can the challenge offered by this new scientific discipline can be taken up with any hope of success.

The present programme reflects this necessity quite excellently and takes it into consideration. I would therefore like to most sincerely thank the Organizing Committee, and especially the chairmann of the workshop, Prof. Janusz Kowalik from Washington State University, who had to bear the heavy burden of preparing this workshop's comprehensive programme.

I hope that the workshop takes an interesting, stimulating and, naturally, successful course. I would like to wish you, ladies and gentlemen, a pleasant stay at the Jülich

Research Centre and in the imperial city of Aachen.

The door to a new scientific world has been flung open, let us enter into it together. Great opportunities, challenges and surprises are ahead of us.

Thank you very much, ladies und gentlemen, I declare the workshop open.

KEYNOTE ADDRESS

Science, Industry and the New Japanese Challenge

Kenneth G. Wilson

Newman Laboratory of Nuclear Studies
Cornell University, Ithaca, NY 14853

Abstract

The Japanese super-speed computer project, recently begun, has generated pressure for a response in the United States and other countries. The background for the Japanese project is the worldwide effort to computerize four hundred years of science, in support of industrial applications of science. In the U.S. a number of barriers are slowing progress of the computerization process. The barriers include software problems, lack of U.S. university participation in the computerization effort, poor matching of resources to needs, etc. The computer revolution is also part of the background for the Japanese project, and problems caused by the computer revolution, such as inadequate education, also require attention. Specific recommendations to overcome these barriers are proposed. Computer-assisted instruction meeting the standards set by Professor Arnold Arons combined with teacher retraining would help science education. A national computer communications network for basic and applied research would greatly improve technology transfer within the United States for an absurdly low cost; Britain already is developing such a network. The diverse groups engaged in the computerization of science need a sense of community which a national network would provide. They also need more decision-making power, and more effective sharing of resources. The U.S. government should establish the network and provide seed money to help private industry, universities and government laboratories collectively implement the other recommendations.

NATO ASI Series, Vol. F7
High-Speed Computation. Edited by J. S. Kowalik
© Springer-Verlag Berlin Heidelberg 1984

I. Introduction and Objectives

The pace of world technological development is presently mainly
dictated by Japan; other nations must keep up or risk the loss of major
markets. The past successes of Japan in consumer electronics, automobiles, and computer components has focused attention on Japan's next
targets. Recently they have started two new national projects, both
concerned with computers: the Super-speed Computer project[1] and the 5th
Generation Computer project.[2] These projects have received considerable
publicity in the press[3] and have generated strong pressures for a
response in the U.S. and other nations.

The increasing availability of computers is causing a revolution in
human life comparable to the introduction of the wheel or the industrial
revolution. Some of the changes being brought about by the computer are
extraordinarily complex. The popular descriptions of the new Japanese
challenges[3] have largely missed the point, because the challenges must
be understood in the context of the changes that the computer revolution
is bringing about. The press reports did not provide this background.
No intelligent response can be formulated without an understanding of
the likely implications of the Japanese projects. Furthermore, at least
in the U.S., there are severe shortages of capital, manpower, and
management attention, all of which are required to deal with the problem.
Any response needs to be very carefully thought out to achieve maximum
impact at modest cost. (The shortage of management attention is simply
the fact that high level managers of major bureaucracies, including the
U.S. government, are faced with far more decisions than they can possibly
handle.)

For the past twenty years or so an effort has been underway to computerize four hundred years of world-wide scientific research. The purpose of the computerization effort is to make scientific knowledge and wisdom available for industrial applications, including the search for and recovery of natural resources (such as oil), product design (automobiles, aircraft, computers, food products, and many others), manufacturing process design and control, etc. An example where the computerization process is very highly developed is structural analysis. Structural analysis is used to determine whether product designs have adequate strength to stand up in their intended use. Computer programs for structural analysis[4] are in use throughout industry in the design of automobiles, aircraft, bridges, etc. These computer programs are based on Newton's laws of mechanical motion and many years of scientific research and engineering development following from Newton's Laws.

The Japanese Super-Speed Computing project has as its goal the design of computers for scientific applications which would be about one hundred times more powerful than today's most powerful supercomputers, today's supercomputers being the Cray-1 and Cray X-MP from Cray Research Inc., the Control Data Corporation CDC 205, the Denelcor HEP[5], and (in some respects) the Floating Point Systems FPS-164.[6] There are a number of more special-purpose systems[7]. The Japanese effort is important for the computerization of science because programs based on scientific knowledge (such as the structural analysis programs) can press the limits of today's supercomputers. There are many scientific applications which are not even feasible on today's computers but might become so if the Japanese project is successful.[8]

Thus the background for the Japanese Super-Speed computing project

that needs to be understood is the computerization of science —
Where does it stand today? Where is it going in the future? How
important is it? etc.

The computerization of science is in total chaos. There are many
diverse groups that contribute to the computerization process: scientists
and engineers in many academic disciplines, who do not speak to each
other; industrial scientists and engineers in many different industrial
groupings, their work often veiled by industrial secrecy; national
laboratories carrying out their own missions, some of which are classified
for military reasons. The U.S. computer manufacturers who sell supercomputers for scientific applications have little understanding of the
scientific market they serve; they even violate the basic principle of
computer marketing which is to provide software compatible systems with
a range of capabilities and price tags. It is virtually hopeless to
give an overview of the present state of the computerization of science
today because the relevant information is scattered among these diverse
groups and much of it is inaccessible.

I have been studying the present condition of the computerization
and its future, for about three years. Despite the chaos, I believe one
can give an overview of the computerization process itself. In this
paper I will try to provide this overview. Special emphasis will be
given to barriers which are slowing progress and recommendations for
overcoming these barriers. The importance of overcoming them is twofold.
Firstly, computerized scientific knowledge is a critically needed
resource to assist industrial development, in the U.S. and elsewhere.
Barriers which slow the computerization of science also slow economic
recovery of the U.S. and the global economies. Secondly, the barriers I

will describe double as barriers to the sales of supercomputers. As a result the U.S. computer industry unanimously characterizes the super-computer market as small and with high risk. As I will discuss, removing the barriers should create an enormous supercomputer market. This market will require that supercomputers with the power the Japanese plan be built by the thousands by mass-production techniques. I see little evidence that the U.S. computer industry is prepared to serve this mass market.

The discussion in this paper will focus on U.S. problems, needs, and opportunities. I restrict the discussion to the U.S. because most of my experience and expertise applies only to the U.S. The bulk of the supercomputer industry today is in the U.S., in addition a number of the barriers I will describe take different forms in different countries due to cultural differences between nations, different legal and economic systems, etc. I have participated in discussions about supercomputers in Britain, Sweden, and France, and one of my earlier papers on the subject is published in Recherche.[9] I expect my present analysis will be helpful for other countries besides the U.S., probably more so than if I tried to write from a global rather than a U.S. perspective, once readers have isolated the parts of this paper that apply to their home countries.

In the past three years I have visited many corporations including Exxon, Schlumberger-Doll Research, Chevron, Lockheed, Dupont, IBM, Floating Point Systems, Corning Glass Works, etc. and have met with representatives of many other firms. I have attended or addressed many conferences including several organized by the Los Alamos and Livermore Laboratories. I have addressed a meeting of the Business-Higher Education

Forum. I have served on two government panels concerned with computing issues, most notably the Lax Panel assembled by the National Science Foundation and the Department of Defense, which reported back (among other things) that the U.S. lead in supercomputers would be lost to Japan if nothing was done.[10] Two years earlier I participated in the "Press Panel" reporting to the National Science Foundation about computational physics. The Press panel report is still eminently worth reading.[11] I have talked with many government officials and testified before Congress.[12] I have actively studied computer science and talked with many computer scientists, as well as scientists from many areas.

In Section II some general characteristics of the computing scene will be described, and three general problems discussed. These problems are: science training, the need for a national computer communications network serving basic and applied research and the role of universities in the computer market.

In Section III, I discuss several major barriers slowing progress of this computerization: software problems, lack of university participation, the enormous resources needed to get computerization started in a new scientific area, and the lack of trained manpower.

In Section IV the relevant projects in Japan are reviewed briefly.

In Section V, I make recommendations for overcoming these barriers — the basic proposal is to build a single community from the diverse groups in industry, university, and government that are concerned with the computerization of science, and give this community more freedom to allocate the resources that are potentially available to it.

Section VI provides recommendations and comments on possible U.S.

government actions.

Section VII is an afterword, on battling for the changes recommended in this paper.

II.   The Computer Revolution: General Observations
and Recommendations

A.   General Observations

In this part I will discuss some general issues related to the computer revolution, and then consider three areas that provide part of the background for questions of technological change. The three areas are science training, computer networks, and the role of universities in the computing market.

One characteristic of the computer revolution is that while computers are making extraordinary advances possible, achievement of these advances is very difficult. Workers in the computing field have become skeptical of any claims about what the computer can accomplish that has not already been demonstrated. "It can't be done" is a phrase I hear repeatedly in conversations with the computer-wise. However, because of the rapid pace overall of the computer revolution, advances that "can't be done" according to almost everybody have been done in a considerable number of cases, but only by one or two people. News of these developments has not gotten out yet. In formulating a response to the Japanese challenge, enormous sums of money can be saved simply by identifying those few people who have already made major breakthroughs, verifying that their claimed advances have actually taken place, and then following up their work. An example will be cited shortly.

Another characteristic of the computer revolution is that computer planning requires continuing major adjustments to market advances. Over about a three-year time period the computer jargon (such as the term "supercomputer") is itself totally redefined. People with responsibility for this planning have to spend major amounts of time keeping up with market developments through daily reading of the trade press and informal information exchanges with other knowledgeable persons. Effective computer planning, in my observation, has to be carried out by full time computing personnel in close cooperation with actual users of the computers in question, with an absolute minimum of interference from high levels of management. This is possible only when there is agreement at all levels on a long-term context and general budgetary guidelines within which detailed planning shifts can be made without higher level approvals and without the costly delays required to seek such approvals. This in turn requires careful budget projections, including the recog- nition that budgets that have increased year by year in the past will continue to grow; the alternative is continual budget-busting pressures which consume enormous amounts of everybodies' time. Proper computer planning is a crucial part of an effective response to Japan, as I will discuss later.

A third characteristic of the computer revolution is that computers greatly enhance the economic value of trained, intelligent manpower and womanpower. People who have been trained to understand the complex aspects of a particular discipline or economic activity can greatly increase their ability to manage this complexity, by using computers. This is true whether the activity in question is in science, engineering, education, communications, product repair, human management, or whatever. This characteristic has upgraded job training requirements at all levels and has created major pressures on world educational systems to be more effective.

B.   Science Training and Computer Assisted Instruction

The talent and creativity of the U.S. population is the most important asset the U.S. has. If this asset is wasted due to inadequate education, nothing else the U.S. does matters very much. Much has been said about this issue, which I do not need to repeat.   However, there is something that needs to be said about the teaching of science. Most scientists and teachers would agree that teaching students to think scientifically has to be done by trained teachers; computers cannot help. This is a perfect example of a generally held belief which is false.

Professor Arnold Arons, recently retired from the University of Washington at Seattle, has a lifetime of experience in teaching basic science, including students who would flunk any standard college courses. He and his colleague, Lillian McDermott, have found that for these students it becomes necessary to talk to them on a one-on-one basis, asking questions which bring forth their misconceptions about basic technical terms such as velocity or acceleration, and then confronting the students with daily experiences that force the students to see for themselves the fuzziness in their thinking. This must be followed by lengthy rehearsing of the student in usage of the terms in different contexts.[13] That these "Socratic Dialogues" are needed should come as no surprise. However, there is no way the U.S. educational system can afford to supply a one-to-one teacher to student ratio in order to reach students by this method. Because of this, Professor Arons has been working with Professor Alfred Bork of the University of California at Irvine, building computerized versions of his Socratic Dialogues.[14]

Professor Arons' computerized dialogues operate on inexpensive computers which means they could be made available in every classroom in the country. The procedure is that a question appears on the computer screen; the student types in an answer, and the computer proceeds to ask another question based on the student's reply.

These dialogues are extremely difficult to write because every wrong answer the student might come up with must be anticipated and a subsequent dialogue constructed for the answer. As a result, preparing these modules requires a team of about six people (for example, one faculty person, two graduate student teaching assistants, and several undergraduate programmers) and the team cannot be expected to produce more than about one lesson every one to two years.[15] Even with this slow development rate, good computer modules can pay for themselves many times over through their widespread use.

There needs to be further development of these dialogues by younger people, people who have been trained to write them to Professor Arons' standards, by someone with Professor Arons' skills.

Widespread use of these dialogues in schools and colleges could uncover a lot of science talent that presently is lost due to lack of proper teaching. They can be used to develop scientific thinking in students who presently get by (or flunk) through memorization of formulae; above all they can build the confidence of students that they can master basic science even if they are not among the quickest members of a school class.

There may be other computer-assisted modules being written which I am unaware of, yet are the equal, or even better than those of Professor Arons. What is really important is to demand that instruction modules

used in schools or universities meet or exceed the standards that
Professor Arons has set.

I don't advocate that computer-assisted instruction modules, even
when developed, replace good science teachers. Instead they will make
science teachers more productive. The computer modules have infinite
patience with slow learners, can provide routine drill to entire classes,
and can help with grading chores, etc. The science teachers thereby
would be able to handle more students than is now the case (hopefully
for a higher salary!) yet would have more time per student to spend on
the critical tasks: using the teacher's understanding of science to
lead students through individual roadblocks, motivating all students to
stick to work, etc.

Professors Arons and McDermott have been retraining school teachers
at all levels for science teaching jobs, and have shown that with the
right training many more current teachers can be good or even superb
science teachers than at present. They use Socratic Dialogues heavily
in their retraining program.[16] The cutbacks in the late '70's in the
Science teaching program of the National Science Foundation has severely
restricted their activities. It is time for both private and public
funding sources to bring the program at the University of Washington
back to full strength and expand programs of a similar nature at other
universities. The combination of teacher retraining and computer-
assisted instruction, if both are carried out to Professor Arons' standards,
would revolutionize science teaching in the U.S. Sputnik failed to
achieve this revolution in the '60's; a second failure in the 1980's can
hardly be tolerated.

C.   A National Network for Science

The most profound aspect of the computer revolution is the marriage
of the computer with high speed electronic communications, to form
computer communications networks.   The astonishing capabilities of such
networks for information transfer was first demonstrated by ARPANET,
established about 1970 by the Defense Advanced Research Projects Agency.[17]
On the ARPANET there are electronic "bulletin boards", classified by
subject.   Anyone on ARPANET who has need for information can post his/
her request on the appropriate bulletin board.   For instance, the
question might be "who can provide a driver program for the XYZ disk?"
This question would be placed on the disk drivers bulletin board. Experts
on disk drivers scan the information requests on this bulletin board and
reply, even if the reply is only to suggest another expert. If experts
do not reply, they may cease to be known as experts!

By using the ARPANET bulletin boards it is possible to find exactly
the person who has the information one is after, selected from thousands
of ARPANET users all over the country.

There is a vast amount of information contained within the U.S.
university community; but it is virtually inaccessible — either written
down in obscure journals or not yet written at all.   This information
seems sometimes to be better known to Japan than to U.S. industry.   A
communications network on the model of ARPANET, linking all university
members and relevant industry personnel, could greatly increase the
accessibility of knowledge contained in the U.S. universities.   This
knowledge is in the public domain and largely developed at Government
expense through U.S. support of basic research.   Making this knowledge
more easily accessible to U.S. industry would greatly enhance the value

of universities to the economy as a whole.

Incredibly, the idea of a national U.S. communications network, linking university and industry scientists and engineers, is treated in the U.S. as a pipe dream[18]. The ARPANET has been in existence for over thirteen years, but is restricted to computer scientists and electrical engineers with major defense contracts. The National Science Foundation has sponsored an add-on to the ARPANET, called CSNET, to link more computer scientists. The Department of Energy runs a network, but only for researchers engaged in plasma fusion research with Department of Energy grants.[19] Other, more informal networks such as USENET and BITNET[20], also have limited accessibility. Meanwhile a national computer network is developing in Britain.

It should not cost more than one hundred million dollars per year to finance a national information exchange network, with network terminals on the desks of all university faculty and academic staff engaged in basic research.[21] This seems a very small price to pay considering that the U.S. has already invested tens of billions of dollars supporting the generation of scientific knowledge in U.S. universities, and my guess is that the value of making this knowledge more accessible to U.S. industry is measured in the hundreds of billions of dollars.

The only agency with the proper mandate to establish such a network is the National Science Foundation. Unfortunately, the Foundation is likely to move very slowly on building a national network, in order to avoid any chance that money appears to have been diverted from existing NSF programs in order to pay for the network.

It is very urgent that any group concerned with U.S. economic productivity put pressure on the National Science Foundation, the White House, and Congress to build the network today. Five or ten years from now will be too late.

Private industry needs to lay plans for relevant scientific, engineering, and marketing employees to have access to the proposed national network. The barrier to these plans is industrial security. It is my belief that in most cases industrial computing systems containing proprietary or sensitive information should not be connected to the network because of the security problem[22]. Instead, employees should have terminals connected directly to the network, (just as they have telephones connected to the U.S. telephone system), or else these terminals should connect to the network through isolated computers which are not a part of company computing systems.

D. Universities in the Computing Market

A university professor is usually not needed to help sell a new brand of cereal. With computers, the situation is different. Digital Equipment Corporation (DEC) is the second leading U.S. manufacturer of computers;[23] they got there with a major boost from universities. Firstly, a generation of students learned the usefulness of DEC minicomputers in university laboratories; moving on to industry after graduation they recognized opportunities to use microcomputers and inclined towards DEC to fulfill these opportunities. More recently a generation of engineering students have been trained on VAX superminicomputers from DEC and are now helping to swell industrial orders for VAX's.

Universities help computing industry marketing in a number of ways.

They can make use of a new computing system before the hardware and software are reliable enough for commercial use. Commercial customers often look to early university installations for practical information about a computing system — they ask questions such as "What is it? What is it good for? What problems have you had with it? What are the alternatives?" etc. Faculty and students can find new uses for the computing system. Students benefit from training on the new system; at the same time they provide extra manpower to help outlast problems that inevitably accompany any new system. Universities can develop new software concepts that help extend the range of usefulness of the system. At Cornell I participated in the purchase and early use of a Floating Point Systems AP-190L Array Processor, and have seen all these activities:[24] Potential commercial customers frequently call the support group at Cornell that operates the Array Processor. Cornell developed the first FORTRAN compiler (a major piece of systems software) for the Array Processor. A number of graduate student theses have been completed with its help. Cornell's experience with the AP-190L helped lay the basis for Floating Point Systems's second product: the FPS-164.

The supercomputer market has been severely depressed, in part by not having access to the university market. Sales of these machines have been well below the potential demand; a primary reason has been lack of access to these systems by universities, which has meant no students receive training for these systems, no faculty develop new applications, universities are not developing new software for them, etc. Supercomputers were recently installed at Colorado State University, the University of Minnesota, and Purdue University, but these installations were too few, too late, and mostly have too expensive user charges to change this situation. Moreover, supercomputers are needed at top ranked universities such as M.I.T., Stanford, Cal Tech, Cornell, University of Illinois, etc., none of which presently has one.

The source of this problem of access is a policy of the U.S. Government and the universities themselves that 0% of basic university research dollars be allocated to pay the costs of large scale scientific simulations. See Sec. III-D.

A consequence of the small supercomputer market is that companies serving this market are very reluctant to make major investments for the future. Public statements from Cray Research, CDC, and IBM incessantly emphasize the theme that the supercomputer market is small and high risk;[25] they use this claim as an excuse for not building scientific computers that truly push the limits of current technology.

One unfortunate suggestion often taken seriously is that business should donate computers which are past their prime to universities. Fortunately, universities can rarely afford the maintenance costs of out-of-date systems, for none of the benefits I have described above ensue when the computers in use in universities are already obsolete. What is worse, students trained on obsolete computers are way behind the technology by the time they graduate, due to the rapid development of computer technology in the meantime. One doesn't want graduates demanding VAX's in industry when newer, better technology is available. I can imagine few more effective ways of slowing technology growth in the U.S. than using universities as a used computer dump.

The supercomputer market has also been limited by the marketing myopia of the U.S. manufacturers themselves. They started out with systems with an entry level price tag of $15 million, which can only be bought with the signature of a senior vice president of a major corporation or an Act of Congress. The first principle of computer marketing requires that such systems be the top of a line of less powerful, less expensive, software compatible systems, so that customers can get a start on these systems without a major effort to sell top management on a $15 million purchase. (This effort usually takes YEARS!) Today, an entry level supercomputer can cost somewhat less than $15 million, but many high level managers now have the $15 million figure permanently engraved in their minds. There ought to be minicomputer priced systems with the architecture of the Cray, CDC, or Denelcor supercomputers.

III. Computerization of Science

A. The Build-Up of Scientific Computing

Embedded in the current world-wide competition is a human undertaking of staggering scope. The undertaking is to embody four hundred years of scientific inquiry and wisdom into computer programs which aid searches for natural resources, industrial product development, and product manufacture.

Already, major advances in design and manufacturing capability have been achieved by computerization supported by scientific knowledge. For example, Newton's Laws of mechanics are the basis for "structural analysis" programs widely used throughout industry, as part of computer-aided engineering. Scientific Laws covering gas flows are the basis for programs extensively used in design of aircraft, to predict their actual flight characteristics. These examples are only the beginning, incorporating only a tiny fraction of the world's scientific knowledge. Further revolutionary advances in the industrial world should follow, for example, from computerization of scientific understanding of atoms and molecules, since most properties of materials and their chemical reactions are determined by the laws of atomic behavior. However, I cannot in one paragraph give even a hint of the range of topics covered in the world's libraries of scientific books and journals or in the minds of tens of thousands of living scientists. All of this encyclopaedic wisdom is potentially harnessable for practical use via the computer.

At the scientific end of this undertaking one sees the world's scientists engaged in open but competitive scientific inquiry and international collaboration to extend the world's reservoir of scientific understanding. Computerization of either past scientific results or current hypotheses now aids in this effort, especially in Europe and Japan where major computing resources are made available for fundamental scientific investigations. (For reasons to be discussed later, the U.S. presently discourages computer use in basic academic science).

At the other end of the computerization of scientific knowledge one sees engineers using computers to help meet the increasingly complex demands placed on industrial design and engineering.[26] These demands result from the need to be competitive on a global scale. This need leaves very small tolerance for design errors despite conflicting requirements of low cost, high quality, energy efficiency, environmental compatibility, etc. In addition scientific help is essential to enable industrial product development to keep pace with shortened time scales for R. and D. combined with rapid product evolution. At this end proprietary design and engineering efforts are the key to market success and as such are a critical part of the competitive economic scene. The majority of U.S. industry depends to some degree on the computerized application of science, at Philip Morris and Kraft Foods as well as Exxon and Boeing.

Computer programs based on scientific knowledge often are major consumers of computing resources. Their use is helping to swell the total scientific and engineering computing demands of industry. Today, major companies buy multimillion dollar mainframes the way ordinary people buy soap. Although the bulk of mainframe usage is for business data processing the percentage of usage of these systems for scientific/ engineering purposes is considerable and growing. In addition, industry is beginning to buy supercomputers dedicated to scientific applications too demanding to run at all on a conventional mainframe. The $15 to $20 million pricetag of supercomputers has in the past been a major hurdle for potential industrial customers, even major oil companies; but recently the costs of entry level supercomputers has decreased and the industrial supercomputer market is starting to grow rapidly. In addition, the high growth rate overall of expenditures for scientific and engineering computing should in time make $15 to $20 million a normal rather than an exceptional price for an industrial supercomputer purchase. On top of these simple extrapolations from present patterns of computer usage there are major scientific applications which await giant increases in capability beyond today's most powerful systems. This includes many problems requiring a fully three dimensional treatment (an example is three-dimensional processing in oil exploration) and most problems at the atomic and molecular level.

I expect that within a decade industry will require thousands of supercomputers dedicated to scientific and engineering applications with capabilities thousands of times greater than the most powerful systems

available today. The supercomputer market will itself have a value (I
believe) of tens of billions of dollars and the importance of these
systems to industrial profits will be measured in the hundreds of billions
of dollars. The first figure is based on my extrapolation from present
mainframe markets, including the impact of new opportunities and other
developments mentioned later. The second figure is based on my estimate
that a company will not go through the trauma of a multimillion dollar
computer purchase unless the expected profits resulting from the purchase
are a factor of 10 higher.

The buildup of scientific computing in industry over the last two
decades has proceeded largely hidden from the international basic research
community. For example, structural analysis was a well-established part
of engineering long before computers were developed; the building of
structural analysis programs did not require much new scientific input.
The national laboratories employed scientists to help with applications
of science starting with the simulations needed for weapons development
at Los Alamos in World War II. However, until very recently the efforts
at the national laboratories were also largely hidden from the rest of
the basic research community.

At the present time the insular, ivory tower atmosphere of basic
scientific research is facing a spectacular invasion from the real
world. The national laboratories are discovering that their own research
cannot progress satisfactorily without more exchanges with basic university
research and training programs. But far more important, the multibillion
dollar industrial scientific computing effort is about to place multi-
billion dollar demands on academic scientific research and training
programs. The reason for this is that the science needed by industry

runs the gamut of scientific understanding — Maxwell's equations for
electromagnetic phenomena, the laws of fluid and gas flows, and above
all the laws of atomic and molecular physics. Scientists are only now
beginning to learn how to use all these laws in concert in problems of
real-life complexity. For example, while the laws of atomic physics
were developed fifty years ago, they were only fully understood in very
simple examples such as the hydrogen atom. Due to basic research underway today one can contemplate applying basic science to the bulk of the
materials problems industries face; to bring off these applications will
require incredibly powerful computers (which modern technology makes
possible but the computing industry has been laggard in supplying)
combined with breakthroughs in research. There are, I believe, enough
opportunities for industrial applications of existing science so that
access to current basic research will be of multibillion dollar importance
to industry and the pressures to get on with further breakthroughs
needed by industry will be immense.

The academic community is not ready for this invasion. The invasion
concerns primarily the theoretical science community, who are expected
by their experimental colleagues to work only with pencil and paper, not
computers. Academic theorists receive only a tiny fraction of existing
research budgets, and in many cases have more computing power available
to them at home on their children's home computer than at their office.
Since I have had advanced warning of this invasion, I have been trying
to help increase the computing capabilities available to the Cornell
theory community. I now assume that our computing budget will soon be
at the level of $10 million/year or higher. It is a strange exercise
since I have been used to scrabbling for tens of thousands of dollars.

Most of my colleages, who have even less, are finding it very difficult to accept my vision of the future, and are reluctant to make immediate sacrifices which are needed to prepare for that future.

B.   The FORTRAN Barrier

There is a very serious barrier that is today blocking the whole process of computerization of science and subsequent exploitation of this computerization in industry. This barrier occurs in the way that the scientific computer programs are written. When scientists explain their work to each other, they do this using a mixture of mathematics and human language (the standard language for scientists the world over is currently English.) The most effective scientific expositions are carefully broken down into chapters of a textbook or sections of a scientific article which fellow scientists can master chapter by chapter or section by section. Unfortunately, the current language predominantly used by scientific programmers to address computers, namely FORTRAN, is neither a human language nor a mathematical language. The worst aspect of FORTRAN is that the ideas underlying a FORTRAN program get all jumbled up in the FORTRAN description. Many different ideas usually are needed to build major scientific programs, which the scientist would normally explain in separate chapters. However, each and every line of a FORTRAN program typically draws on many of these ideas at once, making documentation or reading or modification of a FORTRAN program an endlessly difficult, time consuming, and frustrating task. To make matters worse, there is a very great pressure to optimize these programs to minimize their running costs; this optimization is usually done relative to a specific computing system, including its precise arrangements for data storage and graphics display. Both the writing of FORTRAN and its optimization are highly error-prone processes; full confidence in these programs can rest heavily on twenty years of usage of them, combined with hundreds of man-years spent improving and optimizing these programs and then discovering and removing errors.

There are two consequences of the "FORTRAN barrier". The first is that programs presently running on a specific mainframe often cannot be moved to a more powerful supercomputer even when growing usage of the program has made the mainframe inadequate, and even when a major product line is at stake. The effort and the delays involved in moving the program and then re-establishing confidence in it are too overwhelming to contemplate. The second consequence is that there is now a very major reluctance to build new industrial applications programs, just because of the enormity of such tasks. This is especially true in cases where it is not certain that present computers are powerful enough to handle the application, once the program is established. The combined effect of these two consequences has been to depress the supercomputer market by at least an order of magnitude. It is extremely difficult to persuade a senior vice president of a major corporation to sign for a $15 million supercomputer when it is not clear that any existing programs can be moved over to it or that any new applications will be developed for it on a reasonable time scale.

The FORTRAN barrier is starting to crumble. First of all, there is a trend to industry to make use of "third party" software. For example, there are several structural analysis packages such as NASTRAN from MacNeil Schwendler Corp. and ANSYS from Swanson Associates. These packages have been reworked so that they are logically structured and modular enough, despite being written in FORTRAN, to be adaptable to different computing systems. They are currently available in versions for supercomputers, mainframes or attached processors. The existence of these third party packages can be a powerful incentive for industrial purchase of a supercomputer or high performance attached processor. Unfortunately, the establishment of a commercial company to build and support a portable science-based package is about the last step in the long process of bringing a piece of scientific knowledge to the computer; the FORTRAN bottleneck is still very much present in earlier stages of computerization where commercial viability of the software is not assured, or where the application is internal to a single company.

The second source of hope is rather more profound. Modern computer science has started to develop a startling array of ideas for easing the difficulties of interacting with a computer. These ideas include many different language frameworks; they also include ideas from the so-called artificial intelligence community. The basic idea that appeals to me in artificial intelligence, as applied to computer programming, is to study the decisions a person makes while designing a computer program. Then one tries to provide computerized help in making these decisions as well as in generating a computer program once the decisions are made.[27]

Unfortunately, recent developments in computer science followed a long period of gestation during which modern computer science became very isolated from the many worlds of specific computer applications and from the computer manufacturers. This isolation seems to exist whether the computer scientists live in universities, industrial laboratories or whatever. Computer scientists speak a language which is unintelligible to the average scientific programmer or computer designer. Because of this isolation, the strange languages and other products of computer science do not fully meet the needs of specific application areas and are largely ignored by the real scientific world. A way must be found to bring modern computer science ideas to bear on the fundamental practical problem, namely to enable programmers to specify completely their programs (including optimization strategies) in a civilized, human readable form close to the familiar languages of English and mathematics. The translation process from such a specification to an actual computer program should be handled as far as possible by the computer itself.

A related source of revolutionary approaches to computer programming is the personal computer world. The availability of graphics in both personal computers and scientific workstations is opening up whole new ways to address the computer, illustrated for example by the VISICALC program and its follow-ons. Scientific programming is far more complex than most personal computer applications but is still likely to be profoundly changed by the use of graphics, for example, its ability to accept and display mathematical notation.

C. The Learning Curve Barrier

Another problem in the computerization of science is the enormous computing requirements needed to start computerization of a new area of science. There is a "learning curve" in the computerization business, just as there is in manufacturing. Once computerization of a particular scientific application has been demonstrated, continued development of the application can bring the computing demands for the application down by factors of one hundred, one thousand, or more. A clear example of this is provided in the aircraft industry. The computing requirements at the NASA Ames Laboratory, where many initiatives in aerodynamic computation begin, are considerably more severe than within the aircraft industry itself. In early stages of computerization, the best numerical approximations have yet to be discovered and researchers have to be super-cautious in seeking out numerical errors precisely because the approximations are poor; the resulting computing demands are prodigious. In contrast the pressures for more computing power in industry tend to result mostly from the need for shortened turn around time and increased numbers of runs on highly mature scientific applications. Scientists and engineers in industry who need computing power to get a new application started do not, in my experience, get much sympathy in industrial budget planning.

D.   The Barrier of Academic Inertia

There is a barrier to progress which is most pronounced in the United States although I see it in various guises in other countries as well. I will discuss only the U.S. situation. The barrier is that most U.S. university scientists are not participating in the computerization effort. What is worse, they are not preparing their graduate students to participate either. There are exceptions to this situation; more importantly, there is a whole generation of young scientists in universities who want to be involved in the computerization process but cannot because the universities do not have the necessary computers themselves. The universities do not provide access to computers outside the universities either.

The situation up to the present, has been as follows. By mutual agreement between senior university scientists and the National Science Foundation, computer equipment and computer usage charges receives the lowest priority in the granting of research funds, lower than

instrumentation grants or salary awards, or travel, or whatever. An
expensive computing equipment request is normally granted only when it
is needed for routine data analysis in connection with even more expensive
experimental equipment. As a result, there are superminis such as
Digital Equipment Corporation's VAX fairly widely available in major
universities, but their predominant use is for data analysis rather than
for making predictions based on scientific knowledge. Theorists, who
are the type of scientists most likely to be involved in the computerization process, are expected to compute, if at all, at no cost to the
university research community. They may use spare time on a local VAX,
or they can seek time from the national laboratories (especially Livermore
or Los Alamos). Nowadays they often go abroad, to Japan or Germany,
where large-scale computing is freely available to visiting U.S. scientists.
The one exception to this picture is in the atmospheric sciences;
theoretical studies in atmospheric science are encouraged on the supercomputer at the National Center for Atmospheric Research (NCAR), which
is funded by the NSF.

The origin of this situation is worth describing. For over three
hundred years, science has made progress through experimental investigation and analytic theoretical analysis. From World War II until the
last few years, the United States has been the leader in these conventional scientific modes. The results have been spectacular, both in
terms of scientific understanding of nature and practical economic
benefits. However, the economic benefits have come with a time delay,
often twenty years or more. For example, the laser emerged from basic
research in the late 1950's; it was the subject of the 1981 Nobel award.
It is now evident that the laser (combined with optical fibers) will be

part of an incredible revolution in communications — thereby underlying a hundred billion dollar industry. However, it is now 1983 and this revolution hasn't quite happened yet — all we know is that it is coming. Because of this long time delay, the academic scientific community has been relatively isolated from the commercial world that is the ultimate economic beneficiary of science. The academic community, especially its leading senior scientists, have fought hard to maintain adequate funding for traditional basic research; despite this the funding was eroded continuously during the 1970's resulting in today's obsolescent instrumentation and inadequate faculty positions for young scientists. The academic view has been (and remains) that theoretical computing is unnecessary and would be, if given higher priority, a disastrous drain on research budgets.

University faculty have another major responsibility, namely the training of undergraduate and graduate students. Their view here is simple. The training programs at major universities are designed to meet the needs of future Nobel Prize winners, with the exceptions of courses for non-science majors at the freshman or sophomore levels. While not everyone taking these courses will actually be a Nobel winner, it is believed that the training they receive is still reasonable. Undergraduate and graduate students often help with computerized data analysis, but it is assumed that no specific training in computing is required for this — they can read a book about FORTRAN if they have not already picked it up.

It is time to make supercomputing fully available to the theoretical science and engineering community in universities. There are two reasons for this. One is that large scale computing is now essential

for continued progress in many areas of theoretical basic research. If
the plugs were pulled on the world's big computers research would cease
in important subfields of elementary particle theory, astrophysics,
surface science, turbulence, etc. For example, thirty years of experimental studies of short-lived relatives of the proton and neutron has
resulted in a theory of nuclear forces, called "Quantum Chromodynamics".
This theory is too complex to be solved by analytic means, and young
theorists all over the globe have been struggling to gain better understanding of it by computer simulation.[28] It is already clear that
present day computers are inadequate for this problem, and some of the
most determined theorists are now designing computers themselves in
order to obtain the computing power that current technology makes
possible but is not yet supplied commercially.[29] Without computers it
is unlikely that we will ever find out whether Quantum Chromodynamics
correctly describes thirty years of experiments. The struggle of
theorists to obtain computer time at national laboratories or abroad or
by building their own, is simply the struggle to keep major research
areas like Quantum Chromodynamics alive. The academic community understands very well that many experimental disciplines will die without
adequate experimental equipment. This community is unfortunately not
yet ready to concede that adequate computing equipment is equally important
for many theoretical research areas.

The other reason for making supercomputing equipment available in
univesities is to enable universities to participate fully in the supercomputer market, as explained in Section II.D. The most important
university function in the market is the training of students both to
recognize opportunities for the application of supercomputers and to be

able to carry out these applications. Preparing for the use of supercomputers in scientific or engineering applications typically requires
Ph.D. level training; some companies (such as Schlumberger-Doll Research)
mostly hire scientists with several years of experience in basic research
beyond the Ph.D. Ph.D. training is organized as an apprenticeship in
basic research, in fact, much of university research is carried out by
Ph.D. candidates. Hence it is important to encourage university researchers
to use supercomputers in their research, when this makes sense, in order
that graduate students carrying out this research gain first hand
experience with large scale computing. It is important that universities
have access to the most powerful computers currently available rather
than aged supercomputers which no longer are commercially viable, both
because the computing problems of basic research require the most powerful
computers obtainable and because of all the practical reasons explained
in II.D.

There are now a reasonable number of people in the National Science
Foundation who are willing to change past policies, and designate a
small percentage of the NSF budget for theoretical computing, the way
percentages are designated for materials science, mathematics, and other
NSF programs. It is not clear that the academic community that advises
NSF will support such a designation, since it means the percentages of
the budget allocated to existing NSF programs will be slightly decreased.

E.   Interdisciplinary Chaos

There are many diverse groups engaged in the computerization of
science, in universities, industry, and national laboratories. There is
no sense of cohesion or common purpose among these groups. There is
no common meeting ground where these groups could get together and

discover their common interests. Instead they meet in hundreds of disconnected meetings, sponsored by hundreds of distinct societies. The Society for Exploration Geophysicists, The Society for Quantum Chemistry, the Cray User's group, the Society for Industrial and Applied Mathematics, the American Association for the Advancement of Science, the Society for Computer Simulation, etc. ,all have members heavily engaged in the computerization of science. Within universities, the faculty members rarely cross departmental boundaries, even though they may share common problems in areas like fluid dynamics, materials science, or they may share common computing needs. The scientists and engineers or computing personnel engaged in the computerization of science have, I find, very little overall sense of the enterprise they are a part of. Most of them see only the day-to-day problems of the little corner of science or engineering or computer design they are currently engaged in. They struggle to maintain their little niche; they do not see the big picture, nor do they give much attention to the major problems I discuss. This makes it difficult to get any of these major problems dealt with.

F.   The Training Barrier

Even if the barriers I have described are eliminated there remains the basic problem of education. The growth in scientific computing in industry will create extraordinary demands for Ph.D. physicists and other scientists. Far too few scientists are being trained at the Ph.D. level to meet future demand. Most universities (including Cornell) train fewer Ph.D.'s today than in the late sixties. Physicists will be especially needed because all branches of science reduce ultimately to the laws of physics. For example, biology deals with cells and life built up from cells; but as one tries to understand cells in detail one must often deal with the molecules making up a cell; to understand the molecules, especially to use computers to predict their properties, one must deal with the atoms making up the molecule or even the individual electrons in the atoms. To apply the computer means using Newton's Laws or the laws of Quantum Mechanics. In consequence, physicists will often be working side by side with chemists, molecular biologists and cell biologists to computerize important biological problems.

It will not be enough to increase opportunities for graduate education in science. More recruits to science are needed at all levels from kindergarten through the graduate level, and a revolutionary improvement in science training is needed to achieve an overall increase in scientifically trained manpower for industry.

Few people appreciate the changing hiring patterns being generated by the computerization of science. The Schlumberger-Doll Research Center and Exxon Corp. are seeking high quality physicists with several years of experience in world class basic research BEYOND the Ph.D. The two most promising Ph.D's in numerical astrophysics at Cornell in the past few years were hired by General Electric Company and Kodak, Inc.

IV. Developments in Japan

There are four programs underway in Japan that bear watching.

The first program is the provision of major computing resources to Japanese universities. At present the universities are served by many Japanese mainframes. University users in Japan are charged only about 1/100th the costs that U.S. university users must pay for comparable time on a U.S. university computer. In the near future, several Japanese manufacturers will place early production models of supercomputers on the university network; this means university use of these systems can begin immediately. Even more importantly, student training in the use of these supercomputers can begin immediately. There is a commitment to explore fundamental scientific problems in Japan using these computers , for example, in atomic and molecular science. No such commitment exists in the U.S.

The second program is the development in Japan of supercomputers by Japanese manufacturers. In particular, several of these supercomputers are claimed to be IBM-compatible. How successful the IBM-compatibility will be, I cannot tell yet, but if it is truly effective the Japanese supercomputers could handle far more of the existing U.S. scientific and engineering computing load than any U.S. supercomputer. Thus the Japanese could enter a far larger U.S. market than U.S. supercomputer manufacturers enjoy, obtaining a revenue base permitting far more investment in future technology than any U.S. supercomputer manufacturer is making.

The third program is the Japanese Super-Speed computing project. This is a research project sponsored jointly by the Japanese Government and the major Japanese manufacturers, aimed at designing a supercomputer one hundred times more powerful than existing systems by 1990. It is this project which is setting the time scale for U.S. action. In particular it means the Japanese are seeking a major improvement in super-computer performance without waiting for evidence that there will be an adequate market for their new system. CDC has indicated that they will try to match the Japanese goals; but questions of performance are not at the heart of the issue. The Japanese often take over an international high technology market simply by being the only supplier with enough capacity to meet market demand. I expect that if the Super-Speed computer can be mass produced for reasonable cost, it will find a market in the thousands, due to the broad range of scientific applications it will make possible. In any case the 1990 market for supercomputers will be much larger than today's due to natural growth. Competition for this market is likely to be settled in favor of whichever manufacturer has the capability to deliver thousands of supercomputers.

The fourth program is the Japanese "5th Generation" computer project. This is another MITI-sponsored affair aimed at incorporating artificial intelligence into computing systems with logical inference capability used for natural language interpretation and the like. It is not quite clear to me what this project portends. The 5th generation team will learn a lot of advanced computer science. It will bear watching if the team achieves major rapport with important application areas. Outside of this one project, Japanese software goals seem very practical but unadventurous, such as building very high quality FORTRAN compilers for their supercomputers.

In summary, Japan is making four smart moves that could bring them to leadership in key areas of computerization of science, as well as dominance of the supercomputer market at just about the time market demands explode.

V.   Recommendations for Action in the United States

In previous sections of this paper, I have given the background for a response to the Japanese Super-Computing project. In this Section I shall describe my own recommendations for action in the United States.

My principal recommendation is that the many disparate groups involved in the computerization of science should develop a sense of community. This community includes scientists and engineers from many scientific, engineering, agricultural, and medical disciplines. The community overlaps universities, industry, and government laboratories. The community includes the designers of scientific computers and the marketing organizations for these computers. The community includes applied mathematicians and computer scientists; it includes computing support staff who support scientific computing systems.

This scientific/engineering computing community has specific needs: for information exchange, for resources (manpower, financial resources, educational resources, and computing equipment), and for decision-making power. It needs better mechanisms for incorporation of new technology than presently exist.

The most fundamental need of the scientific/engineering community is for a computer communications network serving the entire community; a computer communications network is by far the most effective framework for exchange of information within the community, and for establishing a sense of community among all its diverse members. The network should also provide remote computing access and file transfer capability, so that community members in diverse locations can carry out cooperative computing projects; such a network would allow economies of scale in meeting computing demands, especially from universities.

There are other ways to support information exchange. There needs to be a trade show specifically for scientific and engineering computing; I have written to AFIPS (the organization that runs the National Computer Conference) requesting that they sponsor such a show. There need to be large, interdisciplinary conferences where all the diverse groups in the community can come together; one such conference is planned to be held in Washington in June of 1984.

There need to be interdisciplinary umbrella organizations in universities with strong industrial ties, to unite different academic disciplines and bring together industrial and university scientists and engineers. Models for such organizations include the Center for Integrated

Systems Studies at Stanford and the Materials Science Center and Sub-Micron Facility at Cornell, but neither of these models are targeted at scientific/engineering computing. I am helping to plan a "Theory and Simulation Science Center" at Cornell, as the kind of center which will bring together the research and graduate training programs of greatest relevance to the scientific/engineering computing community. The Theory and Simulation Science Center can hopefully serve as a model for similar organizations at other campuses.

Planning for new buildings at universities can also help bring diverse groups together. Many of the disciplines concerned with scientific and engineering computing, especially computer science, electrical engineering, and computing support groups, will require major additional space to accommodate their growth over the next decade.

There is a widespread need for resources within the scientific/ engineering computing community. The totality of resources that might be made available to the community is large — from the major industrial expenditures on scientific and engineering computing to the large numbers of students and junior staff in universities that would like to partici-pate in community activities. Unfortunately these resources are not distributed very effectively — industrial budgets are often locked into data processing mainframes; university students and junior staff often cannot participate due to lack of access to computing equipment.

I recommend that more of the decisions about resource allocation be in the hands of the community itself rather than outsiders with relatively less understanding of the communities' needs and opportunities. Too many decisions are made by senior faculty instead of junior faculty or students,by senior managers in industry instead of by scientists, engineers, and support staff at a lower level, by Acts of Congress instead of informed agency personnel. High-level personnel should be involved in the overall framework — for overall budget decisions, for overall organizational questions. For example, there should be high-level decisions in universities, industry, and government agencies (such as the National Science Foundation) to have separate budgets for scientific and engineering computing which are distinct from data processing budgets (in the industrial and university cases) or scientific research budgets (at the National Science Foundation). There should be realistic growth projections built into these budgets to prevent massive amounts of wasted time spent in budget-busting or penny-pinching. The detailed allocation of these budgets need to be in the hands of people who keep up with technological developments — in the scientific computing market and in the computerization of science. There needs to be a practical understanding by senior management (in universities, government, and industry) of the results to be expected from the scientific/engineering computing community, so that the community can be responsible for budget and other resource allocations and not be second-guessed about these decisions as long as reasonable results are forthcoming. I have seen many examples where normal managerial arrangements were ineffective at solving scientific computing resource problems, causing both immense waste of managers' time and continuing deterioration of a scientific computing environment, rather than any benefit. I have seen many examples in universities where a graduate student or even an undergraduate handled all computing decisions with great success. Most of my direct experience is with universities or government agencies but I have had enough industrial involvement to know that many corporations need to move scientific computing decisions lower down the corporate ladder, including even the decision whether or not to buy supercomputers.

One type of decision that arises repeatedly is whether or not to aggregate. Industries face decisions as to whether to jointly sponsor research or proceed independently; whether to develop software separately or share it from a common third party source, etc. University personnel face decisions whether to acquire separate minicomputers or get together to obtain a supercomputer. Another type of question is whether to encourage lots of small companies to serve a particular need, versus a small number of large corporations. There are too many barriers distorting these decisions; antitrust problems facing industry, departmental boundaries in universities, etc. Above all there are barriers to aggregation caused by the desire of all organizations to hoard their own resources. I urge all parties involved — universities, industries, and government, to ease the problems of resource sharing. Private companies should (in my view) plan to spend a portion of their scientific/ engineering computing budgets outside of the company — on university-industry collaborations, on third-party software, or whatever; the scientific/engineering computing community within industry should have a strong voice in such external expenditures. Universities should encourage resource sharing, between departments (for example in joint computing support projects) and with industry. Interdisciplinary centers interface more effectively with industry than individual departments. Through these centers universities can promote greatly increased interchange of people and information between industry and universities.

There needs to be greater attention given to the process by which major new computer technology enters production use within the scientific/

engineering computing community. Computer manufacturers seem to dump new products onto the market with no thought given to the problems of winning market acceptance for them. A variety of organizations have born the brunt of years of instability that characterized the early years of the CDC 7600, the IBM 360 series, the Cray-1, etc. Few of these organizations are eager to repeat their experiences. In addition, as computers become more complex, the market for these computers becomes increasingly dependent on the existence of trained manpower who know what the new computers are good for and how to run them.

The main problems with new computing systems concern their software. Ideally, new computers would be software-compatible upgrades of old ones. Unfortunately, the long-established mainframe lines are increasing in power far too slowly to meet current demands, and fundamental technological limits are blocking rapid future development of systems like the IBM 370 series. The current vector supercomputers such as the Cray or CDC 200 series seem equally doomed to fall short, to be replaced by a great variety of parallel computing architectures. The Denelcor HEP may be a harbinger of architectures to come.

The logical place to try out new computing systems with new software is in the universities, so that training of students on these new systems can begin as early as possible. I explained the benefits of early university involvement in these systems in Section IID. Unfortunately, universities rarely have the resources to operate an early production model of a new computer, even if they can scrape together the funds to buy it. I think it would pay both the industrial users of computing and the computing manufacturers to place a higher value on early university trials of a new computing system than is now the case. Interdisciplinary centers at universities could sponsor early acquisition of innovative computer hardware and software; such projects would I think be an attractive feature of industrial associates programs for these centers. Such industrial associates programs would help interested industries gain early information about forthcoming commercial computing systems, as well as gaining access to manpower trained on the new systems.

There will continue to be organizations other than universities that accept early delivery on specific systems, such as the NASA Ames Laboratory. But the need for training of students on new computing systems is now too acute not to use universities as much as possible as the main location for new computing technology.

Another very critical need is for universities to experiment with new ways to train students to write software. The parallel architectures to come will seriously strain the current FORTRAN based frameworks for building scientific software. It is especially important that universities that combine top quality science and computer science departments encourage interdisciplinary projects combining both computer scientists and scientists to attack the FORTRAN barrier.

V.   What the U.S. Government Can Do

There are likely to be U.S. government initiatives in the 1985 budget to supply supercomputing access to U.S. universities. These initiatives will have to be planned rather carefully, if the most important needs are to be met.

The highest priority for government action, I insist, is to build a national computer network for basic and industrial research supporting interdisciplinary communication, remote-computing access, and file transfer, following the example of Britain.   In particular, the National Science Foundation should establish overall planning for this network and should finance university access to this network. This network should have much higher priority than the provision of supercomputers on the network; there should be no stinting on network funding regardless of what other programs are sacrificed to cover the network's cost. See Sections IIC and V.

Secondly, one of the primary aims of the government initiatives should be to encourage the nation's top-ranked research universities to build up their internal scientific computing resources to a level about one thousand times greater than the capacity of current supercomputers. These universities should also develop the capability to accept major computing systems early in their lifetime. This buildup should take place, I recommend, over roughly a five-year period. At the same time universities should be establishing much greater collaboration with industry in scientific and engineering training and research programs that feed the computerization of science.   I believe that government support of this buildup would best be supplied in the form of seed money that would be discontinued if it is not heavily matched, after one or two years delay, from private sources. The seed money should support university-wide planning for scientific computing networks within each university, training programs focused on these networks, and inter-disciplinary university organizations that can interface effectively with industry. It may be necessary, as an intermediate palliative, to establish national supercomputing centers serving university needs. The worst mistake the government could make is to establish national supercom-puting centers on the model of the Plasma Fusion Energy center at Livermore without at the same time providing seed money for internal university development. National centers will be necessary to serve individual university users at universities which bungle their internal planning or are too small to build adequate internal computing services. However, major research universities like Cornell need the freedom and encouragement to build their own computing support with innovative approaches targeted to individual university needs that national computing centers cannot match. For example, a four thousand processor system is being planned to meet some of Cornell's needs starting in 1987.[30] This system is both too risky and too limited in purpose for any national center to be willing to consider, despite its extraordinary potential (greater than any currently planned commercial system known to me).

I expect to raise a fair proportion of the support for this system from private sources, as part of my efforts to make sure that Cornell is in full partnership with private industry in activities related to the computerization of science. Government seed money for this program would make my efforts to raise private support much easier. The two extremes of _full_ government support (through a national center buying and operating the four thousand processor system) or _no_ government support at all would each very much _weaken_ my ability to achieve full partnership with private industry.

One problem with government planning for supercomputing is that the current government planning committees do not take account of private sector needs in their planning. I have met many of the members of these committees; they have not thought through the impact that increasing use of science in industry accompanied by rapidly expanding multi-billion dollar scientific computing budgets will have. These government planners, in my experience, have no concept of the magnitude of the demands industry

will shortly make on the major U.S. universities, as industry discovers
it can no longer survive on minimally trained manpower and internal
industrial research. One can hardly blame the planners for these over-
sights. The computer industry should be a major voice warning government
about these developments. Instead the computing industry continues to
insist that the supercomputer market is small with minimal private
sector demand into the forseeable future. Government planners presently
refer mostly to conditions and needs at the national laboratories as
their principal source of planning information. Government planners are
also insensitive to the time delays of university training programs.
Ph.D. training takes four or five years; when postdoctoral fellowships
and junior faculty experience are also required training for industry,
the total training time is close to a decade. To carry out this training,
universities must have adequate computing power close to a decade in
advance of industrial need for the resulting manpower. To meet these
university needs takes much bolder planning than I have seen.

One reason I consider it unlikely that the government will provide
the seed money I recommend for university development is that I can find
no bureaucratic support for such a program. I have found four individuals
in the government with a sufficiently broad mandate to be able to consider
a seed money program, namely the President's Science Advisor, the head
of the National Science Foundation, the Undersecretary of Defense for
Research and Engineering, and the Undersecretary of Commerce for
Productivity, Research and Innovation. Unfortunately, beneath these
individuals there are agencies and programs serving specific disciplines
and missions, with minimal capability for cooperation. These agencies
and programs prefer mission or discipline-oriented supercomputer programs

like the Plasma Fusion network or the National Center for Atmospheric Research as opposed to university-wide programs at a single university. Thus I very much fear that the U.S. government response to the Japanese Super-speed Computing project will be predominantly to establish national supercomputer centers for specific disciplines, with conservative, general purpose computer acquisition programs, combined with a network which is seriously underfunded for university network access needs and with very little seed money at all to encourage university computing build-ups and university-industry partnerships. Even in these circumstances, I expect to continue my efforts to ensure that Cornell has adequate computing support and interdisciplinary organization to play a full role in the computerization of science, comparable if not superior to the roles of major European or Japanese universities. I expect to win government support for this program despite bureaucratic bottlenecks (as I have in the past) because it is too embarrassing for agencies like the NSF if they refuse such support. However, unless something is done Cornell is likely to become unique among U.S. universities in possessing these capabilities I am seeking. If my own efforts fail the U.S. universities would then fall too far behind U.S. industrial needs to remain a serious force in the computerization effort, and would, as one consequence, lose many of their young faculty theorists to industry.

VII. Afterword: Keeping up the Fight

I have painted a grim picture of the present state of the computerization of science in the United States. Many people in industry, universities, and government are battling for change, and every day more people recognize the need for these changes. I have found a willingness to accept major changes at all levels from Congressmen and heads of

corporations to ordinary citizens, all of whom recognize the profound
challenge that today's international economic competition poses for the
U.S. This willingness means major changes can be accomplished if people
fight for them.

One danger is, that people pressing for change will give up, or
accept unsatisfactory solutions. For example, hastily built modules
for an entire science course should be rejected; instead each computer
lesson should be required to meet Professor Arons' standards. Researchers
should not settle for a small share of a Cray-1 at a national center
when they need a large share of a system with one thousand times more
power. Small fixes to FORTRAN should not be accepted when a major upgrade
in programming capability is required. When computing issues arise (or
should arise) in committees that don't want to face them, the issues
should be fought through even if one gets glared at by every other
member of the committee. (I have faced this situation myself.) A
one-time computer appropriation should not be accepted when there is a
need for a percentage of a research or computing budget to be designated
permanently for scientific computing support. Halfway measures will not
solve current U.S. economic difficulties, and in the long-term will
generate less support than programs which fully meet U.S. needs.

Many people have helped me come to grips with the problems of large-
scale scientific computing. However, my wife, Alison Brown, deserves
special mention for her own professional efforts and for putting me in
touch with computer science.

References

1. See, e.g. B. L. Buzbee, R. H. Ewald, and W. J. Worlton, "Japanese Supercomputer Technology", Science 218, 1189 (1982).

2. See, e.g. L. R. Harris, Fifth Generation Foundations, Datamation 29, No. 7, p.148.

3. See e.g., "With Stakes High, Race is on for Fastest Computer of All", New York Times, February 1, 1983, C1; and "The Race for the Supercomputer" Newsweek, July 4, 1983, p.58.

4. For example, NASTRAN from MacNeal-Schwendler Corp. (see J. F. Gloudeman, this issue); ANSYS from Swanson Associates, P.O. Box 65, Houston, Pennsylvania, 15342.

5. See, e.g. H. F. Jordan this issue.

6. The FPS-164 is not a supercomputer, but it is often under consideration as a less costly alternative (by a factor of 10) with the same cost effectiveness. Scientific third party software packages like NASTRAN and ANSYS or the circuit simulation program SPICE, are available on the FPS-164. It is regrettable that Cray and CDC do not produce supercomputer-compatible systems with the same price and performance as the FPS-164: see the very end of Section II.

7. For example the ICL DAP (K. G. Bowler and G. S. Pawley, this issue), the Goodyear Aerospace MPP, high performance array processor from Star Technologies, CSPI, and Floating Point Systems, etc.

8. See, e.g., the papers by V. L. Peterson, and Fuss and Tull, this issue; the whole area of simulations at the atomic and molecular level also require much greater power than is available today.

9. K. G. Wilson, "La Recherche a hesoin d'un grand programme d'informatique scientifique, Recherche 14, 1004 (1983).

10. Report of the Panel on Large-Scale Computing in Science and Engineering, NSF 83-13.

11. W. H. Press et al., Propspectus for Computational Physics, Report by the Subcommittee on Computational Facilities for Theoretical Research to the Advisory Committee for Physics, Division of Physics, National Science Foundation, March 15 1981.

12. Testimony by K. Wilson before the U.S. House of Representatives, Committee on Science and Technology, Congressional Record for February 23, 1983.

13. See e.g. A. B. Arons, in Daedalus, (Spring 1983), p.91 and A. B. Arons, Amer. J. Phys. 44, 834 (1976).

14. A. M. Bork, Am. J. Phys. $\underline{47}$, 5 (1979).

15. This is the current rate of production of Professor Bork's group on difficult lessons.

16. See ref. 13 and L. C. McDermott, Am. J. Phys. $\underline{42}$, 668, 737 (1974); ibid. $\underline{44}$, 434 (1976).

17. I was unable to find any reference describing the success of ARPANET in non-technical terms.

18. See, e.g., question by Congressman G. Brown to K. Wilson, ref. 12.

19. See D. Fuss and C. G. Tull, in this issue.

20. Ira H. Fuchs, Bitnet —"Because It's Time", IBM Perspectives in Computing $\underline{3}$, No. 1 (1983).

21. I estimate the cost of connecting a scientist to the network per year can vary roughly from $1,000 to $10,000 depending on facilities provided; this means $100 million per year would allow the connection of 10,000 to 100,000 scientists to the network.

22. See e.g. R. T. Moulton,"Network Security", Datamation, $\underline{29}$, No. 7, p. 121 (1983).

23. See, e.g. Datamation "The Leading U.S. DP Companies" Vol. 29, No. 6, p.96 (1983).

24. See, e.g. K. G. Wilson, "Experiences with a Floating Point Systems Array Processor", in Parallel Computations, G. Rodrigue, Editor, (Academic, New York, 1982), p.279.

25. Most recently, the speech by William Norris, Chairman of Control Data Corporation, to the meeting "Frontiers of Supercomputing" (August 1983 at Los Alamos Laboratory).

26. The next few paragraphs are based on personal observations of the industrial computing scene by the author. One source of further information would be the market research firms covering the scientific market.

27. See, e.g. R. C. Waters, "The Programmer's Apprentice: Knowledge based Editing," IEEE Trans. Software Eng. SE-8, 1-11 (1982).

28. M. Creutz, L. Jacobs, and C. Rebbi, Physics Reports (to appear).

29. See e.g. M. Creutz, "Doing Physics with Computers — High Energy Physics", Physics Today $\underline{36}$, No. 5, p.35 (1983).

30. Floating Point Systems has been collaborating with Cornell on assessing the feasibility of such a system.

PART 1

HARDWARE SYSTEMS

LARGE-SCALE AND HIGH-SPEED MULTIPROCESSOR SYSTEM FOR SCIENTIFIC
APPLICATIONS: CRAY X-MP SERIES

Steve S. Chen

Cray Research, Inc.

Chippewa Falls, WI

1. Overview of CRAY X-MP System

A. General-purpose multiprocessor system for multitasking applications.

* Run independent tasks of different jobs on multiple processors.
  Program compatibility (with CRAY-1) is maintained for all tasks.
* Run related tasks of single job on multiple processors.
    - Loosely-coupled tasks communicating through shared
      memory.
    - Tightly-coupled tasks communicating through shared
      registers.
* Small overhead of task initiation for multitasking, $O(1\,\mu s)$ to
  $O(1 ms)$, depending on granularity of the tasks and software im-
  plementation techniques.
* Flexible architecture concept for processor clustering.
    - All processors are identical and symmetric in their
      programming functions, i.e., there is no permanent
      master/slave relation existing between all processors.
    - A cluster of k processors: $(0 \le k \le p)$ can be assigned to
      perform a single task, where $p = 2$ is the number of physical
      processors in the system.
    - Up to $p + 1$ processor clusters can be assigned by the
      operating system.
    - Each cluster contains a unique set of shared data and
      synchronization registers for the inter-communication of
      all processors in a cluster.
    - Each processor in a cluster can run in either monitor or
      user mode controlled by the operating system.
    - Each processor in a cluster can asynchronously perform
      either scalar or vector operations dictated by user
      programs.
    - Any processor running in monitor mode can interrupt any
      other processor and cause it to switch from user mode to
      monitor mode.
    - Built-in detection of system deadlock within the cluster.

NATO ASI Series, Vol. F7
High-Speed Computation. Edited by J. S. Kowalik
© Springer-Verlag Berlin Heidelberg 1984

* Faster exchange for switching machine state between tasks.
* Hardware supports separation of memory segments for each user's data and program to facilitate the concurrent programming.

B. General-purpose multiprocessor system for compute-bound and I/O-bound applications.

* All processors share a central bipolar memory (4MW), organized in m=32 interleaved memory banks (twice that of CRAY-1). All banks can be accessed independently and in parallel during each machine clock period. Each processor has four parallel memory ports (four times that of CRAY-1) connected to this central memory, two for vector fetches, one for vector store, and one for independent I/O operations. The multiport memory has built-in conflict resolution hardware to minimize the delay and maintain the integrity of all memory references to the same bank in the same time, from all processor's ports. The interleaved and efficient multiport memory design, coupled with shorter memory cycle time, provide a high-performance and balanced memory organization with sufficient bandwidth (eight times that of CRAY-1) to support simultaneous high-speed CPU and I/O operations.

* New, large, CPU-driven Solid-state Storage Device (SSD) is designed as an integral part of the mainframe with very high block transfer rate. This can be used as a fast-access device for user large pre-staged or intermediate files generated and manipulated repetitively by user programs, or used by the system for job "swapping" space and temporary storage of system programs. The SSD design with its large size (32MW), very fast data transfer speed (maximum rate 10 Gb/sec, and typical rate 1000 MB/sec, 250 times faster than disk), and much shorter access time (less than .5 ms, 100 times faster than disk), coupled with the high-performance multiprocessor design, will enable the user to explore new application algorithms for solving bigger and more sophisticated problems in science and engineering which they could not attempt before.

* The I/O Subsystem, which is an integral part of the CRAY X-MP System, also contributes to the system's overall performance. The I/O Subsystem (compatible with CRAY-1/S) offers parallel streaming of disk drives, I/O buffering (8MW max. size) for disk-resident and Buffer Memory-resident datasets, high-performance on-line tape handling, and common device for front-end system

communication, networking, or specialized data acquisition. The
IOP design enables faster and more efficient asynchronous I/O
operations for data access and deposition of initial and final
outputs through high-speed channels (each channel has maximum rate
850 Mb/sec, and typical rate 40 MB/sec, 10 times faster than disk),
while relieving the CPUs to perform computation-intensive
operations.

C. General-purpose multiprocessor system for scalar and vector
applications.

*   All processors are controlled synchronously by a central clock
    with improved cycle time = 9.5 ns (vs. 12.5 ns of CRAY-1).
*   The scalar performance of each processor is improved through
    faster machine clock, shorter memory access time, and larger
    instruction buffers (twice that of CRAY-1).
*   The vector performance of each processor is improved through
    faster machine clock, parallel memory ports, and hardware
    automatic "flexible chaining" features. These new features allow
    simultaneous memory fetches, arithmetic, and memory store
    operations in a series of related vector operations (this
    contrasts to the "fixed chaining" and uni-directional vector
    fetch/store in CRAY-1). As a result, the processor design
    provides higher speed and more balanced vector processing
    capabilities for both long and short vectors, characterized by
    heavy register-to-register or heavy memory-to-memory vector
    operations.
*   The processor design is well-balanced for processing both scalar
    and vector codes. The overall effective performance of each proc-
    essor in execution of typical user programs with interspersing
    scalar and vector codes (usually short vectors) is ensured through
    fast data flow between scalar and vector functional units, short
    memory access time for vector and scalar references, as well as
    small start-up time for scalar and vector operations. As a result
    of this unique design characteristic, the machine can perform very
    well in real programming environments using standard compiler,
    without resorting to enormous amount of hand-coding or even
    restructuring of the original application algorithms.
    Certainly, as the code is more vectorized, and the vector length is
    becoming longer, an even better performance can be achieved.

2. CRAY X-MP MULTIPROCESSOR

IOS   CPUs   SSD

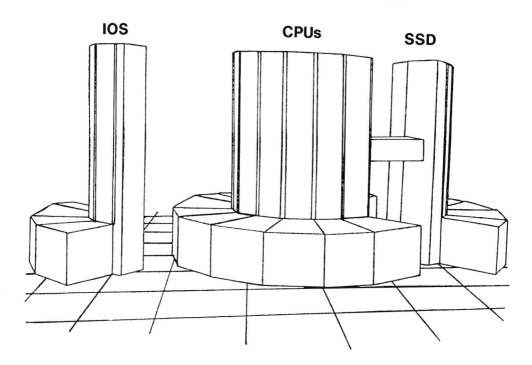

3. CRAY X-MP OVERALL SYSTEM ORGANIZATION

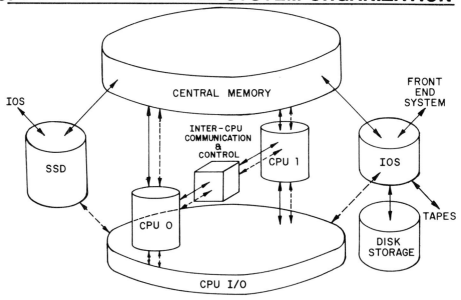

————— DATA PATH
- - - - - CONTROL PATH

4. CRAY X-MP   DATA FLOW

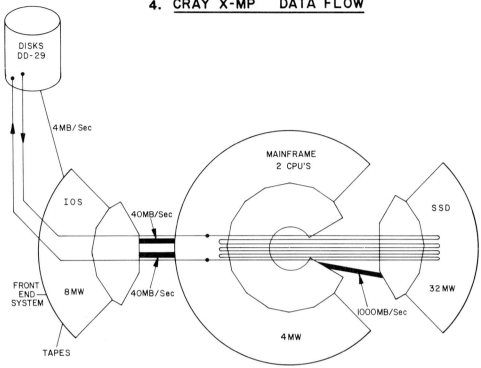

5. SSD CONCEPT

CPU	I/O		I/O	
&				
DISK	USER	USER		USER

CPU	I/O	I/O	I/O	I/O
&	-	-	-	-
SSD	USER	USER	USER	USER	USER

SSD

Used as disk

FUNCTIONS   as extension of central memory

DUE to very short access time: < .5 ms

very fast transfer rate: 1000 MB/SEC

APPLICATION for BIGGER, MORE COMPLEX
problems, which was NOT achievable
before

6. SSD USAGE

Add one JCL card for each temporary
file used.

EXAMPLE:

```
    JOB, --.
    ACCOUNT, --.
    CFT.
→   ASSIGN, DN=FT01, DV=SSD-0-20.
    LDR.
    /EOF
    ⋮
    WRITE(1) A,B,C
    REWIND(1)
    READ(1) A,B,C
    ⋮
    /EOF
```

– NO PROGRAM CHANGES REQUIRED
– FORMATTED OR BINARY I/O
– BLOCKED OR UNBLOCKED I/O
– RANDOM OR SEQUENTIAL I/O

7. VECTOR COMPUTATIONS

$$\bar{A} = \bar{B} + s * \bar{D}$$

FETCH $\bar{B}$ } CRAY-1 1ST CHAIN

FETCH $\bar{D}$

MULTIPLY } CRAY-1 2ND CHAIN

ADD

STORE $\bar{A}$ } CRAY-1 3RD CHAIN

CRAY X-MP ONE CHAIN

NOTES:

1. Using 3 memory ports per processor

2. Hardware automatically "chains" through all five vector operations such that one result per clock period can be delivered

8. VECTOR LOOP FAMILIES BENCHMARK TIMINGS ON X-MP

	1-CPU		
	SHORT VECTOR (VL = 8)	MEDIUM VECTOR (VL = 128)	LONG VECTOR (VL = 1024)
A=B	1.1	1.8	2.1
A=B+C	1.2	2.2	2.7
A=B*C	1.5	2.6	3.3
A=B/C	1.5	1.9	2.0
A=B+C+D	1.5	2.7	3.2
A=B+C*D	1.4	2.9	3.6
A=B+s*D	1.3	3.0	4.0
A=B+C+D+E	1.3	2.3	2.7
A=B+C+D*E	1.6	2.5	2.9
A=B*C+D*E	1.3	2.5	3.1
A=B+C*D+E*F	1.5	2.1	2.2
	1.5	2.5	3.0

(Unit based on compiler generated code running on 1/S)

9. SCIENTIFIC LIBRARY (CAL) BENCHMARK TIMINGS ON X-MP

CODE	(1-CPU X)/1S SPEEDUP FACTOR	
SSUM	1.36	
SDOT	2.26	
SAXPY	4.04	
FOLR (•)	5.93	(3.40)
FOLRN (•)	7.32	(1.94)
GATHER	2.55	
SCATTER	2.48	
MXM	1.33	
MXMA	1.42	
MINV	2.18	
CFFT2	2.16	
CRFFT2	2.12	
RCFFT2	2.11	

(•) New vector algorithms used on X only; the number in ( ) indicates the speedup when vector algorithms are applied to both the X and S

10. GENERAL LINEAR ALGEBRA (FORTRAN) BENCHMARK TIMING ON X-MP

CODE	(1-CPU X)/1S SPEEDUP FACTOR
SGEFA	2.77
SGECO	2.75
SGESL	2.84
SGEDI	2.63
TRED2	3.08
TRED1	2.08
TRBAK1	3.27

11. CRAY X-MP OVERALL PERFORMANCE

1-CPU RATE$_1$ (PEAK 210 MFLOPS)

    MINIMUM: 1

    TYPICAL: SCALAR-DOMINATED   1.5
                VECTOR-DOMINATED 2.0

    MAXIMUM: 4

2-CPU RATE$_2$ (PEAK 420 MFLOPS)

    MINIMUM: 2

    TYPICAL: SCALAR-DOMINATED   3.0
                VECTOR-DOMINATED 4.0

    MAXIMUM: 8

I/O RATE$_3$

	ACCESS TIME	TRANSFER RATE
DISK	1	1
SSD	.01	250

NOTES: 1. Unit based on compiler generated code running on 1/S. TYPICAL refers to small-to-medium size vectors encountered in typical programs

        2. Assuming two CPU's are dedicated to multitasking of a single large job

        3. Unit based on measured time per sector

12. MULTITASKING ON THE CRAY X-MP MULTIPROCESSOR

OFFERS:

- The exploitation of another dimension of parallelism beyond vector processing

- A natural way for scientists and engineers to view their problems

- An opportunity for numerical analysts to explore new and faster parallel algorithms

- A convenient way for programmers to express concurrency in their programs

- Improved performance at several levels

13. TWO DIMENSIONS OF PARALLELISM

MULTITASKING

↑

    HIGHER level parallelism

    independent ALGORITHMS

    JOB/PROGRAM/LOOP oriented

    SINGLE and MULTI-JOB performance

                LOWER level parallelism

                independent OPERATIONS

                STATEMENT oriented

                SINGLE JOB performance

→

SEQUENTIAL   VECTORIZATION
(SCALAR)   (VECTOR)

14. MULTITASKING - EXPLOITING PARALLELISM AT SEVERAL LEVELS

(Conceptual Examples)

1. **Multitasking at the job level (1)**

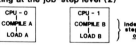

2. **Multitasking at the job-step level (2)**

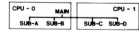

3. **Multitasking at the program level (3)**

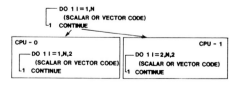

4. **Multitasking at the loop level (4)**

      ┌─ DO 1 I=1,N
      │   (SCALAR OR VECTOR CODE)
      └1 CONTINUE

CPU - 0	CPU - 1
┌─ DO 1 I=1,N,2 │ (SCALAR OR VECTOR CODE) └1 CONTINUE	┌─ DO 1 I=2,N,2 │ (SCALAR OR VECTOR CODE) └1 CONTINUE

NOTES: 1. SW support available now
       2. Need further feasibility study
       3., 4. SW support for user-directed multitasking available now

66

15. MULTITASKING OF VECTOR CODE

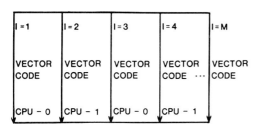

Example:

```
       DO 2 I = 1,M
            .
            .
         DO 1 J = 1,N          } VECTOR
    1      A(I,J) = B(I,J) + C(I,J)  } CODE
            .
            .
       2 CONTINUE
```

16. MULTITASKING OF SCALAR CODE

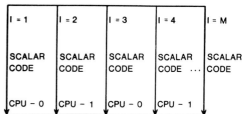

Example:

```
       DO 2 I = 1,M
            .
            .
         DO 1 J = 1,N          } SCALAR
    1      A(I,J) = A(I,J-1)•A(I,J)  } CODE
            .
            .
       2 CONTINUE
```

17. MULTITASKING BY PROCESSOR PIPELINING

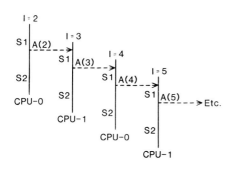

Example:

```
       DO 1 I = 2,N

       A(I) = A(I-1)∗B(I)       S1

       D(I) = A(I)+C(I)         S2

    1 CONTINUE
```

18. MULTITASKING VS. VECTORIZATION FOR THE CRAY X-MP

-Vectorization offers a speedup of up to 10-20 over scalar processing, depending on actual code and vector length

- Multitasking offers an additional speedup of Sp ≤ 2 , depending on task size and relative multitasking overhead

- Total speedup over scalar processing
  = SPEEDUP (MULTITASKING)•SPEEDUP (VECTORIZATION)
  e.g.= Sp•(10-20)=18-38 : ASSUMING Sp=1.8-1.9

- A general guideline: first, partition tasks at the highest possible level to apply multitasking, and then vectorize each task as much as possible

19. X-MP MULTITASKING PERFORMANCE

- Multitasking is running on the X-MP.

- Multitasking has been demonstrated with PIC code, SPECTRAL code and MG3D code.

- For two processors the speedup is 1.8 - 1.9 over one processor.

- Parallelism is at a high level – program modification is minimal.

- Multitasking overhead with the X-MP hardware/software is negligible.

20. PIC

- A particle-in-cell simulation program for electro/magneto static interaction between collisionless beams of plasma

- Parallelism occurs in the independent tracking of particles, and the evaluation of total charge distribution

- Multitasking accounts for 96% of the execution time of a model experiment involving 37,000 particles, and 50 time steps

- 1-CPU execution time = 22.5 seconds on X-MP

- 2-CPU execution time = 12.1 seconds on X-MP

Actual 2-CPU speedup = 1.86 over 1-CPU

21. SPECTRAL

- This is a benchmark code for short term weather forecast

- Parallelism occurs on the latitude level, i.e., the outermost loop inside each time step

- Multitasking accounts for 98% of the execution time of a model experiment involving a global grid structure with 160 latitude by 192 longitude points, and 200 time steps

- 1-CPU execution time = 380.8 seconds on X-MP

- 2-CPU execution time = 201.2 seconds on X-MP

Actual 2-CPU speedup = 1.89 over 1-CPU

22. MG3D

- A seismic 3-D migration code to construct underground reflector structure.

- Parallelism occurs in the decoupled frequency domain at each depth level, after Fourier Transform over time.

- Multitasking accounts for 98% of the execution time of a model experiment involving 200 x 200 traces, with 1024 time samples for each trace, and 1000 depth level.

  - Total computation = 1.5×10^{12} FLOPS
  - Total I/O = 40×10^9 Words

- 1-CPU execution time = 23.8 hours with disk

  = 3.58 hours with SSD

  (6.6 times speedup over 1-CPU with disk)

- 2-CPU execution time = 1.89 hours with SSD

  (12.6 times speedup over 1-CPU with disk)

Actual 2-CPU speedup = 1.89 over 1-CPU

SIMPLICITY AND FLEXIBILITY IN CONCURRENT COMPUTER ARCHITECTURE

Wolfgang Händler
Institut für Mathematische Maschinen und Datenverarbeitung
Martensstrasse 3
D - 8520 Erlangen
F. R. Germany

1. Obstacles to innovative concurrent computer architecture

The speed-up of a p-concurrent computer device is generally not equivalent to p and a higher availability of an ensemble of p structures is not evidently given by itself. Beyond it there is no real direct way to solve the problem of "full employment" regarding the p structures with respect to certain given algorithms or procedures /1/.

According to Charles Vick /2/ "I've always felt that the challenge to map an inherently parallel problem space into a parallel solution space with as few artificial transformations as possible represents one of the most interesting challenges that a computer scientist or engineer could ask for".

As a consequence of VLSI-technology many possibilities are given. However, not having suited theories for solving arbitrary problems on a multiplicity of elementary (not necessarily simple) structures, we have no chance to utilize these possibilities.

Up to now a general line has not been found. The obstacles to a variable "parallelization" (bringing a problem into a form, where many parts (tasks) of it can be computed or executed simultaneously) can be characterized as follows (compare /3/ and /4/).

1. Multiprocessors become unmasterably complex (Complexity myth)
2. Speed-up of a multiprocessor (or parallel processor) with n units becomes only about $\log_2 n$ (Minsky's conjecture)
3. A Princeton-Type-Computer (Processor) is not an appropriate starting point for building up multiprocessors (Myth of the von Neumann bottleneck).

NATO ASI Series, Vol. F7
High-Speed Computation. Edited by J. S. Kowalik
© Springer-Verlag Berlin Heidelberg 1984

4. Any computer essentially deviating from the conventional Princeton line becomes necessarily a special purpose computer, which reaches an outstanding performance only with respect to specific problems (Myth of the unavoidability of specialization).
5. Parallel programs are qualitatively different from sequential programs (Myth 1, as discussed by Anita Jones and Peter Schwarz /4/.
6. Parallel programs are intrinsically more difficult to write than sequential software (Myth 2, in /4/).
7. Multiprocessors are doomed to waste substantial resources owing to synchronization (Myth 3, in /4/).
8. Cost c for a conventional Princeton-Type Processor results in a performance proportional to c^2 (double cost results in four times the performance etc.). In contrast to it in multiprocessors double cost brings about at most double performance (however, compare 2). ("Grosch's Law")
9. Multiprocessors are more reliable than uniprocessors (Myth 4, in /4/).

While the mythoi 1 - 7 are negative and sceptical statements, the mythos 9 (myth 4 of Anita Jones) is an optimistic statement or an overestimation which can become true only with careful analysis and appropriate software. Mythos 8 reinforces Mythos 2, saying that it is an uneconomic affair to go into parallelism.

In the following we continue to discuss the mythoi more in detail.

Concerning 1
Multiprocessors have generally a great number of parts (units) which have to be interconnected, while uniprocessors have only very few. The number of possible interconnections between n units is proportional to p^2 (or p (p - 1)). In consequence cost of connective hardware increases with the power of two and above it the control will increase equally intolerably.

The "Timids", i.e. early multiprocessors with $p \leq 4$, seem to certify this statement.

Comment: To connect "everything with everything" therefore cannot be a reasonable concept. Connections must be restricted to a certain defined neighborhood, see chapter 2, in order to achieve reasonable cost, control, fault tolerance and traffic characteristics.

Concerning 2

Data must be distributed, must be collected, and must be interchanged between the p units, while this is not necessary in conventional uni-processors. M. Minsky /5/ argues therefore that a considerable amount of time is spent always for communication in multiprocessors as well as in parallel processors. His conjecture for an average possible speed-up is $\log_2 p$ which is a very discouraging figure in particular for great p. It would mean, that it is unreasonable to build up multiprocessors at all and in particular those for great p.

Comment: Experiments and investigations have shown meanwhile that Minsky´s conjecture is too pessimistic in general. Possible speedups can considerably vary from application to application. The experience shows that speed-up distinctly above $\log_2 p$ can always be achieved.
From a certain p on - dependent on the specific application - the speed-up becomes uneconomic. One has to decide each case (or application) on its own [+)].
It seems to be rewarding to search for more rigorous estimations and possibly theorems with respect to speed-ups in multiprocessors and parallel processors /6/.

Concerning 3

With the seventies criticism came up concerning the Princeton-Type Computer /7/ (or von Neumann Computer). With respect to programming activities and control one was considering what is called the "semantic gap".It was stated that the infrastructure of a Princeton-Processor is not well suited to algorithmic structures. With respect to hardware and in particular to traffic one criticized what is called the "von Neumann-bottle-neck". Just with the last argument we might come to the conclusion that it is unreasonable to build up multiprocessors.

Comment: While the semantic gap leads to a development, which is called "applicative programming" or "functional programming" which will not be subject of this paper, the "von Neumann-bottle-neck" is not prohibitive with respect to multiprocessor conception. The bottle-neck is not an inherent property of the Princeton-Processor. Rather it is a question of appropriate connections, data-paths and synchronization, i.e. it is a problem, which can be solved independently for multiprocessors. Above it data flow can be realized in multiprocessors which is one basis for bridging the semantic gap /8/.

[+)] Compare also another paper which is in preparation by W. Henning, also IMMD.

Concerning 4
A specialization seems to be unavoidable, looking e.g. to ILLIAC/IV.
This computer has an excellent performance processing regular data of a
multiplicity of 64. Nevertheless there are instances, where some or all
of the ALUs (Arithmetic and Logic Units) are unused. Above it large
classes of problems are entirely unsuited to ILLIAC IV ! Other examples
are e.g. STARAN and PEPE, which in this sense are "Specialists". In
unfavourable situations a majority of hardware is "unemployed". This
must be avoided by choosing only well suited problems with respect to
such a specific computer.

Comment: Nevertheless this kind of specialization can be avoided by
striving for flexibility, versatility and adaptability in computer
architecture. An once existing hardware must be made ready for manifold
utilization. If this can be done in runtime then it is called "dynamic
architecture" (comp. /3/, /9/ where the specific kind of utilization
again is called "operation mode".

Concerning 5 (taken over literally from A. Jones and P. Schwarz /4/).
"Parallel programs are qualitatively different from sequential programs. This myth is false. But parallel programs are quantitatively
different. The result is a shift in emphasis, not a radical change. For
example, consider synchronization; the same primitives found in uniprocessor operating systems are also used on multiprocessors. However most
of the concern in the uniprocessor case has been with the "wake-up"
policy, which determines how many and which particular waiting
processes may continue when a synchronization event is signalled. In
contrast, in the multiprocessor it is the associated "resource" policy
that is of interest. The resource policy determines which resources a
process may continue to hold while waiting to pass a synchronization
point".

Concerning 6 (taken over literally from /4/).
"Parallel programs are intrinsically more difficult to write than
sequential software. We found this myth to be false most of the time.
Using current programming disciplines and object-oriented operating
systems, one need rarely consider the behavior of anything other than a
sequential program. The rare exceptions are in programs that directly
manipulate physical devices. Timing bugs may arise. Only in such cases
need one consider the action of multiple executing entities. However,
when such occasions do arise, it is extremely difficult to understand
multiple simultaneous threads of execution".

Concerning 7 (taken over literally from /4/).
"Multiprocessors are doomed to waste substantial resources owing to synchronization. This myth is fallacious. Measurements on locking within the HYDRA operating system show that if data are locked instead of critical code sections, synchronization can be negligible. In measurements involving 14 processors, idleness due to locking consumed less than 1 percent of the processors".

Concerning 8
Grosch´s law (comp. /3/, as it is called, reflects the situation in the Sixties where small additional features like index registers, cache registers and certain refinements in control always resulted in a considerable success. Many of such steps of refinement - amounting once again the cost of the non-improved processor - could result in a four-fold performance (as compared with the non-improved processor).

Comment: For many reasons this "law" is no longer valid. Many of the refinements have become standards and to introduce other proved to be not as favourable as c^2, because physical laws and in particular speed of light set limits to further improvements.

Concerning 9 (taken over literally from /4/).
"Multiprocessors are more reliable than uniprocessors. Stated more generally, physically distributed systems are more reliable. This myth is also false. Physical distribution does not automatically lead to a more reliable system unless the software is also logically distributed. Both HYDRA and PLURIBUS illustrate that with care and forethought a system with high availability can be built. Integrity is a much more difficult objective to achieve. The long-known method of checkpointing may be used to attain integrity at a very gross level but when the system is reset many changes are lost. Integrity at a finer grain is yet to be accomplished".
Mythoi have generally a long life. They must be recognized and unmasked in our case in order to reach a better starting point for viable multiprocessor and parallel-processor solutions.

2. New Concepts in Computer Architecture

This chapter summarizes new concepts, developments, and experience, which are suited to conquer the forementioned obstacles and mythoi, not forming, a (1 to 1) correspondence, however. The concepts fall mainly in two categories, namely ´simplicity´ and ´flexibility´.

2.1 Simplicity

Regarding simplicity some keywords are:
    tight coupling with multiports   Fig. 1
    restricted neighborhood   Fig. 2
    regularity and homogenity   Fig. 3
    hierarchy   Fig. 4
    space-sharing   Fig. 5
    size-independent topology   Fig. 6
(where there is not given an order or rank).

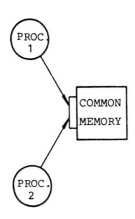

Fig. 1: Tight coupling with multiports

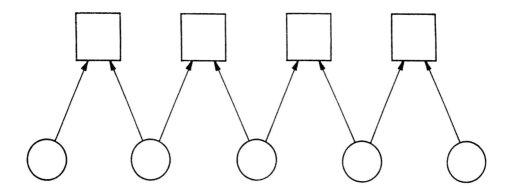

Fig. 2: Restricted neighbourhood

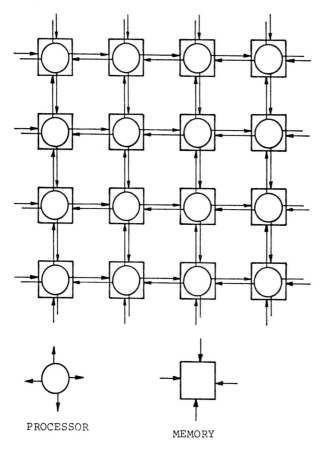

PROCESSOR

MEMORY

Fig. 3: Regularity and homogeneity

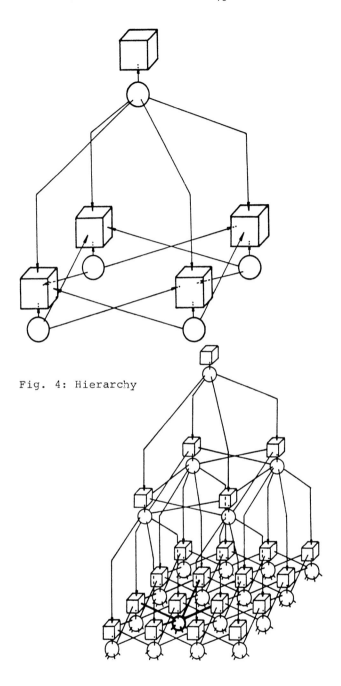

Fig. 4: Hierarchy

Fig. 5: "Space-Sharing" (or Resource Sharing) substitutes the former concept of "Time Sharing". The lowest layer of processors form the working area (resp. 4, 16, 64, 256 etc. processors). The other upper layers are dedicated to a global operating system.

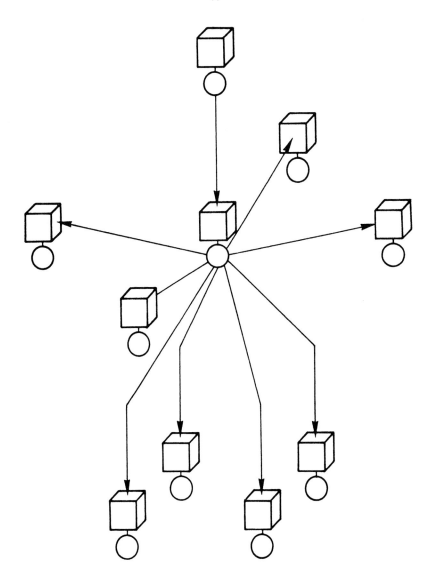

Fig. 6: Size independent topology

2.1.1 With multiports as entrance to memory blocks is introduced a minimum of problems regarding communication and logic synchronization of a multitude of processors. All current methods for communicative and logic synchronization can be applied without essential restrictions. In some cases additional hardware can be provided for interrupt functions.

2.1.2 It is not reasonable to realize all possible connections between processors. With 1024 processors for instance one would have to provide a multiport with an 1024-port at the entrance of each memory block. This is an unrealistic and expensive unit particularly if the memory block is comparably small. Therefore one has normally - and in particular with an increasing number of processors - to provide a restricted neighborhood-topology. For the sake of simplicity one unique type of multiport should be designed, preferably with a number 2^d of inputs. Preliminary experience shows, that in the context of typical applications d may be reasonably chosen 2, 3, or 4. Investigations for some more specific problems like Fast Fourier-Transform /10/ show a considerable adaptability of a restricted-neighborhood-topology to a majority of problems. Above it some theoretical investigations e.g. by Galil et Paul /1/ show that some regular and homogeneous topologies fulfil considerably the requirements with respect to a general exchange of data.

2.1.3 Regularity and homogeneity are asked for with respect to easy mastering of

1. Production (fabrication in particular with respect to VLSI-design)
2. Verification/Checking
3. Programming/Programming tools
4. Systolic computation /11/.

In most cases a rectangular array of processors and/or ALUs is most appropriate, as it can be derived from the algorithmic scheme of Relaxation methods, where at any time preferably data are taken by a respective processor (i,k) from locations (i-1,k),(i+1,k),(i,k-1),(i,k+1).

Similar results can be obtained e.g. from the application of Matrix-Multiplication-Methods, Matrix-Inversion-Methods and from Fast-Fourier-Transform, which always demand highly regular data-exchange. This is valid in particular in the case of systolic processes, where hexagonal (and other regular) connections are appropriate. As an essential point one can state that regularity and homogeneity are mainly directed to the requirements of data-exchange in multiprocessors and/or ALU-arrays.

2.1.4 Tasks and data have initially to be distributed in multiprocessor systems. In particular data have to be distributed in the case of parallel processors. In the case of multiprocessors this would lead to a control unit, which can broadcast all tasks approximately at the same time to all processors, which seems to contradict fundamentally 2.1.2.

Another possibility would be to feed in the tasks, data etc. by one particular processor (possibly one, which is located in the "centre" of the regular structure, compare 2.1.3). This would mean in the rectangular case that broadcasting would consume a time which depends on the square-root of the number of processors involved: p (particular considerations could be made in the case of an other regular array of processors).

To improve this figure one has to introduce another principle of "space-sharing" (compare 2.1.5). The job of broadcasting can be allocated to particular processors, which are connected hierarchically in certain regular layers to the originally two-dimensional array of processors (or ALUs). The simplest imagination shows a third dimension, in which all control functions place (fig. 4) /12/. Assuming such a hierarchical structure above the regular two-dimensional working space one concentrates all distributing functions, broadcastings, scheduling etc. in the upper regions of the pyramid. To distribute (or broadcast) something then consumes time in order of $\log_2 q = 1/2 \log_2 q$ (instead of q, as pointed out above for the two-dimensional case).

Regular rectangular, hexagonal or e.q. octogonal structures were described in contrast to it as suited for computing on respective data structures like matrices. Hierarchical structures are needed for control purposes and - as we have seen - for exchange of data between processors which are not immediate neighbors. Requirements for immediate data-exchange on the one hand and for control (as well as for long range data-exchange) on the other hand seem to be incompatible first of all.

Nevertheless may find a consistent structure - as shown above -, which combines the two requirements in that every horizontal cut of the structure shows a homogeneous, regular shape, while every vertical cut results in a hierarchical shape, which shows - neglecting horizontal connections - a tree structure, where every node is connected with four subordinated nodes and with one superior node. Just this tree-substructure shows also a regularity but not a homogeneous [+] one.

Regularity, homogeneity (2.1.3) and hierarchy (2.1.4) as developed here implicate two other properties which nevertheless are fortunately most favourable. The additional properties as a consequence are discussed in 2.1.5 and 2.1.6.

2.1.5 The system developed so far shows a multitude of processors mainly bounded by two structures a horizontal (regular-homogeneous) one (2.1.3) and a vertical (hierarchical) one (2.1.4). Considering the lowest horizontal structure it is clear that not the whole layer of (with their connections) will be utilized at any time. Rather a natural job stream of applications will demand at any time for a specific partition into subsets of processors. Each subset performing tasks independently from the others. Instead of time-sharing with respect to the single processors the tasks are distributed onto the array of the lowest layer. This means space-sharing with respect to application programs. Nevertheless the task of distribution itself is done by a specific processor or by a certain group of processors of superior layers (fig. 5).
So we have - in the vertical direction - a partition again between the Operating System and the many application tasks. The Operating System itself can be divided into many specific tasks like scheduling, distribution of data and tasks, evaluation of status reports and e.g. accounting (if necessary), which are spread out onto the superior layers of the pyramid.

In general therefore we allocate tasks to processors, which hold these tasks for a longer period than this usually will happen with conventional single processors. During the execution of a program no task scheduling is necessary. Nevertheless data have to move from task to task and so from one processor to the next one /13/, regarding one subset of processors.

[+] Of course: this statement would really depend on more rigorous definitions, which are not given here. This paper is rather directed to an immediate comprehension.

2.1.6 Finally the structure - so far developed - is size-independent because having a certain deepness of the pyramid (a sufficient number of layers) the local connection-topology of one processor (node of the structure) remains the same for all lower layers e.g. 9 connections [+)] for the shown example (fig. 6).
Most other concepts for multiprocessors have in contrast to it the property that the number of connections increases with p^2 again (p: number of processors) for the whole configuration and with p with respect to one processor.

With a "size-independent" topology configurations can be built up on different sizes without any change in technology. This presents a substantial realization of the concept to spread out the performance by multiplying equal units of one unique technology.

2.2 Flexibility

It is worthwhile, to remind of some earlier concepts of flexibility which came up with computers and computing. The following milestones may be noted in this context

1941 Program control: Konrad Zuse demonstrates the first programmable computer Z 3
1946 Modifiable stored program: Burks, Goldstine and von Neumann create the idea of a stored program, which itself can be modified by another program
1951 Universal non dedicated bus: Connections between various parts of a computer become flexible (MIT's Whirlwind Computer)
1951 Microprogrammability: Maurice Wilkes creates the flexible control device, which facilitates design, construction, maintenance, and adaptability of computers
1960 Polymorphy: Units of computer like memory blocks, processors, I/O-devices etc. can be combined more flexibly according to the respective need and to the ever changing need during the life time cycle
1960 Fixed plus variable structure: E. Estrin develops the concept of adaptable hardware, which can be adjusted to the respective need of a given application or algorithm
[+)] Each processor is connected to the local memory block allocated to it (it's not a private memory!)

ca. 1974 Dynamic Computer Architecture: Kartashev and Kartashev propose, to make interchangeable wordlengths, number of ALUs and
numbers of processors.

Evidently these concepts are upwards compatible. Altogether they offer
an impression of greatest possible flexibility with respect to computers. Nevertheless the concept of Estrin /14/ as well as the concept of
Kartashev and Kartashev /9/ are not accepted and not realized so far.

Besides there are some other concepts which may be considered in this
context, i.e.

2.2.1   Classical universal processor (Princeton)
2.2.2   Advanced universal processor (General register set)
2.2.3   Higher Level Language processor (Burroughs)
2.2.4   IPL-processor (List processing concept)
2.2.5   Demand-driven-processor (Berkling et al.)
2.2.6   Data-driven or Data-flow-processor (Dennis)
2.2.7   Associative/parallel processor (STARAN)
2.2.8   Cellular processor (Legendi)
2.2.9   Objectoriented processor (iAPX 432)
2.2.10   Digital differential analyzer (DDA)

Up to now mainly the type of the advanced universal processor (as a
descendant of the classical universal processor) dominates the scene in
an average computing centre. Also the type of the higher level language
processor has its own adherents. All other types, and in particular
data-flow-processors and associative processors have their specific
adgerents, while only a very few examples are realized [+)].
The following thesises are given for a flexible and versatile Computer
Architecture:

a) The <Operation Modes> 2.2.1 til 2.2.10 are pairwise compatible
b) A processor can be designed in a manner that the given hardware
   always can be utilized in a multitude of <Operation Modes> according
   to the respective program under consideration.
c) In the case an interchange of Operation Modes is performed by an
   auxiliary program in runtime, the Computer Architecture is called a
   dynamic [+)] one. (The auxiliary program may be called for a part of
   O.S.)

[+)]   Kartashev and Kartashev have called their specific concept <Dynamic
   Computer Architecture>. In this paper we use the same term with a
   slightly changed meaning.

d) A splitting of a system into one <host> on the one hand and into a <specialist> on the other hand can be avoided by an appropriate design according to a) til c). (Compare myth 4 in chapter 1.)

As a consequence of a) til d) a unique Operating System can be supported, which supervises the system in the usual way. While a Host/Specialist splitting gives an additional load with respect to communication, data transfer and synchronization between both (Host-Specialist), such an unique Operating System, residing on a Dynamic Computer Hardware offers many advantages.

Compatibility and as a consequence of it the unification of concepts 2.2.1 til 2.2.9 should be discussed to some extent, while it is impossible to cover all aspects of the ongoing research. Most of the respective research has to be done in the future. In this paper we endeavour to sketch the main points.

It has been shown in other papers (/15/ til /17/), that the Conventional Processor - mainly characterized by 2.2.1 and 2.2.2 (universal processors) and often also by elements of the HLL processors - can be extended in order to cover also the Associative/Parallel Processor according to 2.2.7 (similar to STARAN). In this specific case data are stored, interpreted and processed in an unique processor in either way. This happens by filling up the Instruction Code, utilizing existing microprogramming devices and by designing an extra turntable (hardware) which simplifies the necessary conversion of data (compare fig. 7).
This conversion from horizontal (conventional) data format to vertical (new associative/parallel) data format is executed predominantly only in the context of I/O processes.
Taking many such processors configuring a Multiprocessor by connecting them across multiport-memories (compare in particular 2.1.1 and 2.1.2), concepts of Demand-Driven-Processor [++] (2.2.5) and Data-Driven-Processor (2.2.6) can be approximated on such a structure /18/. Approximation in this context means a certain deviation with respect to known papers on the subject (and in particular those from J. Dennis /8/). Most papers on Data-Flow up to now deal with operands and operations in the order of machine instructions and with problems to parallelize on this level (grain-of-sand-level). Other papers occasionally have criticized

[+]   Kartashev and Kartashev have called their specific concept <Dynamic Computer Architecture>. In this paper we use the same term with a slightly changed meaning.
[++]   also called Reduction Machine

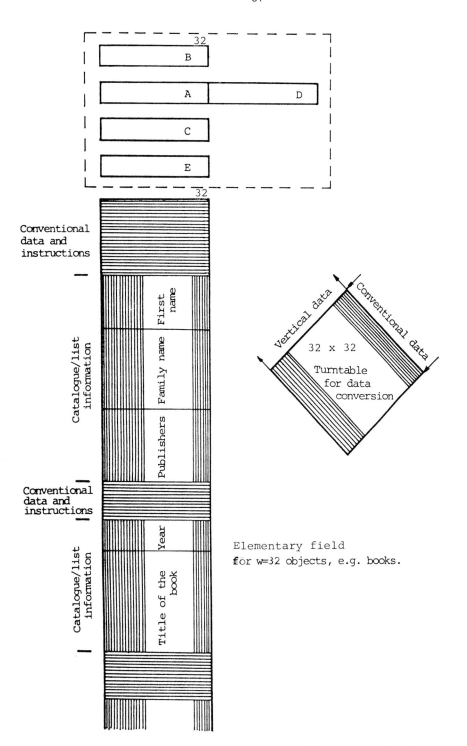

Fig. 7: Vertical processing with a 32 bit conventional processor, equipped by a microprogrammed, additional instruction code, resulting in parallel and associative computing.

just this point and stated that such a partition is far too atomic. An appropriate step into a more feasible direction seems to be to raise the whole consideration into a higher level and in particular into task level /19/. The step from instruction level to the task level seems to fit also in an other contemporary concept, namely in <Object-oriented Architecture> 2.2.9 /20/.

Tasks or more general <Objects> with their specific functions which are allowed to be applied to them are then allocated to specific memory blocks, which connect processors working on the objects.

Up to now we have slightly outlined a unification of 2.2.1, 2.2.2, 2.2.3, 2.2.5, 2.2.6, 2.2.7 and 2.2.9. In favour of comprehensibility we relinquish some more details, which are under investigation now, and solutions which have beend already found. Final remarks can be made on concepts 2.2.4 (IPL-Processor) and 2.2.8 (Cellular Processor) instead.

Apart from the fact that List-Oriented Processors (2.2.4) have been recently designed by utilization of microprocessors in consideration of microprogramming devices, it is to remark that they are very close in a natural way to HLL-Processors (2.2.3) on the one hand and to Data-Flow-Processors (2.2.6) on the other hand. Applications which are suited to a List-Oriented Processor are in most cases also suited to Associative/Parallel-Processors (2.2.7).
In such a way the proposed unified processor offers a lot of new insight into computing. The Operation Mode may be exchanged several times during runtime of one application program.
It remains to show, how the concept of Cellular Processor (2.2.8) can be unified with all other concepts. For this reason we consider a 32 x 32-field (array) of elements (as an example). First of all these (1024) elements may be thought of being register elements (dynamic or static).

Realizing the connection between neighboring elements we have the usual register set (32 cells, each one with a wordlength of 32 as an example with respect to concepts 2.2.1, 2.2.2 and 2.2.3). Making available also a ´vertical´ access to the field (fig. 7), we have at the same time a realization of the turntable which was mentioned above in the context of an Associative/Parallel-Processor (2.2.7). All other earlier statements are still valid, so that also the other concepts and in particular 2.2.5 (Demand-Driven-Processor) and 2.2.6 (Data-Driven-Processor) are covered. Finally we extend now the elements (each one as an own entity) to a real <cellular element> in the sense of 2.2.7 /21/.

3. Outlook

Nowadays computer architecture is excellently suited to VLSI-[+] and even WSI[++]-Technology considering in particular regularity, homogeneity, hierarchy and in general simplicity (as pointed out in Section 2.1). In such a way the next step in direction of more flexibility in Computer Architecture can be taken into account and seems to be realistic (Fig.8).

[+] VLSI: Very Large Scale Integration /22/
[++] WSI: Wafer Scale Integration /23/
    A planar multitude of VLSI´s as they appear as a consequence of the production process, can be considered as a unit of higher order.

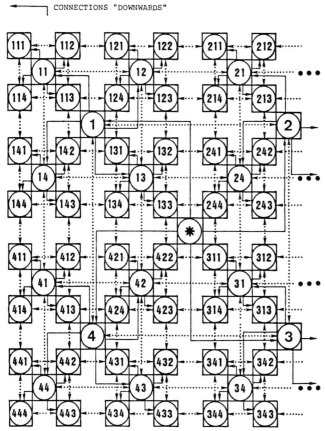

Fig.8: The pyramid transformed onto a plane (for Wafer-Scale-Integration). Compare fig.4 and fig.5 .

References

/1/ Galil, Z., W. Paul: Effizienz paralleler Rechner; In: Brauer, W. (Hrsg.) Informatik Fachbereiche, Vol. 33: GI - 10. Jahrestagung, Wilhelm R. (Hrsg.), pp. 54 - 64, Springer Verlag 1980

/2/ Vick, C.R.: Research and Development in Computer Technology. How do we follow the last act? (Keynote address); In: Proc. 1978 International Conference on Parallel Processing, pp. 1 - 5, G. J. Lipovski ed., IEEE/ACM Catalog No. 78CH1321-9C

/3/ Händler, W.: Innovative computer architecture - how to increase parallelism but not complexity; In: Evans, D.J. (ed.): Parallel Processing Systems; Cambridge University Press, Cambridge 1982, pp. 1 - 41
    or: Händler, W.: Technology in Computing and Architectural Considerations; In: Proceedings SEAS Anniversary Meeting 81, Nice Vol. 1 (1981) 17 - 38

/4/ Jones, A. and P. Schwartz: Experiences Using Multiprocessor Systems - A Status Report; Computing Surveys Vol. 12 (1980) No. 2, pp. 121 - 165

/5/ Minski, M., S. Papert: On some associative, parallel and analog computations; In: Associative Information Techniques, edit. E. J. Jacobs Elsevier, New York, 1971

/6/ Kuck, D.: The Structure of Computers and Computing; John Wiley and Sons Inc. 1978, Vol. 1

/7/ Backus, J.: Can Programming be liberated from the von Neumann style? A functional style and its algebra of programs; CACM 21 (1978), pp. 613 - 614

/8/ Dennis, J. B.: Data Flow Supercomputers; Computer 13 (1980), pp. 48 - 56

/9/ Kartashev, S. I. and Kartashev, S. P.; Kartashev, S. I. ed.: "Designing and Programming Modern Computers and Systems", Vol. 1, LSI modular computer systems; Prentice Hall, Inc., Englewood Cliffs, New Jersey 07632, 1982

/10/ Arnold, F., L. Benker, M. Grütz: Die Fast Fourier Transformation und Möglichkeiten ihrer Implementierung auf EGPA; Arbeitsbereichte des IMMD, Vol. 10 (1977) No. 14, University of Erlangen-Nürnberg

/11/ Kung, H.T.: The structure of parallel algorithms; In: Advances in Computers, Vol. 19, edited by Marshall C. Jovits, 1980, pp. 65 - 112

/12/ Händler, W., F. Hofmann and H.J. Schneider: A general purpose array with a broad spectrum of applications; In: Proceedings of the Workshop on Computer Architecture IFB, Springer-Verlag Vol. 4 (1975), pp. 1 - 335 (and numerous further publications of the Project EGPA)

/13/ Kneißl, F.: Realisierung von Makro-Datenflußmechanismen auf hierarchischen Mehrrechnersystemen; Dissertation, University of Erlangen-Nürnberg, 1982

/14/ Estrin, G.: Organization of computer systems: The fixed plus variable structure computer; In: Proceedings of Western Joint Comput. Conf. 1960, pp. 30 - 40

/15/ Händler, W.,: "Unconventional Computation by Conventional Equipment", Arbeitsberichte des IMMD, Vol. 7 (1974) No. 2, University of Erlangen-Nürnberg

/16/ Bode, A., Händler, W.: "Some results on associative processing by extending a microprogrammed general purpose processor"; 6th workshop on computer architecture for non numerical processing, Hyeres INRIA, ISBN 2-7261-0260-3 (1981)

/17/ Albert, B.; Bode, A.; Händler, W.: "A Case study in Vertical Migration: The Implementation of a Dedicated Associative Instruction Set"; In: Microprocessing and Microprogramming, 8 (1981) 257 - 262, North-Holland

/18/ Treleaven, P.C.: Taxonomy of data driven and demand driven
     computer architecture; In: Workshop on Taxonomy in Computer Archi-
     tecture, pp. 107 - 124, Nürnberg, F.R. Germany, June 9, 1981
     Blaauw, G. W., W. Händler (ed.): Arbeitsberichte des IMMD, Vol. 14
     (1981) No. 8, University of Erlangen-Nürnberg
/19/ Jones, A. K., K. Schwans: TASK forces: distributed software for
     solving problems of substantial size; In: 4th int. conference on
     software engineering, pp. 315 - 330, ACM/SIGSOFT, Munich, Germany,
     Sept. 1979
/20/ intel: iAPX 432 01 iAPX 432 02 VLSI general data processor, preli-
     minary data sheet
/21/ Legendi, T.: Cellular algorithms and their verification; In:
     Lecture Notes in Computer Science, Vol. 111, pp. 167 - 188 CONPAR
     81, Proceedings, Nürnberg, June 10 - 12 (1981), edited by W.
     Händler, Springer-Verlag, Berlin-Heidelberg-New York 1981
/22/ Mead, C. A. and L. Conway: Introduction to VLSI Systems; Addison-
     Wesley, 1980
/23/ Aubusson, R. C. and I. Catt: Wafer Scale Integration: a New Ap-
     proach; ESSCIRC 77, pp. 76 - 78

DISTRIBUTED ARRAY PROCESSOR, ARCHITECTURE AND PERFORMANCE

S.F. Reddaway
International Computers Limited
Stevenage
England

1. INTRODUCTION

The origin of the DAP (Distributed Array Processor) architecture lay in matching
the capabilities of rapidly advancing semi-conductor technology with some real
world problems. A major feature that suited both the technology and the
applications was parallelism, and the design adopted was a large array of bit-
organised processing elements (PEs), each having both storage and processing. The
emphasis was on simplicity, generality and flexibility.

The approach is consistently parallel throughout and by-passes many of the problems
associated with grafting some parallelism onto heavily ingrained sequential
practices. In particular, a parallel language (DAP-Fortran) is a key component
providing both natural parallel application programming and efficient hardware
execution. The approach is a more radical departure than that adopted by vector
machines, which leads to both advantages and disadvantages.

Vector machines emphasise arithmetic performance, especially floating point
multiply and add/subtract on one (or at most two) precisions. DAP is very flexible
 with respect to number representation and precision, with full trade-offs against
speed and storage space. In a wider sense the bit organisation gives generality of
function as we shall see. This means that DAP performance on a complete algorithm
or application is often much more impressive than the raw MFLOPS processing power.

The simple nature of the bit-organisation means that hardware development is
relatively cheap and quick and the result relatively cheap to manufacture and
maintain. An emphasis has been cost-effective power, rather than power-at-any-
price.

NATO ASI Series, Vol. F7
High-Speed Computation. Edited by J. S. Kowalik
© Springer-Verlag Berlin Heidelberg 1984

An important aspect is the balance between storage and raw processing power. In many applications, a large store is of very great value. Considerable emphasis has therefore been given to providing a large store, even at the expense of processing power, to enable effective problem solving.

2.   DAP ARCHITECTURE

This has been described elsewhere (references 1,2,3) so this account is brief.

DAP is an SIMD machine with a large array of simple bit-organised PEs under the control of a Master Control Unit (MCU). Connectivity is of 3 kinds, the first 2 giving the array a 2D (square) organisation.

    a)   2D nearest neighbour connections, including wrap-around cyclic connections.

    b)   Row and column highways terminating on one of a set of MCU registers. As well as bit-vector transfers between an MCU register and any chosen row or column, a bit-vector can be replicated to make a bit-matrix and a bit-matrix can be condensed to a bit-vector by ANDing along rows or columns. If the latter is followed by a jump dependent on the MCU register being all True, a branch depending on a condition being True throughout the array has taken only two machine instructions.

    c)   A data bit can be broadcast to all PEs.

The store is 3D, formed by the 2D array of PEs each having a few thousand bits of store. Data can be stored and processed in many layouts, but only 2 basic modes are supported in DAP-Fortran. In vertical mode, each number is held entirely within one PE store, and the numbers stored in corresponding sets of addresses in each PE form a matrix of numbers; processing is parallel across all the numbers, but serial through the bits. In horizontal mode, a number is stored along a row of PEs at the same store address. A vector consists of a number in each row at the same address; vectors are processed essentially in parallel, with the one-bit adders in each PE being able to form a word adder along the rows. However, the processing rate for vectors is considerably slower than for matrices despite one vector operation taking considerably less time than one matrix operation. Scalars are held in horizontal mode, and processed in either the MCU or the array. Any precisions or data type (e.g. integer, floating point) can be used.

3. FIRST GENERATION DAPs

3.1 Hardware

This machine had 4096 PEs (64x64) each with 4K bits of store, later enhanceable to 16K bits. (i.e. 2MBytes enhancable to 8 MBytes). The store forms part of an ICL 2900 mainframe, which acts as a host. The DAP cycle time is 200 nsecs.

3.2 Software

This is discussed more fully in reference 4. In DAP-Fortran (reference 5), operations may be performed on three kinds of atom: Matrix, Vector and Scalar. The Matrix and Vector atoms match the DAP size: 64x64 elements and 64 elements respectively. Indexed sets of these atoms are allowed in a similar way to Fortran's indexed sets of scalars. Many precisions are supported, in 8-bit increments. As well as element by element parallel operations on arrays, there are several intrinsic functions for data reorganisation and for mixed rank operations, such as MAX or SUM of an array.

A powerful language feature is the use of Boolean arrays to control the assignment of results.

Programs in DAP-Fortran tend to be clear and concise leading to high programmer productivity. The elegance of some algorithmic constructs was a major inspiration to the forthcoming array extensions in ANSI Fortran 8X.

3.3 Basic Performance

As part of the system software, operations such as multiply or MAX have been programmed in the DAP assembly language APAL (reference 6). For example, store to store performance on 40-bit floating point matrix operations is about 20 MFLOPS for addition, and 10 MFLOPS for multiplication. Staying with 40 bits, better performance is shown by other operations: 20 MFLOPS for squaring, 15 MFLOPS for square root (this is the rate at which square roots are produced - equivalent to about 100 MFLOPS) and 60 MFLOPS for MAX (equivalent to over 200 MIPS). Also extremely fast are exponential, logarithm, trigonometrical functions and random number generation, which, along with square root and MAX, take good advantage of the bit-organisation.

Fixed point add is many times faster than floating point, and multiplication of a matrix by a scalar can be several times faster than matrix-matrix. Lower precision operations can be much faster, with multiply and related operations varying as roughly the square of the precision. Trick operations, such as changing the sign of floating point arrays, can achieve 10,000 MFLOPS. All the above performance rates include the option of local activity control.

Other less arithmetically oriented operations can be extremely fast, such as moving arrays, sorting and scanning data, compressing and expanding data, processing of Boolean and symbol arrays.

4.   PERFORMANCE OF FIRST GENERATION DAPS

The first customer installation was at QMC (Queen Mary College of London University) in 1980 with the aim of providing a national service to the academic community. The machine has recently been enlarged from 2 MBytes to 8 MBytes. There are some 400 users, doing a wide range of mainly scientific applications. In all there is now an installed base of 5 machines. As expected, performance relative to other machines varies widely and, because the programs are different, is often not easy to measure.

Many of the reported results fall in the range 0.1 to 6x CRAY-1 (or the rough equivalent on other machines). As expected, performance on arithmetic applications is better than the raw MFLOPS figures would suggest. The best performances are for physical simulations that involve Boolean arrays; the array processing here is very fast even in DAP-Fortran, and APAL could offer a further order of magnitude improvement in these cases.

It is interesting that in the early days there was considerable theoretical criticism of DAP concerning lack of high performance on "scalar processing", even on generally favourable problems, and that this would be a dominating bottleneck. (For example, if 20% of work is "scalar", and array processing is, say, 100 times faster than scalar, then only 4% of the theoretical array performance would be achieved). In general, where complete applications have been written for the DAP, this has not happened. There are wide variations, but fairly typical is an equal number of matrix, vector and scalar operations. (The situation is complicated by scalar-matrix, scalar-vector and Boolean operations as well as data movement and control overheads). If one further assumes that the matrix operation effectively replaces only 2000 operations (instead of 4096) in the best scalar code, then the scalar operation is only 0.05% of the work (rather than the critics' 20%) and the vector operation, if it replaces 50 operations, is only 2.5% of the work. Put another way, 99.95% parallelism is indicated. In terms of DAP time, assuming matrix/vector/scalar operation times are in the ratio 10:2:1, then 15% of time is vector and 8% is scalar (rather than the critics' 96%). The effective "MFLOPS rates" would be 40% of theoretical.

An actual example is inverting a matrix (64x64 for simplicity) with full pivoting. The DAP code has been given elsewhere (reference 1), and the required operations per step can be summarised as:

    1 Matrix $\pm$
    1 Scalar-vector divide
    1 extract the pivot row and expand to a matrix
    1 extract the pivot column and expand (after the above division)
        to a matrix
    1 extract the pivot element from the pivot column
    1 maximum element (matrix-scalar)
    Some Boolean work

At the end, the rows and columns are re-ordered to take account of pivoting. The truly scalar work is almost negligible – extracting the pivot element from the pivot column, and expanding the scalar into a vector. This takes only about 1% of the DAP time. Extracting and expanding the pivot rows and pivot column and the scalar-vector divide are "vector operations" and take about 20% of the time. The Boolean work (mostly), maximum element and reordering are to do with pivoting and take about 20% of the time; this fraction is much less than for a serial machine. This example can be viewed as virtually 100% parallel, and the effective "MFLOPS rate" is about 79% of theoretical without pivoting and about 59% with pivoting. (The best serial codes need nearly as many arithmetic operations as this parallel code).

The above matrix inversion with full pivoting runs about an order of magnitude faster on the DAP than an equivalent code on a CDC 7600, and is one of many examples of performance being much better than indicated by peak arithmetic rates. Far from the supposed scalar content usually causing DAP applications performance to be worse than indicated by raw arithmetic there have often been reverse effects due to various causes.

Cases vary widely and not all algorithms map well onto DAP. However, the early criticism in terms of _scalar_ performance appears to have been misconceived. It seems to have largely derived from experience of Fortran codes on early vector machines, where everything not performed in vector instructions was called scalar. Much of this was things like loop control, indexing, end effects and boundary conditions rather than essential scalar floating point arithmetic. (The latter is what DAP is weakest at; some of the scalar control operations are fast). The amount of loop control and indexing would be quite large on vector machines due to DO loops iterating most naturally over only one dimension of the problem at a time. Once a problem is structured to use DAP matrix processing, the time for residual loop control or matrix indexing is small compared to the matrix arithmetic; there is not much of it, and the pace of matrix operations is comparatively leisurely.

Boundary conditions usually have only minor effects. Either certain things are not done at boundaries, which can be controlled very easily, or something extra is required which can usually be dealt with effectively by conditional operations. The latter also arise in the very important case of data dependent conditional operations. One example is pivoting. A very different example is the highly conditional operations in meteorological "physics" codes which are highly dependent on the local presence of cloud, rain or ice. A Fortran code will vectorise poorly due to many tests and branches. With DAP a superset code is written which deals with all cases by using the Boolean matrices obtained from the tests to turn PE activities on and off. This is extremely fast, and although at times there may be very few PEs active, there is no code branching and execution speed is data independent. This is an example of the associative processing of arbitrary sub-sets of data, which can be very powerful. The effect of this kind of highly conditional processing is usually to improve DAP performance compared with other machines. A meteorological physics benchmark coded for DAP had several times better performance than the more regular "dynamics" part of the benchmark; as well as the "conditional" effect, logarithms and Table Look Up contributed to this good performance. (Similar superset conditional array processing can be applied in commercial data processing such as data validation or payroll).

Other key factors are choice of algorithm and good top-down mapping onto DAP and DAP-Fortran; good choices here result in clear and easy coding as well as good performance. It is often constructive to consider problems that are larger than the minimum size that spans the DAP array. ("Oversize problems"). There is a spectrum from the serial emphasis of grossly oversize problems to a parallel emphasis for problems of minimum size. In the four examples that follow it is advantageous to squash an oversize problem into the array such that several neighbouring points are in the same PE. (This is known as "crinkled" mapping). This minimises both data movement and the effects of boundaries between sub-matrices. (In other contexts an oversize matrix can advantageously be divided into sub-matrix "sheets" that match the hardware array).

4.1 ADI

Here the solution of tridiagonal sets of equations has a parallel formulation in which log n more arithmetic is done than for the serial formulation (reference 7). However, increasingly oversize mappings look progressively more like the serial formulation and the excess work decreases.

4.2 Multi-Grid

Here an "exact fit" problem causes all except the finest grid to have wasted PEs. A problem oversize by a factor of only 2 or 4, spends most of its time in the finest two or three grids, which have no wasted PEs.

4.3 FFT

FFTs with one point per PE have been programmed and run on DAP. Having two points per PE is better because each PE performs a complete "butterfly" which enables considerable reduction in arithmetic and routing. Further gains can be achieved by further increasing the number of points/PE, with fewer multiplications (and more of those remaining being the faster scalar-matrix type) and less routing. More points per PE can either be achieved with larger transforms, or, more often, by doing many transforms in parallel; the individual transforms are becoming more serial. The extreme case is a complete transform in every PE, for which performance is several times better than with one point per PE. Because additions predominate over multiplications, fixed point arithmetic further substantially improves performance, and this suits most signal and image processing. As an example, 4096 64-point complex FFTs with 16-bit fixed point output precision, programmed in APAL, take only 20 msec; this corresponds to about 300 million arithmetic operations per second. With bulk FFTs some further advantage could be obtained with Winograd transforms.

4.4   Convolution by Fermat Number Transform

The solution of many problems can be formulated in terms of a convolution algorithm. Poisson's equation in some circumstances is one example, and there are several in signal processing. Another example is very high precision multiplication. Convolution in turn has efficient solutions in terms of transforms like the FFT and FNT (Fermat Number Transforms, reference 8). FNTs have the advantage that multiplications are eliminated (except for the one essential for the convolution) and they produce an exact result; this makes them attractive for multiplication. One use of very high precision multiplication is in testing Mersenne numbers for primality, using the Lucas-Lehmer test. In searching for such new primes large numbers of multiplications of the order of 100,000 bits are required.

On conventional number crunchers, most testing to date has used direct multiplication methods with the fast arithmetic facilities. A "divide and conquer" algorithm has also recently been used on CRAY-1 with a slight improvement, and a transform algorithm has very recently been used on CYBER 205 with some further improvement. From complexity theory the latter two algorithms should be much faster, but because they put more emphasis on fixed point addition and less on multiplication, the multiplication hardware favoured the basically slower direct method.

On DAP, the absence of multiplication hardware means performance reflects complexity theory much more closely. The FNT method has been implemented, and is about 100 times faster than the direct method. It is nearly twice as fast as a transform method on Cyber 205 and about four times faster than the direct method on CRAY-1. The FNT replaces ordinary arithmetic by fixed point add/subtracts which have some rather unusual carry and shift requirements. These can be handled better on the bit-organised DAP than on conventional word-organised hardware.

5.   SUPERCOMPUTER MARKET

The market for machines with the emphasis on high performance 64-bit floating point multiply and add is well established, notwithstanding the fact that they are often not well matched to algorithms. Such a market might be attacked by a multi-bit DAP development. Unpublished work on PEs with a small locally addressable fast store and dealing with 4 or 8 bits at a time have shown the possibility of 100-200 times performance improvement per PE on high precision floating point, with 10-20 times more hardware per PE. Some simplicity, flexibility and generality is lost, and the control side needs to move fast to keep up, but there is still more flexibility than in word organised machines.

An interesting question is how many applications really require very large machines. Mostly the requirement is for throughput rather than very fast absolute execution speed. In any event, the latter is often not achieved on big machines because of time sharing. Smaller machines under the control of smaller groups can serve many needs for large-scale cost-effective processing.

6.   SECOND GENERATION DAPS

Development work is proceeding on a much smaller and cheaper DAP with fewer PEs and more integration, attachable to the PERQ single user workstation. An interesting area is signal processing and other high data rate applications. Good graphics will allow close interaction with programs which will often increase productivity.

Signal and image processing usually involve lower precision than number crunching and a variety of algorithmic techniques including highly data dependent Boolean processing. In this area, the competition is often from special hardware, with several different pieces of hardware for different stages of processing. With DAP, programmable power that can give powerful performance on many different stages can lead to a powerful and flexible "one-box" approach. The special hardware may be better at particular parts, but the DAP is often better overall, and alterable into the bargain.

As part of a very powerful single user workstation the array processor can contribute to a wide range of powerful functions to give high performance man-machine interaction, as well as providing powerful numerical processing.

98

7. REFERENCES

1. Flanders P.M., Hunt D.J., Parkinson D., Reddaway S.F.
"Efficient High Speed Computing With The Distributed Array Processor"
Proc. Conf. on High Speed Computer and Algorithm Organisation.
Academic Press Inc, 1977

2. Hunt D.J., Reddaway S.F.
"Distributing Processing Power In memory" in "The Fifth Generation Computer
Project" Pergamon Infotech Ltd. 1983

3. Parkinson D.
"The Distributed Array Processor (DAP)"
to be published in "Computer Physics Communications", 1983

4. Flanders P.M.
"Fortran Extensions For A Highly Parallel Processor" in "Supercomputers"
Infotech International. 1979

5. International Computers Limited
"DAP: Fortran Language" Technical Publication No. 6918. 1979

6. International Computers Limited
"DAP: APAL Language" Technical Publication No. 6919. 1979

7. Hunt D.J., Webb S.J., Wilson A.
"Application of a Parallel Processor to the Solution of Finite Difference
Problems" In "Elliptic Problem Solvers"
M.H. Schultz (ed). Academic Press 1981

8. McClellan J.H., Rader C.M.
"Number Theory in Digital Signal Processing"
Prentice Hall Inc. 1979

Japanese Project on Fifth Generation Computer Systems

Tohru Moto-oka

The Department of Electrical Engineering

The University of Tokyo, Tokyo, Japan.

1 INTRODUCTION

The Fifth Generation computers are defined as the computers which will be used predominantly in 1990s. Supercomputers will be used in scientific and engineering calculations and simulations. Database machines and present mainframe computers will be networked in order to organize worldwide information systems. Many microcomputers will be used as system elements in various social systems. However, many computer industries are already earnestly developing these computers for future use.

Non-numeric data processing, including symbol processing and applied artificial intelligence, will play more important roles than at present in the future information processing field. Non-numeric data such as sentences, speeches, graphes, and images will be used in tremendous volume compared to numerical data. Computers are expected to deal with non-numeric data mainly in future applications. However, present computers have much less capability in non-numeric data processing than in numeric data processing.

In the Japanese national project on Fifth Generation Computer Systems(FGCS), the knowledge information processing systems which are consisted of non-numeric data dedicated computers such as inference machines, knowlege base machines and intelligent man-machine interface machines will be developed.

This project started in April 1982, and is expected to run in 10 years. The initial step is the preliminary three years stage in which the project is being dealt with mainly by the Institution of New Gen-

eration Computer Technology(ICOT). ICOT was organized with the support
from the Ministry of International Trade and Industry(MITI) and eight
leading electronic manufactures in Japan. Many scientists and
engineers support this project through the organization of advisory
groups.

The objective of this project is to realize new computer systems to
meet the anticipated requirements of the 1990s. Roles that FGCS are
expected to play include the following:

1 To enhance productivity in low-productivity areas among non-
standardized operations in the tertiary industries.

2 To overcome constraints on resources and energy by minimizing
energy consumption and control for optimization of energy conversion efficiencies.

3 To realize medical, educational, and other support systems for
solving ever more complex, multifaceted, social problems including
but not limited to, transition to an elderly society.

4 To contribute to international society and to help internation-
alization of Japanese society through international cooperation,
machine translation, and in other ways.

For this objective, an environment will have to be created in which
men and computers find it easy to communicate freely using a wide
variety of information media, such as speech, text and graphs, and
being supported by knowledge such as common sense.

2 TECHNICAL BACKGROUND

The design philosophy behind conventional von Neumann computers was
based on using a minimum of hardware to configure systems of maximum
simplicity, capable of efficient processing using adequate software,
because in von Neumann's day hardware was expensive, bulky, short-

lived, and consumed a lot of power. From this viewpoint, the stored-program, sequentially-controlled systems were superior and high speeds and large capacities were pursued for economic reasons, resulting in the emergence of today's giant computers.

The key factors leading to the necessity for rethinking the conventional computer design philosophy just described include the following:

1 Device speeds are approaching the limit imposed by the speed of light.

2 The emergence of VLSI reduces hardware costs substantially, and an environment permitting the use of as much hardware as is required will shortly be feasible.

3 To take advantage of the effect of VLSI mass production, it will be necessary to pursue parallel processing.

4 Current computers are extremely weak in basic functions for processing speech, text, graphs, picture images and other non-numerical data, and for artificial intelligence type processing such as inference, association, and learning.

Computers, as the name implies were designed as machines to perform numerical computations. Computer applications have, however, expanded without major changes in design philosophy, into such fields as control systems, processing of multi-information media, database and artificial intelligence systems. However, for computers to be employed at numerous application levels in the 1990s, they must evolve from machines centered around numerical computations to machines that can assess the meaning of information and understand the problems to be solved. For this evolution, in the immediate future, the following will be required.

1 Realization of basic mechanisms for inference, association, and learning in hardware, making them the core functions of the Fifth Generation computers.

2 Prepation of basic artificial intelligence software in order to fully utilize the above functions.

3 Realization of basic mechanism for retrieving and managing knowledge base in hardware and software.

4 Advantageous use of pattern recognition and artificial intelligence research achievements, in order to realize man/machine interfaces that are natural to man.

5 Realization of support systems for resolving the 'software crisis' and enhancing software production.

In order to solve these problems faced by current computer technologies, achievements in related technologies such as VLSI technology, software engineering, and artificial intelligence research will have to be integrated, and the interim achievements of this project will be fed back to these technologies so that they can continue to advance.

3 RESEARCH AND DEVELOPMENT TARGETS

Knowledge information processing systems (KIPS) which will be composed of FGCSs will be based on innovative theories and technologies, and hence capable of accommodating such functions, as intelligent conversation functions and inference functions employing knowledge bases.

The functions of FGCSs may be roughly classified as follows.

1 Problem-solving and inference

2 Knowledge-base management

3   Intelligent interface

These functions will be realized by making individual software and
hardware systems correspond. A conceptual image of the system is shown
in Figure 1. In this diagram, the modeling (software) system is the
project's ultimate target for software development, and the machine
(hardware) system the ultimate target for hardware development. The
upper half of the modeling system circle corresponds to the problem-
solving and inference functions, the lower half to the knowledge-base
management function. The portion that overlaps the human system circle
on the left corresponds to the intelligent interface function. The
diagram also illustrates that the intelligent interface function
relies heavily on the two former groups of functions. This diagram
shows how the emphasis in computer systems will have shifted
decisively towards the human system by significant enhancement of the
logic level of the hardware system and by the positioning of the
modeling system between the hardware and users.

The interface between the software and hardware systems will be the
kernel language. The entire software system will be realized in the
kernel language, and the hardware system will directly execute the
kernel language.

4   THE PROBLEM-SOLVING AND INFERENCE SYSTEM

In research into and development of the problem-solving and inference machine (known simply as the inference machine), the target will
be to develop a hardware mechanism that supports the basic functions
of inference based on the kernel language specification and its computation model.

This hardware mechanism will eventually be integrated with the
hardware mechanisms used to support the knowledge base (the target of
the knowledge base machine research and development) and intelligent

interfaces (the target of the high-performance interface equipment research and development). The overall aim is to realize a prototype FGCS.

The maximum capability of the inference machine will be from 100 MLIPS to 1 GLIPS. The inference executing speed, 1 LIPS (logical inference per second), denotes one syllogistic inference operation per second. One inference operation, executed by a current computer is believed to require 100 to 1000 steps; thus, 1 LIPS corresponds to 100 to 1000 instr/sec. The current generation machines are rated at 10^4 to 10^5 LIPS.

To realize such performance capabilities, the essential research and development will concentrate not only on speeding up the basic devices, but also on high-level parallel architectures to support the symbol processing that is the key to inference. A hardware architecture suited to the new parallel inferences based on the data-flow control mechanism and abstract data type mechanisms will be researched and developed.

The target scale for the hardware encompasses ultimately about 1000 processing elements, and the requisite VLSI manufacturing technology for such hardware will be researched and developed.

The ultimate goal in research into the problem-solving and inference mechanism is a cooperative problem-solving system. In such a system, a single problem will be solved by two or more problem-solving systems cooperating with each other.

A system, for instance, will be conceived as a problem-solving system using large knowledge bases, in which large-scale external databases will function like libraries. In other words, the knowledge bases management system having inference functions (corresponding to the library user) and the large-scale databases (corresponding to the library) will both be part of the problem-solving inference system, and will cooperate in solving problems. Another example is a medical diagnosing system where a diagnosis is made in the same way as a physician and a surgeon might cooperate to make a diagnosis. For this purpose, it will be necessary to develop a meta-inference system that performs inferences on the inference processes of individual problem-solving systems and on the knowledge possessed by the individual systems. The meta-inference system will need to have not only deductive functions but also such higher level functions as common inference, inductive inference, analogical inference, and other tacit inferences, and work will also be done on mechanisms for these functions. The functions will be realized as software in the kernel language. Corresponding to the basic deductive process, this language will be syllogistic, and classified in a logic programming language. Together with the kernel language, several functions will be realized for controlling trial-and-error type programs.

5 THE KNOWLEDGE BASE SYSTEMS

The intention of software for the knowledge base management function will be to establish knowledge information processing technology, where the targets will be development of knowledge representation systems, knowledge base design and maintenance support systems, large-scale knowledge base systems, knowledge acquisition experimental systems, and distributed knowledge management systems. These systems will then be integrated into a cooperative problem-solving system. One particularly important aim will be semi-automated knowledge acquisition, that is, systems will be equipped with a certain level of learning functions.

For the knowledge base management function, relational database interfaces and consistency testing functions will have to be realized in the kernel language.

Research into and development of the knowledge base machine will aim at developing a hardware mechanism that fulfills the demands for knowledge representation systems and large-scale knowledge base systems, and is capable of efficiently supporting storage, retrieval, and renewal of a large volume of knowledge data. This mechanism will ultimately be integrated in the prototype FGCS.

Regarding the target knowledge base management function in research into and development of the knowledge base machine, the aim in performance capabilities based on a database machine with a 100 to 1000 Gbyte capacity, will be to retrieve the knowledge bases required for answering a question within a few seconds.

To realize such performance capabilities, a parallel architecture capable of speedily supporting the symbol processing function intended to handle a large capacity data management function and knowledge data will be indispensable. Research and development will be conducted for a parallel processing hardware architecture intended for parallel processing of new knowledge bases, and which is based on a relational database machine that includes a high-performance hierarchical memory system, and a mechanism for parallel relational operations and knowledge operations.

Research and development will also be done on the VLSI techniques required for building large-capacity silicon disks and processing elements for knowledge operations.

6 THE INTELLIGENT INTERFACE SYSTEM

The intelligent interface function will have to be capable of handling man/machine communication in natural languages, speech, graphs, and picture images so that information can be exchanged in a way natural to a man. As natural language processing provides the basis for translation, English and other languages are to be included as well as Japanese in the objects for processing. Ultimately, the system will cover a basic vocabulary (excluding technical terms) of up to 10,000 words and up to 2000 grammatical rules, with a 99% accuracy in syntactic analysis. The fewer the grammatical rules, the higher the system capabilities.

On speech processing, speech input and output systems will be developed. The object of speech inputs will be continuous speech in Japanese standard pronunciation by multiple speakers, and the aims here will be a vocabulary of 50,000 words, a 95% recognition rate for individual words, and recognition and processing three times the real time of speech, though this may vary somewhat depending on hardware capabilities. As for processing of graphs and picture images, the target system to be developed will be capable of structurally storing roughly 10,000 pieces of graph and image information and utilizing them for knowledge information processing.

Meanwhile, there will also be researches into and developments of dedicated hardware processors and high performance interface equipment for efficiently executing processing of speech, graph, and image data. Furthermore, methods for exchanging informations that are natural to a man, through parallel utilization of such multiple media data, will have to be established.

7 BASIC CONFIGURATION OF THE FGCS

The software and hardware systems that realize the three functions mentioned above will be coupled to form a general-purpose machine. Its conceptual structure is shown in Figure 2.

Because, in actual use, a variety of performance capabilities will be required of each of the three functions, the configuration will have to be flexible enough to provide not only the general-purpose machine, but also various system configurations to accommodate the various performance capabilities required by individual applications, that is, specific function intensive machines in which some functions are enhanced.

These machines will have the Fifth Generation Computer kernel

language as their common machine language, and they will be interconnected in networks to form a distributed processing system.

8 BASIC APPLICATION SYSTEMS IN FGCS

Several basic application systems will be developed with the intention of demonstrating on the usefulness of the FGCS and the system
evaluation. These are machine translation systems, consultation systems, intelligent programming system and an intelligent VLSI-CAD system.

Machine translation systems and various consultation systems, which
are expected to be the most widely used in the 1990s, will be
developed as basic applications systems.

Systems programmers will produce programs in the kernel language
itself. The programmers of the expert systems will make programs using
knowledge representation languages. Consultation systems will communicate with the user in a somewhat restricted natural language, speech,
graphs, or images.

The targets of intelligent programming system will be the development of procedures for automated synthesis of programs through a
knowledge engineering approach, and software-developing consultation
systems. These developments will derive from the kernel language
founded on a new philosophy and modular programming founded on the
abstraction method. Specific targets will be business processing,
robot control programs, and other fields where software is repeatedly
produced in many different environments, and basic modules will be
developed for software in these fields. Other aims will be management
of algorithm banks for the modules and development of synthesizing
systems for unified module levels. In particular, support of the program design, debugging, and enhancement stages that constitute the
majority of current software development efforts will be strengthened
and an attempt will be made to increase current software productivity

by a factor of 10 or greater.

In building these machines, implementation in VLSIs will be mandatory to avoid oversized systems, and research and development on the
necessary VLSI technology for compactness and reliability will also be
implemented. Improvements and expansions to the architecture will
have to be dealt with promptly, and design and evaluation data for the
hardware aimed at structuring knowledge bases will also be accumulated
for use in designing future VLSIs. Therefore, intelligent VLSI-CAD
system plays an important role in both the research environment during
the developing period and the typical application system in FGCS.

9 RESEARCH AND DEVELOPMENT APPROACHES IN THE INITIAL STAGE

(1) Parallel inference machine

The parallel inference machine, together with the knowledge base
machine constitutes the core of the Fifth Generation Computer
hardware. Research objectives at the initial stage are to collect
accurate and various data, either by experiment or by simulation, sufficient to evaluate various alternative approaches. Also to experimentally develop sub-modules necessary for research and development in
the intermediate stage of an inference machine which constitutes a
small-scale experimental subsystem in VLSI chips with a parallel
inference control mechanism and which will be composed of a large
number of modules.

Since this theme needs the most advanced development in the Fifth
Generation Project, the work substance of its conceptual design and
functional design is different from those in conventional development.
The research effort in 1982 was focused on clarification of the goals
and the exploration of various approaches to achieve the goals.

To be concrete, if the execution control mechanism for the basic
parallel inference mechanism is adapted to the present Prolog specification, it may not be possible to run problem solving and inference

programs on the inference subsystem to be developed in the intermediate stage. Therefore, an architecture is necessary which contains execution control mechanisms for various inference methods. Emphasis is placed on the study of such an architecture.

(2) Knowledge base machine

In the initial stage, following points receives special emphasis.

1 Architectures of knowledge-base basic mechanism, parallel relational and knowledge operation mechanism, relational data base mechanism and operational experiment simulators are investigated experimentally developed, and evaluated. Basic technologies for highly parallel relational operation mechanism are established. Highly parallel relational and knowledge operation mechanism, which will receive emphasis in the intermediate stage, is proposed.

2 Various experiments, operational simulation, evaluation data collection, measurements and so on are performed for research and development of the knowledge base machine. Based on these results functions necessary to support knowledge operation using relational algebra operation, and the architecture necessary to implement those functions are proposed.

3 At the last phase in the initial stage, the relational data base mechanism will be realized as the kernel system of knowledge base machine. Moreover, the system will be connected through the local area network (LAN) to the sequential inference machine in order to test and evaluate the knowledge base machine in an operational environment.

4 For the purposes of efficient acquisition storage and management of a large amount of knowledge, hierarchical memory must be developed as a basic hardware requirement. Its development will be treated in the operation experiment simulator.

(3) Basic software system

The item consists of the following five components:
Fifth Generation kernel language, problem solving and inference
software module, knowledge base management software module, intelligent interface software module, and intelligent programming software
module. Design philosophy for each component is described below.

The Fifth Generation kernel language is the basic programming
language for all other modules. Its specification is closely related
to other modules. Modular representation of knowledge and concurrent
programming feature should be extracted as a requirement for the problem solving and inference software modules.

Next, design of the problem-solving and inference software module
has been carried out initially as two separate sub-modules. One for
parallel inference basic software and the other for problem-solving
basic software. However, it has become clear that most of the results
of the investigation on parallel inference basic software can be
reflected in the Fifth Generation kernel language. It is clear that
emphasis in the development of this sub-module, therefore should be
shifted to higher level inference mechanisms centering around default
reasoning and hypothetical reasoning.

The knowledge base management software module consists of a large-
scale relational data base management program and knowledge representation system. The present target in the study and survey of the
large-scale relational data base management program is the experimental development and use of a relational data base and data base
management program. The underlying objective is development of
software technologies required to link the relational data base
machine to the sequential inference machine. In particular, our goal
is to develop a query system for a data base, including the natural
language interface.

The Knowledge base management software module will be composed of the following three systems:

  1 large-scale relational data base management program.

  2 knowledge representation system.

  3 knowledge utilization system.

In order to achieve computer capability which understands natural language, the following two targets are set for the initial stage for the intelligent interface software module.

  1 high level syntactic analysis program

  2 semantic analysis/dictionary pilot system.

Finally, the intelligent programming software module consists of two parts, that is, modular programming basic software, which can be practically used in in a short time, and a software verification management program, which is a long-range research goal. The modular programming basic software is implemented in the kernel language in the sequential inference machine as a programming system to support software development in logic programming language.

(4) Sequential Inference Machine(SIM)

The sequential inference machine is also called pilot model for software development developed in the initial stage of the project to provide researchers with an efficient programming environment for software and hardware research. This machine is a computer specialized for use with a programming language called KLØ, which is an extension of a logic programming language Prolog. The target performance in execution of the first model is as fast as the Prolog running on the DEC System 2060 and its extended model will be ten times faster than the first model. The memory capacity is also planned to be at least ten times larger than that of the DEC 2060.

The practical use of this system is development of various small to medium sized software for research purposes. Since modification and extension are frequently repeated in this type of work, it is important to provide the researchers with a good programming environment for exclusively individual use. To meet this requirement, this system is implemented as a personal computer with high level man- machine interface. A distributed processing architecture connected through a local area network is proposed for system architecture, since distributed processing is suited to the cooperative work of software development and effective use of input/output devices. However, the system will be also used in the stand-alone mode. The second objective of the system is research and experimentation tools for relatively large sized software, such as natural language processing and expert systems. For this purpose, the system is needed to process a large-scale program rapidly and efficiently.

10 CONCLUSION

The research and development targets of the FGCS project are such core functions of knowledge information processing as problem-solving and inference systems and knowledge base systems, that cannot be handled within the framework of conventional computer systems.

These is no precedent for this innovative and large scale research and development project anywhere in the world. We will therefore be obliged to move toward the target systems through a lengthy process of trial and error, producing many original ideas along the way.

The research and development period set for this project is 10 years, divided, into the initial stage (three years), the middle stage (four years), and the final stage (three years) as shown in Figure 3.

114

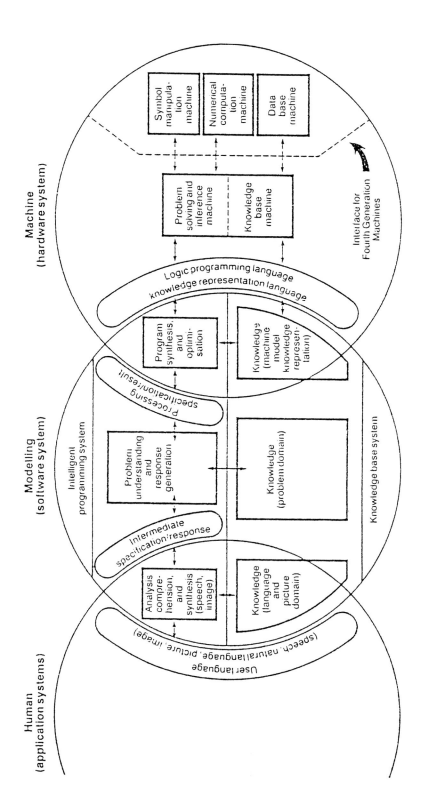

Figure 1 : Conceptual diagram of a Fifth Generation Computer System as viewd
from the standpoint of programming

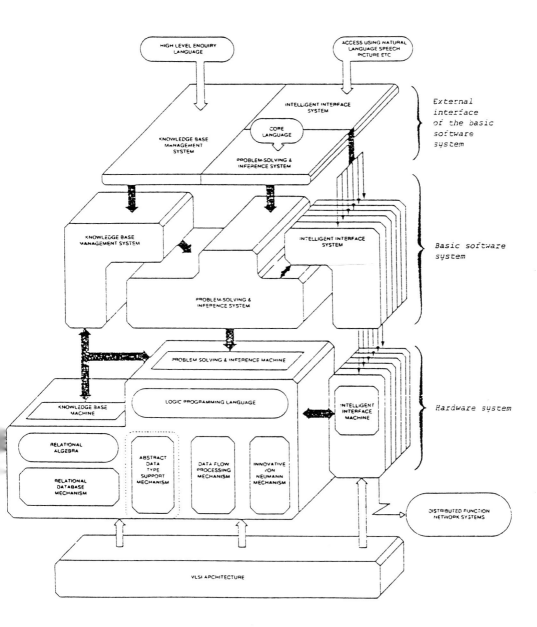

Figure 2: Basic configuration of the Fifth Generation Computer Systems

116

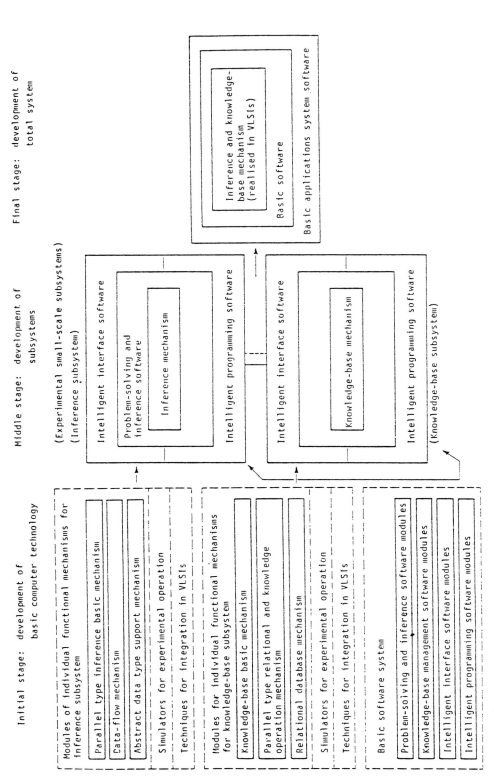

Figure 3: Stages of Fifth Generation Computer research and development

JAPANESE SUPER-SPEED COMPUTER PROJECT

Hiroshi Kashiwagi
Electrotechnical Laboratory
Sakura-mura, Niihari-gun
Ibaragi-ken, Japan

I. INTRODUCTION

Under the auspices of the Ministry of International Trade and
Industry (MITI), a national project started in January 1982 to develop
the High-Speed Computing System for Scientific and Technological Use
(to be called Super-Speed Computer System throughout this paper). The
performance target for the final system is 10 Billion FLOPS (10 GFLOPS).
This project is scheduled to be completed in FY1989 and has a total
budget of 23 Billion Yen (approximately 100 Million Dollars).

This paper describes the outline of the project, the summary of
the current level of development in the supercomputers and related
technologies in Japan which this project is based on. This paper also
reviews the activities in FY 1982, mainly in the area of the architecture and applications.

II. MAJOR APPLICATION FIELDS AND COMPUTATIONAL
REQUIREMENTS IN JAPAN

Atmospheric sciences, aerodynamics and nuclear energy researches
are some of the typical application fields in Japan where the large
scale numerical computations are required. In atmospheric sciences,
the National Weather Bureau and the Meteorological Research Institute,
mainly conduct researches on the numerical weather prediction as well

NATO ASI Series, Vol. F7
High-Speed Computation. Edited by J. S. Kowalik
© Springer-Verlag Berlin Heidelberg 1984

as the climatology. In aerodynamics, the National Aerospace Laboratory
of the Science and Technology Agency have been conducting researches
toward the wind tunnel simulator for the future design of aircrafts.
In the area of nuclear energy research, the Japan Atomic Energy
Research Institute (JAERI) and the Institute of Plasma Physics of
Nagoya University have been conducting researches on large scale
plasma simulations.

At present, these institutes perform most of the numerical
simulations on the large scale general purpose computers, but they are
considering the installation of the commercially available supercomputers in the near future.

III. OUTLINE OF PROJECT

1. TARGETS AND KEY ACTIVITIES

The computational requirements in the application fields such as
those given above are expected to grow enormously in the future. In
order to meet the anticipated requirements 10 years from now in the
application fields of the national interest, the target of the National
Super-Speed Computer Project has been set to 10 Billion FLOPS (10
GFLOPS). The total budget of the project is 23 Billion Yen and the
project is to be completed in FY1989.

This project involves the following three key activities;
research and development of the parallel architecture and the software,
research and development of the new devices with high speed and high
level of integration, and construction and evaluation of the final
system with the super-speed computing engine.

Research and development activities in the parallel architecture
will include the study of various architectures to achieve 10 Billion
FLOPS, together with the hierarchical memory structure to meet the
demands of high data transfer rate, system control methodology as well
as the software development to efficiently utilize such high performance
system.

In the area of the new devices, Josephson junction (JJ), High-Electron-Mobility-Transistor (HEMT) and GaAs devices have been selected as viable candidates for the high speed devices. Both the logic and the memory devices are to be explored in this project. The targets of the new devices are shown in the following table.

Targets of New Devices

Logic Devices	Delay Time: Integration:	10 ps/gate (JJ, HEMT) 30 ps/gate (GaAs) 3,000 gates/chip
Memory Devices	Access Time: Integration:	10 ns 16 K bits/chip

The final system will consist of the front end processor, high speed parallel processing system, high speed, high capacity memory system and the pre/post processing systems for image processing and so forth. The development of the front end processor is not included in the project: a commercially available system will be procured.

The research and development activities for the final system includes the following items: the logic design methodology for the new devices, CAD system to simulate the vast amount of logic data, packaging and cooling technologies and the system testing methodology under very low temperature environment.

2. SCHEDULE

Figure 1. shows the schedule of the project. Basic researches on the new architecture and the new devices already started in January 1982, while the study on the final system is scheduled to start in FY1984.

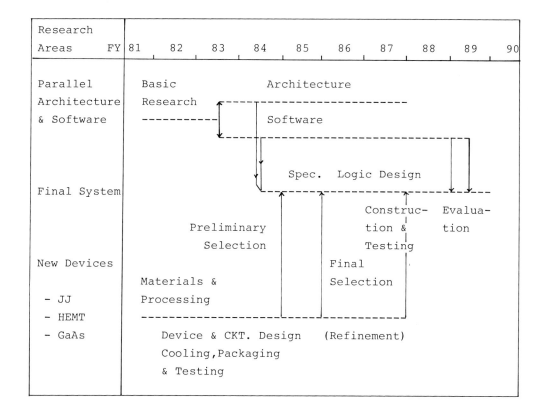

Figure 1:   Schedule of Super-Speed Computer Project

IV. SUPERCOMPUTERS AND NEW DEVICE TECHNOLOGIES IN JAPAN

    This project is based on the background technologies in the
supercomputers and the new devices in Japan. This section summarizes
the state-of-the-art in these areas.

1. SUPERCOMPUTERS

    Research and development of the pipeline architecture have been
mainly conducted by Japanese computer manufacturers. In 1982

announcements of the full scale supercomputers, FACOM VP-100/VP-200
and HITAC S-810 Model 10/Model 20 were made. Very recently, NEC
Supercomputer SX-1/SX-2 also entered the market. The peak performances of VP-200, S-810 Model 20 and SX-2 are 533 MFLOPS, 630 MFLOPS
and 1,300 MFLOPS, respectively. In developing these supercomputers,
main emphasis has been put on the well-balanced hardware and software
designs for the highest possible utilization of parallelism in users'
programs. All three systems employ the pipeline architecture with
multiple arithmetic pipeline units which can operate simultaneously.
FORTRAN has been adopted as the main programming language for these
supercomputers, and very sophisticated compilers are now being
developed, which will allow the detection of parallelisms in users'
programs as much as possible. FACOM and HITAC systems will be
operational in the 3rd or 4th quarter of 1983, whereas the NEC's
system will be operational in the 1st quarter of 1985.

On the other hand, the parallel computers of various architectures (SIMD, MIMD and Dataflow) have been explored mainly by the
universities and national research institutes. Several experimental
systems have been developed, but no full scale system has been built
yet. We expect the future development in this area.

2. ADVANCED DEVICES

Silicon devices are widely used in the supercomputers mentioned
above. The typical gate delay is 350 pico seconds for the ECL logic
LSI's used in the main portion of those systems. At present, research
and development on silicon VLSI's are extensively conducted by the
computer manufacturers. It will be difficult, however, to realize
LSI's which possess both very high speed and very high level of
integration in the near future; even if the fine pattern fabrication
techniques make further progress, the physical properties of the
silicon material will impose significant limitations on the device
performance.

In order to overcome such barriers, researches on the new
devices with the superior physical properties to silicon, e.g. the
Josephson junction device, High-Electron-Mobility-Transistor (HEMT)
device and GaAs device, are pursued in Japan.

Research on the Josephson junction device in Japan includes the

fabrication of the experimental chips such as a 4 bit full adder with
23 Four-Junction-Logic (4JL) gates and a 64 bit static RAM. The HEMT
device is a new type of the III-V compound semiconductor device
announced in Japan in 1980. The recent progress of the HEMT technology includes a 12.8 pico second gate delay time in the 27-stage
ring oscillator at the liquid nitrogen temperature, 77 K. As for the
GaAs device, a 16 bit by 16 bit multiplier chip with more than 3000
gate density and a 1K bit static RAM are some of the state-of-the-art
devices fabricated.

V. ACTIVITIES IN FY1982

The activities of the project in FY1982 were mainly concerned
with the basic researches both in the architecture and in the new
devices.

1. ARCHITECTURE

In the area of the architecture, the main subjects were the
analysis of parallelism in the application codes, and the investigation and the evaluation of basic hardware organizations for parallel
processing. In order to explore parallelism in the frequently used
algorithms, typical sample codes have been gathered for analysis from
several national research institutes in the following application
fields: meteorology, aerodynamics, nuclear energy, molecular science,
structure analysis and so forth. The results of the study indicate
that the analyzed codes fall into one of the three categories: the
continuum model, the particle model and the engineering model
(discrete model).

The first category includes the codes which deal with the time
integration of the flow problems such as the plasma MHD code, the
weather code, the aerodynamic code, all of which have a very high
degree of explicit parallelism; they can be processed very efficiently
on the pipeline or SIMD machines, for example.

The second category includes the codes which simulate the
particle aspects of the physical phenomena. Typical examples are the

particle simulations of plasma and the Monte Carlo simulations of neutrons and photons for shielding calculations. In the former case, both the phase for computing the movement of particles and that for computing the interacting fields individually have a very high degree of parallelism, but interfaces of such computational phases involve so called the nonlinear indexing and the recursion. In the latter case, programs are highly sequential due to many branches, although each particle moves independently and the inherent parallelism is high.

The third category includes the discretized models of various kinds, especially those for the practical systems. Codes for nuclear safety analysis, load flow analysis and circuit analysis are typical examples. These codes may be characterized by many local and independent computations, combined with the global solution of the simultaneous linear/nonlinear equations. Large-sized random sparse matrices are involved in this category. The algorithms employed in these codes in general do not exhibit high degree of parallelism.

Research is being continued on the alternative algorithms for those which have been found to have a low degree of parallelism.

The main research subject in the basic hardware organization was the investigation of architectures optimized for specific application problems. Based on the analysis of the algorithms, several architectures have been proposed. It has been pointed out that the parallelism at the procedure level is important in the second or the third categories. This year's activity did not include, however, the software aspects of the parallel processing, such as the distribution of array data to multiple local memories for SIMD architecture. The activities in FY1983 and on will include the refinement of the proposed architectures with the consideration of the software aspects as well. The outcome of the researches on the parallel architecture will be reflected to the study of the final system.

2. NEW DEVICE TECHNOLOGIES

In the area of the new device technologies, the main subjects for basic research were: the materials and fabrication process techniques, device and circuit design, testing and packaging methods.

With regard to the Josephson junction device, it is especially

important to realize higher reproducibility of the junctions, higher
reliability against the thermal cycling and good electrical
characteristics. The superconducting materials which have been
selected for research are lead alloy and niobium.

With regard to the HEMT device, main efforts have been put on
how to form crystal layers with very high electron mobility on the
semi-insulating GaAs substrates of large diameter. Research is
continued on the development of the Molecular-Beam-Epitaxy(MBE)
techniques to produce various kinds of the modulation doped GaAs/n-
AlGaAs hetero-junction structures.

With regard to the GaAs device, major research subject was the
enhancement of the process yield.

In addition to the materials and process techniques stated
above, researches on the device structures and circuit configuration,
high density packaging and testing methodology for the ultra high
speed devices were also conducted for each of the three new devices.

VI. CONCLUSIONS

The main efforts of research and development activities of the
project have been devoted toward the new devices, especially in the
material and process techniques, since the start of the project. This
basic research phase will continue throughout FY1983. The final
evaluation of the new devices is scheduled in the FY1985-FY1986 time
frame.

The basic research phase will also continue in the area of the
architecture; the architecture for the final system is still quite
dependent on the progress in the new devices and on the outcome of the
analysis of the parallel algorithms in the major applications as well.
The preliminary selection of the architecture for the final system is
scheduled in FY1984.

We have described in this paper the outline of the National
Super-Speed Computer Project, with an emphasis on the architecture and

the applications. In order to meet the challenging goal of 10 Billion FLOPS performance, both the architecture and the new devices are to be explored simultaneously. It should be noted that the final system is regarded as a scientific demonstration system; further refinement will be necessary to make it a commercial product. Besides its objective of satisfying the national needs, this project will also contribute to the society through solving the problems in the wide area of scientific and technological applications.

ACKNOWLEDGEMENT

The author wishes to thank Dr. Kenichi Miura of Fujitsu Limited for very useful discussions and comments. The author also wishes to thank the members of the Scientific Computer Research Association for contributing to this project and for providing materials for this paper.

FACOM VECTOR PROCESSOR VP-100/VP-200

Kenichi Miura and Keiichiro Uchida
Mainframe Division
Fujitsu Limited
Kawasaki, Japan

1. Introduction

In 1982 Fujitsu announced two models of the FACOM Vector
Processor, VP-100 and VP-200, for large scale scientific and engineering computations. These machines both employ the pipeline architecture with multiple pipeline units which can operate concurrently.
The maximum performances of VP-100 and VP-200 are 267 MFLOPS and 533
MFLOPS, respectively. VP-200 allows up to 256M bytes of the main
storage. In developing the FACOM Vector Processor, we have also
incorporated several advanced features of vector processing, in order
to achieve very high average performance for FORTRAN programs in wide
range of scientific and engineering applications. This paper describes our design approach, technologies, architecture and software of
the FACOM Vector Processor, with an emphasis on the implementation of
the advanced features from the view points of hardware and software.

2. Design Approach of FACOM Vector Processor

Development of the supercomputers have been mainly motivated by
the needs to perform large scale simulations of physical models such
as hydrodynamics, numerical weather prediction and nuclear energy
researches. As the extremely powerful computational capabilities of
the supercomputers attracted attentions from various branches of
science and industry, however, the market started to proliferate;

structural analysis, VLSI design, oil reservoir simulations, nuclear plant simulations, utilities and quantum chemistry, just to name a few. This trend, in return, has created demands for supercomputers which can handle various kinds of users' programs efficiently.

Prior to designing the FACOM Vector Processor, we have analyzed more than 1,000 FORTRAN programs in the typical application areas. The main purposes of this study were to clarify the common characteristics encountered in the scientific and engineering computations, and to obtain useful feedbacks to the architecture and the compiler design. The detailed results of this study have been published [1]. We just summarize here the conclusions which we have obtained from this study.

Although high speed components, high degree of parallelism and/or pipelining and large-sized main memory are the basic requirements to stretch the computational capabilities of a supercomputer, the following advanced features in architecture are also important for such a machine to be versatile enough for wide range of applications;

(1) Efficient processing of DO loops which contain IF statements,
(2) Powerful vector editing capabilities,
(3) Efficient utilization of the vector registers,
(4) Highly concurrent vector-vector and scalar-vector operations.

These advanced features greatly increase the so-called "vectorization ratio" for practical application programs. Subsequent sections will describe how we have developed FACOM Vector Processor along the line of this approach; especially how we have incorporated the technology, the architecture and the software (i.e., Fujitsu's vectorizing compiler FORTRAN77/VP) in implementing the above features.

3. Technology

We have fully utilized Fujitsu's latest technologies in the FACOM Vector Processor. The gate-array logic LSI's contain 400 gates per chip, and some special functional LSI's such as the register files contain 1,300 gates. Signal propagation delay per gate of the LSI's are 350 pico seconds for both types. The high-speed memory LSI's

containing 4K bits per module with an access time of 5.5 nanoseconds
are used where extreme high speed is necessary. Up to 121 LSI's can
be mounted on a 29cm by 31 cm 14-layered printed circuit board called
MCC (Multi Chip Carrier). Logic LSI's and memory LSI's can be mixed
on the same MCC. 13 such MCC's are mounted horizontally in a $(50 \text{ cm})^3$
cube, called stack. We have employed the forced air cooling technique
throughout the system. These technologies have all been well-proven
with Fujitsu's FACOM M-380 mainframes. It is with these technologies
that we could realize a 7.5 nanosecond clock for the vector unit and
15 nanosecond clock for the scalar unit.

As for the main storage, we have employed 64K bit MOS Static RAM
LSI's with 55 nanosecond chip access time. The main storage unit for
VP-200 can accommodate as large as 256M bytes with such high density
devices.

4. Architecture

This section describes the structure and basic functions of the
Vector Processor. Advanced features will be separately described in
sections 5.   The FACOM Vector Processor consists of the scalar unit,
the vector unit and the main storage unit (Fig.1).

4.1. Scalar Unit

The scalar unit fetches and decodes all the instructions.
There are 277 instructions, of which 195 are scalar type and 82 are
vector type. When an instruction is scalar type, it is executed in the
scalar unit, otherwise issued to the vector unit. The scalar unit has
16 general purpose registers, 8 floating point registers, and 64k
bytes of cache memory.

4.2. Vector Unit

The vector unit mainly consists of six functional pipeline
units, Vector Registers and Mask Registers. The functional pipeline
units are: Add/Logical Pipe, Multiply Pipe, Divide Pipe, Mask Pipe and
two Load/Store Pipes. The first three pipes are for arithmetic

operations, any two of which can operate concurrently. All the
floating-point arithmetic operations are performed in double-precision
(64 bits). The operands and the results for all the vector arithmetic
operations are assumed to be in the 256 Vector Registers. Load/Store
Pipes take care of data transfer between the main storage and the
Vector Registers; they are both bidirectional.

For VP-200, the throughputs of Add/Logical Pipe and Multiply
Pipe are 267 MFLOPS each, whereas that of the Divide pipe is 38
MFLOPS. Hence 533 MFLOPS maximum throughput, when the Add/Logical and
the Multiply pipes are linked together. Each of the two Load/Store
Pipes has the data bandwidth of 32 bytes/15 nanoseconds, or equivalently, 267 M words/ second in either direction. This rate matches the
the maximum throughputs of the arithmetic pipelines. The total
capacity of the Vector Registers is 64K Bytes, with the basic hardware
vector length of 32 double-precision words. Vector Registers of this
capacity can greatly reduce the data traffic to and from the main
storage unit. As for VP-100, the throughputs of the pipeline units
and the total size of Vector Registers are half of the figures given
above.

In order to control conditional vector operations and vector
editing functions, bit strings (called mask vectors) are also
provided. 256 Mask Registers (16-bits each for VP-100 and 32 bits
each for VP-200) store mask vectors, and Mask Pipe performs logical
operations associated with the mask vectors. More about these will be
described in section 5.

4.3. Main Storage Unit

As described earlier, the maximum capacity of the main storage
is 256 M Bytes for VP-200, with 256-way interleave, or 128 M Bytes for
VP-100, with 128-way interleave. Possible vector accesses are
contiguous, constant-strided and indirect addressing.

5. Advanced Features in architecture

This section describes how the advanced features, as listed in section 2, have been implemented in the FACOM Vector Processor from architectural point of view.

5.1. Conditional Vector Operations

The results of the application program study indicates that the conditional statements are frequently encountered within DO loops. The upwind differencing is a typical example. The FACOM Vector Processor provides three different methods to efficiently execute vector operations involving certain conditional branches: masked arithmetic operations, compress/expand functions and vector indirect addressing.

In the case of the masked arithmetic operations, Add/Logical Pipe generates mask vectors which indicate the TRUE/FALSE values of conditional statements, and the arithmetic pipeline units take such mask vectors via Mask Registers as the control inputs. The arithmetic pipeline units store the results back to Vector Registers only for the vector elements having "1"'s in the corresponding locations of the mask vector: old values are retained, otherwise (Fig. 2a). Note that for a given vector length, the execution time of a masked arithmetic operation is constant regardless of the ratio of TRUE values to the vector length (called "true ratio").

Two other methods utilize the vector editing functions, which we will describe in the following subsection. In short, those vector elements which meet the given condition are brought into new vectors prior to vector arithmetic operations. In contrast to the masked operation, the execution time of a conditional arithmetic operations with these two methods depends on the true ratio.

5.2. Vector Editing Functions

The FACOM Vector Processor provides two kinds of editing functions: compress/expand operations and vector indirect addressing. These functions can be used not only for the conditional vector operations, but for sparse matrix computations and other data editing applications.

Vectors on Vector Registers can be edited by compress and expand functions using Load/Store Pipes as data alignment circuits; no access

to the main storage is involved in these cases. Compressing a vector
A under a mask M means that the elements of A marked with "1"'s in the
corresponding locations of the mask vector M are copied into another
vector B, where these elements are stored in contiguous locations with
their order preserved (Fig. 2b). Expanding a vector means the
opposite operation.

In the vector indirect addressing, on the other hand, a vector J
on Vector Registers holds the indices for the elements of another
vector A stored in the main memory, which is to be loaded into vector
B defined on Vector Registers. Namely, B(I)=A(J(I)) (Fig. 3c). This
is a very versatile and powerful operation, since the order of the
elements can be scrambled in any manner. The data transfer rate for
vector indirect addressing, however, is lower than that for the
contiguous vectors, due to possible bank and/or bus conflicts.

5.3. Dynamically Reconfigurable Vector Registers

One of the most unique features of the FACOM Vector Processor
is the dynamically reconfigurable Vector Registers. The results of
our study indicate that the requirements for the length and the number
of vector registers vary from one programs to another, or even within
a program. To make the best utilization of the total capacity of 64K
bytes for VP-200, for example, the Vector Registers may be concatinated
to take the following configurations: 32(length)x256(total number),
64x128, 128x64,......,1,024x8. The length of Vector Registers is
specified by a special register, and it can be altered by an instruction
in the program.

5.4. High Level Concurrency

The FACOM Vector Processor allows concurrent operations at
various levels (Fig. 3). In the vector unit, five functional pipeline
units can operate concurrently: two out of three arithmetic pipes, two
Load/Store Pipes and Mask Pipe. Furthermore, vector operands associated
with consecutive instructions can flow continuously through each of
the arithmetic pipes. This implies that the start-up time for vector
operations can be effectively masked out.

The vector unit and the scalar unit can also operate concurrently.
Without such feature, the scalar operations between the vector opera-

tions could cause considerable performance degradation. Serialization instructions are provided to preserve the data dependency relations among instructions.

6. Vectorizing Compiler--- FORTRAN77/VP

A vectorizing compiler, FORTRAN77/VP, is now being developed for the FACOM Vector Processor. FORTRAN77 has been chosen as the language for this machine, so that the large software assets can become readily available. In order to obtain high vectorization ratio for wide range of application programs, FORTRAN77/VP compiler vectorizes not only the simple DO loops but nested DO loops and the macro operations such as the inner product efficiently. It also detects and separates the recurrences. These general techniques have been reported in Ref. [1]. We will discuss, in the following four subsections, the techniques which are related to the advanced features in sections 2 and 5. We will also discuss other unique features of FORTRAN77/VP in the final subsection.

6.1. Vectorization of IF Statements

The results of our study indicate that the true ratio of conditional statements widely varies from one case to another. In fact, the true ratio and the relative frequency of load/store instruction executions over the total instruction executions within a DO loop are the two key parameters in selecting the best among the three methods described in 5.1. If the true ratio is medium to high, the masked arithmetic operation is the best; otherwise, the compress/expand method is the best when the frequency of load/store operations is low, and the indirect addressing the best when such frequency is high. The FORTRAN77/VP compiler analyzes each DO loop, compares the estimated execution times for all three methods and selects the one which yields the shortest time.

6.2. Vector Editing Functions

When vector compress/expand functions are used for conditional vector operations, two steps are usually involved: mask vector generation, and actual operations. Frequently used mask patterns may be stored in Mask Registers to skip the first step. When the indirect addressing is used for the same purpose, on the other hand, three steps are involved: mask vector generation, index list vector generation from the mask vector, and actual data transfer between the Vector Register and the main storage. In this case, index vectors rather than the mask vectors may be stored for frequently used access patterns.

6.3. Optimal Register Assignments

In order to best utilize the dynamically reconfigurable Vector Registers, the compiler must know the frequently used hardware vector length for each program, or even within one program the vector length may have to be adjusted. When the vector length is too short, load/ store instructions will have to be issued more frequently, whereas if it is unnecessarily long, the number of available vectors will decrease and resulting in frequent load/store operation again. In general, the compiler puts a higher priority on the number of vectors rather than the length in searching for the best register configuration.

6.4. Pipeline Parallelization

The compiler performs the extensive dataflow analysis of the FORTRAN source programs and schedules the instruction stream, so that the vector arithmetic pipeline units are kept as busy as possible. This process includes the reordering of instruction sequence, balanced assignments of two Load/Store Pipes, and insertion of serialization instructions wherever necessary.

6.5. Other Features of Software

Ease of use is another objective of the compiler. FORTRAN77/VP provides debugging aids, a performance analyzer, an interactive vectorizer, and a vectorized version of the scientific subroutine library (called SSL II/VP). One of the unique features is the inter-active vectorizer. This software is a tuning tool to improve the vectorization ratio of user programs via TSS terminals. For example, a programmer can provide the compiler such useful information as the estimated true ratios of the conditional statements, the estimated hardware vector lengths, and so forth.

7. Parallel Algorithm Study

We are also developing various kinds of parallel algorithms tailored for the FACOM VP100/200 architecture, which can provide nearly maximal performances for specific applications. Some such examples are: Sparse Linear Equation Solver, FFT and Table-lookup.

8. Conclusions

In this paper we have outlined the technologies, the architecture and the software of the FACOM Vector Processor, VP-100/VP-200. We have pointed out the advanced features, which will significantly improve the average performance for the practical application programs, and also described how such features have been implemented in hardware and software. At the time of preparing this paper, the FACOM Vector Processor is in the final stage of the system testing. We have also started running some benchmark programs. The first customer shipment in Japan is scheduled in the 4th quarter of 1983.

Acknowledgements

The authors wish to express their thanks to Messrs. Y.Tanakura and S. Kamiya of Software Division, and Mr. M. Shinohara of the Mainframe Division for valuable discussions and comments.

Reference

[1] S. Kamiya et. al. :"Practical Vectorization Techniques for The FACOM VP", IFIP Congress, Paris France, September 1983.

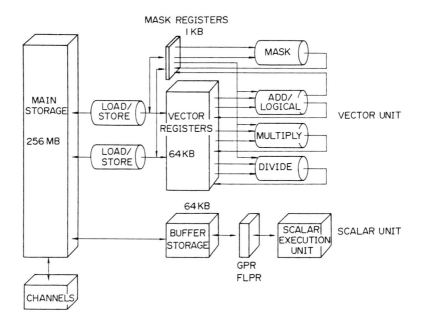

Figure 1. FACOM Vector Processor Block Diagram

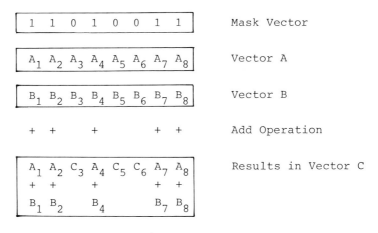

(a) Masked Operation

Figure 2. Three Methods for Conditional Vector
Operations

```
┌─────────────────────────┐
│ 1  1  0  1  0  0  1  1   │   Mask Vector
└─────────────────────────┘

┌─────────────────────────┐
│ A₁ A₂ A₃ A₄ A₅ A₆ A₇ A₈ │   Vector A
└─────────────────────────┘
┌─────────────────────────┐
│ B₁ B₂ B₃ B₄ B₅ B₆ B₇ B₈ │   Vector B
└─────────────────────────┘


┌─────────────────────┐
│ A₁ A₂ A₄ A₇ A₈      │   Compress A
└─────────────────────┘
┌─────────────────────┐
│ B₁ B₂ B₄ B₇ B₈      │   Compress B
└─────────────────────┘

   +  +  +  +  +           Add Operation
```

(b) Compress Operation

```
┌─────────────────────────┐
│ 1  1  0  1  0  0  1  1   │   Mask Vector
└─────────────────────────┘

┌─────────────────────┐
│ 1  2  4  7  8       │   List Vector J Generation
└─────────────────────┘

┌─────────────────────┐
│ A₁ A₂ A₄ A₇ A₈      │   Indirect Vector Load A
└─────────────────────┘
┌─────────────────────┐
│ B₁ B₂ B₄ B₇ B₈      │   Indirect Vector Load B
└─────────────────────┘

   +  +  +  +  +           Add Operation
```

(c) Vector Indirect Addressing

Figure 2.   Three Methods for Processing Conditional
            Vector Operations (Continued)

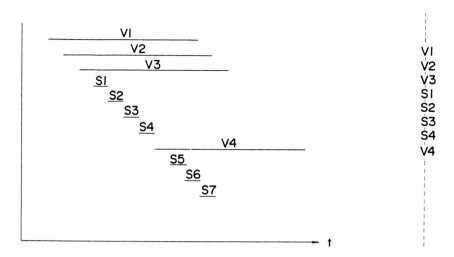

Figure 3.   Concurrent Processing of Scalar and
            Vector Instructions

Latency and HEP

Burton J. Smith
Denelcor, Inc.
17000 East Ohio Place
Aurora, CO   80017

Abstract - The HEP parallel computer system is able to overcome most
of the undesirable effects of latency by pipelining, but without the
usual consequences. The reasons for HEP's latency tolerance may be
found in a few unusual features of the HEP architecture, one of which
seems contradictory; the HEP has very low latency process
synchronization and communication facilities compared to other MIMD
machines.   These features allow a high degree of parallelism to be
sustained.

Introduction

The HEP parallel computer system [6,7] is able to overcome most
of the undesirable effects of latency by pipelining, but without the
usual consequences. For example, a vector pipelined architecture
must have a short pipeline (low latency) to have good performance on
short vectors, but the HEP achieves excellent performance even on
scalar codes using a typical data memory pipeline length of about 20
instruction segments.   To cite another example, the register
operation pipeline in HEP is 8 segments long, significantly longer
than most of the pipelines in a Cray 1, but the HEP closely
approaches its peak processing rate on a much broader class of
problems than just those considered "vectorizable" [1,2,4,5].

The reasons for HEP's latency tolerance may be found in a few
unusual features of the HEP architecture, one of which seems
contradictory; the HEP has very low latency process synchronization
and communication facilities compared to other MIMD machines.   The
HEP is closer architecturally to data flow computers than to
conventional MIMD computers in the way it exploits relatively high
latency instruction execution.

Latency and Pipelining

One way to explain why latency is so harmful in single instruction stream (SI) computers is to say that dependencies in the programs prevent sufficient concurrency to keep the processor busy. Unfortunately, many of the dependencies in typical SI programs result from the need to transform the algorithm into SI-executable form and not from data dependencies present in the algorithm. While an SI computer may have fully pipelined or parallel functional units and plenty of registers to avoid dependencies due to conflicts for those resources, the single program counter is an unavoidable bottleneck. The dependencies due to the program counter include not just the traditional conditional branch problems but a broader class of dependencies resulting merely from the fact that the SI model of computation requires that any side effect of an instruction must be able to affect subsequent instructions. Perhaps the most important and obvious dependency of this kind might be called the memory dependency: data writes and reads at a given memory location must occur in the order issued.

When vector instructions are incorporated in an SI architecture, the effects of latency can be reduced to some extent through the use of pipelining. It is not an accident that the two most highly successful vector architectures, the Cray 1 and the Cyber 205, use pipelined, rather than parallel, processing elements to accomplish vector operations. Pipelined vector SI computers partially solve the latency problems caused by memory dependencies, this primarily because the components of the vectors are loaded and stored at disjoint memory locations. Unfortunately, the presence of short vector and scalar operations in an algorithm reduces the effectiveness of pipelining as a way of concealing latency effects. In addition, the larger the memory of such a computer becomes, the longer the pipelines must be to access it and the worse the performance becomes on short vectors.

In a multiple instruction stream (MI) computer, latency effects due to memory dependencies still exist but are for the most part only local to a particular instruction stream. In a sense, the memory dependency situation for MI computers is very similar to that for vector SI computers; as long as the memory locations are disjoint, there are no memory dependencies between instruction streams any more

than there are between components of a vector. This property allows
the memory references of the HEP system, a scalar MI computer, to be
pipelined in the same way that the components of a vector are
pipelined.

It is also possible to dynamically vary the number of
instruction streams in a pipelined MI design like HEP, just as one
can easily vary the lengths of vectors in a pipelined vector SI
computer. The effects are analogous. The more instruction streams
(the longer the vectors), the more latency can be hidden and
therefore the longer the pipeline can be. Unlike the pipelined
vector SI case, however, the applicability and usefulness of
pipelined MI parallelism is not directly determined by vector length
but by another factor applicable to MI computers generally, namely
how many instructions can a stream execute before it must communicate
with another stream [3]. Put another way, the key performance
limiting factor for MI computers is this: How much performance is
lost implementing inter-stream memory dependencies?

Inter-Stream Dependencies

Ideally, the only MI inter-stream memory dependencies that
should occur in a program correspond to data dependencies present in
the original algorithm. Memory organization and size constraints,
programmer decisions, compiler implementation decisions, and other
factors typically add additional memory dependencies, but these will
be ignored; we will assume that all memory dependencies are due to
data dependencies. The implementation of an algorithm on MI hardware
requires the (usually heuristic) scheduling of the algorithm on the
instruction streams available. If the number of instruction streams
is variable, this may be exploited to improve the schedule. The
scheduling may be accomplished by a compiler, by the programmer, or
by a combination of the two; however it is done, the objective is
obviously to reduce the total execution time of the program. If the
parallelism available in the computer is sufficiently high, there
will be an optimum number of instruction streams for that algorithm
on that computer, and attempts to further increase speed through
parallelism will be more than offset by the increased cost of
implementing the additional inter-stream data dependencies.

There are two kinds of prices that may be paid when exchanging an intra-stream for an inter-stream data dependency: increased latency and reduced parallelism. The increased latency price is paid in proportion to the required number of additional instructions needed by either the sending or the receiving instruction stream (this overhead also has the effect of reducing parallelism slightly), and in proportion to any pure (pipelined) delay between one instruction stream and another for either communication or synchronization. The reduced parallelism price is paid especially when a critical section is employed either to manage a scarce resource used in the implementation of the data dependencies (e.g. the ability to interrupt another processor) or to actually implement the dependencies, but in a naive way (e.g., controlling all accesses to mesh points in an iterative algorithm with a single monitor).

The effect of increased latency is not to directly increase the execution time of every algorithm, but to restrict the amount of parallelism that can be obtained on some algorithms before waiting (and therefore reduced parallelism) occurs. For example, an inter-stream data dependency implementation having a sufficiently high bandwidth but a latency of several hundred instruction times is not particularly suitable for the execution of parallel back substitution against a small upper triangular matrix; the net effect would be manifested as reduced parallelism simply because the data dependency graph of the back substitution algorithm exhibits high connectivity. On the other hand, high latency would not dramatically influence the degree of parallelism that could be obtained for a time independent, complex geometry Monte Carlo simulation whose data dependency graph resembles a number of simple chains joined at their terminal ends. In sum, the effect of high latency for inter-stream data dependencies in an MI computer architecture is only to restrict its applicability to a narrow class of algorithms.

Reduced parallelism, unlike increased latency, has an undesirable effect on the execution rate of essentially all algorithms, and an architecture which must significantly reduce parallelism to implement each inter-stream data dependency is really not much of an MI computer. One probably should use its instruction streams to run independent user programs rather than try to use it as a parallel processor.

The way in which the HEP implements inter-stream data dependencies is by using a distributed shared memory equipped with a "full/empty" bit at each memory word. This bit can be used to enforce alternation of reads and writes, among other things. Unlike most schemes, there is no overhead whatsoever for single producer, single comsumer inter-stream dependencies. The latency is quite low, just two instruction times (one load plus one store), and the only reduction in parallelism that occurs is due to memory bank conflicts. Given these properties, one would anticipate that the HEP is effective on a very broad class of algorithms, and this has indeed proven to be true. It is usually not a good idea to create and destroy HEP processes to enforce the synchronization of an inter-stream dependency, but rather to let the processes busy wait for "full" or "empty". Even though the additional overhead required to destroy and then recreate a process can be quite small, the condition in which there is no actual waiting for "full" or "empty" occurs so often in reasonably well-designed programs that a net reduction in performance will usually result if a "fork/join" approach is taken.

Conclusions

The use of pipelining to avoid the undesirable effects of latency is possible in MIMD as well as in data flow computers. To accomplish this, sufficient parallelism is necessary; the key ingredient required to achieve this parallelism is an effective and economical way of implementing inter-stream dependencies. The HEP system is a good example of how this can be done.

References

1. Gentzsch, W., "Benchmark Results on Physical Flow Problems,"
    this proceedings.

2. Grit, D. H. and McGraw, J. R., "Programming Divide and Conquer
    on a Multiprocessor", Report UCRL-88710, Lawrence Livermore
    National Laboratory (May 1983).

3. Hockney, R. W., "Performance of Parallel Computers", this
    proceedings.

4. Jordan, H. F., "Performance Measurements on HEP-A Pipelined MIMD
    Computer", Proceedings of the 10th Annual International
    Symposium on Computer Architecture, (June 1983).

5. Kowalik, J. S., Lord, R. E., and Kumar, S. P., "Design and
    Performance of Algorithms for MIMD Parallel Computers",
    this proceedings.

6. Smith, B. J., "A Pipelined, Shared Resource MIMD Computer",
    Proceedings of the 1978 International Conference on
    Parallel Processing (August 1978), pp. 6-8.

7. Smith, B. J., "Architecture and Applications of the HEP
    Multiprocessor Computer System", Proceedings of the Society
    of Photo-Optical Instrumentation Engineers, Volume 298,
    Real-Time Signal Processing IV (August 1981), pp. 241-248.

THE S-1 Mark IIA SUPERCOMPUTER

P. Michael Farmwald

Lawrence Livermore National Laboratory, Livermore, California

Abstract

This paper describes the S-1 Mark IIA Multiprocessor System. It is composed of up to 16 supercomputer class uniprocessors with multiple local caches, an extremely large, medium-latency high-bandwidth shared memory, and a low-latency synchronization mechanism for passing short messages. The system is applicable to a wide variety of applications, including large-scale physical simulation, real-time command and control and program development in a time-sharing environment. The hardware organization, its implications, and software supporting the efficient utilization of the multiprocessor are discussed.

Introduction

The S-1 Project[1] is engaged in the development of advanced digital processing technology for potential application in the military and scientific communities. Current work being sponsored by the U.S. Navy and the Department of Energy involves the design and development of extremely high performance, general purpose computers (S-1) and multiprocessor interconnection technologies.

The reasons for development of multiprocessors have been widely discussed; chief among them are reliability, economy and scale. We place heavy — though not exclusive — emphasis on the issue of scale.

Today, there are a number of important problems for which manual solution is infeasible, yet cannot be handled by existing computers because they have insufficent computing power.[2] As an example, the ability to provide an accurate two week weather forecast would have extraordinary economic leverage. It would allow farmers to select optimal times for planting and harvesting, and provide substantial warning of natural disasters to minimize loss of life and property. The latest computational methods for weather prediction are believed to be adequate for the task; unfortunately, they overwhelm the computing and storage capacity that is available today. Development of new oil and mineral resources is of vital national importance. Much of the exploration being conducted involves seismic data processing, and employs vast computer resources. Effective utilization of the new semiconductor technology, specifically very large scale integration (VLSI), is limited by our ability

NATO ASI Series, Vol. F7
High-Speed Computation. Edited by J. S. Kowalik
© Springer-Verlag Berlin Heidelberg 1984

to design and debug circuits involving hundreds of thousands of transistors. Computer-aided design techniques, such as the Project's SCALD system,[3] have been demonstrated to greatly reduce development time of new digital systems; however, their use is effectively limited to designs of moderate size because of capacity limitations. Similar limitations are seen in a variety of military applications.

Given a particular logic technology, there is a limit to performance that can be obtained regardless of the complexity of cleverness of the processor design. Today's fastest processors using commercially available components have a peak performance in the 10-40 MIPS (million instruction per second) regime for scalar operations and 100-400 MFLOPS (million floating point operations per second) for vector operations. A multiprocessor, however, can exceed the inherent limitations on a single processor by performing computations in parallel.

Multiprocessor systems which have been demonstrated to date fall into roughly two categories. The first includes systems that have a large number of small scale processors (minicomputers or microcomputers). Examples include most of the early research multi-processors such as CM*. Aggregate system performance is limited because of the limited performance of the processing elements, and the limited number of processing elements connected together. The second category encompasses systems that have a small number of medium scale processors (small mainframes). This approach has been taken in several commercial offerings that provide cost effective performance enhancement for batch or time-sharing applications through dual-processor configurations. Aggregate system performance is not an issue in these systems as they are used to run more jobs rather than a single job faster.

The S-1 Project is taking the approach of assembling a multiprocessor consisting of up to sixteen uniprocessors, each of which have a performance comparable to that of the fastest supercomputers. This paper will address four topics: design of the uniprocessors, the multiprocessor architecture, operating system support, and the tools for partitioning single problems for a multiprocessor.

Uniprocessors

For use in the multiprocessor, we are developing a family of processors having similar architectures, but differing implementation technology. Each successive family member is intended to make maximally effective use of the then available logic families. Such a succession of processors is required in order to maintain the multiprocessor's edge. Advances in semiconductors are occurring at such a rapid rate that a multiprocessor tied to one particular technology would soon be made obsolete by single processors having an order of magnitude greater speed.

The first generation of the S-1 family of processors is the Mark I, which has been operational since 1977. Implemented in ECL-10K medium scale integrated circuits (MSI), it is roughly equivalent in processing power to one-third of a CDC 7600. The second generation, the Mark IIA, is currently undergoing initial checkout. Through use of extensive hardware support for vector and floating point computations, and faster logic (ECL-100K MSI), it is expected to achieve performance comparable to existing supercomputers such as the Cray-1. Future generations are planned that will follow the leading edge of implementation technologies to obtain ever increasing performance and ever decreasing cost, power and space requirements. The S-1 Mark V, targeted for development in the 1986 time frame, is intended to be a "supercomputer on a wafer" with performance several times that of the Mark IIA.

Unlike traditional supercomputers which sacrifice functionality for performance, the architecture of the S-1 uniprocessors has been designed to be easy and efficient to use for a wide variety of applications. In this, it closely resembles the highly popular mini-mainframes which stress flexibility over performance.

The architecture was designed with a number of goals in mind. First, it must be suitable for high performance implementation; second, it must be simple for a high level language (e.g. Ada) compiler to make effective use of the instruction set; and third, it must provide a comprehensive set of data types and operations so that the programmer can select the arithmetic precision appropriate to a problem.

In addition to the usual general purpose features, the S-1 architecture has incorporated a number of special purpose operations to provide especially high performance for its anticipated applications. Many scientific codes make heavy use of elementary functions such as sine, cosine, exponentials, and logarithms. The architecture provides these functions as single instructions, and the Mark IIA has special hardware to permit these instructions to execute at about the same speed as a simple multiply. An extensive vector instruction set is provided to enhance performance on problems that manipulate large arrays of data. Special vector instructions are provided for signal processing applications. Examples include FFT's and filtering operations. Matrix operations are also supported, including matrix multiply and generalized transpose. Vector instructions execute with a one element step size to simplify the design of the cache on the Mark IIA. In cases where the problem requires non-unity step sizes, the transpose instruction can be used to extract the relevant elements into a unity step size temporary vector. Some indication of the performance of a Mark IIA uniprocessor prototype is given in tables 1 and 2.

The S-1 architecture provides the user with a large, segmented virtual address space spanning 2 billion 9-bit bytes of data. Memory capacity on this scale is crucial for the effective solution of large problems such as three-dimensional physical simulations. The large address space allows all the problem data to reside directly in memory in the obvious fashion, and eliminates the programming contrivances needed to explicitly manage multiple types of computer system storage (i.e., manually swapping data to and from a disk file). A virtual memory mechanism maps the virtual address space to physical memory. In the event that the user's memory requirements exceed physical capacity, it is possible for the operating system to simulate the additional memory with a slight performance penalty; this avoids the problem of a program "falling off a memory cliff". With today's rapidly decreasing costs of memory, however, it is becoming economically feasible to purchase sufficient memory to meet the requirements of even the largest programs.

Instruction (H-halfword, S-singleword, D-doubleword)	Vector Time	Scalar Time	Latency
Move (HSD)	40 ns	80 ns	160 ns
Shift (HSD)	40 ns	80 ns	160 ns
Load Byte (SD)	40 ns	80 ns	160 ns
Floating-point Add (HSD)	40 ns	80 ns	160 ns
Floating-point Multiply (HS)	40 ns	80 ns	240 ns
Floating-point Multiply (D)	80 ns	80 ns	240 ns
Floating-point Reciprocate (HS)	40 ns	80 ns	240 ns
Floating-point Square Root (HS)	40 ns	80 ns	240 ns
Floating-point Reciprocate (D)	120 ns	560 ns	720 ns
Floating-point Sine (HS)	80 ns	480 ns	560 ns

Performance of Selected Mark IIA Instructions
Table 1

Instruction (H-halfword, S-singleword)	Time per Iteration
1024 Point Complex Floating-point FFT (H)	2.1 ms
1024 Point Complex Floating-point FFT (S)	5.4 ms

Performance of Selected Mark IIA Signal Processing Instructions
Table 2

Multiprocessor Systems

The S-1 Mark IIA Multiprocessor System is a MIMD (multiple instruction, multiple data) stream organization. The multiprocessor currently being built at the Lawrence Livermore National Laboratory consists of 16 Mark IIA processors, connected together with a crossbar switch as shown in Figure 1.

A crossbar is the highest possible performance interconnection network, with a direct logical connection from each processor to each memory bank. Given that high performance processing elements are being used, the cost of the crossbar switch turns out to only be a few percent of the system cost, making it the obvious choice for use. The use of slower-growth, distributed interconnection networks is under consideration for future systems.

To the programmer, the S-1 Multiprocessor looks like 16 identical processors executing out of a very large (up to 16 billion bytes) common memory. The processors always get the latest value associated with a memory location, and instructions operate in a read-modify-write fashion. All of the complexity of moving results between different processors and between processors and memories are completely handled by the hardware in an invisible (except for timing) fashion.

In order to speed up effective memory access times, the processor keeps the most-recently referenced memory locations in cache memories, which are very high-speed local memories contained inside of the processors. Each processor has two cache memories, a data cache of size 64K bytes (increased to 256K bytes on the third and later processors), and an instruction cache of size 16K bytes. Both caches use a set size of four and a line size of 64 bytes. Furthermore, both caches are capable of reading up to sixteen sequential bytes in a single cycle, including accesses that straddle line and page boundaries. The cache accesses are included in the normal pipeline sequence. When the processor wants to use a location that is not contained in one of the caches, the processor goes out to the main memory to see if the desired location is stored there. If so, it reads the 64 bytes around the location of interest, and stores them in its cache for future use, removing the 64 bytes that haven't been referenced for the longest period of time. If the location that is desired is contained in the cache of another processor, the requesting processor will ask the processor that has the location in its cache to remove it from its cache, and to transmit the data to the requesting processor.

The technique by which the hardware automatically keeps track of shared data in a multiprocessor with caches is called cache coherence.[4] Associated with each block of 64 bytes in main memory are an additional 17-bits that specify the current "ownership" of the block. There is one bit for each of the 16 processors in the multiprocessor which is set

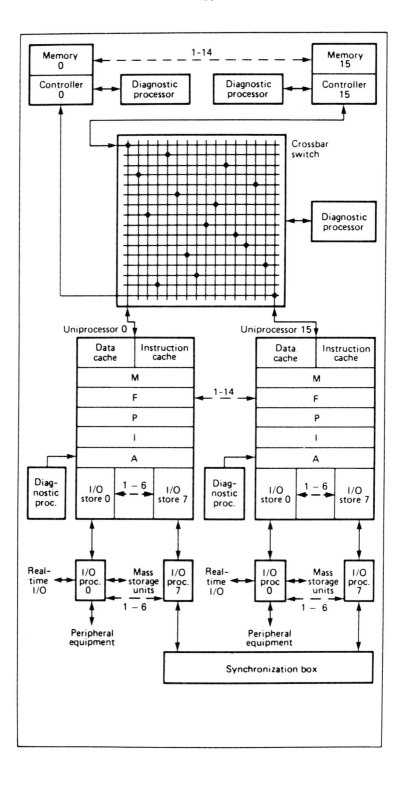

if the corresponding processor has a copy of the block in its cache, and the 17th bit says that somebody has a copy of the block for write access. Multiple processors are allowed to have copies of a block for each access, but only one processor is allowed to have a block for write access.

The use of shared memory to provide high speed synchronization and low latency data transmission (less than a microsecond) is difficult. For problems which require very close cooperation between the processing elements, a special set of hardware implemented queue instructions is provided. These instructions allow one processor to put computed results into a queue for another processor, which takes values and does further computation. We have found that this can substantially speed up processing in some algorithms, e.g. those which involve wavefront computations.

Operating System Support

In order to provide a workable software base for experimentation, the S-1 Project has undertaken the development of a new operating system, called Amber, that is intended to provide a flexible interface to the multiprocessing capabilities of the system.

The basic design goal of Amber is to support a widely varying community of users — including real-time, computation-intensive, and time-sharing — on one system. We see this as particularly important since it allows for extensive sharing of effort, both in the development of system software and applications software. Often several operating systems are developed for new computers, one for each major class of application. When this occurs, there is little motivation to share development effort between the different operating systems. Facilities with common functions are implemented multiple times with different interfaces for each operating system. This not only increases the total development burden, but also limits the rate at which the system matures, since a smaller user group is available to test out the system. On the other hand, when there is a single multi-function operating system, tools such as compilers, debuggers and file maintenance utilities can be readily shared between different applications. More important is the fact that libraries developed by user groups can be shared as well. There is, however, a danger in the development of a multi-function system; the system may not fulfill any of the requirements well. To avoid this problem, Amber has a modular layering of functions. The lowest levels of the system provide only atomic functions that can be implemented efficiently; higher levels of the system incorporate the more complex functions which are specific to particular applications. Commonality is therefore retained, but an application need only invoke the functions necessary to it.

The central example of this kind of layering of function exists in the scheduler. The low level scheduler provides an efficient mechanism for short-term scheduling of tasks on a single processor. The basic algorithm is a simple priority scheduling algorithm with round-robin queues. Within a single priority level, each task may run until it must wait for some external event, or an assigned run quantum expires, at which time it is moved to the end of the queue. Tasks may be assigned to different priority levels depending on their relative importance or real-time constraints. For example, in a time-sharing system normal user tasks might be given priority over batch jobs, and relinquish priority to tasks which must respond to external interrupts in a certain length of time. The high level scheduler implements higher level, policy-oriented scheduling functions, by manipulating the parameters of the low level scheduler, such as task priority or quantum size. The simplest example of such a scheduling policy is for "real-time" jobs. Here the policy is simple: select the priority that the job is to have, and assign it to a processor. More complex policies occur in batch or time-sharing systems, where it may be desirable to load-share across all the processors in the system or to guarantee a particular job a certain fraction of system resources. In contrast to the low level scheduler, which makes assignments on millisecond timescales, the policy decisions are made on second or minute timescales and can therefore be relatively computationally expensive without unduly affecting system response.

The low level scheduler enforces a dedicated processor assignment for each task given to it, rather than scheduling each task to the next available processor. This means that processors may lie idle in the system while there are tasks ready to run. While this may seem unfortunate at first glance, there is in fact strong motivation to restrict tasks to single processors in the short run. First, the I/O architecture of the S-1 attaches peripherals through dual-port memories to a particular processor. A task whose purpose is to control a peripheral can only run on the processor to which the peripheral is attached; the task's processor assignment must reflect this fact. Second, the internal processor caches are very large, and as a task runs it builds up a substantial investment in data that has been locally cached. If its execution were to be moved to a different processor, the data would have to be swapped back to main memory and then swapped into the cache of the new processor. Consequently, if tasks are moved from one processor to another on a short time scale, a noticeable performance degradation results. By performing processor reassignment on a relatively long time scale, the effect is trivialized. Third, to support parallelism between tasks working on the same problem, it is necessary to insure concurrency of execution. By assigning each such task to its own processor, we can do so without use of a complex algorithm which would interfere with the simple requirements of other applications.

One of the important features of the S-1 multiprocessor is the large shared memory which permits high bandwidth communications between tasks. Access to the shared memory is provided in two ways: sharing of entire address spaces, and sharing of specific data objects.

The address space of a task encompases all data to which it has access; this includes program instructions, common blocks, and local variables. In many operating systems, each task is assigned a unique address space (usually called a core image). Each task sees its own private copy of all programs and data. Modifcations made are not apparent to other tasks. In Amber it is possible for two or more tasks to share the same address space, i.e., identically the same physical storage. As a result, a modification to data made by one task is immediately visible to another, even if the tasks reside on different processors. Such shared data may be used as semaphores or locks to synchronize the execution of the tasks or as shared data bases to be concurrently processed by the tasks.

While there are uses for sharing entire address spaces — for instance, the semantics of Ada require tasks to execute in the same address space — there is added protection in only sharing that portion of address which is actually common. For this, Amber implements segmentation. A segment is little more than an ordinary file, except that a task can instruct that a file be mapped into its address space so that it may be directly modified. When two tasks both map the same segment, they share a single physical copy, while other portions of the address space stay private. Thus, a task is protected against inadvertent modifications to its private state. The segmentation mechanism can provide further intertask protection as well. The modes of access (read, write) that a task is permitted to a segment is the same as the normal file protection. It is then possible, for example, to set up — and enforce — a reader/writer relationship between two tasks by granting one read/write access on the segment, and the other only read access.

The inherent redundancy of the multiprocessors is often used to obtain increased reliability and availabiliy. Amber uses a facility called dynamic reconfiguration to exploit the redundant components of the S-1 Multiprocessor. At any time, Amber is capable of providing service with only a partially operating configuration, and it is possible to dynamically change the configuration without halting the system. If a memory box is to be removed, data in that box are moved either to another box or to disk and the virtual memory mapping updated to reflect their new location. If a processor is to be removed, tasks on that processor are halted and redistributed to other processors for execution. When a memory or a processor is added, it is added to the pool of system resources and is assigned as needed.

A Multiprocessor Software Tool

The construction and maintenance of large application programs for a multiprocessor system presents many problems. The details of the multiprocessor system may greatly influence the structure of the software that yields the best performance. For instance, the algorithm that is fastest on a uniprocessor may not exploit the capabilities of a multiprocessor as well as one tailored for parallelism. In addition, the number of processors available on a time-shared (or gracefully degrading) multiprocessor may vary with time, with different algorithms being appropriate for different load factors and numbers of processors.

Thus, it is desirable to maintain a single source which works well on many configurations. However, including too many details of how to best perform a task may lead to unreadable, unmodifiable, and untransportable programs. The approach taken in the Paralyzer, a tool being developed by the S-1 Project, is to split programs into two conceptual pieces. One part describes the "how" of the computation, which includes the basic data and control flow of the algorithm. The second part is the "where" of the computation. This basically specifies what processors are to run the computations, as well as modifying the control and data flow of the first section in ways appropriate to the hardware available. The intent is that the first section is relatively machine and configuration independent, whereas the second is completely driven by the computation resources.

The current version of the Paralyzer uses Pascal as the source language, and is implemented as a source-to-source translator. Special Pascal comments are used to describe some of the "where". The special comments and the "where" description file are implemented in Maclisp (a variant of Lisp) — thus a complete programming language is available for program manipulation. A library of routines have been written in Maclisp to implement the most common kinds of transformations.

A simple example of a transformation performed by the Paralyzer involves partitioning the processing of a matrix among several processors. The directives in the special comments instruct that the matrix be divided into several equal sections, along columnar boundaries, and that each section be given to a separate processor for parallel execution. Such a transformation is feasible when the computation of a single matrix element depends only on other elements in the same column, not on elements in the same row. This restriction insures that a single processor has all the data it needs to perform its part of the computation. When other dependencies exist in data, other more complicated transformations are called for.

In addition to generating code for uniprocessor and multiprocessor systems, the Paralyzer has been used to generate code for simulation purposes. For instance, instead of generating variable references, the Paralyzer can generate calls to routines that allow the cache and memory performance of the algorithm to be determined.

Summary

The S-1 Multiprocessor System is a new step in the development of high-performance computer systems. It combines many cost-effective supercomputers with the interconnection hardware and software to effectively utilize those processors on a single problem. The goal is to provide the capability to solve challenging real problems of interest to real users.

Acknowledgments

Work performed under the auspices of the U.S. Department of Energy by the Lawrence Livermore National Laboratory under contract number W-7405-ENG-48, with support from the Naval Electronic Systems Command and the Office of Naval Research.

References

1. S-1 Project Staff, "Advanced Digital Processor Technology Base Development for Navy Applications: The S-1 Project," Lawrence Livermore National Laboratory, Report UCID 18038 (1978).

2. Levine, R. D., "Supercomputers," *Scientific American*, Vol. 246, No. 1, January 1982.

3. McWilliams, T. M., Widdoes, L. C., "The SCALD Physical Design Subsystem," Proceedings of the 15th Annual Design Automation Conference, Las Vegas, 1978 (IEEE, ACM, New York, 1978) p. 271.

4. Censier, L. M. and Feaurier, P. A., "A New Solution to Coherence Problems in Multicache Systems," *IEEE Transactions on Computers*, C27 (12), 1112 (1978).

PART 2

PERFORMANCE AND CAPABILITIES
OF COMPUTER SYSTEMS

PERFORMANCE OF PARALLEL COMPUTERS

R. W. Hockney
Computer Science Department,
Reading University,
Reading, Berks. UK, RG6 2AX.

Abstract:

The performance of some of the parallel computers discussed at this workshop are compared using the characterization with the two parameters $(r_\infty, n_{1/2})$. This characterization, originally developed for SIMD architectures, is tentatively extended to MIMD computers, and we give some data for the Denelcor HEP. All the varied computers can be compared by plotting their positions on the plane of the two parameters, the so-called "Spectrum of Computers". Some generalizations concerning the behaviour of the computers can be drawn from their relative positions on this diagram.

I. INTRODUCTION

In this workshop a wide variety of parallel computer architectures have been described, and there is a need to compare them on a common and quantitative basis. The maximum performance in millions of floating-point operations per second (megaflops) is a single parameter figure-of-merit, but this gives no measure of the effect of vector-length on the performance. To overcome this, Hockney and Jesshope [1] have introduced a two-parameter description, where the second parameter, $n_{1/2}$, is the vector length that is necessary to achieve half the maximum performance. This description, which is briefly reviewed in section II, was devised to fit well the highly successful pipelined architectures with vector instructions, and can also be interpreted to measure the average performance of arrays of processors working from a common instruction stream. Both these computer architectures have a single stream of instructions and fall in the SIMD class of Flynn [2].

The appearance of the Denelcor HEP computer [3] with its multiple instruction streams, raises the question whether the same two-parameter description can be used to characterize such MIMD computers. In section III we indicate how the definition of the parameters can be extended in a useful way to include MIMD architectures. The Denelcor HEP is particularly interesting because it not only combines pipelining and replication in its physical design, it is also programmable to have a variable number of instruction streams. Thus it can be both a uni- or multi-processor, and act like a pipelined or array-like architecture. In section IV we try to represent all these possibilities by appropriate choices of the parameters r_∞ and $n_{1/2}$.

In section V we plot all the computers on the $(n_{1/2}, r_\infty)$ parameter plane - the so-called "Spectrum of Computers" - and draw some general conclusions on the comparative behaviour of the computers from their relative positions on this plane. Of course, one cannot possibly represent all the features of a complex computer by only two parameters; after all, it takes several volumes of manuals, and thousands of words and numbers to describe any computer in reasonable detail. The

NATO ASI Series, Vol. F7
High-Speed Computation. Edited by J. S. Kowalik
© Springer-Verlag Berlin Heidelberg 1984

purpose of this paper is to show how far this particular two-parameter description can be usefully taken.

II. THE PARAMETERS r_∞ and $n_{1/2}$

It has been shown by Hockney and Jesshope [1] how both pipelined vector computers like the CRAY-1 and CYBER 205, and array-like computers such as the ICL DAP, can be compared on a common basis by considering the timing equation for a vector operation. If this is given the generic form:

$$t = r_\infty^{-1}(n+n_{1/2}) \tag{1}$$

then the two parameters $n_{1/2}$ and r_∞ completely characterize the timing behaviour. The parameters are defined as:

r_∞: **(maximum or asymptotic performance)** the maximum number of elemental arithmetic operations (i.e. operations between pairs of numbers) per second, usually measured in megaflops. This occurs for infinite vector length on the generic computer.

$n_{1/2}$: **(half-performance length)** the vector length required to achieve half the maximum performance

Alternatively, for array-like computers, the timing expression is more usefully written as:

$$t = \pi^{-1}(1+n/n_{1/2}) \tag{2}$$

where

π: **(specific performance)** is defined as the ratio $r_\infty/n_{1/2}$.

An array-like design such as the ICL DAP [1] with N processors is included in the formalism by taking either $n_{1/2}=N/2$ if $n>N$, or $n_{1/2}=\infty$ if there are always enough processors, i.e. when $n\leqslant N$. The value of π is the inverse of the time for one parallel operation of the array.

The significance of the above parameters is as follows:

$n_{1/2}$: measures how parallel the computer appears to the user, and varies from $n_{1/2}=0$ for a serial computer, to $n_{1/2}=\infty$ for an infinitely parallel array. It is also the parameter that measures the effect of vector length on the performance of an algorithm, and therefore determines the choice of the best algorithm on a particular computer.

r_∞: measures the performance of a computer on long vectors (i.e. those for which $n>n_{1/2}$).

π: measures the performance of a computer on short vectors (i.e. those for which $n<n_{1/2}$). Note that for an array-like computer with enough processors ($n\leqslant N$), $n_{1/2}=\infty$ and all vectors are short.

The above characterization was used to compare the CRAY-1, CYBER

205 and ICL DAP on a common basis, and implicitly assumed that there was a single stream of vector instructions, in each of which all the arithmetic operations between the elements of the vectors were the same. This is indeed the case with these computers, and others of the same general type, namely SIMD architectures. In fact, neither of these assumptions is necessary to the analysis, which can be applied equally well to the more general MIMD architectures, as we now describe.

III. MIMD COMPUTERS AND ALGORITHMS

MIMD computers can certainly be characterized in the same way as SIMD computers, because they too can be programmed to perform a vector operation. The only question is whether such a characterization is useful. Ones first thought is that it would not be, because the strength of a multi-instruction stream architecture is that it can perform quite dissimilar tasks in parallel; and this would not be used in a vector operation because the same operation is applied to all elements of the vector. However, if we interpret a vector operation in a generalized sense as representing all the arithmetic work between two synchronization points in an MIMD program, then $n_{1/2}$ will measure the overhead of synchronization; that is to say how much arithmetic must exist between synchronization points, before the time spent on it equals the time spent on synchronization.

It is clear that the penalty that is paid for the generality of an MIMD architecture is the cost of synchronization, and we propose to use the parameter $n_{1/2}$ to measure this overhead. As this synchronization is necessarily achieved by user instructions, it is likely to be substantial and dependent on the type of software used. We would therefore expect to obtain different values from assembly code than from a compiled language. On the other hand, the amount of arithmetic that can be placed between synchronization points (on MIMD computers this is the equivalent of vector length), is likely to be very much greater than the vector length in the corresponding SIMD program. In any event one needs a quantitative measure of the synchronization overhead in order to judge the timing of an MIMD program. We believe, that when appropriately defined, the parameter $n_{1/2}$ can play this role.

We therefore define $n_{1/2}$ for an MIMD computer as the amount of arithmetic that must be performed between two successive synchronization points of a program in order to achieve half the maximum performance of the computer. The synchronization points would typically be the FORK initiating several independent parallel processes which execute concurrently, and the following JOIN at which the program waits for all the processes to finish. The amount of arithmetic means the number of floating-point operations between pairs of numbers, otherwise known as the scalar, serial or elemental operations' count. With this definition Eqn.(1) and Eqn. (2) still apply, with t being the time elapsed between the FORK and corresponding JOIN in the program. If a program is defined as a sequence of such FORK/JOIN synchronization points, then the total execution time, T, of a MIMD program can be expressed as:

$$T = r_{\infty}^{-1}(s+n_{1/2}q) \qquad (3)$$

where:

s is the total amount of arithmetic in the program

q is the number of sequential FORK/JOIN pairs that makeup the program

This is the same formula that has been previously used for the vector computers, except that q in the vector case was the number of vector operations in the program.

We will see in section IV that r_∞ and $n_{1/2}$ may depend on the number of parallel processes that are created in the FORK, so that if this varies in an MIMD program, these parameters cannot be treated as constants. In this case one may either use reasonable average values for them if the variation is small, or if the variation is large evaluate a sum with different values of r_∞ and $n_{1/2}$ for each FORK/JOIN of the algorithm.

$$T = \sum_{i=1}^{i=q} r_{\infty,i}^{-1} (n_i + n_{1/2,i}) \tag{4}$$

where:

q is the number of FORK/JOIN pairs

$r_{\infty,i}$ is the r_∞ for the ith FORK/JOIN

$n_{1/2,i}$ is the $n_{1/2}$ for the ith FORK/JOIN

If we wish $n_{1/2}$ to measure the synchronization overhead of an MIMD program, we must measure it in a situation where other aspects of parallel programming do not impinge. We refer to such matters as the efficiency with which the work can be scheduled amongst the available processes or processors. These are the more usual concerns of those designing algorithms for parallel computers, and are measured by the SPEEDUP, S_p, and the EFFICIENCY, E_p as defined by Kuck [4]. The synchronization overhead that we wish to measure is an additional penalty to that of inefficient scheduling, and must be measured in a situation where the scheduling is perfect, i.e. when $S_p = p$ and $E_p = 1$. The simplest such situation to imagine is the programming of a single vector operation on an MIMD computer in which the vector length is an integral multiple of the number of processors. Fitting the measured time as a function of vector length to Eqn. (1), will provide the values of the parameters that we require, in exactly the same way as was done for SIMD computers. Thus although the choice of a single vector operation at first seems an artificially simple test for an MIMD computer, it in fact turns out to be exactly the test that we want in order to measure the synchronization overhead.

The SPEEDUP and EFFICIENCY measures of Kuck are properties of the algorithm, being measures of the efficiency with which a particular algorithm uses the available resources in processors or instruction streams. The half-performance length, $n_{1/2}$, on the other hand, is a property of the computer hardware and system software (assemblers and compilers). It measures the overhead associated with using multiple instruction streams – they do not come for free. Preferably this overhead, and therefore $n_{1/2}$, should be as small as possible; in any case $n_{1/2}$ tells the programmer how much arithmetic he must put between a FORK/JOIN pair on a particular MIMD computer, if he is to obtain more than 50% of the advertised performance, even using an algorithm with perfect scheduling. In the next section we apply these ideas to the Denelcor HEP.

IV. CHARACTERIZING THE HEP

The Denelcor Heterogeneous Element Processor or HEP consists of up to 16 Process Execution Modules (PEMs) connected via a packet switch network to up to 128 Data Modules (DMs). Each PEM may have from one to 50 user instruction streams, which can be distributed amongst up to 7 user tasks. For our purposes we need only a single task which is to evaluate the element by element product of two vectors. The type of arithmetic operation chosen (discounting division) is irrelevant, since all operations take the same time on the HEP.

A new instruction stream (called a process) is initiated with the machine instruction (or FORTRAN statement) CREATE, which creates a new program status word (PSW) for the new instruction stream and inserts it into the process queue. When the PSW for a process is in the process queue, it is said to be an active process. It remains so, until either the process is completed (a successful QUIT instruction or FORTRAN RETURN statement is executed), or the PSW leaves the process queue whilst it is waiting for data from Data Memory (see next paragraph under "wave-off").

In the case of a single task, the process queue may be thought of as a circular queue of up to 50 PSWs, each of which contains the program counter for its process. The program counter points, in the usual way, to the location in memory where the next instruction for that process is to be found. The minimum length of the process queue is eight; and if less than eight processes are active, there will be some empty slots in the queue. These slots can be filled by creating additional processes (until eight are active) without changing the length of the queue or the timing of the other processes. When more than eight processes have been created, the length of the queue is increased, and becomes equal to the number of active processes. The time between the execution of successive instructions in any one process is correspondingly increased, and its processing rate is inversely proportional to the length of the queue, that is to say to the number of active processes.

The process queue circulates through an eight stage pipeline with a transit time of 100ns (the clock period) across each stage. All register-to-register instructions are executed in the 800ns that the PSW takes to pass through the pipeline, and the program counter of each PSW is updated as it passes out of the pipeline. PSWs referring to instructions that access Data Memory, are removed from the process queue until the data they require has been obtained from Data Memory via the switch. Such PSWs are said to be "waved off", and may typically have to wait 2400ns before the data is available. At this time, execution of the waved-off process is continued by reinserting its PSW into the process queue.

If only one process is active, there is only one PSW in the process queue; and this PSW executes one instruction every 800ns as it continuously circulates around the eight stage pipeline. Working in this mode of operation, the HEP is acting like a classical von Neumann serial SISD computer with an instruction time of 800ns, and processing rate of 1.25 Mips (millions of instructions per second). The timing is governed exactly by Eqn. (1) with:

$$r_\infty = 1.25 \text{ Mips}, \qquad n_{1/2} = 0$$

Provided there are eight or less active processes, the PSW for each process still circulates once every 800ns, giving a processing rate of 1.25 Mips per process. If there are less than eight active processes, the pipeline is not full; and extra processes may be created to fill the empty stages of the pipeline, without changing the overall execution time. The total instruction processing rate is then proportional to the number of active processes, up to the maximum of eight processes. At this point the pipeline is full, and the processing rate is at its maximum of 10 Mips. In this mode of operation, the HEP is acting like an MIMD array of processors, in which the processing rate is proportional to the number of processors in the array.

When eight or more processes are active, the pipeline is full and there can be no further increase in the total processing rate. For example, if the number of active processes is doubled, the processing rate for each process is halved, leaving the total processing rate for all processes unchanged. This is because the PSWs are in a circular queue, and if we double the length of this queue, we double the time interval between the execution of successive instructions of any process, thus halving the processing rate per process. In this mode of operation, the HEP is acting like a pipelined computer (which indeed, in hardware terms, it is), completing one instruction every clock period of 100ns. This is a total processing rate of 10 Mips, independent of the number of active processes and of the way the instructions are distributed amongst the processes (provided, of course, there are more than the eight processes active that are necessary to fill the pipeline).

The above discussion shows that the HEP behaves like a serial computer, an MIMD array of processors, or a pipelined computer as the number of active processes is, respectively, one, less than, or greater than eight. This behaviour can be summarized by the following choice of parameters:

$$r_\infty = 1.25 p_a \text{ Mips}, \qquad n_{1/2} = (p_a - 1)(p_a + a)/2a \qquad p_a \leqslant a \qquad (5)$$

$$r_\infty = 10 \quad \text{Mips}, \qquad n_{1/2} = a - 1 \qquad\qquad p_a \geqslant a$$

where:

a is the length of the instruction pipeline (a=8 for HEP)

p_a is the number of active processes

These expressions are obtained by considering the timing of the HEP pipeline as a function of the total number of instructions, n, and fitting the best straight line of the form of Eqn. (1). The parameters in Eqn. (5) express the basic hardware capability of the HEP, and represent the best possible performance. We present them because they show rather nicely the smooth transition that the HEP makes between being a serial, array or pipelined processor. The above values of the parameters, however, are not appropriate for use in any real programming situation because they do not include the substantial time that is required to create and synchronize a multi-process program. Nor do they take into account the fact that, on average, several instructions will be required for every floating-point operation.

We now consider the more realistic case of the timing for a FORTRAN program to perform one vector operation, taking into account process creation and synchronization. The possible overlapping of

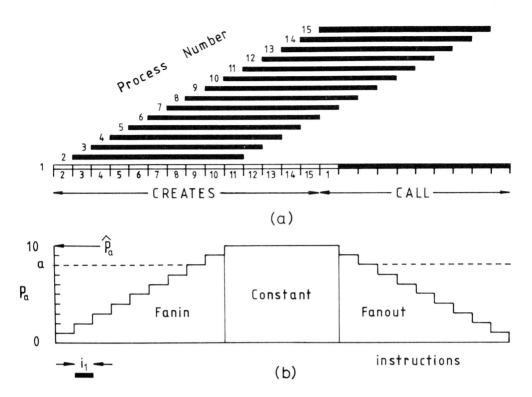

Fig. 1. Timing diagram for the implementation of a single vector operation on the Denelcor HEP. (a) Timing sequence for the creation and call of p=15 processes, open bar: instructions for create or call with process number involved; solid bar: instructions executed within subroutine. (b) Variation of the number of active processes, P_a throughout the task; showing the fanin, constant and fanout phases. Dotted line is the time interval between instructions of any process in clock periods. Horizontal axis in units of i_1, the number of instructions required to create or call a subroutine. Diagram drawn for b=10.

instructions is shown in Fig. 1, and the resulting timing line in Fig. 2. The following notation is used:

i_1 - number of instructions per FORTRAN CREATE statement

i_2 - number of instructions for synchronization in created subroutine

i_3 - number of instructions per floating-operation (flop)

i_4 - number of instructions for loop setup in created subroutine

$i_5 = i_2 + i_4$ - number of instructions for sync/setup

$i_6 = i_5 + \frac{n}{p} i_3$ - number of instructions executed within the subroutine and for convenience we also define:

$j_1 = i_1/i_3$ - flop per CREATE

$j_5 = i_5/i_3$ - flop per sync/setup

In Fig. 1(a) we plot number of instructions along the horizontal axis and process number along the vertical. The execution of instructions by each process is shown by a horizontal bar at the appropriate vertical level, and in a horizontal position where logically the instructions can first be executed. The instructions lying vertically above each other are those occupying the process queue at any particular time. They are executed in the order bottom-to-top in each vertical line, then left-to-right progressing vertical line by vertical line. Thus, the number of horizontal bars crossing any vertical line is the number of active processes. This is plotted in Fig. 1(b) as the solid line, together with the time interval between instructions (dotted line).

Process number 1 is the main control process and is assumed to have already been created. It is shown as the bottom horizontal bar in Fig. 1(a). A FORTRAN subroutine is also assumed to exist that calculates n/p of the elemental products. This subroutine will be executed once in each of p processes, thus completing the task. Initially processes 2 to p are created with p-1 FORTRAN CREATE statements, each of which takes i_1 HEP machine instructions in process 1 (see Fig. 1(a), and note that the horizontal axis is marked off in units of i_1 instructions). Immediately after this, the pth and last execution of the subroutine is initiated with a CALL of the subroutine in process 1 (a CREATE is not appropriate, because process 1 has already been created).

The FORTRAN CREATE statement is syntactically equivalent to a CALL statement. It creates a new process and begins executing the instructions of the subroutine, which are in the form of reentrant code that can be shared by all the processes. On executing the RETURN statement of a created subroutine, the process that was created is terminated by removing its PSW from the process queue.

Since process number 1 starts last, and all the processes are of the same length, it is clear that process number 1 finishes last. The time for the whole task may therefore be found by calculating the elapsed time for process number 1. Processes number 2 to p will finish at staggered times before process number 1, as shown in the Fig. 1(a). Because of this, the number of active processes will increase at the beginning, remain constant for a period in the middle, and decrease down to one towards the end. We refer to these as the fanin, constant, and fanout phases. Sometimes the constant phase does not exit , and there is only a fanin and fanout phase. The time for process number 1 is computed by considering each phase; and summing the number of instructions in process 1 times the number of active processes if the number of active processes is greater than or equal to eight, or the number of instructions in process 1 times eight if the number of active processes is less than eight. This gives the time for the whole task in units of the clock period. The results of these calculations are shown in Figs. 2 to 4.

Figure 2 shows time as a function of vector length for a constant number of created processes. It is composed of two straight line segments to the left and right of the line $n=n_1$, where:

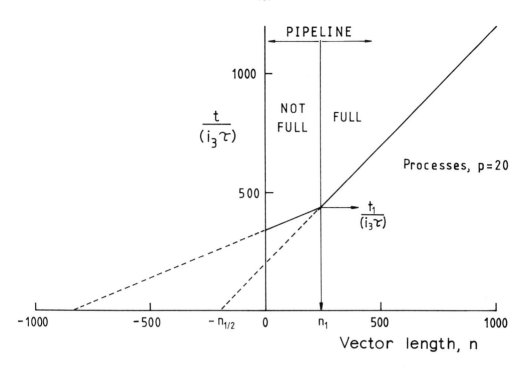

Fig. 2. Time to perform a single vector operation on the Denelcor HEP, as a function of vector length, n, for p=20 processes. (Using also $j_1 = j_5 = 2$.)

$$n_1 = p((a-1)j_1 - j_5) \qquad (6)$$

The maximum number of active processes (i.e. the number in the constant phase) is given by:

$$\hat{p}_a = \min(b,p) \qquad (7)$$

where

$$b = (j_5 + \frac{n}{p})/j_1 + 1$$

For $n < n_1$ the pipeline is never full, i.e. $\hat{p}_a < a$, and we find:

$$r_\infty = \frac{p}{a} \frac{\tau^{-1}}{i_3}, \qquad n_{1/2} = p(j_1 p + j_5) \qquad (8)$$

For $n > n_1$ the pipeline is full in the constant phase, i.e. $\hat{p}_a \geq a$, and we find:

$$r_\infty = \frac{\tau^{-1}}{i_3}, \qquad n_{1/2} = (j_1 + j_5)p + a(a-1)j_1 \qquad (9)$$

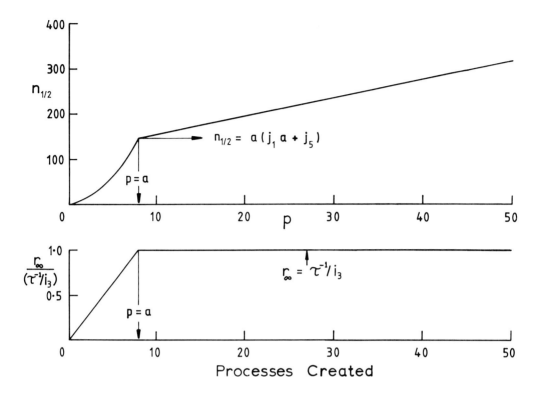

Fig. 3. Theoretical values of The half-performance length, $n_{1/2}$, and asymptotic performance, r_∞ of the Denelcor HEP, as a function of the number of processes created, p. (Using also $j_1=j_5=2$.)

These theoretical values of r_∞ and $n_{1/2}$ are shown in Fig. 3, where we have taken as reasonable values $j_1=j_5=2$ and a=8. For p<a there is always a quadratic variation of $n_{1/2}$ with p, because not enough processes have been created to fill the pipeline. For p>a there is either a quadratic or linear variation depending on the vector length. If $n>n_1$ the pipeline is full in the constant phase, and $n_{1/2}$ is a linear function of p. If $n<n_1$ the pipeline is never full, because the vector is not long enough; the variation is then quadratic. A good program would always be organized to have long enough vectors to fill the pipeline, and the quadratic variation for p>a is not likely to arise in practice. For this reason it is not shown in Fig. 3.

If, alternatively, we consider time as a function of the number processes created, p, we obtain Fig. 4. There are now three regions in the diagram separated by the lines $p=p_1$ and $p=p_2$, where:

$$p_1=a, \qquad p_2=\frac{n}{(a-1)j_1-j_5} \qquad (10)$$

To the left of p_1 and to the right of p_2, the pipeline is never full,

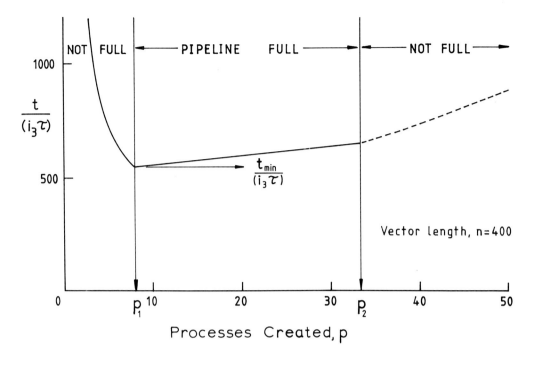

Fig. 4. The time to perform a single vector operation on the Denelcor HEP, as a function of the number of processes created. The vector length n=400, and $j_1=j_5=2$. The dotted part of the curve is not expected to be used in practice.

and the timing follows the curve:

$$t=a\left[\frac{n}{p}+j_1p+j_5\right]i_3\tau \tag{11}$$

To the left of p_1, the pipeline is never full because not enough processes have been created. To the right of p_2, the pipeline is never full because the vector length, n, is insufficiently long to keep eight processes active, out of the many more that have been created.

Between p_1 and p_2 the pipeline is full in the constant phase, and the time varies linearly with the number of processes created:

$$t=[n+(j_1+j_5)p+a(a-1)j_1]i_3\tau \tag{12}$$

The minimum execution time for any n occurs when $p=p_1=a$, then $t=t_{min}$ where:

$$t_{min}=(n+j_1a^2+j_5a)i_3\tau \tag{13}$$

It would appear from this analysis that there is no virtue in creating
more than eight processes (a=8), because the time in Fig. 4 increases
past this point. In practice, it is usually found worth while to
create somewhat more than eight processes, so that the number of
active processes does not fall below eight, even when some PSWs are
waved-off to await Data Memory accesses. We can take this into account
by regarding a as an effective pipeline length, given by the minimum
of a measured (t vs. p) curve like Fig. 4.

V.   THE SPECTRUM OF COMPUTERS

The derivation, or measurement, of the above two performance parameters enables us to compare computers by plotting their values on the
$(n_{1/2}, r_\infty)$ plane. This has the advantage of separating computers that
would otherwise appear very similar when compared on the basis of the
parameter r_∞ alone, as is usually done. It is important also because
the parameter $n_{1/2}$ measures either the amount of parallelism or the
amount of overhead in the architecture, and this is a number that it
is important to know; for example, because it determines the choice of
the best algorithm on a particular computer (see reference [1], page
267). Hockney and Jesshope [1] have described this parameter plane as
the "Spectrum of Computers" because the computers are spread out horizontally according to their value of $n_{1/2}$, as is shown in Fig. 5. Here
we find the more serial computers (small $n_{1/2}$) to the left, and the more
parallel computers (large $n_{1/2}$) to the right.

By definition, computers only work at more than 50% of their maximum advertised performance on vectors longer than their value of $n_{1/2}$.
Since problems satisfying this condition are only a subset of all
problems, we can also regard the $n_{1/2}$ axis as varying from the more general purpose computers on the left, to the more special purpose to the
right. This is only a statement about the effect of vector length on
performance, and should not be taken out of context as a more general
statement. Computers to the right of the diagram which are special
purpose from the vector-length point of view, may be highly flexible
and general purpose in other respects. An example is the ICL DAP that
lies well to the right of the diagram ($n_{1/2}$=2048), but is also highly
flexible because it is user programmable at the bit level. We believe,
however, that it is generally true to say that computers to the left
of the diagram can perform well on the general workload of an installation without reprogramming, whereas computers to the right of the
diagram are likely to require considerable problem reformulation and
reprogramming before their performance comes close to their value of
r_∞. The fact that the CYBER 205 and the ICL DAP usually require this
extensive reprogramming of existing codes, whereas the CRAY-1 does
not, is an example of this phenomenon.

A high value of parallelism is not desirable for its own sake, as
it carries with it the above penalties. It represents an overhead,
namely the overhead of requiring long vectors for efficient operation,
that most users could well do without. Consequently, one could say
that the goal of computer architecture should be to achieve the maximum performance with the least possible parallelism, that is to say
to achieve a design that lies as far as possible to the top left of
the spectrum. Constant values of specific performance, π, run diagonally from the bottom left to the top right. Thus a necessary condition for reaching the goal is that the specific performance be as

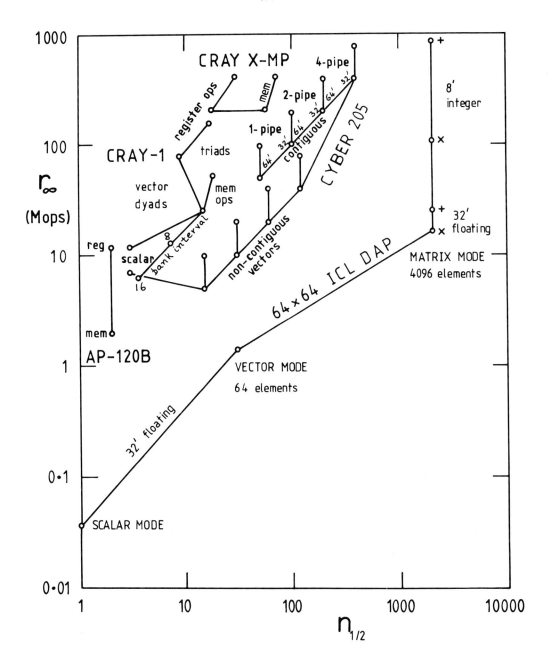

Fig. 5. The Spectrum of Computers showing the CRAY-1, CRAY X-MP, CDC CYBER 205, ICL DAP and FPS AP-120B.

large as possible.

Versions of the "Spectrum of Computers" have been given in references [1] and [4]. In Fig. 5. we show an updated version with the CRAY-1, CRAY X-MP, CYBER 205 and ICL DAP. In the constellation of points for the CRAY-1 the difference in performance between dyadic and triadic operations, and between register-to-register, main-memory-to-main-memory, and scalar operations are shown by plotting separately the performance in these different circumstances. The limited bandwidth to main memory (only one memory access pipeline) means that the performance of memory-to-memory operations is only about one third that of register-to-register operations. The $n_{1/2}$ for memory-to-memory operations is greater than that for register-to-register operations because of the extra time required to get data from memory. Memory bank conflicts are also a problem, and there is severe performance degradation if the memory bank interval between successive elements of the vectors is 8 or 16 (the number of memory banks in the machine). The effect of this is shown in the figure for the case of dyadic memory-to-memory operations, but applies equally to the other modes of operation.

The CRAY X-MP has three pipelines to memory for each of its two CPUs, and may therefore support memory-to-memory vector operations at the full speed of the arithmetic pipelines. The $n_{1/2}$ for memory-to-memory operations is larger than that for register-to-register operations because of the time required to get the data from memory. The machine also has a shorter clock period than the CRAY-1 (9.5ns compared to 12.5ns on the CRAY-1). Both these improvements are taken into account in plotting the points for the CRAY X-MP. It is also assumed that both CPUs can be used to increase the performance of the machine on one problem, although to our knowledge the software for this is not yet available.

The points for the CDC CYBER 205 appear as two combs which show the performance for a 1-, 2-, or 4-pipe machine for both 32-bit and 64-bit arithmetic. The upper comb represents the performance on contiguous vectors, that is to say those in which successive elements are stored in successive memory locations, and the lower comb applies when this is not the case. In the latter non-contiguous case we include the time to gather the two input vectors into contiguous form, and the time to scatter the result vector to the non-contiguous format. Of course, in a sensibly organized program such scatters and gathers would only be necessary occasionally, and not before and after every vector operation, as we assume here. The two combs should therefore be thought of as limiting cases. No program can perform better than the upper comb or worse than the lower, and actual programs will perform somewhere in between. The degradation of performance for non-contiguous vectors on the CYBER 205 arises because of memory bank conflicts, and parallels the bank interval degradation of the CRAY-1. The CYBER 205 has no vector registers and there are therefore no points for register-to-register operation.

The ICL Distributed Array Processor (DAP) provides for scalar, vector (64 elements), and matrix (64×64 elements) modes of arithmetic, and the performance for each of these is shown separately in Fig. 5 for 32-bit floating-point arithmetic. The strength of the machine, however, is in logic and short word-length integer arithmetic in matrix mode, when the ability to program the machine at the bit level can be utilized. In this mode, performance in the region of 1000 Mops is possible.

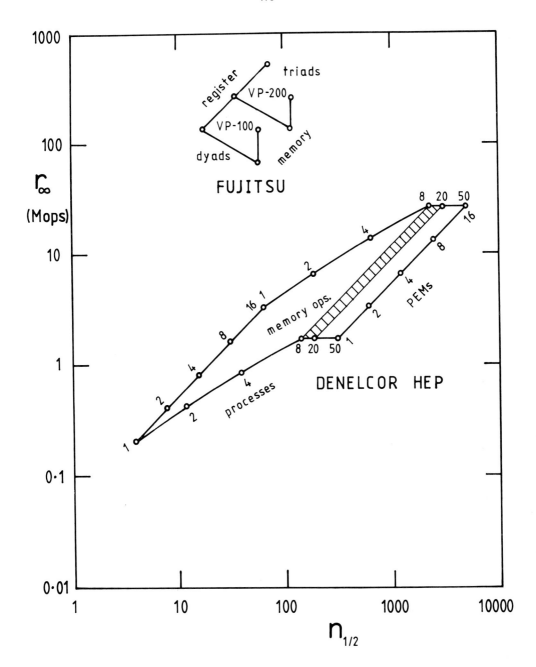

Fig. 6. The Spectrum of Computers showing the Denelcor HEP and Fujitsu VP-100 and VP-200.

In Fig. 6. we show the performance of the DENELCOR HEP and the FUJITSU VP-100/VP-200. The HEP is shown as a box in roughly the same position in the spectrum as the ICL DAP. The variation in performance with the number of processes is given along the bottom and top sides, and the variation with the number of PEMs along the left and right sides. To obtain these points, we have used the results of section IV with $j_1=2, j_5=2,$ and $i_3=6$. Slightly different assumptions would lead to somewhat different positions for the box, but not fundamentally change the picture. We see that the r_∞ in megaflops is considerably less than the instruction rate of 10 Mips per PEM, because only a fraction of instructions can, in practice, be floating-point. Unlike the vector computers (the CRAYs and CYBER 205s), the HEP has no explicit vector instructions, and the operations on each element of the vectors must be explicitly programmed. The arithmetic pipelines of the vector computers produce one floating-point result every clock period, whereas the pipeline of the HEP completes an instruction every clock period, only some of which will be floating-point. The effect of increasing the number of PEMs is to increase both r_∞ and $n_{1/2}$ by the factor of increase, leaving the specific performance π unchanged (see reference [1], page 122).

The variation of performance with the number of processes is also shown. For the reasons given in section IV the number of processes is likely to lie between 8 and 20, which we indicate by the shaded portion of the box. Other parts of the performance box are of theoretical rather than practical importance. Working in this region, the value of $n_{1/2}$ is, like the CYBER 205, around 100. Problems should therefore be organized such that the vector length is substantially greater than 100, preferably several thousand. This can present a problem on the CYBER 205 because it is necessary for all the operations between elements of the vectors to be the same. However, on the HEP, we can interpret a vector operation in a generalized sense, as meaning all the arithmetic between FORK/JOIN synchronization points (see section III). It is thus much easier to obtain long vectors on the HEP than it is on the CYBER 205. It is also easier on the HEP to obtain long generalized vectors by parallelizing the problem at the highest possible level, rather than at the lowest. By this we mean that it is best to divide the overall problem into large independent segments that can be executed simultaneously by separate processes, rather than to look at an existing vector formulation and to spread each mathematical vector operation over many processes, as would be done on a vector computer. The approach to programming on the HEP is therefore quite different from that used on a vector computer.

The FUJITSU VP-100 and VP-200 vector computers are shown at the top of Fig. 6. Comparison with Fig. 5 shows that they have properties lying between those of the CRAY X-MP and the CYBER 205. For register-to-register operations the VP-100 and VP-200 have a performance similar to the CRAY X-MP, whereas their memory-to-memory operation is similar to that for contiguous vectors on, respectively, the 1-, and 2-pipe CYBER 205 in 64-bit mode. The FUJITSU machines have two access pipelines to memory, compared with three on the CRAY X-MP. However, there is 8 or 16 times the vector register space on the FUJITSU machines, making main memory references less frequent. These two effects probably balance out. The performance on actual problems will lie between that for register and that for memory operations, and the large vector register store is likely to give an average performance on many problems approaching that for register operations. The memory-to-memory points on the FUJITSU machines thus represent a worst case situation. However, the contiguous vector performance on the CYBER 205, to which they are similar, represents a best case situation, as not all vectors are likely to be contiguous.

VI. CONCLUSIONS

We have compared a number of the computers discussed at this workshop on a uniform basis, using the spectrum of computers defined by the two performance parameters r_∞ and $n_{1/2}$. The definition of $n_{1/2}$ has been interpreted in a new way that is appropriate for MIMD computers such as the Denelcor HEP, and a theoretical analysis of the performance of this computer has been given. Values of the parameters have also been given for the Fujitsu VP-100 and VP-200. These have been derived from various descriptions and presentations that have been made in the past year. We conclude that the two-dimensional spectrum of computers is a useful diagram to use to compare the performance of these new computers with the familiar CRAY-1, CYBER 205 and ICL DAP.

ACKNOWLEDGEMENTS

The author wishes to thank Mr Dave Snelling of Denelcor and Mr Makoto Shinohara of Fujitsu Ltd. for providing information on the HEP and VP-100/VP-200 respectively, and generally helping with his understanding of these machines. Discussions with Mr N. C. W. Mayes during the course of a HEP simulation project have also been most valuable.

REFERENCES

[1]   R. W. Hockney and C. R. Jesshope, _Parallel Computers - Architecture, Programming and Algorithms_, Bristol: Adam Hilger, 1981. (Distributed in North and South America by Heyden & Son., Philadelphia).

[2]   M. J. Flynn, "Some Computer Organizations and their Effectiveness", _IEEE Trans. Comput._, vol. C-21, pp 948-960, 1972.

[3]   B. J. Smith, "A Pipelined, Shared Resource MIMD Computer", _Proc. 1978 Intl. Conf. on Parallel Processing_, pp 6-8, 1978.

[4]   R. W. Hockney, "Characterizing Computers and Optimizing the FACR(1) Poisson-Solver on Parallel Unicomputers", _IEEE Trans. Comput._, to appear, 1983.

PERFORMANCE MODELLING AND EVALUATION
FOR CONCURRENT COMPUTER ARCHITECTURES

Ulrich Herzog

Institut für Mathematische Maschinen und Datenverarbeitung
Universität Erlangen-Nürnberg, 8520 Erlangen, Germany

Abstract

Skilful computer system modelling and performance evaluation techniques
are needed for concurrent computer architectures. They allow to accurately determine characteristic performance values, to find potential
hardware- and software-bottlenecks; they also help to efficiently
distribute and schedule user tasks.

We briefly survey important performance problems for concurrent computer
architectures and their solution. We also summarize the basic ideas of
the EGPA multiprocessor project which forced us to search for new performance modelling and evaluation techniques.

Table of Contents

NATO ASI Series, Vol. F7
High-Speed Computation. Edited by J. S. Kowalik
© Springer-Verlag Berlin Heidelberg 1984

1. Introduction

Performance modelling and evaluation means to describe, to analyze
and to optimize the flow of data and control information in computer
systems. Performance characteristics, such as utilization, throughput
or response time give information about the efficiency of the hardware/
software-structure and allow the detection and elimination of bottlenecks. Therefore, performance modelling and evaluation is needed from
the initial conception of a systems architectural design to its daily
operation after installation [1,2].

Multiprocessor computer systems with two or three processing units have
been built since many years: Independent user tasks share hardware
resources and processor time. Therefore, using a multiprocessor is
usually better than configuring the processors as uniprocessors and
partition the workload between them [3]. Sharing of resources, however,
means also conflicts and this problem is modelled and analyzed in
section 3.

Rather than running independent tasks on different processors one also
tries in modern multiprocessor concepts to take advantage of the
parallelism inherent in many problems: It may be possible to split
the application program up into a number of subtasks and run subtasks
concurrently, thus reducing the overall execution time. Then, however,
difficult coordination problems (synchronization between subtasks, data
and code sharing, etc.) may occur. The modelling and evaluation of these
performance problems are surveyed in section 4.

Since our investigations were initiated and influenced by the EGPA-
project, a three Million Dollar Project at the University of Erlangen-
Nürnberg, we outline first the EGPA-architecture. However, the performance modelling and evaluation methods are applicable to many multiprocessor computer systems.

2. The Hierarchical Multiprocessor Array EGPA

The Erlangen general purpose array, EGPA, is a "three-dimensional"
processor array which has the structure of a pyramid (see Fig. 1).
The central architectural idea of the EGPA structure is to concentrate
the administrative work in the top of the pyramid or in the higher
levels, e.g., I/O operations and operating system functions, while the
lower and larger processor-planes have to process user problems in
parallel. Another essential aim of EGPA is to achieve unconventional
computing with conventional hardware by linking conventional processors

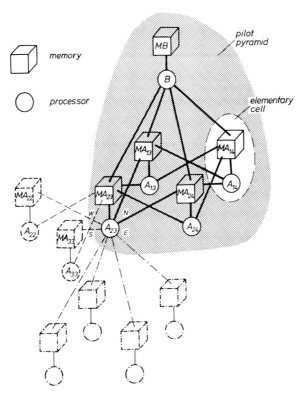

Fig. 1. One elementary pyramid of the EGPA system. Possible
extensions to other elementary pyramids within the
A-array (---) and to a lower level (-.-) indicate the
constant local complexity: no matter how large or small
the pyramid is, a processor (e.g. A_{23}) is interconnected
to no more than nine memories. Memories need have only six
ports, since there is only one interconnection to a processor in the next higher level.

and memories in such a way that they build up a freely extensible
cellular structure [4]. The elementary cell consists of a processor
and a memory; the elementary structure is a pyramid having 1 top and 4
bottom cells. The free extensibility of the array is a means for
achieving higher computing power by adding more processors and memories
to the system without changing the structure of the elementary cells
and the number of their links to neighbour cells. This has been called
constant local complexity and linear global complexity because the
overall complexity of hardware and software is expected to grow only
linearly with the number of elementary cells in the pyramid [4], [5].
In Fig. 1 it is the elementary cell (MA_{23}, A_{23}) which demonstrates the
maximum necessary number of links radiating from (MA_{23}, A_{23}).

These local links interconnect a given processor (e.g., A_{23}) with the memories MA_{13}, MA_{24}, MA_{33}, MA_{22} of its "northern", eastern", "southern" and "western" neighbors and with the memories of the four immediately subordinated processors in the next lower level. In each level, all processors at the borders of the array are connected with their "neighbors" at the opposite border to form a toroidal closing of this level. At the moment, all experimental studies are done with an elementary (pilot-) pyramid consisting of one B-processor and four A-processors, (see bold lines in Fig. 1). This pilot pyramid is made up of commercially available computers (32 bit, microprogrammable processors, multiport memories) because we expect microcomputers of the mid-1980's to have comparable features.

The EGPA pyramid is under the control of a hierarchical multiprocessor operating system, an extension of the original multiprogramming operating system. Its main functions are performed in the top level processor (B) responsible for the overall organization and I/O activities of an elementary pyramid. Low level processors (A), performing application programs, are driven by simple monoprogramming.

The pilot implementation is operational since 1980, cf. fig. 2., and many application programs are being implemented. Hardware structure, system software as well as application programs are being analyzed by means of hardware- and software measurements and our modelling technique, as well.

Fig. 2.   The pilot implementation EGPA and
           hardware-monitor ZM III.

Future plans aim at the implementation of a much larger system with powerful microprocessors. For more details on the pilot implementation and future plans, cf. lit [4, 6, 7].

3. Modelling Classical Multiprocessor Systems With Independent User Tasks

3.1. General Remarks

Multiprocessor systems with some few processing units have been built since many years. The most commonly quoted reasons are robustness and throughput [3]:

Given that the workload at an installation is larger than what the largest uniprocessor can handle, there are two possibilities

A) We use several uniprocessors and partition the workload between them; the corresponding queuing model consists of c identical single server systems and performance characteristics may be ontained by classical results from queuing theory.

B) We use a multiprocessor system, i.e. several processing units under a single operating system; accordingly, multiserver queuing models may be used to analyze the system's performance.

The speedup S is defined as the expected response time ratio

$$S = \frac{E[T_R, \text{ several uniprocessors}]}{E[T_R, \text{ multiprocessor}]} ,$$

and numerical values may be obtained readily using standard queuing tables as well as newest results from literature [8]. Figure 3 shows some typical results.

All these results - obtained under simple or general stochastic assumptions - prognosticate assymptotic speedup S. From real system measurements, however, we know that they are too optimistic because of additional multiprocessor overhead. Each processor in a multiprocessor configuration performs worse then when it is a uniprocessor configuration. The principal reasons are

- contention for memory
- lockouts for critical sections
- more complex scheduling
- communication delays.

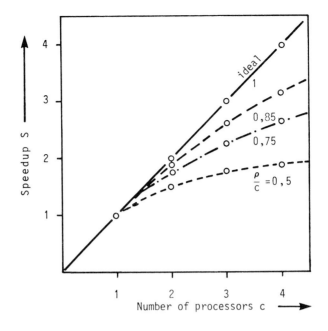

Fig. 3: Speedup for multiprocessor configurations, example.
(φ utilization, exponential assumptions for both
interarrival times, of tasks and processing times)

Taking into account the influence of shared resources is demonstrated
next by memory contention models.

3.2. Memory Interference

Memory conflicts may occur whenever two or more processors attempt to
gain access to the same memory module simultaneously. The effect of
memory conflicts, referred to as memory interference, may decrease
the execution rate of each processor significantly. Much attention has
been paid to the analysis of this phenomena and may be summarized as
follows [7, 9]:

Processor behavior is described as a stochastic process. Each memory
access is followed by a certain amount of processing time. No distinction is made between a memory access to fetch instructions and a memory
access to fetch or store operands, nor between the processing time to
decode an instruction and the processing time corresponding to its

execution. This simplification results in an "unit instruction" which
was first proposed by Strecker. The rewrite time does not need to be
considered because it is overlapped with the next cycle.

T_a and T_p, the memory access and processing time of the unit instructions are assumed to be discrete or continuous random variables.

If two or more processors simultaneously request the same memory unit,
only one of these requests can be served. There exist no priorities
between the processors, but each has equal probability of success.
The deferred processors are queued up to be served in subsequent memory
cycles.

Combining these assumptions with the actual structure of our multiprocessor system, the queueing network model of Fig. 4 reflects the
system behavior: three processors access their own as well as other
memories.

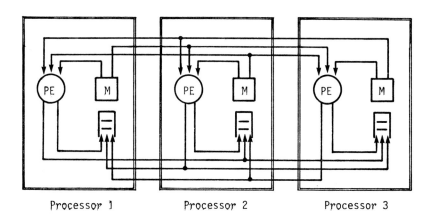

Processor 1   Processor 2   Processor 3

Fig. 4. Modeling of memory conflicts for a symmetric
         multiprocessor system (Processing Elements, Memories)

The interference measure I shows how many percent longer is the
expected execution time $\tilde{E}[T_i]$ of an instruction in a conflicting
situation compared to its expected conflict-free execution time
$E[T_i]$:

$$I = \frac{\tilde{E}[T_i] - E[T_i]}{E[T_i]}$$

It can be shown that the interference I depends on the actual value
of memory access time T_a and processing time T_p only through the

184

instruction service time ratio γ :

$$\gamma = \frac{E[T_A]}{E[T_P]}$$

and the access probability P_A to each memory block. Embedding these
results from the memory interference model into the classical multiserver results from above, realistic speed up values may be obtained.
Figure 5. shows speedup values in case of an extreme example: all
processors access the same memory block. It is demonstrated how each

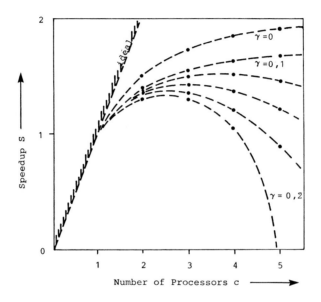

Fig. 5.: Speedup S for multiprocessor configurations taking
into account memory conflicts (extreme example
where all processors access the same memory block;
γ instruction service time ration).

additional processor contributes relatively less to the overall performance; the curve may even drop again, the famous breakdown phenomena of multiprocessor projects with an unbalanced hardware- and/or
software structure.

4. Modelling Progressive Multiprocessor Concepts

4.1. General Remarks

In the classical modelling technique one usually assumes concurrent
processes to be independent of each other; on the other hand side
it is also standard to assume processes, being dependent on each
other, - e.g. I/O and CPU phases - take a sequential turn. Little
research considers I/O and CPU overlap and recognizes that programs
may be decomposed into well defined cooperating subtasks and processed concurrently.

Modern multiprocessor projects such as CM* [10], SMS [11] and EGPA
take advantage of the inherent parallelism of many application
programs. Therefore, the response time for each application may be
reduced drastically. Then, however, difficult coordination problems
may occur and have to be considered in modelling such systems:

- synchronization between tasks and subtasks
- process communication delays
- data and code sharing problems.

Results on the modelling and analysis of these phenomena have been
published in quite some publications, cf. [12 - 15]. However, the main
objective of performance modelling is not analysis but synthesis,
synthesis of optimal structures and operating modes:

Ho do we find a multiprocessor-configuration best suited for a
distinct spectrum of applications? How to allocate functions and
data to different processors and memory modules? How to schedule
tasks and subtasks, globally as well as locally. We next describe a
basic optimization problem; more details may be found in [16, 17].

4.2. Synthesis of optimal schedules for a given program structure

Be given a hierarchically organized computer system like EGPA or
SMS and a socalled type-1-program structure, cf. figure 6.

Assume that subtasks S_o and S_{n+1} may be performed only by the top-
processor and subtasks S_1 to S_n by array processors. Distribution
functions $F_{S_i}(t)$ and mean application values $E[T_{S_i}]$ for the processing time of all subtasks are known (e.g. from measurement),
they may be identical for subtasks S_1 to S_n, $(F_S(t), E[T_S])$, as often
in reality.

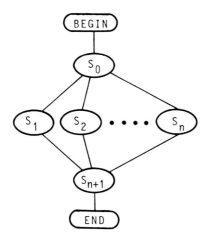

Fig. 6. Type-1-program structure

Obviously, the overall execution time is a minimum when all subtasks S_1 to S_n are executed concurrently on n application processors, only if there is zero communication overhead.

Experiences with the EGPA-pilot implementation and other multiprocessors show that communication overhead due to signalling and data transfers between the coordinating B-processor to the application processors may be considerable and depends on the number of application processors to be controlled. In other words the optimum number of application processors, depends on the communication ration α

$$\alpha = \frac{E[Tov]}{E[Ts]}$$

where $E[Tov]$ is the mean communication overhead to access an array processor.

Consequently the search for the most suitable schedule may be formulated as an optimization problem [16]. Figures 7 and 8 show some typical results for the cycle time and speedup. These examples demonstrate that the optimal number of active array processors depends heavily on the communication ratio but also on the type of

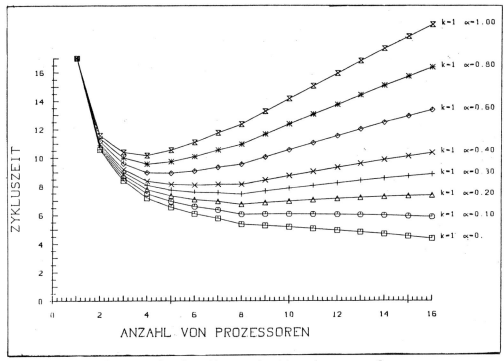

Fig. 7: Example for the cycle time in case of
exponentially distributed processing times
for all subtasks (k=1). The communication
ratio varies between zero and one.

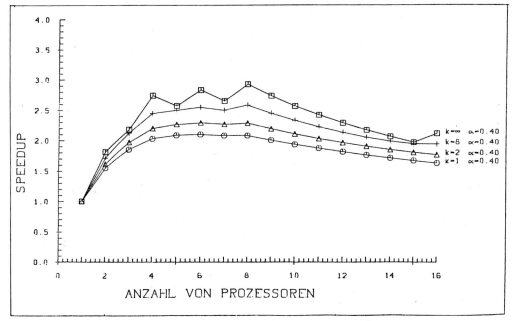

Fig. 8: Example for the speed-up in case of
Erlang-k-distributed processing times for
all subtasks (k=1: exponential; k=∞ constant).

processing time distribution function for the subtasks.

5. Conclusion

We briefly summarized how classical as well as progressive multiprocessor architectures may be modelled accurately. These results allow
to find realistic performance estimates for the efficiency of a
particular hardware/software structure, to detect inherent system
bottlenecks, to find optimal decomposition and scheduling strategies.
Performance evaluation techniques are helpful from the initial conception of an architecture to its daily application. However, a deep
knowledge of real system behavior, a close contact to hardware
engineers, system software designers as well as application programmers is mandatory.

Important results are already available and many activities are summarized in the cited literature. Several directions for future work are
apparent: Generalizations of basic models taking into consideration
more complex hardware structures, operating modes and application
programs.

And there are many challenging problems not yet attact such as systems
with priorities, multi-level hierarchies, global and local schedules
for general program structures.

References:

[1] Agrawala, A.; Herzog, U. (Eds.): Performance Evaluation of Multiple Processor Systems. Special Issue of the IEEE Transactions
on Computers, January 1983.

[2] Kobayashi, H.: Modeling and Analysis - An Introduction to System
Performance Evaluation Methodology, Addison-Wesley, 1978.

[3] Satayanarayan, M.: A Survey of Multiprocessing Systems,
IBM Research Report R C 7346, Yorktown Heights, 1978.

[4] Händler, W.; Hofmann, F.; and Schneider, H.J.: A General Purpose
Array with a Broad Spectrum of Applications. In Proc. 1st Workshop Computer Architecture, Erlangen, W. Germany, May 1975,
Informatik Fachberichte, Vol. 4. Berlin: Springer-Verlag 1976,
pp. 311-334.

[5] Händler, W.: Innovative Computer Architecture - How to Increase
Parallelism but not Complexity. In Parallel Processing Systems,
1980, Proc. Symp. Loughborough Univ. Technol., D.J. Evans, Ed.
England: Cambridge Univ. Press, 1982, pp. 1-41.

[6] Händler, W.; Herzog, U.; Hofmann, F.; Schneider, H.J.; et al: Erlangen General Purpose Array (EGPA). Projektabschlußbericht 1978-1982. Inst. f. Math. Masch. u. Datenverarbeitung, Erlangen 1983.

[7] Fromm, H.J.; Hercksen, U.; Herzog, U.; John, K.H.; Klar, R.; Kleinöder, W.: Experiences with Performance Measurement and Modelling of a Processor Array, IEEE-TC-January, 1983, p. 15-31.

[8] Herzog, U.: Performance Modelling for Multiprocessor-Systems, Fundamental Concepts and Tendencies. Intern. Sem. on Modelling and Performance Evaluation Methodology, 24.-26.1.1983, Paris, Proceedings to be published by Springer.

[9] Fromm, H.J.: Zur Modellierung der Speicherinterferenz bei hierarchisch organisierten Multiprozessor-Systemen Arbeitsberichte des IMMD, Erlangen, Bd. 13, No. 3, 1980.

[10] Jones, A.; Schwarz, P.: Experiences Using Multiprocessor Systems - A Status Report. Computing Surveys, Vol. 12, No. 2, June 1980, p. 121-165.

[11] Kober, R.; Kuznia, C.: SMS 201 - A powerful parallel Processor with 128 Microprocessors. Euromicro, 1979. Amsterdam, North-Holland.

[12] Heidelberger, P.; Trivedi, K.: Analytic Queueing Models of Programs with Internal Concurrency. IEEE-TC-January, 1983.

[13] Herzog, U.; Hoffmann, W.; Kleinöder, W.: Performance Modeling and Evaluation for Hierarchically Organized Multiprocessor Computer Systems. Proc. Int. Conf. on Parallel Processing, Bellaire, 1979, pp. 21-24.

[14] Herzog, U.: Performance Characteristics for Hierarchically Organized Multiprocessor Computer Systems with Generally Distributed Processing Times. Archiv für Electronik und Über-tragungstechnik, Electronics and Communication, 34, 1980, p. 45-51.

[15] Kleinöder, W.: Dissertation Stochastische Bewertung von Auf-gabenstrukturen für hierarchische Mehrrechnersysteme, Arbeitsberichte des IMMD, Erlangen, Bd. 15, No. 10, 1982.

[16] Kleinöder, W.; Herzog, U.: Einführung in die Methodik der Verkehrstheorie und ihre Anwendung bei Multiprozessor-Rechenanlagen, Computing, Suppl. 3, p. 31-64, 1981.

[17] Fromm, H.J.: Dissertation Multiprozessor-Rechenanlagen: Programmstrukturen, Maschinenstrukturen und Zuordnungsprobleme, Arbeitsberichte des IMMD, Erlangen, Bd. 15, No. 5, 1982.

A PERFORMANCE SURVEY OF THE CYBER 205

M. J. Kascic Jr.
Control Data Corporation
Arden Hills, Minnesota   55112

ABSTRACT

With a raw performance measured in the hundreds of millions of floating point operations per second, the CYBER 205 has the potential for
generating qualitatively new computational results. This potential
can be realized only when architectural, syntactic and semantic intelligence cooperate in the problem solution endeavor. While much attention has been paid to the interaction between architectural and syntactic intelligence, the role of semantic intelligence has been
obscured.

We present several examples of CYBER 205 performance to illustrate
the results possible when a semantic algorithm methodology is
employed.

INTRODUCTION

"It was the best of times, it was the worst of times, it was the age
of wisdom, it was the age of foolishness, it was the epoch of belief,
it was the opoch of incredulity, . . ."

These words from Dickens "A Tale of Two Cities" could describe the
present, vis a vis the vector computer. Never before has such computational power existed on the face of this planet and yet never has a
smaller percentage of available power been put to use. There is a
veritable explosion of scholary work and yet day to day "hands on"
programming is done under the rubric of a methodology better suited
to a bygone day. Finally, we have statements ranging from "We can
vectorize anything!" to "Scaler mode plays a critical role in almost
any meaningful calculation."

It is not clear to the author that much progress is being made in
forming a synthesis of these thesis/antithesis combinations. Indeed,

NATO ASI Series, Vol. F7
High-Speed Computation. Edited by J. S. Kowalik
© Springer-Verlag Berlin Heidelberg 1984

it is not clear to the author that much progress is being made in understanding that there is a thesis/antithesis situation.

One type of fallout from this situation is the usage of vocabulary in discussing vector processing as if that vocabulary had univocal meaning when in fact it does not. Take the word "performance" for instance. While it is patently absurd to rate a computer only in terms of its peak processing power, it is equally absurd to rate it only in terms of it's response to outdated programming methodologies armed with artificial syntactic intelligence alone. Thus, while for completeness we will include a discussion of the raw power of the CYBER 205 and some examples of it's response to artificially intelligent, syntactically transformed code structures ("automatically vectorized" code structures), the term "performance" in the title is to be taken to mean that achievable with a higher level of semantic vectorization is applied to a mathematically formulated problem.

It is the author's fond hope that this semantic methodology will provide a means to chart a course between the Scylla of theory: Polyanna theorems that cannot be put to work to solve real problems, and the Charybdis of practice: pessimistic cliches that inhibit the absorption of scholarly work into the everyday computing environment.

For fuller discussion of the interplay among architectural, syntactic and semantic intelligence on the CYBER 205, see (3).

ARCHITECTURAL PERFORMANCE OF THE CYBER 205

Since we are discussing the vector performance of the CYBER 205, we should make clear what a vector is.

Def. Vector - contiguous set of (virtual) memory locations.

When a vector structure is imposed on data, architectural intelligence has the opportunity to utilize its components to the full. This is illustrated by Tables 1 (and 2) which tabulate the raw performance of the CYBER 205 performing a vector addition/multiplication (and linked triad resp.).

TABLE 1.   CYBER 205 VECTOR ADD OR MULTIPLE MEGAFLOP RATE

VECTOR LENGTH	2 PIPE, 64-BIT	4 PIPE, 64-BIT 2 PIPE, 32-BIT	4 PIPE, 32-BIT
32	23.9	27.1	29.1
64	38.6	47.8	54.2
100	49.5	65.8	78.1
250	71.0	109.6	150.6
500	83.1	142.0	219.3
1000	90.7	166.1	284.1
10000	99.0	196.0	384.3
50000	99.8	199.2	396.8

DEF: LINKED TRIAD-TRIADIC COMBINATION OF TWO VECTORS AND ONE
SCALAR THAT CAN BE EVALUATED AS ONE OPERATION.

FOR EXAMPLE: VECTOR + SCALAR * VECTOR
(VECTOR + SCALAR) * VECTOR

TABLE 2.   CYBER 205 LINKED TRIAD MEGAFLOP RATE

VECTOR LENGTH	2 PIPE, 64-BIT	4 PIPE, 64-BIT 2 PIPE, 32-BIT	4 PIPE, 32-BIT
32	31.7	34.4	36.0
64	54.7	63.4	68.8
100	74.1	90.9	102.0
250	119.0	168.9	213.7
500	149.3	238.1	337.8
1000	170.9	298.5	476.2
10000	196.7	386.8	749.1
50000	199.3	397.3	789.3
	200	400	800

Since the vector length at which half the peak performance of the
CYBER 205 is attained is neither too small nor too large, the CYBER
205 is neither a linear extrapolation of a scalar computer, nor is it
a paracomputer. Hopefully, it is a qualitative step forward in
computational performance capability.

SYNTACTIC PERFORMANCE OF THE CYBER 205

While the performance charts in Figures 1 and 2 are an end in themselves to the designer, they are a tabula rasa from the standpoint of
the user, a mere slate upon which to impress problem solution
techniques.

There has been (and still is) much confusion in some circles as to
what the vectorization process is/ought to be. We shall distinguish
two qualitatively different modes of vectorization, namely, syntactic
and semantic. It is not our purpose here to philosophize concerning
the distinction, but rather to make note of it in clarifying exactly
what is entailed in stating performance claims for the CYBER 205.

Syntactic vectorization is the process of recognizing that a vector
data structure already exists, or transforming a scalar data structure
into a vector data structure. This type of vectorization is concerned
with form, not content. It can be done by automatic software, i.e.,
vectorizers, and/or by humans either by rewriting traditional scalar
code so as to make the vectors "visible" to a vectorizer or by using
a vector language to directly express vector constructs.

From the point of view of CYBER 205 performance, the most important
consideration is the capability to transform a non-vector data structure to a vector data structure at vector speed. Otherwise, even if
artificial intelligence finds the right transformation, the transformation time may exceed the time to execute the original scalar
algorithm.

There are three basic capabilities of the CYBER 205 to carry out such
transformations:

1. Control Store - the capability to perform a vector operation under
   control of a bit vector which can select which operands are to be
   stored into the target vector.

2. Compress/Merge - the capability to remove/insert a substructure/
   vector from/into a vector/superstructure under control of a bit
   vector.

3. Gather/Scatter - the capability to remove/insert a substructure/
   vector from/into a vector/superstructure under control of an index
   list.

The control store allows a substructure to be "sensed" while the
compress/merge and gather/scatter allow substructures to be
"realized."

Since the raw performance of these transformations has been discussed
elsewhere (4) let us give two examples of how they affect the vectorization process. First we shall present a table of performance of
two automatic vectorizers on a canonical set of "loops." Then we
shall show in detail how control store allows vectorization of upwind
differencing and more efficient vectorization of a classical marching
kernel. The affect of compress/merge and gather/scatter will be saved
for the next section.

Table 3 contains a table of megaflop rates achieved on the CYBER 205
(2 pipe in 64-bit mode) by two automatic vectorizers, VAST and KAP
(compared to strictly scalar execution) on a canonical set of FORTRAN
DO loops, called the "Livermore" loops. One should keep in mind that
the performance listed is a function of the state of the art of artificial intelligence, the exact form of expression within the loops,
as well as the capability of the CYBER 205. The results are taken
from (1) where the reader is recommended for details.

TABLE 3. CYBER 205 PERFORMANCE OF AUTOMATICALLY VECTORIZED
"LIVERMORE LOOPS"

KERNEL	SCALAR	VAST	KAP	
1	9.6	121.3	120.2	
2	12.3	16.2	76.9	
3	5.9	73.9	76.6	MFLOPS
4	3.3	3.3	17.0	
5	7.9	7.9	5.7	
6	5.2	5.2	6.1	
7	17.0	146.9	144.7	
8	22.4	22.4	15.9	
9	13.0	81.0	81.6	
10	8.6	29.8	30.7	

KERNEL	SCALAR	VAST	KAP
11	1.7	8.5	8.2
12	2.9	77.4	76.0
13	3.1	3.0	4.4
14	5.5	6.9	5.3
15	3.4	3.4	19.3
16	.6	.6	.6
17	4.9	4.9	4.9
18	8.3	42.4	50.1

On the one hand, it is clear that loop #1, a so called hydrodynamic loop is a vector waiting to be vectorized, while loop #16, a Monte Carlo loop defies both vectorizers. Is the poor performance of loop #16 intrinsic to Monte Carlo simulation, or is it also attributable to the theoretical state of AI and/or a practical mismatch between AI capability and the exact mode of expression of the code? This question remains open. But see (2).

In presenting the rest of our examples, we shall not make any direct comparisons with scalar code. The reason for this is that we wish to vectorize an algorithm, not a piece of code. Since there are many ways to express the same algorithm in scalar code leading to different performance regimes each reader must decide for himself/herself the effectiveness of the vectorizations presented.

Upwind differencing is a technique used in fluid dynamics to stabilize differencing in the advection terms. Since this section is devoted to syntactic performance, and not semantic, we will say no more about that aspect. What is important here is that, as is illustrated below, the usual expression of the algorithm involves conditionals. This allows us to introduce:

DEF. Vector Relational - the operation of comparing two data vectors element by element, creating a bit vector with a "1" in a position if a given condition is met and a "0" if not.

The vector relational can be accomplished on the CYBER 205 <u>at the same rate of speed as vector arithmetic</u>. This allows the vectorization of syntactic expressions involving conditionals.

Consider the following expression of upwind differencing:

```
For 2 ≤ J ≤ N
If (VEL(J).GE.0.) DIF(J) = RDEL*(X(J)-X(J-1))
Else                DIF(J) = RDEL*(X(J+1)-X(J))
```

This algorithm is vectorized in three operations:

1. A vector relational creates a bit vector distinguishing the two cases, e.g.,

   VEL(2)≥,0   VEC(3)<0   VEL(4)≥0   . . .
       1   0   1

2. A linked triad calculates the backward difference at each grid point:

   RDEL*(X(2)-X(1))   RDEL*(X(3)-X(2))   RDEL*(X(4)-X(3))   . . .

3. A control store is used to overwrite the backward differences with forward differences at precisely the right grid points:

   RDEL*(X(2)-X(1))   <u>RDEL*(X(4)-X(3))</u>   RDEL*(X(4)-X(3))   . . .

Table 4 contains the performance of this algorithm measured in the <u>number of grid points processed</u> rather than in megaflops.

TABLE 4.   CYBER 205 2 PIPE PERFORMANCE OF UPWIND DIFFERENCING

	64-Bit Mode	32-Bit Mode	
N = 10	2.4	2.5	
50	9.4	10.9	
100	14.6	18.7	Millions of <u>grid</u>
1000	29.6	53.1	<u>points</u> per second
10000	33.3	66.7	

A classical marching algorithm used in time dependent problems as well as in interative steps in elliptic problems can be written:

For $1 \le J,K \le N$

$$Y_{JK} = D_{JK}*X_{JK} + AP_{JK}*X_{J+1,K} + AM_{JK}*X_{J-1,K}$$

$$+ BP_{JK}*X_{J,K+1} + BM_{JK}*X_{J,K-1}$$

where we will assume Dirichlet boundary conditions, which means that a subscript of 0 or N+1 indicates a boundary grid point. The generalization of this algorithm to three dimensions is straightforward.

While the vectorization of this algorithm to length N is obvious, with a little more work, it is possible to achieve vector length N^2 in two dimensions and N^3 in three dimensions.

This is done by noting that the following bit vector "senses" the interior vs. the boundary grid points in 2 dimensions:

$$\underbrace{000 \ldots 0}_{N+2} \ \underbrace{011 \ldots 10}_{N+2} \ \underbrace{011 \ldots 10}_{N+2} \ . \ . \ . \ \underbrace{011 \ldots 10}_{N+2} \ \underbrace{000 \ldots 0}_{N+2}$$

Using this bit vector (and its straightforward generalization to 3 dimensions) it is possible to achieve the performance in Table 5.

TABLE 5. CYBER 205 2-PIPE PERFORMANCE OF MARCHING

	64-Bit Mode	32-Bit Mode	
2 Dimensions			
N = 32	81.3	150.3	
64	91.9	179.6	
128	96.4	191.6	Millions of Floating Point Operations per Second
3 Dimensions			
N = 16	69.0	135.7	
32	83.2	165.9	
64	91.1	181.8	

When the coefficients of the marching are independent of J and K (and
L) performance increases since it is possible to use the linked triad.
Such performance is listed in Table 6.

TABLE 6. CYBER 205 2 PIPE PERFORMANCE OF HOMOGENEOUS MARCHING
(SMOOTHING)

	64-Bit Mode	32-Bit Mode	
2 Dimensions			
N = 32	138.8	245.6	
64	162.8	313.7	
128	172.7	342.0	Millions of Floating Point Operations per Second
3 Dimensions			
N = 16	126.7	246.4	
32	154.2	307.0	
64	168.9	337.1	

SEMANTIC PERFORMANCE OF THE CYBER 205

Semantic vectorization is the process of producing a vector algorithm
from the algebraic expression of an algorithm without any reference
to a pre-existing translation of that algorithm into a scalar data
structure. This may entail transformations that can be justified only
at the mathematical level. Red/black reordering schemes are just such
an example. (It is the author's opinion that the essentially semantic
character of such transformations has not been properly appreciated.)

We shall illustrate the semantic performance of the CYBER 205 by presenting performance results for a sequence of algebraically posed
problems. The sophistication level increases with each succeeding
example leading to a fully vectorized application.

I. We begin with the performance of two algorithms of full linear
algebra. The reader is referred to [4], [5], and [9] for more
details.

TABLE 7.   CYBER 205 2 PIPE PERFORMANCE OF FULL MATRIX TIMES VECTOR

		64-Bit Mode	32-Bit Mode	
N =	100	.28	.23	
	500	3.4	2.2	MSEC
	1000	11.8	6.8	

CYBER 205 2 PIPE PERFORMANCE OF FULL MATRIX SOLUTION

		64-Bit Mode	32-Bit Mode	
N =	100	13.3	11.7	
	500	652.7	444.4	MSEC
	1000	4270.	2603.	

II. The single tridiagonal system, on the other hand, still represents a challenge to vector processing. To see this, note that solution of a full 1000 x 1000 algebraic system of equations demands over 80,000 times as much work as solving a triadiagonal system, but it can be accomplished in merely 8000 times the time.

The reason for this, of course, is that all algorithms for such solution either involve recursion, such as in Gaussian Elimination or involve data motion and vectors of length $N/\log_2 N$, such as cyclic reduction and Swartzrauber/Cramer.

The performance listed in Table 8 was reported in (6). Naive GE stands for Gaussian Elimination using a standard library routine. Unrolled GE for Gaussian Elimination uses tightly coded substitution phases implementing a partial matrix inverse. Swartztrauber/Cramer stands for a vectorized version of Cramer's rule first reported in (10). Measured cyclic reduction stands for a moderately optimized vector/scalar version of cyclic reduction. (We expect to better this performance by about 10% to 15%.)

The details of the cyclic reduction algorithm can be found in (4). However, we should point out here that an integral part of the algorithm is the ability to work with the substructure of even and odd elements of a vector. Although such substructures are not a priori vectors on the CYBER 205, the compress and merge operations allow them to be removed from and inserted into vector structures at vector speed.

TABLE 8. CYBER 205 2 PIPE PERFORMANCE OF SOLUTION OF SINGLE TRIDIAGONAL SYSTEM TIMES IN MICROSECONDS

N	Naive G.E.	Unrolled G.E.	Swartztrauber Cramer	Measured Cyclic Reduction
32	134	134	237	112
64	239	175	309	154
128	447	312	410	209
256	864	589	563	292
512	1700	1140	824	492
1024	3370	2250	1300	673
2048	6700	4460	2240	1130

Finally, one should note that the Gaussian Elimination and cyclic reduction algorithms used above demand a no-pivoting situation such as diagonal dominance. The Swartztrauber/Cramer does not.

We will discuss the case of multiple tridiagonal systems after our discussion of the FFT.

III. The Fast Fourier Transform is a sparse factorization of the Discrete Fourier Transform which reduces the work of matrix multiplication from $O(N^2)$ to $O(N\log_2 N)$ in effecting the algorithm. However, a naive implementation of the algorithm results in a mean vector length of $\log_2 N$ on the CYBER 205. This results from a block even/odd interaction pattern occurring at each level with the size of the block being halfed at each successive level.

Hence, for the early levels a technique is used to calculate the following complex linked triad pair:

$$V_3 = V_1 + S*V_2$$
$$V_4 = V_1 - S*V_2$$

(where V_j and S are complex) using six linked triad operations.

As the block size falls below a certain threshold, the compress operation is used to keep the vector length at N/2 at the cost of data motion.

Details of the analysis can be found in (7). Table 9 lists the performance for a single complex FFT on complex data stored in a vector of reals and a vector of imaginaries.

TABLE 9. CYBER 205 2 PIPE PERFORMANCE OF A SINGLE FFT MILLISECONDS

M =		
	1K	.77
	2K	1.53
	4K	3.11
	8K	6.42
	16K	13.28
	32K	27.52
	64K	56.98

IV. The previous two examples dealt with the performance of a single case of an algorithm. However, in most applications the two previous algorithms are used on many systems simultaneously. In particular an ADI type iterative method calls for the independent solution of M tridiagonal systems of length N where M = N in two dimensions and N^2 in three dimensions. Similarly the separability of the multi-dimensional discrete Fourier transform allows it to be effected by a sequence of one-dimensional transforms.

The algorithmic methodology known as simultaneous solution allows the vectorization of M tridiagonal systems to proceed with vector length M. In the case of M independent FFT's, it yields a vector length of $M\log_2 N$.

Tables 10 and 11 illustrate how the performance increases as the number of systems to be solved increases.

TABLE 10. CYBER 205 2 PIPE PERFORMANCE OF SIMULTANEOUS SUBSTITUTION
          OF M TRIDIAGONAL SYSTEMS - ALL TIMES IN MICRO SECONDS

			64-Bit Mode		32-Bit Mode	
			Time	Time/M	Time	Time/M
N = 32	M =	32	220.	6.9	190	5.9
		1024	1850	1.8	1000	1.0
N = 64	M =	64	540	8.4	440	.4
		2048	7000	3.4	3640	1.8

TABLE 11. CYBER 205 2 PIPE PERFORMANCE OF SIMULTANEOUS FFT OF
          M SYSTEMS TIMES IN MICROSECONDS

			64-Bit Mode		32-Bit Mode	
			Time	Time/M	Time	Time/M
N = 32	M =	32	460	14.4	355	11.1
		1024	4300	4.2	2300	2.2
N = 64	M =	64	1220	19.1	940	14.7
		2048	19450	9.5	10240	5.0
N = 128	M =	128	4280	33.4	2800	21.9
		512	13100	25.6	7200	14.1

V. We shall now combine the algorithmic ideas of the previous
    examples with some mathematical ideas to produce vectorized
    solvers for the discretized versions of two classical PDE's.

    The first example deals the iterative solution of the matrix
    equations which arise from the classical discretization of the
    linear non-homogeneous nonisotropic diffusion equation. (From
    the matrix algebra point of view, this discretization could
    also arise from the Helmholtz equation.)

    Rather than go into the timings of the individual components
    of the total algorithm, let us discuss the computational bound-
    ary conditions that were imposed on the algorithmic process,
    the interaction with mathematical ideas and finally the agree-
    ment of the predicted performance using CYBER 205 vector numer-
    ical linear algebraic formulas with the actual run time
    recorded.

204

The typical second order block centered grid discretization of
the diffusion equation leads to the following set of finite
difference equations when implicit spatial differencing is
employed for numerical stability.

$$TX_{j-\frac{1}{2},k,1} (P^{n+1}_{j-1,k,1} - P^{n+1}_{jkl}) - TX_{j+\frac{1}{2},k,1} (P^{n+1}_{jkl} - P^{n+1}_{j+1,kl})$$

$$+TY_{j,k-\frac{1}{2},1} (P^{n+1}_{j,k-1,1} - P^{n+1}_{jkl}) - TY_{j,k+\frac{1}{2},1} (P^{n+1}_{j,k,1} - P^{n+1}_{j,k+1,1})$$

$$+TZ_{j,k,1-\frac{1}{2}} (P^{n+1}_{j,k,1-1} - P^{n+1}_{jkl}) - TZ_{j,k,1+\frac{1}{2}} (P^{n+1}_{jkl} - P^{n+1}_{j,k,1+1})$$

$$- Q_{jkl} = C (P^{n+1}_{jkl} - P^{n}_{jkl})$$

Figure 1.

The "computational" boundary conditions imposed on the solution
process are:

1. A variant of SOR must be used.

2. Vertical line type SOR is preferable since TZ>>TX or TY.

3. The subroutine embodying the vectorized algorithm must be "user
   friendly" in the sense that input data will enter in standard
   engineering lexicographic order and the solution must be output in the same order.

The influence of mathematics in this solver arises in the consideration of the relaxation process. "Classically" this relaxation process
was done on the lexicographically ordered input data. Unfortunately
this method is highly recursive, i.e., each grid point must wait until
its predecessor is relaxed. This process is depicted in Figure 2 for
a xxx two-dimensional grid.

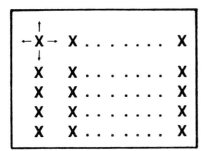 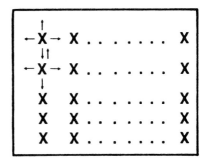

Figure 2.

It is not hard to see that if one imposes a chessboard pattern of red and black squares under the grid that relaxation of the red grid points can be done simultaneously and similarly the black ones. The remarkable fact, and one that depends upon a knowledge of the spectrum of the associated iterative operator, is that asymptotically both methods converge to the right answer at the same rate! This aesthetically pleasing piece of mathematics is due to Young (11). Its computational impact upon the problem at hand is that with proper data reordering, independent grid points of the same color can be processed with vector operations.

The situation is complicated here by computational boundary condition #2. This leads us to a grid coloring scheme illustrated in Figure 3. While the coloring of lines instead of point allows the relaxation to "spread information" faster in the vertical direction, which intuitively matches with the fact that TZ is large, it also couples the grid points in each vertical line by a tridiagonal system.

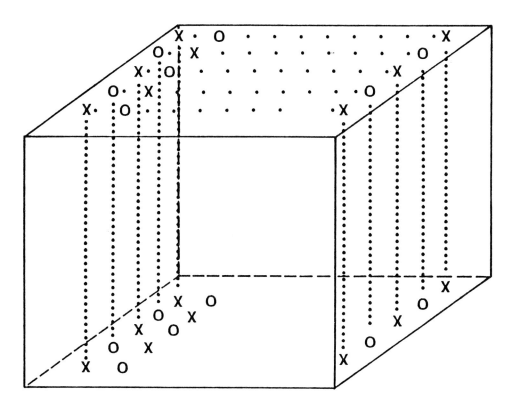

Figure 3.

Thus in order to put together a subroutine that satisfies the computational boundary conditions as well as being totally vectorized, we have the following six steps, where T is the transmissibility matrix, ξ° is the initial guess and ξ is the right hand side. Subscripts 1 and 2 denote red and black values respectively.

207

COMPUTATIONAL ALGORITHM FOR T $\xi = \eta$

I   TRANSFORM T,$\xi°$,η FROM LEXICOGRAPHIC ORDER
TO RED BLACK LINE SS ORDER

II   DO LU DECOMPOSITION OF T

III EACH ITERATION FORM
$$Y_1^{l+1} = \omega\,(\eta_1 - U\xi_2^l) \text{ and}$$
$$y_2^{l+1} = \omega\,(\eta_2 - L\xi_1^{l+1})$$

IV EACH ITERATION SOLVE
$$L_1 U_1 (\xi_1^{l+1} - (1-\omega)\xi_1^l) = y_1^{l+1}$$
$$L_2 U_2 (\xi_2^{l+1} - (1-\omega)\xi_2^l) = y_2^{l+1}$$

V   EVERY SECOND ITERATION FIND $\|\xi_1^{l+1} - \xi_1^l\|\infty$

AND $\|\xi_2^{l+1} - \xi_2^l\|\infty$

AND TEST FOR CONVERGENCE.

VI MERGE ANSWER BACK INTO LEXICOGRAPHIC FORM

Figure 4.

The vectorization methodology for each of the six steps is as follows:

1. Compress operation transforms data from one storage order to the other.

2. The recursion in the LU decomposition is handled by the simultaneous solution methodology, i.e., with data in the RBLSS order the recursion is on vectors of lengths NXNY/2.

3. Control Store allows the interaction with neighbors in other lines to proceed across boundaries yielding a vector length of NXNYNZ/2. The over-relaxation parameter is handled by a linked triad.

4. The recursive substitution is again handled by simultaneous solution yielding a vector length of NXNY/2.

5. The maximum absolute value in a vector can be searched for in one operation.

6. The merge operation puts the answer back into lexicographic order.

Assuming 30 iterations to convergence, the following table compares the theoretically derived run times against the actually measured run times as well as the effective megaflop rate in each case. This effective rate was calculated by dividing the classical flop count by the actual run time. Hence, the overhead induced by the data motion does <u>not</u> appear in the flop count, but <u>does</u> appear in the timing.

TABLE 12. CYBER 205 2 PIPE PERFORMANCE OF SOR DIFFUSION SOLVER IN 64-BIT PRECISION
N = TOTAL NUMBER OF GRID POINTS. ALL TIMES IN MILLISECONDS

N	Theoretical Prediction	Actual Measurement	Average Mflop Rate
220	2.05	2.17	52
1680	9.46	9.56	90.2
8200	42.92	43.04	97.7
51000	254.534	254.534	102.8

Since the mathematical details of the final example are published elsewhere (8), we limit ourselves here to recalling some of the performance levels reached.

TABLE 13. CYBER 205 PERFORMANCE OF MIXED FFT/LULU ALGORITHM FOR POISSON'S EQUATION
ON N^3 GRID IN 64-BIT PRECISION. ALL TIMES IN MILLISECONDS

N	No. of Pipes	Theoretical Prediction	Actual Measurement
32	2	18.69	18.95
64	2	140.97	142.1
64	4	83.86	84.2

<u>BIBLIOGRAPHY</u>

1. C.N. Arnold   "Performance Evaluation of Three Automatic Vectorizer Packages", Control Data Corp.

2. D. Barkai, M. Creutz,   "Wilson Loop Calculation in 4-Dimensional
   & K.J.M. Moriarty   Lattice Gauge Theory on the CYBER 205"
                            Computer Physics Comm. to appear.

3. M.J. Kascic Jr.   "Syntactic and Semantic Vectorization:
                            Whence Cometh Intelligence in Super-
                            computer?" Summer Computer Simulation
                            Conference., Vancouver 1983.

4. M.J. Kascic Jr.   "Vector Processing on the CYBER 200, State
                            of the Art Supercomputer", Infotech,
                            Maindenhead UK 1979.

5. M.J. Kascic Jr.   "Semantic Vectorization Methodology: Full
                            Matrix Algebra Model Problems I and II"
                            CYBER 200 Seminar # SN 4100, Control Data
                            Corp.

6. M.J. Kascic Jr. &   "Tridiagonal Systems and OCI on the CYBER
   J.F. Koehler   200 I" SIAM October 1981.

7. M.J. Kascic Jr.   "A Fundamentally Fast Treatment of the
                            Discrete Fourier Transform: CYBER 200
                            Seminar #SN 4100 Control Data Corporation.

8. M.J. Kascic Jr.   "Anatomy of a Poisson Solver" SIAM June
                            1983.

9. K. Kline et al   "Vector Processing Applied to Boundary
                            Element Algorithms on the CDC CYBER 205:
                            Conf. on Vector and Parallel Processing,
                            Paris March 1983.

10. P. Swartztrauber   "A Parallel Algorithm for Solving General
                            Tridiagonal Equations." Mathematics of
                            Com., Vol. 33, No. 145 January, 1979.

11. D.M. Young   "Iterative Solution of Large Linear Systems"
                            Academic Press 1971.

BENCHMARK RESULTS ON PHYSICAL FLOW PROBLEMS

W. Gentzsch

Deutsche Forschungs- und Versuchs-
anstalt für Luft- und Raumfahrt,
Bunsenstr. 10, D-3400 Göttingen

1. Introduction

This report is a summary of the DFVLR-Reports [1],[2] and [3] all dealing with benchmark results on physical flow problems on modern available supercomputers.

The programs contained in the benchmark can be devided into three classes

- production codes
- fast solvers
- kernels.

From the user's point of view there are a number of points of interest
in connection with the performance of a computer such as

- Scalar performance, which is an important part of the overall efficiency for real production codes (s. [1],[4]).

- Performance on unmodified programs, in order to give some information
  about the payoff the user gets if he does not want to go through the
  trouble of hand tayloring his programs for a specific architecture.

- Performance on handvectorized or handparallelized versions of a
  program, including restructuring or replacing of algorithms, in order
  to match machine architecture.

- Parametric studies, where parameters are for example vector length,
  number of meshpoints or number of processes.

- Measurements on basic kernels to find out what "net" performance
  characteristics for different types and constellations of operations
  can be expected, in order to give the programmer a clue how to ar-
  range his algorithms and group the expressions therein for optimal

NATO ASI Series, Vol. F7
High-Speed Computation. Edited by J. S. Kowalik
© Springer-Verlag Berlin Heidelberg 1984

execution time behavior.

The performance measurements described here do not include investigations of throughput and I/O.

2. Programs contained in the benchmark

In the following we will give a short description of the program. The
reader who is interested in more details is referred to [1] and to the
corresponding literature in [1] and [2].

2.1 Production codes

MHD   Numerical solution of the magnetohydrodynamic equations in two
       dimensions by finite differences and fast explicit superstep method
       in time.

EPS   Second order panel method for the incompressible flow over a thin
       plate.

E2D   Solution of the time dependent 2D- and 3D-Euler equations for the
E3D   axial-symmetric and the fully three dimensional inviscid flow
       field past blunt bodies by a finite difference method (Rusanow-
       algorithm).

WALL   Finite volume technique and MacCormack's time-splitting method for
       the solution of the Navier-Stokes equations for shock boundary
       layer interaction.

D3G   Finite difference solution of the compressible 3D-boundary layer
       equations for laminar and turbulent flow past blunt bodies (with-
       out nose region).

BEUL   Finite volume technique for the 2D-Euler equations for inviscid
       flow past a bulge.

2.2 Fast solvers

MG00   Multigrid methods for the Helmholtz equation on rectangular and
MG01   general domains in two dimensions.

TR3   Finite difference method with cyclic reduction for the Dirichlet problem for Poisson's equation in a rectangle.

MAD   Solution of the Poisson equation in a rectangle by a multigrid and an ADI method.

2.3 Kernels

GEL   Gauss elimination method for the solution of linear systems of equations with full matrices as they occur e.g. in panel methods.

RELAX Successive overrelaxation method for linear systems of equations arising in the numerical solution of the Helmholtz and Poisson equations.

RECURS Collection of 12 fundamental algorithms for the solution of linear systems of equations with sparse matrices.

KERNE Collection of 10 fundamental kernels such as vector addition, multiplication, division, inner product, polynomial evaluation, backward and central differences and combinations of these.

3. Survey of Supercomputers

The benchmark program or at least a subset of them were run on the following machines:

STAR-100 (CDC-Data Center, Arden Hills)	November 1979
CYBER-203 (CDC-Data Center, Arden Hills)	November 1979 and 1980
AMDAHL-470/V6 (DFVLR, Oberpfaffenhofen)	December 1979
CRAY-1 (IPP, Garching)	February 1980
CYBER-205 (CDC-Data Center, Arden Hills)	November 1980
CRAY-1S (Cray-Research, Chippewa Falls)	November 1980
CYBER-76 (RRZN, Hannover)	June 1981
ICL-2960/DAP (Queen Mary's College, London)	September 1981

HITACHI-S9/IAP (HITACHI-Works, Kanagawa)   April   1982
DENELCOR-HEP (DENELCOR-Works, Aurora)   April   1982
IBM-3081 D (DFVLR, Oberpfaffenhofen)   May   1982

Remarks:
- The CYBER-205 was a 2-pipe version.
- The timings of the IBM-3081 reflect the performance of one of the two
  processors (only one processor can work on one task).
- The CRAY-1 was equipped with 16 memory banks, the CRAY-1S only with 8
  banks. The difference in performance was minor (generally less than
  10 per cent on favour of the CRAY-1), so the timings of the CRAY-1S
  were omitted.
- Large arrays had to be put in LCM (Large Core Memory) on the CYBER 76
  causing some loss of performance for some of the production codes.
- The HITACHI-S9/IAP was run with 8 banks and 16-banks of memory with a
  considerable difference in performance on highly vectorized codes.
  Only the timings for 16-bank memory are included in chapter 4. Numbers
  on both configurations, S9 and S9/IAP, can be seen in tables 4,9 and
  11 of chapter 4.
- The benchmark was run on a one-processing-element-version of the
  DENELCOR-HEP.
- Obviously the timings presented below reflect the capabilities of the
  software to make optimal use of the machine architecture as well as
  the capabilities of the architecture itself, even though most of the
  time it is impossible for the user to decide whether the software or
  the hardware is to blame or to praise. In some instances parts of programs were coded in assembler (as on HEP) or standard assembler subroutines were called (as on CRAY) with dramatic performance improvements in some cases. For those machines not described below, it may be
  helpful for the interpretation of the results to list the software
  environment: on the AMDAHL-470/V6 and the IBM-3081 D the benchmark was
  run unter MVS-SE using the HE-FORTRAN IV-Compiler, on the CYBER-76 it
  was run under SCOPE 2.1 using the FORTRAN IV Compiler.

4. Results

In this section we shall present a number of tables which contain timings
of our programs on those machines we have mentioned above. We shall try
to interpret the results, giving explanations wherever possible and/or
necessary. Some observations may be explained in a rather obvious or at

least plausible way, others remain peculiar and are still waiting for
an explanation. Among others we shall attempt to discuss aspects of
speed up and overhead, the effect of vector length and number of processes. All timings are in seconds.

4.1 Fundamental Kernels

We shall discuss the results on HEP separately from the other machines
as, due to the state of the compiler, absolute kernel timings on HEP are
less interesting than the effects of parallelization on execution times.
Notation in table 1:

$<x,y>$ denotes the inner product of array x and y.

$P_9(x)$ denotes the evaluation of a polynomial of ninth degree by
Horner's scheme with the elements of the array x as abscissae.

The collumn OPC contains the number of arithmetic operations per index.
On table 1 measurements of the scalar performance, i.e. performance with
autovectorizer turned off where ever possible, are presented. The author
is aware of the fact that the results are somewhat compiler and instruction scheduler dependent, but believes that at least a clue is necessary
in order to be able to estimate the effective performance of a vector or
parallel machine on a real world problem, which is always a mixture of
scalar and vector (or parallel) performance.

A few points concerning scalar performance seem remarkable:
- S9, CRAY-1, CYBER-205 and CYBER-76 belong to the same class with no
  significant overall advantage to any of the machines. Old CYBER 76
  performs surprisingly well, revealing some resemblance to its younger
  relatives.
- IBM 3081 timings reflect the performance of one of its processors only.

Tables 2,3 and 4 show the results on vectorized kernels. On tables 2 and
3 the timings for vector lengths 100 and 1000 respectively are given in
seconds, on table 4 performance for vector length 1000 is presented in
MFLOPS (millions of floating point operations per second). The (necessarily scalar) results on AMDAHL-470/V6 and IBM-3081 are entered into these
tables for comparison. The results on CYBER-205 reflect the breaking
down of expressions into dyadic operations (timings for expressions are
roughly the sum of timings of its constituting operations), except for
linked triads (kernel 10, also contained in kernel 7) where special
hardware instructions are available.

Table 1: Fundamental kernels. Timings for 10^6 loops in sec. Scalar
kernels (i.e. vectorization turned off), vectorlength
N = 100.

Kernel Type	OPC	AMDAHL V6	IBM 3081	HITAC S9	CRAY-1	CYBER 205	CYBER 76
1 | $x + y$	1	96	66.2	27.4	38.2	36.6	36
2 | $x*y$	1	133	88.6	33.3	39.4	34.4	31
3 | x/y	1	307	166.8	102.4	71.9	118.7	72
4 | $(x-y)*(x+y)$	3	202	111.7	51.4	48.2	38.6	53
5 | $<x,y>$	2	124	92.7	36.4	43.2	34.5	42
6 | $5.(x/z+y*z)$	4	488	258.3	129.4	89.4	130.7	127
7 | $P_9(x)$	20	1686	1030.5	393.8	495.8	346.4	749
8 | $x_i - x_{i-1}$	1	123	67.1	27.0	37.8	34.6	35
9 | $x_{i+1} - 2x_i + x_{i-1}$	3	220	125.4	44.4	50.9	41.7	57
10 | $y + B*x$	2	-	105.3	36.6	44.4	32.6	58

This is not at all true for the CRAY machine: evaluation of kernel 4
(i.e. $(x-y)*(x+y)$) takes only slightly more time than a single add or
multiply, coming close to timings of this kernel on CYBER-205, even
though the CYBER is considerably faster on single operations (factor
of 2-2.5 for N = 100, factor of 4 for N = 1000 over CRAY).

For the S9/IAP the picture is somewhat blurred. Similar phenomena to
those on CYBER-205, as far as composition of expression timings from
timings of single operations might be expected, but cannot be entirely
verified. The perfromance loss on kernel 4 in that sense cannot be fully
explained and may be due to memory bandwidth problems.

Vector division on S9/IAP is rather disappointing with only a minor performance gain in comparison with scalar timings. A significant performance improvement on vector operations was reached by HITACHI by recon-
figuring S9 memory from 8 to 16 way interleaving. Apparently only the
increased memory bandwidth met the requirements of the processing speed
of S9/IAP. In this section only the results on 16 way interleaving
memory are presented.

The speedup on vectorized fundamental kernels for N = 100 over scalar
performance is in the rangs of

    6.6 to 17.2 on CYBER-205
    7.1 to 10.9 on CRAY-1
    1.2 to 4.6 on S9/IAP.

Table 2: Vectorized kernels, N = 100, time in sec for 10^6 loops.

	Kernel Type	OPC	AMDAHL V6	IBM 3081	S9/ IAP	CRAY-1	CYBER 205
1	$x + y$	1	96	66.2	8.7	5.3	2.3
2	$x*y$	1	133	88.6	8.8	5.3	2.0
3	x/y	1	307	166.8	82.9	9.9	7.7
4	$(x-y)*(x+y)$	3	202	111.7	28.3	6.9	6.0
5	$<x,y>$	2	124	92.7	8.0	6.2	4.8
6	$5.(x/z+y*z)$	4	488	258.3	107.9	13.2	13.7
7	$P_9(x)$	20	1686	1030.5	153.3	56.2	33.6
8	$x_i - x_{i-1}$	1	123	67.1	10.2	5.3	2.2
9	$x_{i+1} - 2x_i + x_{i-1}$	3	220	125.4	26.5	8.0	6.3
10	$y + B*x$	2	-	105.3	10.2	7.4	2.6

For N = 1000 a certain performance increase for all vector machines can be observed.

For add and multiply on CYBER-205 about 50% of maximum performance is reached for N = 100 and about 90% for N = 1000. The measured results for this machine are fairly close to the - admittedly coarse - theory, where performance in floating point operations per second is described by the formula

$$FLOPS = NOPI * N / \{C * (S + R * N)\}$$

with the following notation

NOPI : Number of operations per index
N   : Vector length
C   : Cycle time
S   : Overhead (e.g. start up time)
R   : Number of cycles per "result"

(considering examples like inner product, the word "result" has to be handled with a little caution). Startup times for linked triads are higher than for the basic operations mentioned above with the effect of a lower relative performance at e.g. N = 100. This theoretical expectation also is in agreement with the measured numbers.

For the CRAY-machine the phenomena are somewhat heterogeneous: for usual (i.e. FORTRAN) kernels the performance gain on N = 1000 over N = 100 is in the range of 10-20%. For those kernels, however, where assembly subroutines were called (such as inner product and linked triad) improvements of close to a factor of two can be observed. Explanation of these phenomena would require a detailed analysis. The overhead for the evaluation of a vector expression is strongly vector length and expression dependent. Efficient management of vector registers and concurrent use of functional units and memory access also have a decisive influence on the performance.

Surprisingly enough the performance increase on the S9/IAP by changing vector length from 100 to 1000 is almost as difficult to predict as on the CRAY (82% for N = 100, 98% for N = 1000 of max. performance are predicted by the above formula). The measured increase ranges from the order of a few percent for more complex kernels to 17% for addition, 26% for multiplication and 24% for P_9.

Table 3: Vectorized kernels, N = 1000, time in sec for 10^6 loops.

	Kernel Type	OPC	AMDAHL V6	IBM 3081	S9/ IAP	CRAY-1	CYBER 205
1	$x + y$	1	938	665.7	71.9	43.6	11.4
2	$x*y$	1	1344	890.0	65.1	44.0	11.1
3	x/y	1	3228	1662.4	813.5	88.2	63.9
4	$(x-y)*(x+y)$	3	1808	1120.7	277.1	58.7	33.4
5	$<x,y>$	2	1482	926.9	62.5	30.1	22.7
6	$5.(x/z+y*z)$	4	4983	2606.2	1012.5	119.3	97.1
7	$P_9(x)$	20	15747	10406.1	1176.6	455.3	124.3
8	x_i-x_{i-1}	1	917	685.2	77.1	44.1	11.3
9	$x_{i+1}-2x_i+x_{i-1}$	3	1685	1292.5	249.0	71.3	33.2
10	$y+B*x$	2	-	1060.8	76.6	47.3	11.6

Table 4 contains performance data on fundamental kernels for vector length N = 1000 measured in MFLOPS. The numbers for the vector machines in this table are more or less close to the maximum performance for the respective expression. For a 2-pipe-version of a CYBER-205 the asymptotic speed for add and multiply is 100 MFLOPS and 200 MFLOPS for linked triads.

At first glance the reader may be disappointed by the MFLOPS-rates of the CRAY for add, mult (he may be tempted to expect 80 MFLOPS). A detailed analysis (see e.g. [1]) shows that almost 3 out of 4 cycles are overhead for simple vector operations, the main ingredients of which are filling and emptying of registers, filling of the pipeline and memory access.

As soon as intermediate results can be kept in vector registers and are
reused by subsequent instructions the performance improvement may well
be a factor of three over simple operations.
On the S9/IAP simple operations approach the theoretical value: of 16.7
MFLOPS. Inner product and linked triad exceed this limit due to overlapped execution on high speed and standard arithmetic. On the other
hand a performance loss for more complex operations can be observed.

Table 4: Vectorized kernels, N = 1000, performance in MFLOPS.

	Kernel Type	AMDAHL V6	IBM 3081	S9	S9/ IAP	CRAY-1	CYBER 205
1	$x + y$	1.07	1.50	3.65	13.91	22.94	87.72
2	$x*y$	0.74	1.12	3.00	15.36	22.73	90.09
3	x/y	0.31	0.60	0.98	1.23	11.34	15.65
4	$(x-y)*(x+y)$	1.66	2.68	5.84	10.83	51.11	89.82
5	$<x,y>$	1.35	2.16	5.49	32.00	66.45	88.11
6	$5.(x/z+y*z)$	0.80	1.53	3.10	3.95	33.53	41.19
7	$P_9(x)$	1.27	1.92	5.08	17.00	43.93	160.90
8	$x_i - x_{i-1}$	1.09	1.46	3.70	12.97	22.60	88.50
9	$x_{i+1} - 2x_i + x_{i-1}$	1.78	2.32	6.76	12.05	42.08	90.36
10	$y+B*x$	-	1.89	5.46	26.11	42.28	178.57

In table 5 we shall present the timings for fundamental kernels on HEP
for array sizes of 100 and 1000. The simple loops contained in the
kernel program are converted in a rather standard way to a "fork and
join" where the workload is distributed among the processes by "self
scheduling" [3].
The timings show some more or less expected phenomena and some peculiarities:
For the addition of 100 operand pairs timings for 10 processes are generally 10% better than for 20 processes, which sounds reasonable as 10
adds per process are executed with a smaller relative create-overhead
for 10 processes. The speedup of parallel execution of 10 processes over
sequential execution ranges from factors of 2.5 for simple loops up to
3.5 for more complex ones and down to 1.4 for the scalar product.

Table 5: Fundamental kernels on HEP.

	N = 100	sequential	parallel	
			NPROC=20	NPROC=10
1	$x + y$	1663.1	707.8	639.0
2	$x*y$	1663.1	702.4	639.0
3	x/y	1743.1	711.1	621.6
4	$(x-y)*(x+y)$	2253.1	716.7	664.2
5	$<x,y>$	1725.5	1284.9	1228.5
6	$5.(x/z+y*z)$	2333.1	759.3	655.8
7	$P_9(x)$	19242.3	11003.3	7066.3
8	$x_i - x_{i-1}$	1646.6	695.7	635.7
9	$x_{i+1} - 2x_i + x_{i-1}$	1885.7	714.0	640.0
10	$y+B*x$	1823.1	707.1	630.8
	N = 1000			
1	$x + y$	16514.5	5042.9	4223.3
2	$x*y$	16514.5	5040.0	4223.3
3	x/y	17314.5	4590.0	4245.0
4	$(x-y)*(x+y)$	22414.5	4831.3	4393.8
5	$<x,y>$	17116.9	11546.3	10829.9
6	$5.(x/z+y*z)$	23214.5	4846.8	4455.0
7	$P_9(x)$	191143.7	48188.7	44194.7
8	$x_i - x_{i-1}$	16498.0	5005.1	4293.1
9	$x_{i+1} - 2x_i + x_{i-1}$	19077.1	4886.1	4295.0
10	$y+B*x$	18114.5	5934.9	4316.1

The disappointing behaviour of the inner product may be explained as
follows: synchronization for the asynchronous "sum" - variable for every
index, as it was done in the benchmark, certainly was not the smartest
way to realize the inner product. Collecting sums per process in local
variables and adding the results into an asynchronous variable after the
work per process is basically done would certainly improve the performance. The same would probably hold true, had the order of the loops in
P_9 been reversed and the outer loop been parallelized.
Changing array sizes to N = 1000 the factors parallel over sequential
improve somewhat (3.9 for simple loops, 5.2 for complex ones, 1.6 for
inner product). Only slight further changes occur when N is increased
to 5000 or 10000. Apparently the synchronization overhead for each index

spoils the factor of 8-10 which is to be expected by the architecture of the machine (and is in fact achieved for production codes). Surprising is the observation that the numbers for NPROC = 20 are still considerably slower (upto 16%) than those for NPROC = 10. Timings for complicated expressions are in the same range as for simple ones, indicating that loop and synchronization overhead are responsible for performance losses to a large extent.

4.2 Algorithms for sparse systems

The following subroutines of RECURS have been tested on the IBM-3081 and the CRAY-1 of the DFVLR in Oberpfaffenhofen, and the CYBER 205 of the University of Bochum. For details see [5]:

SOR   - point successive overrelaxation
SORRB   - red-black or checkerboard SOR
SLOR   - line SOR
SLORZ   - ZEBRA SLOR
VSLORZ - SLORZ with simultaneous treatment of the Thomas-algorithms
ISLORZ - SLORZ with iterative treatment of the Thomas-algorithms
CSLORZ - SLORZ with cyclic reduction for the Thomas-algorithms
LJAC   - line Jacobi
JACCG   - point Jacobi with conjugate gradient acceleration
ADILJ   - alternating direction implicit with LJAC and relaxation
LJACV   - LJAC with simultaneous treatment of the Thomas-algorithms
ADIV   - ADILJ with simultaneous Thomas in x, iterative Thomas in y
          for the CYBER and cyclic reduction in y for the CRAY.

Table 6 shows the CPU-times in sec for the discretized model problem

$$u_{xx} + u_{yy} = 1, \quad (x,y) \in G$$

$$u(x,y) = \frac{1}{4}(x^2+y^2) , \quad (x,y) \in \dot{G}$$

where $G = \{(x,y)/0<x<1, \ 0<y<1\}$ and $\dot{G}$ is the boundary for two different grids of 33 * 33 resp. 65 * 65 gridpoints.

The times for LJACV are estimated with the aid of LJAC* (SLORZ/VSLORZ), similar for ADIV with 0.5*ADI* (SLORZ/VSLORZ+SLORZ/ISLORZ) for the CYBER and 0.5*ADI* (SLORZ/VSLORZ+SLORZ/CSLORZ) for the CRAY.

222

Table 6: CPU-times in sec for the model problem.

| | | IBM-3081 | | CRAY - 1 | | CYBER 205 | |
		33	65	33	65	33	65
SOR		0.22	1.80	0.061	0.691	0.049	0.473
SORRB		0.16	1.30	0.015	0.082	0.008	0.052
SLOR		0.30	2.41	0.061	0.445	0.071	0.459
SLORZ		0.23	1.84	0.045	0.338	0.056	0.345
VSLORZ		0.22	1.81	0.016	0.089	0.036	0.159
ISLORZ		0.68	5.47	0.072	0.378	0.078	0.376
CSLORZ		0.61	4.40	0.052	0.278	0.134	0.690
LJAC		2.03	23.57	0.557	6.062	0.599	6.070
JACCG		0.51	4.20	0.027	0.177	0.013	0.098
ADILJ		0.54	3.93	0.120	0.824	0.136	0.879
LJACV		-	-	0.199	1.595	0.400	2.760
ADIV		-	-	0.065	0.329	0.123	0.561

Here the best methods for the solution of a single differential equation are SORRB, VSLORZ and JACCG. Because of the somewhat complicate indexing (running across the Thomas-algorithms), VSLORZ is not optimal for the CYBER which is a memory-to-memory machine. For the memory-to-register CRAY, VSLORZ is very suitable. If no optimal relaxation factor is available, JACCG seems a good alternative for both CRAY and CYBER. Here the CYBER gains by its very fast Q8SDOT-hardware instruction for the dot-products in the algorithm. To enlighten these features, table 7 shows the factors IBM:CRAY and IBM:CYBER for selected methods.

It is important to note that the vector lengths in SORRB are 16 resp. 32 for the CRAY and 512 resp. 2048 for the CYBER, in VSLORZ and LJACV 16 resp. 32, in ISLORZ, CSLORZ and ADIV 32 resp. 64 for both machines and in JACCG 32 resp. 64 for the CRAY and 512 resp. 2048 for the CYBER. However, the CYBER reaches half of its maximum speed for vector lengths of about 100 and 90% for vector length of about 1000 which by far is not yet reached in most of the programs. Vector lengths of 16 and 32 result in performance rates of about 15 resp. 25% for a two pipe CYBER, while the CRAY for vector lengths of 16 and 32 reaches about 70 resp. 85% of its maximum speed.

Table 7: Speed-up factors against the IBM-3081.

	CRAY-1		CYBER 205	
	33	65	33	65
SORRB	10.7	15.9	20.5	24.9
VSLORZ	13.8	20.3	6.1	11.4
ISLORZ	9.4	14.5	8.7	14.6
CSLORZ	11.7	15.8	4.6	6.4
ADIV	8.3	11.9	4.4	7.0
LJACV	10.2	14.8	5.1	8.5
JACCG	18.9	23.7	38.4	42.8

Another interesting aspect is the realized profit of the different algorithms for one and the same computer. In table 8 the profit for implementing the simultaneous Thomas-algorithms in SLORZ, which then results in VSLORZ, is a factor of 3.8 on the CRAY for a 65 * 65 grid but improves nothing on the scalar IBM:

Table 8: Profit for vectorization.

		FACTOR	IBM-3081		CRAY-1		CYBER 205	
			33	65	33	65	33	65
ST	VSLORZ/SLORZ		1	1	2.8	3.8	1.5	2.2
RB	SORRB/SOR		1.4	1.4	4.1	8.4	6.3	9.1
ZE	SLORZ/SLOR		1.3	1.3	1.4	1.3	1.3	1.3
IT	ISLORZ/SLORZ		0.3	0.3	0.6	0.9	0.7	0.9
CT	CSLORZ/SLORZ		0.4	0.4	0.9	1.2	0.4	0.5

In table 8 ST means simultaneous Thomas-algorithms, RB red-black, ZE Zebra, IT iterative Thomas and CT means cyclic reduction for the recurrences in the Thomas-algorithm. For IT and CT, the gain in performance considerably grows for large $M > 128$. Again the implementation of a red-black pattern for a single differential equation seems to be the most promising one. In the case of a system of nonlinear differential equations, as they often occur e.g. in fluid mechanics or magnetohydrodynamics, point methods converge very slowly and a much better way is to use Richtmyer's algorithm for systems with block tridiagonal matrices for which all the line methods described above will carry over. Evidently the implementation of these modified Richtmyer algorithms on vectorcomputers is more difficult and will be discussed in a future note.

4.3 Handvectorized programs

Timings on those production codes, fast solvers or kernels that were
"hand taylored" in order to fit the respective architectures are presented in this section. In some instances restructured versions for
vectorization purposes also ran faster on scalar machines than the original version. Therefore the results of the most successful versions
are shown.
On the other hand it may be interesting to know what the reward for going
through the pain of rewriting a program may be. A comparison between
timings of original versions with autovectorization employed versus
rewritten versions shows that for production codes and fast solvers the
following factors can be attained (depending on the vector length and
degree of vectorization).

    CYBER-205 : 2.5 - 5.4 (mean value 4.2)
    CRAY-1   : 1   - 3.3 (mean value 2.3).

Care should be taken when interpreting these numbers as they do not reflect vector over scalar performance because the autovectorizer sometimes
did a respectable job on the original programs (as was the case with the
MHD program on the CRAY where the whole code was autovectorized right
away). For the S9/IAP timings of the original versions are not available.
On the other hand comparisons of the performance of S9 with and without
IAP on identical versions yield factors in the range of 1.6 to 2.1 (mean
value 1.8) on production codes and fast solvers.
For nonfundamental kernels (like GEL or RELAX) factors are in the range
of:

    CYBER-205 : 11.2 - 22.1 (mean value: 16.7)
    CRAY-1   :   2.0 - 4.2 (mean value: 3.2)

whereas comparison between S9/IAP yields factors between 1.0 - 4.0 (mean
value: 2.5).

For the HEP the factors of parallelized over sequential production codes
range from 5.8 to 9.1 with a mean value of 7.8.

225

Table 9: Handtaylored programmes.

	AMDAHL V6	IBM 3081	S9	S9/ IAP	CRAY-1	CYBER 205	CYBER 76
MHD12	4.4	2.6	0.99	0.54	0.24	0.18	--
MHD22	15.4	10.2	3.50	1.68	0.61	0.38	--
MG00	14.9	8.9	4.19	2.57	0.69	0.65	15.3
EPS4	30.8	20.02	8.12	4.98	3.39	3.04	12.0
EPS7	115.6	80.89	32.69	18.95	11.59	10.20	49.2
GEL100	0.58	0.35	0.14	0.042	0.011*	0.017	--
GEL200	4.58	2.74	1.10	0.269	0.042*	0.08	--
E2D	8.1	4.72	--	--	1.06	1.5	2.43
BEUL	--	81.9	33.16	21.81	--	--	--
RELAX15	2.2	1.30	0.68	0.68	0.16	0.05	--
RELAX63	39.8	21.81	11.41	6.93	1.32	0.44	--

* (using calls of assembly subroutines for linked triads)

Studying the literature dealing with parallelization of fundamental kernels one may gather the impression that parallelization is more cumbersome than e.g. vectorization. This is not necessaryly true for production codes. Examples like the EPS program show that due to the lack of data dependencies the parallelization of a giant loop with lots of scalar subroutine calls contained in it may be a straight forward thing to do, whereas vectorization means introduction of a large number of auxiliary arrays and tracing the index structure of these arrays down to the bottom level of the calling sequence of the scalar subroutines (which may be rather painful). In fact the original version of the program was parallelized rather than the vectorized version because the space that was used for local arrays (one sample for each process) was prohibitive.

Parts of the parallelized MHD program were recoded in HEP-assembler, yielding a factor of approximately 3.5 over pure FORTRAN. For the assembly version 6 MFLOPS are achieved on the 1 PEM-version of the HEP. This relatively high performance can be explained by the fact that the number of arithmetic operations (order of 20) per index is large compared to the loop and synchronization overhead.

Table 10: Parallelized production programs on HEP.

| | | HEP | | | |
	sequential	parallel	AMDAHL		
EPS4	414.0	54.48	30.7	(41.5)**
EPS7	1760.9	192.99	115.6	(178.4)**
MHD12	48.7	8.4	4.4	
MHD62	1549.7	194.33	131.9	
		55.97*		
GEL100	8.53	1.08	0.58	
GEL200	67.31	7.87	4.58	

* a number of subroutines being coded in HEP-assembler
** the numbers in parentheses reflect the times of the original versions on the AMDAHL, the ones that were actually parallelized.

4.4 Parametric Studies

In this section we will present timings on MHD and RELAX programs with the grid size N as parameter (N * N being the number of grid points). In both cases the number of arithmetic operations is roughly proportional to N * N. If T(N) denotes execution time for grid size N, the quotient

$$Q(N) = N * N / T(N)$$

which is proportional to the MFLOPS-rate for a given grid size, shows different behavior on different types of machines:
- For scalar machines Q(N) is roughly a constant function of N.
- For vector machines Q(N) starts with relatively small numbers until it reaches a certain saturation level.
- For the DAP Q(N) grows quadratically.
Remark: For DAP and CRAY a certain "saw tooth" behaviour would be observed as soon as N were to exeed 64.
For the MHD program the vector length is N on the CRAY and N * N on S9/IAP and CYBER-205.
For the RELAX-program vector lengths are N for S9/IAP and CRAY and N*N/2 for CYBER-205 where a red black pattering was applied.

Table 11: Parametric study in dependency upon vector length on an
N * N-grid for RELAX

N	AMDAHL	IBM 3081	S9	S9/ IAP	CRAY-1	CYBER 205
3	0.2	0.12	0.11	0.16	0.03	0.03
7	0.5	0.34	0.21	0.26	0.07	0.03
15	2.2	1.30	0.68	0.68	0.16	0.05
31	9.5	5.42	2.66	2.03	0.44	0.13
63	39.8	21.81	11.41	6.93	1.32	0.44

Table 12: Parametric study in dependency upon vector length on an
N * N-grid for MHD (1000 Iterations, time in sec)

N	AMDAHL	IBM 3081	S9	S9/ IAP	CRAY-1	CYBER 205	DAP*
10	4.4	2.6	0.99	0.54	0.24	0.18	11.0
20	15.4	10.2	3.5	1.68	0.61	0.38	11.0
30	36.3	22.4	7.8	3.47	1.17	0.75	11.0
40	63.8	39.0	13.9	5.94	1.83	1.22	11.0
50	100.1	58.4	22.8	9.09	2.75	1.83	11.0
60	131.9	83.0	33.0	13.06	3.66	2.56	11.0

* 32-BIT-Arithmetic

A more detailed discussion of the DAP results may be found in [2].

5. References

More detailed reference lists may be found at the end of reports [1]
to [3].

[1] Gentzsch, W., Müller-Wichards, D., Weiland, C.:
   Benchmark Results on Physical Flow Problems with the CDC and
   CRAY Vectorcomputers,(in german).
   DFVLR IB 221-82 A 02, Göttingen 1982.

[2] Gentzsch, W.:
   A Survey of the New Vectorcomputers CRAY-1S of CRAY Research,
   CYBER-205 of CDC and the Parallelcomputer DAP of ICL. Architec-
   ture and Programming,(in german).
   DFVLR - FB 82-02, Köln 1982.

[3] Müller-Wichards, D., Gentzsch, W.:
   Performance Comparisons among Several Parallel and Vector Com-
   puters on a Set of Fluid Flow Problems.
   DFVLR IB 262-82 R 01, Göttingen 1982.

[4] Gentzsch, W.:
   High Performance Processing Needs in Fluid Dynamics.
   Proc. of SEAS Spring Meeting 1982, pp. 575-590.

[5] Gentzsch, W.:
   How to Maintain the Efficiency of Highly Serial Algorithms
   Involving Recursions on Vector Computers.
   Proc. of 1. Int. Conf. on Vector and Parallel Methods in
   Scientific Computing, Paris 1983, pp. 79-86.

PARALLEL PROCESSING OF SPARSE STRUCTURES*

David J. Kuck and Daniel D. Gajski
Department of Computer Science
University of Illinois at Urbana-Champaign
1304 West Springfield
Urbana, Illinois 61801-2987

1. Introduction

In [Kuck81], [Kuck82], we presented a relationship between data structures, program structures, and machine structures. Under the assumption that an algorithm or program has been put in parallel form, this relationship holds across a wide range of programming languages and computer architectures. Thus the data, program, and machine structures presented are basic concepts that have many possible implementations. In that paper, the data structures considered were scalar data, array or string data that is accessible with "regular indexing," and "other data" including sparse or "irregularly indexed" arrays, trees, graphs, etc. In this paper, we will consider these other data structures in more detail.

In [Kuck82], program structures are first subdivided into non-loop blocks and blocks enclosed in loops, and then loops are further subdivided according to the kinds of dependence graphs they contain. Three kinds of graphs that exhaust the possibilities are acyclic, linear cyclic, and nonlinear cyclic. A linear cycle is a cycle of dependences in which all right-hand sides consist of linear combinations of left-hand side variables. If a cycle is not linear, it is nonlinear. In this paper, we shall consider these same program structures.

The machine structures considered in [Kuck82] are single and multiple execution array machines (SEA and MEA) and multiple execution scalar (MES) machines. For example, the CDC Cyber 205 is an SEA machine, while the Cray-1 and Livermore S1 are MEA machines. The Denelcor HEP is an MES system. However, in practice only chained multiple-array operations are executed in the Cray-1 and multiple-array processing on the S1 has not yet been demonstrated.

The goal of this paper, together with [Kuck82] and possibly further extensions to other data structures, is not just to provide a taxonomy, but rather to provide an absolute checklist for a given system's functionality, to provide a means for comparing the overall capabilities of various systems and, finally, to provide a basis for deciding what kind of system is required for a particular application as reflected in its programs or algorithms.

The programming language statements used in this paper reflect both the structure of Fig. 1 and the statements used in real machines. Thus, for SEA and MEA systems, loop statements are called *array* or *vector operations* as they are in the parallel and pipeline supercomputers or attached array processors. Linear cyclic statements are called *recurrence* or *reduction operations* as they are in such real systems.

For MES systems, we use the loop control constructs *doall* and *doacr* [Padu79], [Cytr82], [KuPa79]. These both mean that the body of the loop may be assigned to as many processors as the loop limit indicates and that dependences between statements must be satisfied at run time. *doall* is used for acyclic loops and is thus a special case of *doacr* which allows dependence cycles. Thus, *doall* is used merely to illuminate the (not always obvious) acyclic nature of a loop.

This paper will consider sparse data structures that are arrays accessed by control bits and those accessed by tags.

*This work was supported in part by the National Science Foundtion under Grant No. MCS 80-01561, and the U.S. Department of Energy under Contract No. DOE DE-AC02-81ER10822, and Control Data Corporation under Contract No. CDC82-1101.

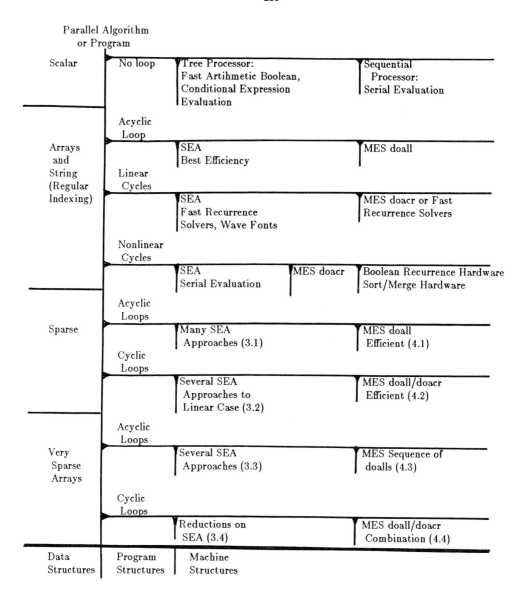

Fig. 1. Data, Program and Machine Structures

The outline of the remainder of this paper is as follows. In Section 2, we give several definitions concerning sparse data structures and MES system synchronization methods. In Section 3, we discuss the details of Fig. 1 with respect to array execution machines (primarily SEA) and in Section 4, we present a similar discussion for MES machines. Section 5 contains a summary and extension remarks.

2. Definitions and Background Ideas

In any computer system that performs more than one operation at a time, there are five distinct phases of data handling and computation: fetching, aligning for processing, processing, aligning for storage, and storage (FAPAS). Each of these is a potential bottleneck and a computer system must be designed so that each is balanced in a bandwidth or capacity sense. In addition to this balance between parts of the system architecture, the architecture itself must be designed to match the data structures and program structures of the computations it is to perform. We shall use Fig. 1 to relate these three key concepts: data structures, program structures, and architectural structures.

There are, of course, many cost-effective approaches to the fast evaluation of particular classes of algorithms. But, generally it is difficult to compare or evaluate various approaches. By using Fig. 1, one can start with algorithms, select data and program structures, and then determine what kinds of architectural features are necessary. Or, one can start with a given architecture and determine the kinds of computations that it can appropriately handle. Notice that programming language details are only incidental to this discussion; the individual constructs of any language can be mapped to particular points in Fig. 1.

Fig. 1 may be interpreted at the level of individual program statements or for larger "chunks" of program, letting the "worst" program and data structure in a "chunk" represent the whole, if it will dominate the required execution time. Similarly, from the architectural point of view, one or more FAPAS stages that dominate the computation time can be used to represent a given computation. This can be a subtle point because the data structure may change as it moves through the FAPAS stages; for example, in the Cray-1, dense arrays may be fetched but only sparsely changed and then stored densely.

The scalar and regular array access parts of Fig. 1 are discussed at length in [Kuck82]. In that discussion, we mentioned the difficulties in executing array operations caused by conditional branching. The essence of the problem is not in the program statement (conditional branch) but rather in the data structure (sparse array), as is clear from similar difficulties caused by data that is input in a sparse form. So, in this paper we will concentrate on the lower parts of Fig. 1 that deal directly with sparse data structures, regardless of their reason for arising.

To understand the meaning of Fig. 1, assume we have a good parallel algorithm or program and wish to decide how it will perform using certain architectural features. If it is a "good" parallel algorithm and its data structures are all scalar, then by definition there will be no loop (iterative or recursive). We can use fast tree processors [Davi72], [Kuhn79], or simply evaluate it serially.

If it has regularly indexed array or string data structures, then one of three program dependence graphs must arise in loops. If the loop has no dependence cycles, an SEA machine can deliver excellent performance (with sufficiently large data structures) as is evidenced in the array processors and vector supercomputers. The MES systems also perform well using doall control. If there is a dependence cycle in which all right-hand side expressions are linear combinations of left-hand side variables (Boolean or arithmetic), we have a linear cycle and many fast algorithms have been developed to solve them on SEA machines [Same77], [WiSa82]. These include simple reductions on most vector supercomputers, general first-order recurrences on the Burroughs BSP, and wave-front algorithms (for high-order recurrences) on parallel processors or systolic arrays. Here again, the MES system offers no particular advantage and similar algorithms may be used, or doacr may be used depending on the details of a given program. If a nonlinear cycle arises, SEA machines are unable to provide any speedup of consequence, but MES machines are often able to provide good speedups via doacr control. It is noteworthy that special cases of Boolean nonlinear recurrences can achieve good speedup via special hardware. General, low-order (<3) Boolean recurrences can be solved by techniques described in [BaGK82] and high-order ones arising in sorting and merging can be handled by Batcher networks [Batc68]. Note that Boolean recurrences arise in many numerical and nonnumerical programs simply due to conditional branching, when the algorithm or program is transformed to its most parallel form

[Kuck76].

The lower parts of Fig. 1 deal with "irregularly" indexed data. For example, the Cyber 205 has difficulties in accessing memory for arrays with anything but stride 1 and the Cray-1 has problems with certain strides (while the situation is reversed between the Cyber 205 and Cray-1 for very sparse array access). Generally, the three program constructs discussed above should be presented here again for each data structure. However, because of the difficulty in handling cyclic dependences and sparse data together, we will combine linear and nonlinear cycles for this discussion.

The following sections of the paper discuss in detail the various cases shown in Fig. 1. Section 3 deals with the SEA processing of sparse arrays and very sparse arrays, while Section 4 deals with these data structures on MES architectures. One can conclude immediately from Fig. 1 that as data structures become more complex, SEA machines become more difficult to exploit and MES systems become more attractive.

2.1. Sparse Array Operations

We will carefully distinguish the informal notion of sparse and dense arrays from the physical representation of arrays in a machine; this may be in memory, processors, or interconnection networks. We will refer to three physical representations of arrays. A *complete array* is represented in such a way that any element's position in the representation determines its indices, and vice versa, and the array contains no null values.

An *expanded array* differs from a complete array only in that it may contain null values. When stored, a *null value* does not affect any memory location. When computed on, it does not affect the result.

A *packed array* has a representation that associates auxiliary information with an array to determine the indices of each element. This information may be in the form of *tag words*, one associated with each packed data word (stored in any order), or it may be a *control bit string* which indicates the position in the complete array of each data element in the ordered, packed array [Kogg81].

Intuitively, from an algorithmic point of view, *dense arrays* contain mostly interesting values (e.g., nonzeros) while *sparse arrays* contain a relatively large number of uninteresting values (e.g., zeros). We shall further distinguish merely sparse arrays from those that are very sparse arrays. Since all of these distinctions are made for purposes of saving memory space and processing time, they must necessarily depend on machine details and hence cannot be defined in absolute terms. Roughly speaking, however, it is probably almost always true that one would treat arrays with 80% to 90% or more of interesting values as dense arrays. Sparse arrays would range from those regarded as dense down to the area of 10% to 30% interesting values. The rest would be treated as *very sparse arrays*.

Notice that in an idealized computer with no overhead time required for accessing sparse arrays, the breakpoints are determined by space requirements only. In this case, sparse arrays would be stored using bit strings and very sparse arrays would use tag words. The exact breakpoints would depend on array sizes and machine details [BaGK83], [Kuck70].

It should also be realized that in real computers various cases arise naturally from program constructs. For example, in SEA machines, conditional branching naturally leads to control bit strings to be used in handling complete arrays. In MES machines, conditional branching in a complete array computation leads to independent address generation for random elements of a complete array; thus, a packed representation of the array (usually with tag words) may be used everywhere but in the memory for bandwidth savings over SEA systems.

When subscripted subscripts (or indirect addressing) appear in a loop on an SEA or MES machine, we naturally are led to tag words and packed representations of complete arrays. If arrays are stored packed, then of course we can process them packed, or we may expand them first.

To compare several approaches to handling sparse and very sparse data, let us consider the following simple model of the flow of data from memory to memory. We will assume here that all data is stored in memory as complete arrays. The data undergoes the five conceptual steps of being fetched, aligned for processing, processed, aligned for storage, and stored as shown in Fig. 2. The data can be converted from complete to packed upon being fetched (as in the MES case) and we denote this by C → P in Fig. 2. Alternatively, it can be converted during alignment for processing as in the Cyber 205 compress and expand case (see Fig. 2). In the Cyber 205 [Cybe81], this is accomplished by a complete memory-to-memory pass, but in principle it is a preprocessing data alignment operation. Next, we see that data is processed either in complete or packed form. After processing, it must be prepared for storage. In the Cray-1 [Cray81], new values are merged in the vector registers with old values fetched from memory. Thus, the new values are made into an expanded array and only the changed positions are written into the old complete array; we denote this by C → E → C in a post-processing alignment step in Fig. 2. In the Cyber 205, hardware is provided to use control bit strings to store only the desired values using a controlled store instruction (cf., Fig. 2). Finally, the Cyber 205, after computing on a packed array in the compress/expand case, expands the packed array in a post-processing alignment and then stores the expanded array.

Thus, we see that a great variety of approaches can be used in dealing with sparse arrays. In later sections, we will discuss these ideas in more detail.

2.2. MES Synchronization

Broadly speaking, there are two classes of methods for ensuring proper synchronization between variables inside loops:

A) Generate-Use Synchronization

Array Representations

System	Computation Type	Fetch	Align	Process	Align	Store
Cray-1	Sparse	C	C	C	C → E → C	C
Cyber 205 (controlled store)	Sparse	C	C	C	C → E	E → C
Cyber 205 (compress/ expand)	Very Sparse	C → P	P	P	P	P → C
Cyber 205 (gather/ scatter	Very Sparse	C → P	P	P	P	P → C
SEA	Sparse or Very Sparse	C → P	P	P	P	P → C
MES	Sparse or Very Sparse	C → P	P	P	P	P → C

Fig. 2. Techniques for Handling Sparse Arrays

The methods in this class guarantee that each dependence arc is satisfied in executing the program. This can be the fastest way to execute a loop in parallel, but it can also become rather complex. At one extreme, we can associate full or empty information with each variable, and also include an integer with each full variable that denotes the number of uses necessary to make it empty. Each time it is read, the count is reduced by one. If implemented in hardware, this can be regarded as "state" or "tag" information that effectively renames a variable dynamically. This can become quite complex if some uses of the variable are executed conditionally.

A practical implementation of this method is to use only a "full" or "empty" bit in conjunction with "test empty-write-set full" and "test full-read-set empty" instruction types as in the Denelcor HEP [Smit82]. If a variable is to be used multiple times, it can first be written to multiple locations, thus implementing a renaming method by use of multiple memory locations.

Another approach to this synchronization method is via the single-assignment rule which disallows multiple writes to any variable. This, of course, obviates the need to count the number of uses of a variable. A variable must be set full before it is used, but emptying and reusing variables are unnecessary concepts.

For straight-line scalar code and most array codes, a compiler or programmer can easily rename variables to satisfy the single-assignment rule. However, if one of several conditional assignments to a variable is desired before it is to be used, they must be lumped into one statement and not spread over several assignment statements in various segments of code, unless greater implementation complexity can be tolerated. The dataflow architectures use languages that require the programmer to obey such rules.

For subscripted subscript array assignments, static renaming is impossible since the particular array elements to be changed are not determined until run-time. Furthermore, data-flow or. single-assignment languages cannot support algorithms or computations that require this concept. For programs that contain multiple assignments to the same array with subscripted subscripts, the methods of this paper are effective, however.

If generate-use synchronization is implemented by some kind of busy-wait operation, it can lead to substantial bandwidth waste. For example, if implemented in the memory, busy-wait synchronization from processor i can consume interconnection network and memory bandwidth until iteration i is reached.

An ideal method of generate-use synchronization is to have a processor that generates a value, trigger a processor that needs it to proceed. This may require interprocessor signalling that is expensive to implement and/or slow, particularly when jobs are dynamically assigned to processors at run-time.

B) Iteration Delay Synchronization

The idea of this method is to delay the initiation of subsequent iterations sufficiently long to guarantee that synchronization of all variables is complete.

Iteration delay synchronization can be implemented in various ways. A simple one is to have each processor execute a no-operation loop for a predetermined number of iterations and then begin a generate-use synchronization procedure. This can lead to performances that are worse than a straight generate-use method, because the delay has to be conservatively chosen and may be much too long on a particular run (e.g., in a loop containing conditional branching). The speed loss due to conservative delays must be balanced against that incurred from lost bandwidth by method A, however.

Using iteration delay synchronization, if a loop of s statements and N iterations is executed using *doacr* control on an MES machine, we can achieve a speedup of $O(Ns/((N-1)d+s))$, where d is the delay between starting successive iterations. Note that if d = 0, we have the *doall* case. By employing generate-use synchronization, it may turn out that some iterations can be started earlier based on run-time tests. This has the effect of reducing (or eliminating) d for particular iterations and thus reducing the (N-1)d term in the speedup denominator. We can rewrite the speedup using a coefficient $0 \leq \alpha \leq 1$ as $O(Ns/((N-1)\alpha d + s))$, where α represents the overall amount of delay we can avoid in executing the whole *doacr*. Clearly, in the best case $\alpha = 0$ and we have achieved the *doall* case. Illustrations of this idea will be presented in Section 4. The above analysis ignores delay factors due to interconnection networks or memories.

C) A third type of synchronization will be used in this paper to synchronize all processors in the system. We call this barrier synchronization, and it is effectively a join of all processors followed by a fork to all processors. We denote it as shown on step 3 of Fig. 4.

3. Parallel Processing on SEA Machines

3.1. Array Operations with Sparse Array-Access

Most pipeline and parallel computer systems built have used control bits or tags to handle sparse arrays. Typically, complete arrays are accessed from a parallel memory and then control bits or tags are applied in the processor(s) (Cray-1, Cyber 205). This wastes memory bandwidth because not all of the data accessed is used. It also may waste processor bandwidth by wasting processor cycles. For example, in parallel machines the normal procedure has been to disable certain processors. In pipeline processors, typically all of the results are computed and the control bits are used to select the desired results for storage.

The above sketch describes exactly the procedure carried out in the memory-to-memory Cyber 205 using controlled stores (cf., Fig. 2). In the register-to-register Cray-1, a vector register merge instruction must be used to form the correct result before storage. Thus, two extra instructions are required--one to fetch 64 elements of the vector into which we will store, and one to merge this with the newly-computed results under bit-vector control. Thus, redundant stores and fetches are carried out (cf., Fig. 2).

A somewhat disruptive side-effect of this arises in handling arithmetic exceptions on the Cray-1. Since control bits are not used in the processing step, spurious arithmetic exceptions may arise (in elements that one does not mean to be computing). Thus, users typically disable interrupts, generate special values (e.g., computed infinity) that are properly used in subsequent operations, and then observe any difficulties in the final results (or at checkpoints). This in effect produces very imprecise interrupts which can be tracked down by rerunning the program with interrupts enabled. On the Cyber 205, in contrast, interrupts are masked by control bits so spurious arithmetic exceptions are suppressed.

The memory/control unit scheme of [BaGK83] can effectively eliminate both memory and processor waste, however. In this method, control bits are generated by evaluating conditional expressions in parallel. Those control bits are stored in a smart memory called the Control Function Compressor (CFC) shown in Fig. 3. Each column in CFC corresponds to a memory/processor module. Each row stores one bit per column. "1"("0") indicates that the corresponding statement is (is not) executed on that iteration. Our CFC supplies the iteration value of the topmost "1" in each column which is subsequently converted into a memory address by the Memory Address Generator (MAG). Therefore, since only those operands that are operated upon are fetched from memories, no memory or processor bandwidth is wasted (except possibly at the end of the array). As long as all complete array indices are linear functions of iteration variables, all operands can be fetched, proper pairs of operands aligned, operated upon, and stored back to memories in parallel. Furthermore, this set of actions can be pipelined at the maximum rate.

3.2. Sparse Recurrences on Array Machines

Parallel linear recurrence solvers may be used on parallel or pipeline processors to achieve substantial speedups [Gajs81]. When systems of the form $x = Ax + c$ have an A matrix that is very sparse (within the diagonals), two possible approaches exist. One is to ignore the sparseness and use standard methods. The other is to try to take advantage of the sparseness to speed up the computation. This alternative, however, can be rather complex to carry out and may yield little advantage.

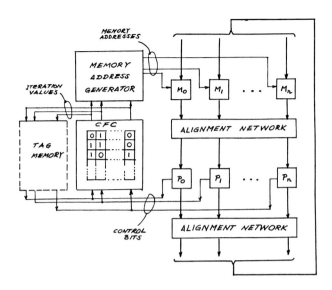

Fig. 3. A Scheme for Handling Sparse Arrays on SEA Machines

If we have a first-order linear recurrence with a number of zeros on the subdiagonal, the recurrence system could be broken into a number of smaller systems, all of which could be solved at once. However, most existing machines can only handle one system at a time, so they must be solved one after the other. Thus, if the complete system of size n can be solved in k log n steps, r derived systems (of equal size) could be solved in perhaps rk log(n/r) steps, which may, in fact, be much more time than k log n.

An additional problem here is that the process of breaking one system into smaller ones may be very time-consuming itself. Commonly, we could expect the A matrix zeros to be determined by conditional branching, so a run-time decision would be required, thus making it even more unlikely that any time can be saved over treating the problem as one big recurrence.

If an architecture allows several recurrences to be evaluated simultaneously and if the breakup process can be handled quickly, then the approach may have some merit, of course. This might be possible on a full-scale implementation of the S1 or other MEA systems.

A special class of linear recurrences is formed by the reductions or remote-term recurrences. Normally, these appear simple compared to the general case discussed above. But when conditionals are included, general recurrences may become simpler to solve, while reductions do not change. Consider the sum-reduction with conditionals:

> **do** $i \leftarrow 1, n$
> **if** $a_i \neq x$
> **then** $t \leftarrow t + a_i$
> **endo**

Notice that there is no possibility of the conditional breaking this dependence chain as there was for a general recurrence. Here the scalar variable t is carried throughout the computation. The computation can, however, be transformed in several ways for possible speedup.

One transformation would be to first pack the a vector to remove all a_i with the value x, producing a vector of length $m \leq n$. The resulting vector could then be reduced in time proportional to log m. Another transformation would be to set to zero all a_i with the value x and then reduce the whole vector in time proportional to log n. Equivalently, a bit-vector can be used to indicate which elements are to be used as operands. Obviously, machine details and the relative values of m and n will dictate which method is faster.

The Cyber 205 has implementations of various reduction instructions and these may also be executed under bit-vector control in time roughly equivalent to that required for dense vector reduction. In the Cray-1, there are no reduction instructions per se. Thus, one must merge zeros into the operand vector under bit-vector control and then carry out the reduction in the ordinary way.

Yet another solution would be to use the Control-Function Compressor shown in Fig. 3. First, control bits are generated by comparing a_i and x for all i. Secondly, each processor sum-reduces all array elements with control bit equal to 1 in one column of the CFC. Thirdly, all partial sums residing in processors are reduced in time proportional to log p, where p is the number of processors. Therefore, the entire reduction can be accomplished in time proportional to $(m/p) + \log p$. In this case, it is assumed that there is approximately an equal number of 1s in each column of the CFC and that array indices are at most a linear function of the iteration variable i.

3.3. Array Operations with Very Sparse Array-Access

3.3.1. Densly Stored Arrays

The Cray-1 does not provide any support for very sparse access. There is only one selective-merge instruction (already mentioned in Section 3.1) which supports all sparse processing. Cyber 205 has two very useful instructions. The gather instruction collects data into a vector register from random locations in the memory through a vector of index values. Similarly, the scatter instruction distributes data into random memory locations. Both instructions are only 2-3 times slower than regular vector instructions that access regular data with stride 1. Gather/scatter instructions are only useful when all index values are different. When dependences are created, the program must be executed sequentially. For example, whenever $f_i = g_j$, for some i and j, dependences are created in the following program:

$$
\begin{aligned}
&\textbf{do } i \leftarrow 1, n \\
S_1:\quad & f_i \leftarrow \dots \\
S_2:\quad & g_i \leftarrow \dots \\
S_3:\quad & A(f_i) \leftarrow x_i \\
S_4:\quad & y_i \leftarrow A(g_i) \\
&\textbf{endo}
\end{aligned}
$$

An approach that allows parallel execution without any knowledge of the f_i is to build hardware capable of breaking any dependences between elements of A, as shown in Fig. 4. For the program segment shown above, we first compute statements S_1 and S_2 and store them in a tag memory with n memory modules. A tag consists of the iteration value and the corresponding value of f_i or g_i. They are stored in the memory module M_i where $i = f_i$ mod n or $i = g_i$ mod n. Those tags are colored in such a way that each statement is assigned one color. Assuming that $f_i = 1, 2, 7, 4, 3, 2$ and $g_i = 6, 1, 4, 2, 4, 4$, for $i = 1, 2, 3, 4, 5, 6$, then the storage map shown in Fig. 4 would be created for a tag memory with four memory modules. This requires a sorting of the size equivalent to the number n of processor/memory elements. However, the sorting time is transparent, since sorting can be overlapped with computation of the next group of $f_i's$ and $g_i's$. Each processor would execute statements S_3 or S_4 using the arguments only from one memory module. The statement S_3 is executed if the tag is of color s_1, and S_4 is executed if the tag carries color s_2.

Although there is no contention in the tag memory, contention may be created in the memory that stores arrays x and y. However, if in any row in the tag memory all iteration values are different, modulo n, then the entire row can be executed at once.

$$\textbf{do} \quad i \leftarrow 1, n$$

$$S_1: \quad f_i \leftarrow \ldots .$$

$$S_2: \quad g_i \leftarrow \ldots .$$

$$S_3: \quad A(f_i) \leftarrow x_i$$

$$S_4: \quad y_i \leftarrow A(g_i)$$

$$\textbf{endo}$$

M_0	M_1	M_2	M_3
$(3,4,s_2)$	$(1,1,s_1)$	$(1,6,s_2)$	$(3,7,s_1)$
$(4,4,s_1)$	$(2,1,s_2)$	$(2,2,s_1)$	$(5,3,s_1)$
$(5,4,s_2)$		$(4,2,s_2)$	
$(6,4,s_2)$		$(6,2,s_1)$	

iteration   color

value

f_i or g_i

Fig. 4. Tag Memory for Execution of Statements
with Subscripted Subscripts

3.3.2. Sparse Processing of Sparsely Stored Arrays

So far we have considered sparse processing of arrays that are stored in complete form. Here, we will consider arrays that are stored in the packed form.

An efficient scheme for processing very sparse arrays is a modification of the description presented in Section 3.2 and shown in Fig. 3. For any given array X, only nonzero elements are stored in the memory. An element x_i is stored in the memory module (i mod n). For each element x_i that is in memory, a tag (i,d) is stored in the tag memory, where d is the displacement of x_i from the earliest element of x stored. For simplicity, we will assume that the tag memory is a separate memory with direct access to CFC (shown dotted in Fig. 3) and that it contains the same number of n memory modules as the main memory. For example, when two arrays, A and B, must be added conditionally and stored into the C array, the addition is actually performed only if there is an A-tag, B-tag, or a C-tag in the tag memory, and the corresponding control bit is 1 in the CFC. A simple way to accomplish the sparse execution is to use the CFC twice: first, to compute new control bits and, secondly, to fetch the memory elements and perform required additions. The first task is accomplished by fetching all control bits with value 1, and computing corresponding index values which are then used to determine by associative search in the tag memory whether corresponding array elements are in the memory. This associative search is over the first couple of elements in the tag memory. For example, if control bits are coming from an IF statement with equal probability for both branches, then only the two or three top elements in tag-memory will be searched on the average. If the A-tag, B-tag, and C-tag are not in the tag memory, the corresponding control bit in the CFC is set to 0. Therefore, when the CFC is used for the second time, either one operand is in the main memory or the result must be zeroed.

This is a very efficient scheme, since only array elements that cause change in the C-array values are ever fetched and operated upon. The price for this efficiency is an overhead consisting of three associative searches of the tag memory. For details, see [BaGK83].

3.4. Recurrence Operations with Very Sparse Array-Access

Recurrences are very difficult to execute efficiently, as already mentioned in Section 3.2. It is even more difficult when the coefficient matrix is stored as a very sparse array.

However, reductions can be handled the same way as described in Section 3.2 (Fig. 3), by first reducing all array elements in one memory module using the Control-Function Compressor and Tag Memory, and then performing a reduction on n partial results generated by n processors.

4. Parallel Processing on MES Machines

4.1. doall with Sparse Array-Access

This case provides one of the standard arguments for an advantage of MES machines over SEA machines. Each processor can follow a different path through a loop body, thus providing more efficient performance than array machines can deliver because of their lock-step behavior.

Prog. 1 will illustrate the method. We consider two methods of executing Prog. 1 using four processors. In Fig. 5, we show generate-use synchronization. Here, *empty* (x) means that users of x must wait until x is assigned a value; it corresponds to setting the state of x to *empty*. On the other hand, *full* (x) means that x can be used at any time; it corresponds to setting the state of x to *full*. We assume that the assignment operation sets the left-hand-side variable to *full* and that all input arrays are initialized to *full*. Notice the barrier synchronization is used here to ensure that all *empty* instructions are executed before any of the subsequent assignments are made. For simplicity, we measure time in terms of statements executed. Fig. 5 shows the fastest possible execution of Prog. 1, because data is used as soon as possible. However, spurious memory requests may be generated in attempting to access variables that are *empty*.

Notice that faster execution is possible if Prog. 1 is restructured properly. One time-step can be saved if the assignments to d_i and a_i are reversed in order. By further perturbing the order of statements across the f_i, the overall time can be reduced to just seven steps.

In Fig. 6, we show iteration-delay synchronization to execute Prog. 1. Here, a compiler can determine that all variables requiring synchronization will have been set *full* if subsequent iterations are delayed by two time steps; regardless of which branch is taken, both a_i and d_i will be ready for use by other processors. Thus, a fixed delay of two statements is provided in Fig. 6. Notice that this leads to a total of eleven time steps in contrast to ten for Fig. 5. This method can be more memory-efficient than the previous because it does not generate any spurious memory requests.

4.2. doacr with Sparse Array-Access

Dependence cycles may be handled using *doacr* in a manner similar to the *doall* discussion of Section 4.1. For dense arrays, a multiprocessor might best use one of the standard fast recurrence solvers for low-order linear systems, but for high-order or nonlinear recurrences, *doacr* is probably preferable. However, when a conditional statement is used with a recurrence, *doacr* may be used in a very efficient manner, regardless of order or linearity. The efficiency of the method does depend on the

Prog. 1

$$\textbf{doall } i \leftarrow 1, 4$$

$$\textbf{if } q_i < r_i$$

$$\textbf{then} \quad a_i \leftarrow b_i + c_i ;$$

$$\textbf{else} \quad d_i \leftarrow e_i + a_{i-1} ;$$

$$a_i \leftarrow m_i + n_i ;$$

$$\textbf{fi}$$

$$f_i \leftarrow a_i + g_i;$$

$$h_i \leftarrow d_{i-1} + g_i;$$

$$\textbf{endoall} ;$$

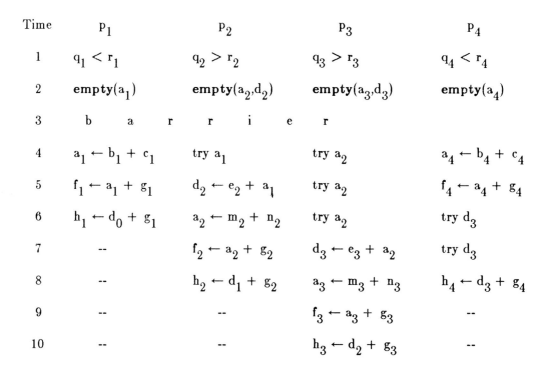

Time	P_1	P_2	P_3	P_4
1	$q_1 < r_1$	$q_2 > r_2$	$q_3 > r_3$	$q_4 < r_4$
2	$\textbf{empty}(a_1)$	$\textbf{empty}(a_2,d_2)$	$\textbf{empty}(a_3,d_3)$	$\textbf{empty}(a_4)$
3	b a r	r i e	r	
4	$a_1 \leftarrow b_1 + c_1$	try a_1	try a_2	$a_4 \leftarrow b_4 + c_4$
5	$f_1 \leftarrow a_1 + g_1$	$d_2 \leftarrow e_2 + a_1$	try a_2	$f_4 \leftarrow a_4 + g_4$
6	$h_1 \leftarrow d_0 + g_1$	$a_2 \leftarrow m_2 + n_2$	try a_2	try d_3
7	--	$f_2 \leftarrow a_2 + g_2$	$d_3 \leftarrow e_3 + a_2$	try d_3
8	--	$h_2 \leftarrow d_1 + g_2$	$a_3 \leftarrow m_3 + n_3$	$h_4 \leftarrow d_3 + g_4$
9	--	--	$f_3 \leftarrow a_3 + g_3$	--
10	--	--	$h_3 \leftarrow d_2 + g_3$	--

Fig. 5. Prog. 1 with Generate-Use Synchronization

Time	P_1	P_2	P_3	P_4
1	$q_1 < r_1$	$q_2 > r_2$	$q_3 > r_3$	$q_4 < r_4$
2	$\text{empty}(a,d_1)$	$\text{empty}(a_2,d_2)$	$\text{empty}(a_3,d_3)$	$\text{empty}(a_4)$
3	$a_1 \leftarrow b_1 + c_1$	$\text{delay}(2)$	$\text{delay}(4)$	$\text{delay}(6)$
4	$f_1 \leftarrow a_1 + g_1$	no op	no op	no op
5	$h_1 \leftarrow d_0 + g_1$	$d_2 \leftarrow e_2 + a_1$	no op	no op
6		$a_2 \leftarrow m_2 + n_2$	no op	no op
7		$f_2 \leftarrow a_2 + g_2$	$d_3 \leftarrow e_3 + a_2$	no op
8		$h_2 \leftarrow d_1 + g_2$	$a_3 \leftarrow m_3 + n_3$	no op
9			$f_3 \leftarrow a_3 + g_3$	$a_4 \leftarrow b_4 + c_4$
10			$h_3 \leftarrow d_2 + g_3$	$f_4 \leftarrow a_4 + g_4$
11				$h_4 \leftarrow d_3 + g_4$

Fig. 6. Prog. 1 with Iteration Delay Synchronization

conditional statement breaking the cycle into a number of short dependence chains. We will use a simple linear recurrence to illustrate the method which simply ripples dependences across processors in a serial manner.

Consider Prog. 2 with two synchronization techniques. Fig. 7 illustrates generate-use synchronization and Fig. 8 illustrates iteration delay synchronization. Notice that for this execution there are two dependence chains, each of length 1. If the chains are not broken by the conditional, the method still yields a good speedup if there are many statements in the loop.

The delay here is one statement per processor, as dictated by the first-order recurrence. If this program were executed on a large number of processors, and if the conditional statement broke the recurrence frequently, the generate-use synchronization could provide a substantially greater speedup (as was indicated in Section 2).

4.3. doall with Very Sparse Array-Access

When irregular subscripts are encountered, severe constraints may be placed on speedup potential. For example, consider the following loop:

```
do   i ← 1, n
     f_i ← ~
     A(f_i) ← ~
endo
```

where there may be other statements in the loop but none involving the A array. If the index f_i forms a set f of distinct integers for all i, then we have a *doall* that can be executed completely in parallel. If not all the f_i are distinct, the loop can be broken into several *doall* loops *to be executed one after the other*. Such knowledge about the f_i could be provided by the user in the form of assertions.

Prog. 2

```
doacr  i ← 1, 4

    if  q_i < r_i

    then  x_i ← x_{i-1} * y_i ;

    else  x_i ← z_i ;

    fi

    w_i ← x_i * a_i ;

endoacr ;
```

Time	p_1	p_2	p_3	p_4
1	$q_1 < r_1$	$q_2 < r_2$	$q_3 > r_3$	$q_4 < r_4$
2	$empty(x_1)$	$empty(x_2)$	$empty(x_3)$	$empty(x_4)$
3	B A R	R I E	R	
4	$x_1 \leftarrow x_0 * y_1$	try x_1	$x_3 \leftarrow z_3$	try x_3
5	$w_1 \leftarrow x_1 * a_1$	$x_2 \leftarrow x_1 * y_2$	$w_3 \leftarrow x_3 * a_3$	$x_4 \leftarrow x_3 * y_4$
6		$w_2 \leftarrow x_2 * a_2$		$w_4 \leftarrow x_4 * a_4$

Fig. 7. Prog. 2 with Generate-Use Synchronization

Time	p_1	p_2	p_3	p_4
1	$q_1 < v_1$	$q_2 < r_2$	$q_3 > r_3$	$q_4 < r_4$
2	$empty(x_1)$	$empty(x_2)$	$empty(x_3)$	$empty(x_4)$
3	$x_1 \leftarrow x_0 * y_1$	delay(1)	delay(2)	delay(3)
4	$w_1 \leftarrow x_1 * a_1$	$x_2 \leftarrow x_1 * y_1$	no op	no op
5		$w_2 \leftarrow x_2 * a_2$	$x_3 \leftarrow z_3$	no op
6			$w_3 \leftarrow x_3 * a_3$	$x_4 \leftarrow x_3 * y_4$
7				$w_4 \leftarrow x_4 * a_4$

Fig. 8. Prog. 2 with Iteration Delay Synchronization

Alternatively, if the f_i are input data, tests could be done at compile time, or in other cases the f_i could be tested after being computed. Lacking any information about the f_i, such a loop must be executed sequentially, unless special hardware is available.

Hardware can be brought to bear on solving this problem in several ways. A modification of the NYU Ultracomputer switch [GoKr81] could handle the above loop by finding for each subset of f with identical elements, those f_i with maximum i values, and storing only these values. This would require a *fetch-and-max* operation to be added to that machine design.

Software approaches can be used on the above loop to examine the set f to determine the first repeated value, break the set just before this value, and execute these index values i as a *doall*. The procedure is repeated when the first *doall* is finished, and so on, until i equals n. Generalizing the procedure to loops with multiple occurrences of an array on the right-hand-side or left-hand-side is not difficult. This can also be implemented in hardware by generalizing the notion of *empty* and *full* to include a number of state bits associated with each memory location, which can be tested before accessing memory. Such an approach is being designed for the Cedar system [YeZh83].

4.4. doacr with Very Sparse Array-Access

Consider the cyclic loop

$$
\begin{aligned}
&\textbf{do} \qquad i \leftarrow 1, n \\
&\qquad\qquad i \leftarrow \sim \\
&\qquad\qquad r_i \leftarrow \sim \\
&\qquad\qquad A(l_i) \leftarrow A(r_i) + \ ... \\
&\textbf{endo}
\end{aligned}
$$

In a number of special cases, we can immediately turn this into a *doall*. These could be asserted by the programmer, or in some cases they could be detected at compile time, or code could be compiled to test the index sets l and r for these cases at run time and execute the *doall* code conditionally. In the general case we must face a recurrence, of course.

The general case can be handled as a *doacr* by a combination of the methods of Sections 4.2 and 4.3 [Kuck83]. By testing the index sets as in Section 4.3, it is possible to break the loop into a series of recurrences, each of which does not contain any output dependences. Thus, the overall computation consists of executing a series of such recurrences. Each such recurrence is handled as in Section 4.2 with generate-use synchronization, since all the v_i values are *full* (initially) except those for which l_1 variables are computed within each recurrence, and for these we must wait. The Cedar system hardware mentioned in Section 4.3 is also being designed to handle this case.

5. Conclusion

The performance of a parallel algorithm or program computation depends strongly on three things: the data structure, the program structure, and the machine structure used. The relationship between these three factors is outlined in Fig. 1 and discussed throughout this paper. A machine designer or machine user would be well-advised to carry out comparisons like those done here for the particular algorithms in which he is interested, before committing himself to one approach or another. While some approaches are more expensive of hardware than others, there can also be tremendous performance differences as a result.

The ideas of this paper can also be carried over to other data structures, e.g., trees, graphs, etc. However, the program structures are exhaustive and apply to all programming languages. Of course, the program structures can be refined to reflect more details in particular cases, as can the machine structures.

6. Acknowledgments

We thank Ron Cytron, Clyde Kruskal, Alex Viedenbaum, and Mike Wolfe for their comments. We especially appreciate the production skills of Mrs. Vivian Alsip and Mrs. June Wingler.

REFERENCES

[BaGK80] U. Banerjee, D. Gajski, and D. Kuck, "Array Machine Control Units for Loops Containing IFs," *Proc. of the 1980 Int'l. Conf. on Parallel Processing,* Harbor Springs, MI, pp. 28-36, Aug. 1980.

[BaGK83] U. Banerjee, D. Gajski, and D. Kuck, "Accessing Sparse Arrays in Parallel Memories," *Journ. of VLSI and Computer Systems,* Vol. 1, No. 1, pp. 69-100, Spring 1983.

[Cray81] Cray Research, Inc., *Cray-1 S Series Hardware Reference Manual,* Pub. No. HR-0808, rev. B-01, Nov. 1981.

[Cybe81] Control Data Corp., *CDC Cyber 200 Model 205 Computer System Hardware Reference Manual,* Pub. No. 60256020, rev. A, March 1981.

[Cytr82] R. G. Cytron, "Improved Compilation Methods for Multiprocessors," M.S. thesis, Univ. of Illinois at Urbana-Champaign, Dept. of Comput. Sci. Rpt. No. 82-1088, May 1982.

[Gajs81] D. D. Gajski, "An Algorithm for Solving Linear Recurrence Systems on Parallel and Pipelined Machines," *IEEE Trans. on Computers,* Vol. C-30, No. 3, pp. 190-206, Mar. 1981.

[GaKP81] D. D. Gajski, D. J. Kuck, and D. A. Padua, "Dependence Driven Computation," *Proc. of the COMPCON 81 Spring Computer Conf.,* San Francisco, CA, pp. 168-172, Feb. 1981.

[GoKr81] A. Gottlieb and C. P. Kruskal, "Coordinating Parallel Processors: A Partial Unification," *Computer Architecture News,* Vol. 9, No. 6, pp. 16-24, Oct. 1981.

[Kogg81] P. M. Kogge, *The Architecture of Pipelined Computers,* McGraw-Hill, 1981.

[Kuck81] D. J. Kuck, "Automatic Program Restructuring for High-Speed Computation," Invited paper, *Proc. of CONPAR 81, Conf. on Analysing Problem-Classes and Programming for Parallel Computing,* Nurnberg, F. R. Germany, ed. by W. Handler, pp. 66-84, June 1981 (Springer-Verlag).

[Kuck82] D. J. Kuck, "High-Speed Machines and Their Compilers," *Proc. of the 1979 Int'l. Conf. on Parallel Processing,* pp. 5-16, Aug. 1979.

[Kuck83] D. J. Kuck, "Sparse Re Solution on Cedar," unpublished memo January 1983.

[Padu79] D. A. Padua Haiek, "Multiprocessors: Discussion of Some Theoretical and Practical Problems," Ph.D. thesis, Univ. of Ill. at Urb.-Champ., Dept. of Comput. Sci. Rpt. No. 79-990, Oct. 1979.

[Smit82] B. S. Smith, "Architecture and Applications of the HEP Multiprocessor Computer System," *Proc. of the Int'l. Society for Optical Engineering,* Vol. 198, pp. 241-248, 1982.

[ZeZh83] P. C. Yew and C. Q. Zhu, Cedar document in preparation, July 1983.

PART 3

ALGORITHMS AND APPLICATIONS

EXPERIENCE IN EXPLOITING LARGE SCALE PARALLELISM

D. Parkinson
Queen Mary College
London

Introduction

A 4096 processor DAP - a SIMD system has been in active use at
Queen Mary College, London, since summer 1980. The machine has
been providing a service to a world wide community in a production
environment. Descriptions of the DAP can be found in [1] and a
recent paper [2] summarises a number of the performance
measurements obtained. In this paper I wish to concentrate on
more general aspects of the experience gained in order that we can
give some insight into the magnetude of the task that must be
tackled if it is ever going to be possible to create transportable
and efficient code across various parallel computers
organisations. The emphasis is on efficiency as there is little
problem in obtaining portability of inefficient programs. The
indications of our current results are that efficient portable
programs will require the development high level languages and
associated compilers/interpretors with the ability to transform
programs with the skill of a high quality mathematician. It is my
belief that it will be a large number of years before suitable
tools are created, in fact so long that we will consider obsolete
current programs in low level languages such as FORTRAN.

This pessimistic prediction is offered as a challenge to the
optimists who seem to believe that either

   a)   one can start with a FORTRAN program and extract the
        parallelism or

   b)   can derive new languages which express all the
        parallelism and then implement these languages
        efficiently.

The rest of the paper will attempt to present some of the
challenges involved in attempting to program a simple problem -
the solution of linear equations on an SIMD system.

NATO ASI Series, Vol. F7
High-Speed Computation. Edited by J. S. Kowalik
© Springer-Verlag Berlin Heidelberg 1984

How do I solve N equations on a given processor system?

The full treatment of the correct strategy for solving N linear
equations on a system with P processors is worthy of a whole book.
There is a growing literature which deals with specific topics,
one of the latest being ref. [3]. Here we can only treat a very
small section of the problem i.e. dense sets of equations on
systems with sufficient memory to hold all the coefficient matrix.

The first problem that comes to the notice of anybody creating a
library routine is the fact that any given processor system has a
fixed maximum number of processors and that this number hardly
ever appears to be the number of processors as recommended by
theory, e.g. ref [3], which examines algorithms with $O(N/2)$
processors. To emphasise the point in a typical day users of the
DAP ask for advice on how to solve 4 equations, 64 equations and
12000 equations! The number of processors is 4096 which is an
apparent mismatch to all these problems. However, very efficient
solutions were found to each case. The case of 4 equations was
resolved when it was discovered that the real problem was to solve
many thousands of independent sets and so a trivial implementation
of a standard serial algorithm was appropriate with each processor
solving completely a given problem. The important lesson being
that one must examine the context in which the problem set - or in
- FORTRAN jargon - we examined an outer loop. There is nothing
unusual about this phenomenon, only in rare cases do we find that
examination of innermost DO loops are adequate to provide adequate
amounts of parallelism. A not uncommon source of parallelism is
only indirectly implied in a program - i.e. that it is going to be
used a number of times and therefore one can consider increasing
the parallelism by doing multiple 'runs' simultaneously - a
beautiful challenge for the believers in automatic program
translation.

The problem with 12000 equations turned out to be really a problem
connected with the solution of a 8^4 mesh with 3 variables at each
cell. This is a very typical so-called sparse matrix problem and
is solved by well understood iterative techniques.

In both extremes of problem size the solution was found by
examining the context in which the problem arose. A general
result of practical parallel processing experience is that it is
even more necessary to examine the problem context than for serial
machines.

Gaussian Elimination on a multiprocessor system

The standard algorithm for solving a set of linear equations is a
fine example of a recursive descent technique. It is convenient
to identify four stages in the algorithm

Given N equations to solve defined by a coefficient matrix A(N,N) and
a RHS vector B(N).

Stage 1   -   Select an equation and a variable which appears
                in that equation - the Pivot equation and the
                Pivot variable.

Stage 2   -   Recast the Pivot equation into the form:
                Pivot variable = linear sum of all the other
                                 variables.

      2a   -   If there is only one equation skip to stage 5.

Stage 3   -   Use the result of stage 2 to eliminate the
                pivot variable from all the other equations.

Stage 4   -   Recursively re-enter the procedure to solve N-1
                unknowns using the coefficient matrix, obtained
                in stage 3.

Stage 5   -   Use the result(s) from stage 4 on the pivot
                equation to evaluate the pivot variable.

Stage 6   -   Exit from this call of the procedure.

Although this recursive definition will appear strange to a
FORTRAN programmer it represents faithfully the standard algorithm
for solving a set of equations with a single right hand side.

We can now examine the algorithm with the view of using it to
solve a given set of equations (N) with a fixed number of
processors (P).

The first thing we should notice is that the algorithm is applied
to a reducing set of equations and so the ratio number of
processors:instantaneous number of equations, is montonically
increasing so that although we may start with the task of solving
say 64 equations with 64 processors we eventually create a
subproblem which requires the solution of 8 equations with 64
processors, i.e. solving N equations with $O(N^2)$ processors and
therefore this task is very relevent even in todays small MIMD
systems.

That observation means that a full treatment of the task should examine the generalised algorithm.

Stage 1   -   Select m equations and m variables - the pivot set.

Stage 2   -   Solve the pivot set in terms of all other variables

    2a   -   If finished go to stage 6.

Stage 3   -   Eliminate the pivot variables from all remaining equations.

Stage 4   -   Re-enter the procedure to solve N-m equations.

Stage 5   -   Use the results from 4 to evaluate the pivot variables.

stage 6   -   Exit from this call of the procedure.

In terms of a more conventional vocabulary the modified algorithm can be viewed as a 'partitioned' or 'block' matrix algorithm using partitions of size m x m. The particular case of 2 x 2 partitions has been extensively studied by Evans and his co-workers [4] under the name of WZ algorithm. On a system with P processors blocks of size $\sqrt{p}$ * $\sqrt{p}$ seem to be optimum.

Before continuing with a discussion of block methods it is best to return to the simpler algorithm and examine the various stages more carefully.

Selection of Pivot Equations

The usual serial strategy for pivoting is column pivoting i.e. selecting the pivot equation to be that equation with the largest element in column one of the coefficient matrix. If we wish to copy this strategy in a parallel environment we have the task of selecting the largest member of a set of N elements using P processors.

The cost of this operation is strongly dependent on system architecture. The most common assumption is that the maximum element of p values held in p processors is computed in a time log p.t where t is some mythical universal operation time used for all operations. In any real system the timing equaiton we have more complex timing equation.

$$\text{Time for maximum} = \left\{ \left\lceil \frac{N}{p} \right\rceil - 1 \right\} t_i + t_p$$

Where $\lceil x \rceil$ implies the first integer $\geqslant x$ and t_i is the comparison time of an individual processor and t_p the time to find the maximum across all processors. The value of t_p depends on the processor connectivity as well as the number of comparisons. For associative processors such as DAP t_p << arithmetic time and can usually be ignored. On a linearly connected set of processors with local memory

$$t_p \sim pt_r + \log_2 p \, t_c$$

Where t_r is the processor to processor routing time and t_c is the comparison time.

If we simplify our discussion to the case where we always have P>N i.e. more processors than equations we see that the cost of stage 1 is either constant, O(N) or O(log N) depending on the exact details of the computer hardware - an unfortunate observation if we are trying to devise a universal parallel algorithm. It must be emphasised that this is a real problem. There are papers in literature which propose special algorithms to avoid pivoting as the authors assume that the operation will be too expensive (takes time O(log N)); such papers must be ignored when we develop routines for a machine like DAP.

Modification of the Pivot Equation

The prime operation of this stage is to divide a row of a matrix by a constant. Many years of experience suggests that we would be best to program this as:

        c ← 1/A(1,1)

        for   i = 2 to n do

        A(1,i) ← A(1,i)*c

There are two assumptions in such coding

        i)   division is more costly than multiplication

        ii) we have a serial computer!

The second assumption only becomes evident when we attempt to time the above algorithm and the alternative

        for   i = 2 to n do

        A(1,i) ← A(i,i)/A(1,1)

The first version takes time td + tm whilst the second version takes time td (td is the division time and tm is the multiply time). Hence totally reasonable serial programming gives a bad parallel algorithm. It should be realised that this timing equation makes the assumption that a single quantity may be extracted from a single processor and broadcast to all other processors in a time short compared with the multiply time - this is not necessarily true for all parallel systems.

Creation of the Reduced Set of Equations

Stage 3 of our operation has the highest degree of parallelism available. The task is to subtract multiples of a 'vector' from a set of 'vectors'. Each of these individual vector operations is well suited to parallel operation. In the case where $P = N$ the processors will be fully utilised. However, as we eliminate more and more variables from the system we will start to under-utilise the processors. At the stage where the number of equations has been reduced to $P/2$ we can simultaneously eliminate a variable in two equations and so go back to full utilisation. This process can be repeated when the number of reduced equations falls to $P/3$ etc. until we reduce our problem to $\sqrt{P}$ equations. The problem of organising and programming this algorithm seems horrifying but would need to be done if one wished to optimally implement this stage on any particular system. An optimal parallel implementation would need to do this somewhere, so there is a challenge for either, for the compiler writer who must detect these options or for the programmer who might wish to explicitly program these stages.

A potential solution to the problem is the partitioned matrix method based on partitions of size $\sqrt{P}*\sqrt{P}$, with the submatrices solved using the Gauss Jordan algorithm. Assympotically the 'efficiency' of such an algorithm is O(1) (in the case of no pivoting). The question is still open on how one can be certain of selecting non singular matrices as pivot sets - as yet little research has been done on this question. Hunt (private communication) has implemented a strategy for doing block matrices but using full column pivoting on the DAP for systems up to size 650 x 650.

Solving P Equations with P^2 processors

As discussed above we can derive this problem as a direct result
of a Gaussian Elimination process or using a partitioned
technique. A single system may be solved more efficiently using the
Gauss-Jordan algorithm [1] as this algorithm requires only half the
number of parallel (multiplication) operations, than the
triangular reduction methods. The cost of implementing a pivot
strategy is highly system dependent - on the DAP pivoting is a
negligible cost so we find no reason to deal with triangular
matrices.

The literature of parallel processing algorithm design has often
turned out to be unhelpful in searching for practical algorithms.
There is a standard parallel computer theoretical model which is
used to evaluate algorithms. Briefly this model assumes:

     i   All arithmetic operations take unit time

    ii   The time to access data is negligible

   iii   The only operations supported are unary or binary

    iv   Arithmetic is 'atomic' e.g. the task of adding
         two numbers cannot be shared amongst the
         processors.

Each and every one of the above assumptions are invalid for bit
organised machines such as DAP and assumptions i and ii will be
incorrect for all practical systems. There is therefore a need
for more complex models so that more realistic algorithm
evaluations can be made. The current model is so bad that it
really only suggests one conclusion - do not construct computers
to which the model can be accurately applied!

There is therefore a need to use more complex models with many
parameters so that more realistic algorithm evaluations can be
made. It is not improbable that efficient portable programs will,
in todays terms, be a collection of routines from which a
selection is made, at execution time. This type of program
already exists in some application areas e.g. molecular orbital
packages which use different sub-programs depending on the
relative magnitude of the problem parameters.

Summary

In this paper we have tried to highlight some of the questions
which arise when one attempts to implement a 'trivial' problem on
a parallel processor with a fixed number of processors. Starting
from the type of programs we associate with serial computation
there appear to be many potential options e.g. very
hardware/system dependent. What is the solution to the problem?
I believe that the solution must lie in the direction of
developing programming tools which operate at a higher level than
is common in the FORTRAN/ALGOL/PASCAL type. Future languages must
include as primitives operations such as solution of equations,
sorting, matrix inversion etc. so that the compiler writers can
choose the optimal implementation for a given architecture. It is
not too improbable that efficient portable programs will really be
a collection of options. Which option to use being chosen at run
time after the program has done some 'measurements' on the
environment.

References

[1]   Flanders, P.M., Hunt, D.J., Reddaway, S.F. and Parkinson,
      D.   'Efficient High Speed Computing with the DAP' in 'High
      Speed Computer and Algorithm Organisation'. Ed. Kuck,
      D.J., Lawrie, D.H. and Sameh, A.H., Academic Press, 1977,
      p. 113-128.

[2]   Parkinson, D., Liddell, H.M. 'The Measurement of
      Performance on a Highly Parallel System'. IEEE
      Trans Comput, vol C-32, p. 32-37, Jan 1983.

[3]   Lord, R.E., Kowalik, J.S. and Kumar, S.P.
      'Solving Linear Algebraic Equations on an MIMD
      Computer'. JACM, vol 32, p. 103-117, 1983.

[4]   Evan, D.J. 'Parallel Numerical Algorithms for
      Linear Systems in Parallel Processing Systems'.
      Ed. D.J. Evans, Cambridge University Press, 1982,
      p. 357-384.

DESIGN AND PERFORMANCE OF ALGORITHMS
FOR MIMD PARALLEL COMPUTERS

J. S. Kowalik
Systems and Computing
Washington State University
Pullman, Washington 99164-1222

R. E. Lord
Computing Service Center
Washington State University
Pullman, Washington 99164-1220

S. P. Kumar
Department of Mathematics and Computer Science
University of Miami
Coral Gables, Florida 33124

The authors have designed and programmed algorithms which utilize MIMD computers for solution of problems in ordinary differential equations and linear equations. In addition to theoretical analysis of their performance, actual peformance was determined by execution of the codes on the Heterogeneous Element Processor (HEP) manufactured by Denelcor, Inc. HEP is a relatively high performance computer of the MIMD type.

We present the techniques used in the design of these algorithms and relate them to the achieved performance. The techniques range from parallelization of existing sequential algorithms to the design of a parallel algorithm which is appropriate only for a multiprocessor computer.

1.   ORDINARY DIFFERENTIAL EQUATIONS.

Ordinary differential equations (ODE) present a natural opportunity for investigating parallel methods for their solution. Parallel electronic analog computers have been commercially available for more than 35 years and are used almost exclusively for the solution of ODE's. Indeed, a very early digital computer (ENIAC) was of parallel design and intended for the solution of ODE's. In addition to this early hardware, considerable attention has been given by researchers to inherently parallel methods of solving ODE's. Nievergelt [1] proposed a method in which parallelism is introduced at the expense of redundancy of computation. Other parallel methods are given by Miranker and Liniger [2] and Worland [3].

NATO ASI Series, Vol. F7
High-Speed Computation. Edited by J. S. Kowalik
© Springer-Verlag Berlin Heidelberg 1984

Our interest in using a modern parallel digital computer to solve ODE's can be expressed in terms of the following questions:

a. Given some measure of the size (eq. the number of independent variables) of a particular set of ODE's, how many parallel processes can be efficiently employed in their solution?

b. What are the benefits of some specific techniques (parallel methods of updating the independent variables and scheduling methods) to increase the parallelism of the solution of ODE's?

c. To what extent do the methods employed lend themselves to the specification of the design of a translator which would process the specification of a set of ODE's into efficient parallel codes?

We chose to investigate two specific instances of ODE's. The first problem was a set of ten nonlinear first order equations which describe the flight characteristics of a ground launch guided missile. A sequential Fortran program of somewhat less than 1000 source lines was available for its solution and the starting point of our investigation. More details on this particular problem together with preliminary results are given in [4]. The second problem was a set of six equations describing a reaction wheel stabilization device. The problem is described in more detail by Grierson, et al., in [5]. A sequential Fortran program for the solution of this second problem was supplied to us by the authors cited in [5].

For both problems, the original solutions employed a fourth-order Runge-Kutta (RK-4) formula for performing integration and we parallelized only the code for computing derivations and updating of the state variables. In addition we coded both of these problems using the parallel predictor-corrector (PPC) method described by Miranker and Liniger [2] in order to evaluate this method. The code for reading initial conditions and parameters as well as the code for producing intermediate and final output was kept in its sequential form. Since, for both these problems, the amount of time devoted to these I/O activities is very low compared with the total solution time, the penalties for remaining sequential in this portion of the code was minimal.

Our initial effort was devoted to partitioning the code for evaluation of derivatives and integration of state variables into several distinct tasks. We chose to parallelize the code at the source level rather than at a machine instruction level in order to be somewhat machine independent and to keep the bookkeeping aspects of producing parallel code at a manageable size.

The determination of how much code constituted a task was based only on judgement but was abounded by consideration that a task consists of at least one source statement and that if the code consisted of any data dependent branches then all of the targets of the branches must also be part of the task. This latter consideration was required since we wished to view the selected tasks as a task system complete with precedence constraints. Following the methods described in Chapter 2 of Coffman and Denning [6] the resultant task system representing the sequential Fortran program was an equivalent maximally parallel task system, and a schedule of this maximally parallel task system would result in our parallel program. The maximally parallel task system is derived by consideration of the memory cells (Fortran variables) which constitute the range and domain of each of the tasks. Two tasks T and $\hat{T}$ can be executed in parallel as long as the intersection of the range of T and the domain of $\hat{T}$, the domain of T and the range of $\hat{T}$, and the range of T and the range of $\hat{T}$ are all empty. Our initial method of determining ranges and domains was by inspection of the source code, but in the later part of our investigation we found that this determination could be made, for the most part, by a program which read the source code and the compiler cross-reference listing. The compiler output was also used to determine an estimate of the execution time of each task by examination of the generated machines instructions.

For the first problem, a total of 40 tasks were identified, ten of which were updating of the dependent variables, one for updating the independent variable time, and the remaining 29 tasks were involved with evaluating the derivatives. Since the computer which we used to execute the parallel code was the Denelcor, Inc. HEP machine, all tasks timing will be in terms of HEP machine instructions. For the most part, HEP executes all instructions in the same amount of time and thus instruction count is a good approximation to execution time. For our task selection, the shortest task was 2 instructions, the longest was 88 instructions and the total task system was 1265 instructions for an average of slightly less than 32 instructions per task. For the second problem, a total of 19 tasks were selected with a minimum of 1 instruction time, a maximum of 43 instruction times and an average of just over 14 instruction times. Figure 1 illustrates the task system selected for the second problem.

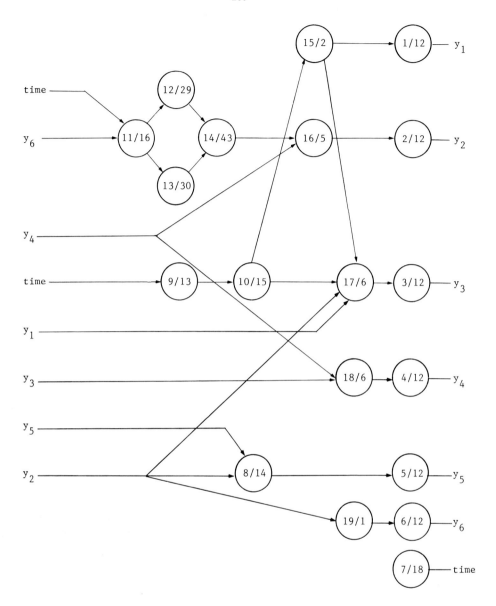

Figure 1. Graph illustrating task system for reaction wheel
where (i/j) is the i-th task of time duration j.

Following the selection of tasks, determination of their precedence constraints and estimating their execution time, our next step is to schedule these tasks for execution by p processors. A simplified illustration of how we might solve ODE on a sequential computer is shown in Figure 2. In this Figure we have indicated that there are some tasks associated with evaluating the derivatives, updating the dependent variables and updating the independent variables. One approach to parallel execution might be to consider those tasks, together with their precedence constraints and execution time, as a task system and schedule them for execution on p processors. A repeated execution of that schedule (until time = endtime) would be a solution to the problem. By means of a simple example, we illustrate that shorter execution times can be achieved by considering the entire problem solution rather than just the interior of the "While" loop. Consider the Van der Pol equations written as two first order equations:

$$\dot{x}_1 = x_2$$

$$\dot{x}_2 = u(1 - x_1^2)x_2 - x_1.$$

```
WHILE time < endtime do

    /*    tasks for derivatives                        */
       TASK 1
       TASK 2
          .
          .
          .
       TASK J
    /*    tasks updating dependent variables           */
       TASK J + 1
          .
          .
          .
       TASK N - 1
    /*    task updating independent variable           */
       TASK N
```

Figure 2. Illustration of code for solving ODE's.

And assume the tasks for its solution are as given below.

Task No.	Description of Tasks	Execution Time
1	Compute $temp_1 = u(1 - x_1^2)$	3
2	Compute $temp_2 = temp_1 * x_2 - x_1$	2
3	Update x_1 based upon x_2	4
4	Update x_2 based upon $temp_2$	4
5	Update independent variable time	1

Figure 3a shows an assignment of these tasks to two processors which is optimal if one only considers the interior of the "While" loop. However, Figure 3b shows an assignment which correctly solves the problem and has shorter period than that of 3a. This later schedule is based upon considering the entire problem rather than just the interior of the "While" loop. The details of the later scheduling technique are given in [7] and it is this technique that we used for developing schedules for both problems.

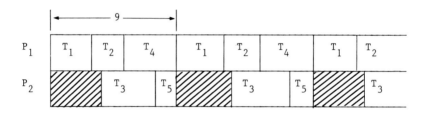

3a.) Scheduling interior of "While" loop.

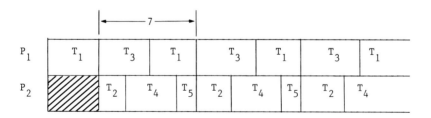

3b.) Scheduling with loop unrolled.

Figure 3. Two schedules for solution of Van der Pol Equation.

The results of applying the above cited scheduling techniques are shown by the graphs of speed-up vs p in Figure 4. In the case of the reaction wheel, our choice of tasks resulted in a maximum speed-up of 4.5. For this problem and choice of task systems, the maximum speed-up obtainable by scheduling only the interior of the "While" loop was 2.4 (53% of the maximum speed-up). For the missile problem, the

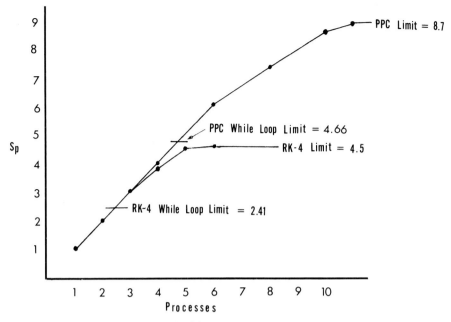

a.) Reaction Wheel Problem

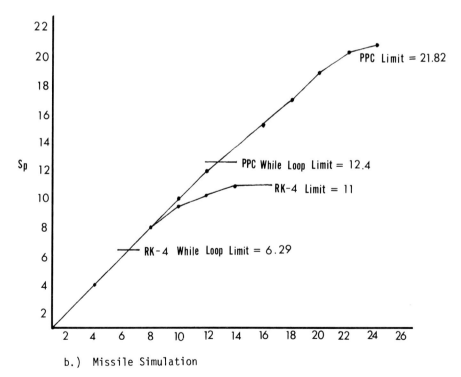

b.) Missile Simulation

Figure 4. Speed-up vs. p Considering Only Scheduling.

maximum speed-up obtainable was 11 and the limiting case for scheduling only the interior of the "While" loop was 6.9 (57% of the maximum).

The next step in the implementation is to insure that the schedules we have developed will not be violated. The synchronization method which we used is based upon a FULL/EMPTY semaphore associated with each variable. This method is easily implemented on the Denelcor HEP computer where a FULL/EMPTY bit is associated with every memory location. If two tasks T_i and T_j have a precedence relation $T_i \lessdot T_j$ then it must be the case that T_i computes some value that T_j uses. If T_i and T_j are assigned to different processes in a particular schedule then, to ensure synchronization, the status of the particular value is set to full by T_i and is emptied by T_j. In the HEP when the synchronization option is selected, a store instruction can only execute when its target memory location is empty and after the execution that location is set full. For load instructions, the load can only execute when the memory location is full and it is set empty upon completion of execution. In Fortran, this option is elected by preceding the variable referenced with a '$' sign. The resultant action is dependent upon whether the reference results in a load or a store instruction.

The method we employed to synchronize these calculations was for each variable in the range of some task to provide a separate semaphored copy of that variable to each process that was assigned one or more tasks with that variable in their domain. For purposes of analysis, the extra instructions required to create these separate semaphored copies of the variable are termed "send penalties". We assume for all tasks, any execution results in a single store instruction for each variable in its range. This was true for all of the tasks which we selected and can easily be enforced for any code with only slight modifications. With the above assumption, the number of send penalties for a variable x is the number of processes less one, which are assigned tasks with x in their domain. For a given variable x, define dx to be the number of tasks with x in its domain, and p to be the number of processors employed in a given schedule. Then the expected number of send penalties for the variable x is:

$$E = p - 1 - p \left(\frac{p - 1}{p} \right)^{dx}$$

For a complete schedule, the number of send penalties is the sum of the number of send penalties for each of the variables. Figure 5 gives the expected number of send penalties with various numbers of processors for variables with degree ranging from dx = 1 to dx = 8.

The importance of the expected number of send penalties is not in their numeric value but is in their form. As Figure 5 illustrates, the synchronization penalty grows most rapidly with small values of p and grows less rapidly with larger values. That is, increasing the amount of parallelism in a particular problem solution does not yield a corresponding increase in synchronization penalty.

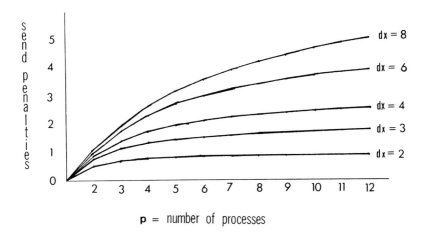

Figure 5. Send Penalties vs. p for Various Degrees.

In addition to the synchronization send penalties, in some cases there will be "receive penalties" which arise in two ways. First, if a variable is in the domain of a task T which is assigned to a different processor than the task T_1 which had that same variable in its range and if T has multiple uses (load instruction) of the variable. In this case a local copy of the·variable is made and the transmitted copy is set empty so that T_1 can update it in a subsequent iteration. For similar reasons, if T_1 and T_2 both have x in their domains and are both assigend to a processor which is different than that to which the task that produces x (tasks with x in its range) is assigned, then a local copy of x is made prior to the execution of either T_1 or T_2. For the two problem solutions which we examined, the number of receive penalties was significantly less than the number of send penalties.

Selected cases of the problems were executed on the Denelcor HEP computer with the following results:

	Reaction Wheel	Missile	
	RK-4	RK-4	PPC
Number of processors	5	8	8
Predicted Results:			
Useful Work*	54	173	346
Scheduling Inefficiencies*	9	19	17
Synchronization*	7	23	58
Speed-up	3.85	6.44	6.57
Actual Results:			
Speed-up	3.60	5.76	6.48

*In HEP machine instructions for one cycle of innermost loop.

In all cases the actual results were somewhat less than the predicted results. This is felt to be because the average execution times were used for the tasks that had variable execution times. In general, a task running longer than average will result in additional execution time (decreased speed-up) while a task running shorter than average will often not result in shortening the problem execution time.

On the basis of the problem we examined, we can answer the original questions as follows:

a. Using sequential methods, i.e., RK-4, for updating the dependent variables we were able to efficiently utilize approximately the same number of processes as the number of first order equations.

b. The parallel predictor-corrector method doubled the amount of parallel code that could be executed efficiently and the scheduling methods we used provided nearly twice the amount of parallelism as scheduling only the interior of the "While" loop.

c. It would seem quite difficult to have the original Fortran source mechanically translated into as efficient a parallel code as that which we produced. However, given some representation of the problem which identifies it as solving ODE's and a clear structure for identifying the derivations such as is provided in the CSSL language [8], knowledge of the design of a translator is available. We expect that the efficiencies of such a translator would be as good as or better than the hand code which we produced.

2. TRIDIAGONAL LINEAR EQUATIONS.

Tridiagonal linear equations appear very frequently in numerical treatment of partial differential equations characterizing continuous fields (see, for example, Vemuri and Karplus [9]). The solution of the single system of tridiagonal equations $A\underline{x} = \underline{d}$ or

$$b_i x_{i-1} + a_i x_i + c_i x_{i+1} = d_i, \qquad 1 \leqslant i \leqslant n$$

where $\qquad x_0 = b_1 = c_n = x_{n+1} = 0,$

presents a challenge to designers of parallel algorithms for multiprocessor systems and pipeline vector computers. Due to the popularity of vector computers such as CRAY-1 and CYBER 205 a substantial amount of research has been done to find a vectorizable algorithm for these equations. The standard Gauss Elimination algorithm is recursive and will not vectorize. An alternate method of cyclic reduction allows for vectorization and runs several times faster on CRAY-1 and CYBER 205 than the standard algorithm. The reader interested in this subject should consult: Kershaw [10], Kascic [11], Jordan [12] and Hockney and Jesshope [13].

Our interest is in exploring theoretically and experimentally a version of Gaussian Elimination suituable for an MIMD machine. We assume that the number of equations n is much larger than the number of processors p, and that pivoting for numerical stability is not required. To illustrate the algorithm we assume that $n = 12$ and $p = 3$. Since we deal with an MIMD machine it is not necessary that $k = n/p$ is an integer, but this choice simplifies our notation. The initial augmented matrix $[A,\underline{d}]$ is partitioned as shown in Figure 6. If each processor concurrently eliminates the elements b_i and c_i in the diagonal block assigned to this processor we get the matrix $[A,\hat{\underline{d}}]$ shown in Figure 7. Processor 2, for example, eliminates b_6, b_7, b_8, c_7, c_6 and c_5, in this order. If we solve $2p - 1 = 5$ linear equations identified by arrows in Figure 7, then the system is decomposed into three separate subsystems that can be solved independently. Clearly, this idea can also be used to solve equations with bidiagonal or banded matrices. Using slightly more sophisticated elimination we can obtain the matrix $[\bar{A},\bar{\underline{d}}]$ shown in Figure 8. In this case only p equations need to be solved before the entire system is decomposed. Processor 2, for example, eliminates b_6, b_7, b_8, c_6, c_5 and c_4, in this order. This elimination was first used by Wang [14] as a part of a different method for SIMD computers.

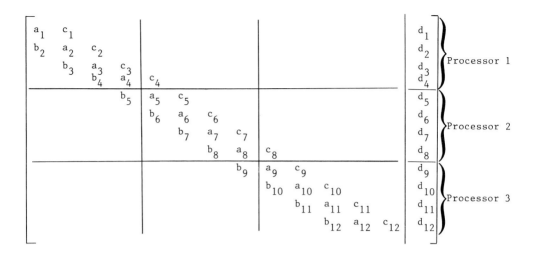

Figure 6.   Intial augmented matrix [A,$\underline{d}$].

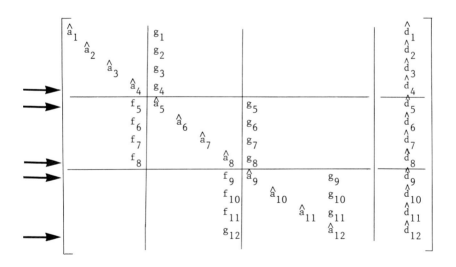

Figure 7.   Final Matrix [A,d].

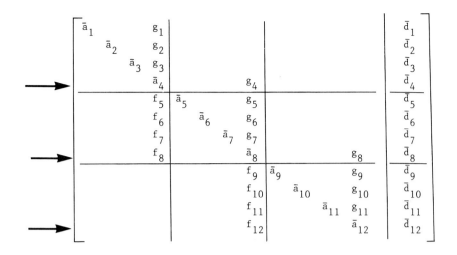

Figure 8. Matrix [A,d].

Figures 9, 10 and 11 show all the steps of the algorithm and the associated operations count. It is assumed that the time for division is twice the time for multiplication, addition or subtraction. This is approximately true for the HEP computer.

Phase 1

Step 1

Processor i, $1 \leqslant i \leqslant p$

Eliminates b_j, $j = (i-1)k+2$, $(i-1)k+3,\ldots,ik$

$f_{(i-1)k+1}$:= $b_{(i-1)k+1}$

For   j   := (i-1)k+2 to ik do

begin

$\quad m_j$:= b_j/a_{j-1}

$\quad a_j$:= $a_j - m_j c_{j-1}$

$\quad f_j$:= $- m_j f_{j-1}$

$\quad d_j$:= $d_j - m_j d_{j-1}$

end

Operation Count*

2k

2k

k

2k

_____

7k + 0(1)

Remark: processor 1 does not calculate f's.

Figure 9.

Step 2

Processor i, $\quad 1 \leqslant i \leqslant p$

Eliminates c_j, $\quad j = ik-2, ik-3, \ldots, (i-1)k+1$

	Operation Count
$g_{ik-1} \quad := \quad c_{ik-1}$ For $\quad j \quad := \quad ik-2$ downto $(i-1)k+1$ Begin	
$\qquad m_j \quad := \quad c_j / a_{j+1}$	$2k$
$\qquad g_j \quad := \quad - m_j g_{j+1}$	k
$\qquad f_j \quad := \quad f_j - m_j f_{j+1}$	$2k$
$\qquad d_j \quad := \quad d_j - m_j d_{j+1}$	$2k$
end	
$\qquad m_i \quad := \quad c_{(i-1)k} / a_{(i-1)k+1}$	
$g_{(i-1)k} \quad := \quad - m_i g_{(i-1)k+1}$	
$a_{(i-1)k} \quad := \quad a_{(i-1)k} - m_i f_{(i-1)k+1}$	
$d_{(i-1)k} \quad := \quad d_{(i-1)k} - m_i d_{(i-1)k+1}$	

$$7k + 0(1)$$

Remark: processor 1 does not calculate f's,
$g_{(i-1)k}$, $a_{(i-1)k}$ and $d_{(i-1)k}$.

Figure 10.

Phase 2

Solve the following p tridiagonal equations:

$$f_i x_{i-k} + a_i x_i + g_i x_{i+k} = d_i$$

where $\qquad i = k, 2k, 3k, \ldots, pk$

and $\qquad f_k = g_{pk} = 0.$

Time complexity $0(p)$ using one processor.

271

Phase 3

Processor i, $1 \leqslant i \leqslant p$
Calculation of the remaining variables.

for j := (i-1)k+1 to ik-1 do $$x_j := \frac{d_j - f_j x_{(i-1)k} - g_j x_{ik}}{a_j}$$	Operations Count $6k + 0(1)$

    Remark: processor 1 does not calculate
            the fx products.

Figure 11.

The total operations count for the i-th processor is $T_i = 20k + 0(1)$, but one processor also solves the p linear equations of phase 2. Hence, the total solution time is

$$T_p = 20k + 0(p) + 0(1).$$

Solving the entire set of n equations with one processor requires the time

$$T_1 = 10n + 0(1)$$

and the potential speed-up is

$$S_p = \frac{T_1}{T_p} \approx \frac{n}{2k + p}.$$

The parallel algorithm (which we will refer to as PTRD) described in Figures 9, 10 and 11 was programmed and run on the HEP computer using HEP Fortran. Using the following notation for the program tasks:

T_1^i: Computation of Step 1 and then of Step 2 of Phase 1, $i = 1,2,...,p$

T_2: Computation of Phase 2

T_3^i: Computation of Phase 3, $i = 1,2,...,p$

first p parallel instruction streams corresponding to p blocks of Figure 6, are created where the i-th stream executes T_1^i. Next, these p streams are joined and only one stream executes T_2 sequentially. Finally, p parallel streams are created again to compute the tasks $T_3^1, T_3^2, \ldots, T_3^p$ in parallel yielding the solution $\underset{\sim}{x}$.

The program PTRD required a negligible amount of synchronization. As shown in Figure 12, synchronization is required only at two points in the complete process which was achieved by using one semaphored variable (based on FULL/EMPTY principle implemented by HEP). Since the time complexity of each of the tasks T_1^i, i = 1,2,...,p is the same, the time taken to join these p tasks is negligible. The same holds for joining the p streams at the end of tasks T_3^i. Program PTRD was run for $12 \leqslant n \leqslant 2000$, $2 \leqslant p \leqslant 12$ and numerical results support our theoretical analysis with a reasonable degree of accuracy. Table 1 presents a comparison between predicted and actual speedup for some of them. Since, on one Processor Element Module (PEM) of HEP, 8 Task Status Words (TSW) can be created during one clock period (100 nsec), the performance of 10 million operations per second can be obtained when at least 8 instruction streams are active. In reality, depending on the data memory access delays, on the average between 8 and 12 parallel streams may give the same performance. Hence, the obtained numerical results up to p = 12 are useful to compare.

The method does not achieve the speedup close to p due to the additional operations required by the parallel algorithm as compared to the sequential Gauss Elimination method. As a first order approximation we can assume that

$$T_p = \frac{T_1(1+r)}{pe}$$

where $r \geqslant 0$ is the redundancy of the parallel algorithm and $0 < e \leqslant 1$ is the efficiency of the processors usage for a given schedule. The value of e measures the average utilization of the p processors which share the workload during the execution time T_p. It follows that

$$S_p = \frac{e}{1+r}$$

where

$$asd = \frac{e}{1+r} \leqslant 1$$

can be called the algorithmic slowdown. In the presented algorithm for tridiagonal equations $r \approx 1$ and $e \approx 1$, and the algorithmic slowdown is approximately 0.5.

Designing efficient parallel algorithms we attempt to maximize asd which for a given problem may be a function of problem size, selected tasks, algorithm and data structures, computer architecture and processors schedule. Other factors which influence the real speedup include: data routing, program and compiler features, and memory contention.

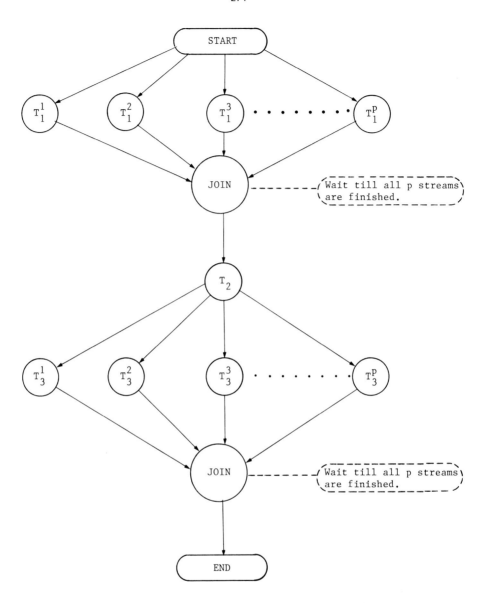

Figure 12. Synchronization points of PTRD.

n	p	S_p	
		PREDICTED	ACTUAL
96	3	1.432835	1.578941
	4	1.846154	1.932581
	6	2.526316	2.325428
	8	3.000000	2.58719
	12	3.428571	2.538620
864	3	1.492228	1.785608
	4	1.981651	2.335110
	6	2.938775	3.369206
	8	3.857142	4.265834
	12	5.538461	5.492768
2000	4	1.992031	2.372852
	5	2.484472	2.926389
	8	3.937007	4.471816
	12	4.878049	5.350523

Table 1

REFERENCES

1. J. Nievergelt, "Parallel Methods for Integrating Ordinary Differential Equations," CACM, Vol. 7, No. 12, December, 1964, pp. 731-733.

2. N. K. Miranker and W. M. Liniger, "Parallel Methods for the Numerical Integration of Ordinary Differential Equations," Math. Comput., Vol. 21, 1967, pp. 303-320.

3. P. B. Worland, "Parallel Methods for the Numerical Solution of Ordinary Differential Equations," IEEE Trans. Comp., Vol. C-25, October, 1976, pp. 1045-1048.

4. R. E. Lord and S. P. Kumar, "Parallel Solution of Flight Simulation Equations," Proceedings of the 1980 Summer Computer Simulation Conference, Seattle, WA, August, 1980, AFIPS Press.

5. W. O. Grierson, D. B. Lipski and N. O. Tiffany, "Simulation Tools: Where Can We Go?" Proceedings of the 1980 Summer Computer Simulation Conference, Seattle, WA, August, 1980, AFIPS Press.

6. E. G. Coffman, Jr. and P. J. Denning, Operating Systems Theory, Prentice-Hall, Englewood Cliffs, NJ, 1974.

7. R. E. Lord, "Scheduling Recurrence Equations for Solution on MIMD Type Computers," Ph.D. Dissertation, Washington State University, Department, of Computer Science, 1976.

8. C. Strauss, Editor, "Continuous Systems Simulation Language," SIMULATION, Vol. 9, No. 6, December, 1967.

9. V. Vemuri and W. J. Karplus, Digital Computer Treatment of Partial Differential Equations, Prentice-Hall, Englewood Cliffs, NJ, 1981.

10. D. Kershaw, "Solution of Single Tridiagonal Linear Systems and Vectorization of the ICCG Algorithm on the CRAY-1," in Parallel Computation, G. Rodrigue, Editor, Academic Press, 1982.

11. M. J. Kascic, "The Trying Tridiagonal System," unpublished manuscript.

12. T. L. Jordan, "A Guide to Parallel Computation and Some CRAY-1 Experiences," in Parallel Computation, G. Rodrigue, Editor, Academic Press, 1982.

13. R. W. Hockney and C. R. Jesshope, Parallel Computers, Adam Hilger Ltd., Bristol, England, 1981.

14. H. H. Wang, "A Parallel Method for Tridiagonal Equations," ACM Transactions on Math. Software, Vol. 7, 1981, pp. 170-183.

VECTORIZATION OF SCIENTIFIC SOFTWARE

Dr. Kenneth W. Neves
Boeing Computer Services Company
Energy Technology Applications Division
Seattle, Washington 98124

ABSTRACT

Scientific computing has become a very broad discipline over the last few decades. The body of scientific software from major industries and various engineering disciplines runs on a great variety of computing equipment ranging from specialized systems (minis or even micros) to large mainframes. In fact, major software packages often outlive several host computers and, in some instances, are converted to several new hardware designs. An ever-increasing percentage of scientific programs are migrating to computers that exploit some form of parallelism in computation to achieve superior performance. Such computers, often called "vector computers," are beginning to exist in sufficient numbers that a trend to move most large application programs to this type of computer is well established. These vector computers, however, bring with their design an "obligation." Quite often, to achieve the dramatic performance increases advertised, the user is obligated to reformulate or at least reorder the computations. The result is even greater software expense in scientific computation. This software expense has become a significant deterrent to widespread usage of supercomputers. As we move toward the age of multiple instruction/multiple data stream (MIMD) architecture, the software deterrent is likely to become more significant.

In this paper we examine aspects of application software on today's vector computers. Part of this discussion will relate to architectural differences found in current vector computers and how these seemingly subtle differences can impact computation. We examine the need to structure and classify elements of scientific computation. The algorithm, and its associate computational kernels and data structure, must be appropriately analyzed. We suggest that algorithm formulation and its substructuring into existing and alternative computational components require more active investigation. This requires a thorough understanding of both hardware and application software.

NATO ASI Series, Vol. F7
High-Speed Computation. Edited by J. S. Kowalik
© Springer-Verlag Berlin Heidelberg 1984

278

BACKGROUND

Today most of the usage of "supercomputers" is in applications that have traditionally been heavy "compute bound" scientific applications. As researchers and
scientists gain access to such machines, a major task is to achieve efficient
implementation of existing scientific application programs. The process at its
most rudimentary level is often called "conversion." It has been fairly well
accepted that conversion by means of obtaining a successful FORTRAN execution of
an existing program on a supercomputer is often not a very acceptable approach to
code conversion unless other steps are taken to achieve efficiency. The "other
steps" to efficiency, however, seem to be obscured by a preoccupation with FORTRAN
optimization.

We have seen the emergence of "vectorizing compilers" as they are distributed by
hardware vendors, the development of FORTRAN preprocessors that "vectorize"
FORTRAN source, papers and reports on compiler inefficiencies (and how to work
around them), and in one case an interactive compiler allowing the user to "fine-
tune" a particular compilation. There is nothing inherently wrong with these
tools. However, their value is many times limited and they are often likely to be
misused. Certainly vectorizing compilers are helpful in achieving effective use of
the hardware, but they are not a panacea. The FORTRAN programmer is somewhat at
the mercy of the compiler if this is the only tool he uses. For example, the
CRAY-1 compiler (level 1.09) can recognize many vector constructs. The following
is one:

```
        DO 10  I = 1,N
            Y(I) = A*X(I) + Y(I)
    10  CONTINUE
```

This statement is compiled using the vector attributes of the assembler as one
would hope. The CRAY-1 compiler, like all compilers, is not perfect. This is
illustrated by the fact that the following loop executes 25% faster.

```
        DO 10  I = 1,N
            Y(I) = A*X(I) + (Y(I))
    10  CONTINUE
```

It would be easy to draw the conclusion from this example that the compiler needs
to be supplemented by a software tool recognizing this deficiency. This, in fact,
is what has given birth to the "vectorizers" alluded to above. We believe this is
the wrong approach because the fundamental principles of vector computation become
obscured and often lost in this interaction and preoccupation with FORTRAN. In
this example, the elementary operation performed (often called a SAXPY) is fundamental and used in many applications. It is reasonable to provide an efficient

implementation of this code as a basic tool for the FORTRAN user. The implementation could be in FORTRAN or not. That is immaterial. The resulting implementation, however, should, on the CRAY-1, address the instruction sequencing problem that the current compiler ignores. If this were done, a good "loop" would be available, but a code using a well-coded SAXPY still may be inefficient! The reason comes from the fact that this loop is often the inner loop of a more complex process. On several architectures it is better to treat the entire nest of loops as the fundamental operation. On the CRAY-1, for example, this could save the large number of memory store/fetch operations that repeated use of SAXPY can cause.

The identification of key computations is nontrivial and architecture-dependent. The FORTRAN language and any reasonable substitute will always have deficiencies. What is needed is an approach that is compatible with FORTRAN (or whatever the accepted scientific language is at the time) and exploits the architectural attributes of the hardware. The answer, in our judgment, lies _above_ the language, not obscured _in_ the language. One must first examine the design of the application, not optimize a FORTRAN expression of the application as it existed on another architecture.

As we will discuss, there are certain fundamental building blocks of algorithm design which account for much (not all) of the computation in many disciplines. These fundamental constructs of computation recur in many algorithms and often hold the key to efficient computation. Just like adds, multiplies, square roots, and other elementary functions pervade computation, so do these higher level functions. Quite often their implementation (whether in assembler or FORTRAN) can be the key to efficiency. What is important is that these fundamental constructs (or kernels) be identified and provided in optimal form as tools to the FORTRAN developer.

It will be observed that these kernels can be misused and that some kernels will not be the best choice on one architecture but may be on another. Thus, a key to this approach is an architectural design phase that can and must take place before detailed machine implementation.

If current trends continue, the FORTRAN programmer will be hopelessly dependent on compiler idiosyncrasies, FORTRAN preprocessors, and/or interactive compilers (which require problem-dependent data to be effective, such as the success rate of an IF-test!). In the following sections we discuss the dependency of algorithms on hardware architecture and describe, through examples, the computational impact of this dependency. We conclude with a more detailed discussion of the above recommended approach.

HARDWARE ARCHITECTURE AND COMPUTING PERFORMANCE

In order to provide a basis of discussion of appropriate scope, we shall confine our discussion to current or near-future architectures typified by single instruction/multiple data stream machines (SIMD). Examples of such machines include the CRAY-1S, CRAY X-MP, CYBER 200's, and the Fujitsu FACOM VP-200. We will make no attempt here to compare these machines. On occasion we may use one or more specific computers to illustrate concepts.

In several architectures there are pipelined functional units which can be used in parallel and/or "chained" to achieve higher performance rates. The difference between designs usually is dependent on the mechanisms used to transfer data from memory to the "vector" units. To describe the architecture of several vector computers is beyond the scope of this paper. The interested reader may find references 1, 2 and 5 acceptable starting points. We shall examine a simple generic model of a vector computer. However, specific computer types will be used in computational examples.

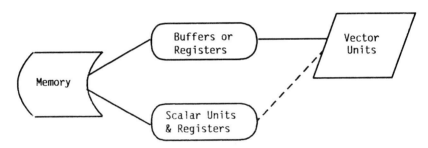

Figure 1. Generic Vector Computer

Four general areas have great impact on algorithm performance and must be considered when designing efficient algorithms for these types of machines. The relative importance of each depends both on the machine and the application as implemented through its underlying algorithms.

- Memory Characteristics: The size of memory and bandwidth to secondary storage are important for applications that are usually memory limited. However, performance for almost all applications depends on the bandwidth and access characteristics between memory and the vector units. For example, several machine designs impose the requirement of regular or contiguous storage of vectors in order to achieve a vector operand fetch at peak rates. An algorithm design that violates such memory requirements can cause severe degradation in performance.

- Buffer/Register Characteristics: The interface between memory and the vector units is usually a buffer or set of vector registers. The characteristics of registers can often affect performance in various ways. A large, richly structured register set can often reduce the memory fetch/store requirements and enhance performance despite other memory bandwidth limitations.

- Scalar and Vector Functional Units: Typically vector machines must perform vector and scalar floating point operations. The vector units are capable of much faster sustained rates of computation when properly used. The greatest speeds are attained by using "long" vector operands. Not all algorithms can be packaged in totally long vector operations. Thus scalar processing plays an important role in some applications. Moreover, the ratio of vector speed to scalar speed can be a significant algorithm design parameter. For example, this ratio was so large for the CDC STAR-100 computer that even algorithms with a relatively large percentage of vector operations had disappointing performance because the portion that required scalar processing was so very slow. Another important parameter is vector startup time. Since the vector computers under discussion exploit parallelism via the pipelining process, their performance is a function of both startup time (the number of machine cycles to configure the pipe and produce the first result) and the asymptotic result rate.

- Instruction Sequencing: More so than on conventional computers, performance on vector computers can be dramatically affected by instruction sequencing at the assembly language level. While this has traditionally been a compiler optimization problem, we have observed that algorithm choice is sometimes the only acceptable means of improving degraded performance. Compiler "tricks" can be applied to some algorithms and not to others. Examples will be given later. This type of architecture dependency is not peculiar to modern vector computers. Even on scalar machines the "unrolling" of loops to gain efficient register use have been employed for some time.

AN EXAMPLE: PATHS TO AND FROM MEMORY

We now examine several basic computations with regard to their sensitivity to one isolated architecture difference--the number of fetch/store paths between memory and the vector units that can be simultaneously employed. One-, two-, and three-path architectures currently exist. In fact, in one design the number of paths is variable depending on whether the operands are contiguous or not. For the first example, we revisit the dense SAXPY computation mentioned earlier.

LOOP 1

```
DO  10   I = 1,N
   Y(I) = A*X(I) + Y(I)
10 CONTINUE
```

To simplify the discussion, assume that the vector load, store, add, and multiply units behave as pipelined vector units with a characteristic performance model given by

$$T = S + K*N ,$$

where T is time, S is a startup time, and N is the number of vector components (in this case specified by the DO loop). We also assume, to simplify the discussion, that each vector unit (after startup) processes one result per machine cycle and that the result of the multiply pipe can be "chained" into the add pipe when appropriate. Under these conditions, a one-path-to-memory machine will require on the order of 3N machine cycles plus startup time to process the computation from memory-to-memory. At face value, a two-path machine should require 2N cycles, but by using double the number of vector operations with vector lengths of N/2, one can achieve an asymptotic rate of 1.5N cycles through proper instruction sequencing. A three-path machine, of course, requires only one set of simultaneous operations and thus can perform this operation in N cycles (again neglecting startup cycles).

One may be tempted to rate the asymptotic performance for this computation as a function of the pipe rate and the number of paths-to-memory. However, this loop (often called the dense SAXPY as named in LINPACK (3) developed at Argonne National Labs) is most often the very inner loop of a nested combination of DO loops. Treated as such, one can often suppress the final store operation and hold the result in a vector register (if the machine has one). The result is a reduction of the required number of memory accesses and significant speed improvement. This process is sometimes referred to as programming at "supervector" rates.

Loop 1, though a fundamental computation, has simple memory requirements. A more complicated loop, illustrative finite difference and finite element techniques, is given below and requires more intricate handling.

LOOP 2

```
DO  10   I = 1 , N
   Z(I) = X(I)*Y(I) + Z(I)
10   CONTINUE
```

Table 1 gives the achievable asymptotic results on several computers for these loops.

CYCLE TIMES (NEGLECTING STARTUP)

	Loop 1		Loop 2	
	Vector	Supervector	Vector	Supervector
1 Path/Reg.	3N	N	4N	2N
2 Path/Reg.	1.5N	N	2N	N
3 Path/Reg.	N	N	1.5N	N
3 Path/Buffer	N	N	2N	2N

TABLE 1

Using the table, one can examine specific machines. Since the CYBER 205 is a buffered memory-to-memory, three-path machine, one cannot employ supervector programming. That is, the peak performance is unavoidably a function of memory access. The above table illustrates the degradation one path to memory can cause (e.g., the CRAY-1). It also illustrates the advantages of having the flexibility to use vector registers. For example, compare the one-path register machine (CRAY-1) to the three-path buffer machine (CYBER 205) on LOOP 2, supervector rate. In this latter case, the CRAY-1 is able to use registers to overcome a single-path memory access limitation.

Both the number of paths to memory and register flexibility have direct impact on more complicated computations than these example loops. A more complex operation such as matrix multiply is directly affected by the limitations of memory access. Sparing detail, there are essentially three ways to order the triply nested loops of matrix multiplication, resulting in three distinct implementations of the same set of computations. The order of computation is different and hence the access of the matrix data in memory varies. Using efficient Cray Assembly Language (CAL) coding, BCS has achieved the following rates of computation on the CRAY-1 for the three implementations (given in millions of floating point operations per second, MFLOPS):

METHOD A: COLUMN ORDERED	50 MFLOPS
METHOD B: INNER PRODUCT	75 MFLOPS
METHOD C: OUTER PRODUCT	150 MFLOPS

This yields a range of efficiency from 32% to 95% of the maximum capacity of the CRAY-1. It is perhaps worthy to note here that the slower algorithm, column ordered, is more often the preferred algorithm on virtual memory machines where minimizing page faults is crucial. It is not likely that a compiler could recognize these facts and switch algorithms at compilation. This will be discussed further when software design is addressed.

So far, we have ignored a very important aspect of efficiency on vector computers, namely, the computation of non-ideal operations. Inherently scalar algorithms and/or processes that involve "short vectors" cannot always be avoided. The next section will discuss this often crucial area.

SCALAR AND SHORT VECTOR PERFORMANCE

Many applications deal with repetitive operations involving short vectors or vectors not regularly stored (i.e., not stored with fixed stride). Examples exist in oil reservoir modeling, structures computations and electric power systems problems. With such problems, the asymptotic rate is not the key factor in performance. If one were to plot the number of computations per second as a function of vector length, the resulting characteristic curve shown in Figure 2 would provide a more useful tool to estimate performance. The terms r_∞ and $n_{\frac{1}{2}}$, following the notation of reference 1, indicate the maximum vector rate and the value of N for which a vector operation achieves one half that rate, respectively.

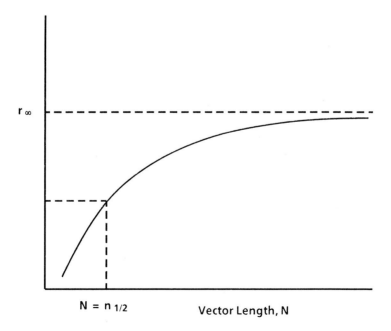

Figure 2. Characteristic Curve for a Vector Operation

The ideal curve is of infinite slope initially, reaching its asymptotic maximum instantly, and would thus perform equally well for short vectors. (Note: This ideal is achieved by scalar computers but at the expense of the asymptotic rate.) To illustrate the effects of operating short of the maximum rate and also to illustrate the use (and misuse) of computational kernels, we shall examine the basic loop of direct sparse matrix factorization. This loop taxes most hardware designs and often provides the most difficult challenge to a compiler. The loop is as follows:

<u>LOOP 3</u>

```
       DO 10 I = 1,N
         J = INDEX(I)
         Y(J) = A*X(I) + Y(J)
   10    CONTINUE
```

This loop is dealing with two types of vectors, large full vectors of length M, and the nonzero elements within these vectors of length N (less than M). On several machines (not all, however) this is inherently not a vector operation. The restrictions on storage often disallow the efficient vector fetch/store of a randomly stored vector such as the nonzeros of vector Y in the above loop. If we treat the entire loop as a vector (composite) operation, it has a characteristic curve as previously described. On the CYBER 205, there are seven different ways to program this loop. The best method is a function of the density of nonzeros, i.e., ratio of M to N. This was also true of the CDC STAR-100. (A complete discussion of the seven methods is given in reference 4.) For a fixed density, the "best" choice changes dramatically between these two machines, largely due to a change in the ratio of vector speed to scalar speed. This poses quite a challenge to the compilers which must decide as a function of M and N which of the several methods it must use. Obviously, the compiler is not privy to the values of M and N. (At least one manufacturer is considering compiler options to allow for the input of this type of information at compile time.)

It is reasonable to approach the above loop by reducing it to a series of "vector" operations. The sequence is as follows:

- GATHER - fetch the elements of a full vector according to the INDEX array into a dense (short) vector YSTAR of length N.

- DENSE SAXPY - perform a dense triad operation using YSTAR and X, storing the result in YSTAR.

- SCATTER - Store the elements of YSTAR into the full vector Y according to the INDEX array.

The results of this approach on various machines are most enlightening. We examine the CRAY-1 results only. Three approaches are compared: 1) CRAY FORTRAN, 2) GATHER/SAXPY/SCATTER (GSS) as described above coded in optimal CRAY assembly language (CAL), and 3) CAL coding of the entire loop. The CAL coding of the entire loop is provided in a library of subroutines called CRAYPACK developed by BCS. The characteristic curves of the three approaches are given in Figure 3.

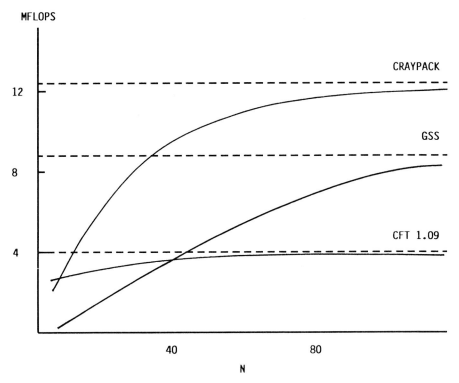

Figure 3. Characteristic Curves for Sparse Loop

The three curves indicate that the highest asymptotic performance is given by method 3. The poorest performance comes from FORTRAN, with GSS somewhere in the middle. However, a computational kernel such as this loop should not be analyzed in isolation. Even though this computation accounts for 80% of the factorization time, it is not clear from asymptotic results alone which approach is best in a given application. Table 2 gives the factorization times in a direct sparse elimination algorithm using the three methods described. Two different problems were used--one derived from an electric power system analysis of the eastern United States power grid, and the other from a finite element formulation of a structural analysis of a geodesic dome. The dimensions of the matrices were 5,300 and 2,132, respectively.

FACTORIZATION TIMES

	POWER PROBLEM	STRUCTURES PROBLEM
FORTRAN	.181 sec.	1.2 sec.
GSS	.240 sec.	0.9 sec.
SAXPYS	.168 sec.	0.6 sec.

TABLE 2

It is of interest to note that the relative performance of the three methods changes between problems. On the power problem the FORTRAN loop outperforms GSS, the optimally coded building block approach (even though the latter had over double the asymptotic rate). This can be explained by the characteristic curves (see Fig. 3) and the fact that, for the power problem, the value of N in the loop during most of the factorization was significantly less than 38, the cross-over point between FORTRAN and GSS. Fortunately, SAXPYS has the higher asymptotic rate as well as the shortest startup time (i.e., using the terminology of reference 1), the smallest $n_{\frac{1}{2}}$ and largest asymptotic rate) and, therefore, is preferred over a large problem class. On the CYBER 200 series no single method is best for all densities on both machines (203, 205).

This example illustrates several important facts that are, in our opinion, critical to achieving high performance on vector processors.

• Many, if not all, important mathematical algorithms have critical key computations that consume a great percentage of processing time.

• Key computational kernels must be handled optimally to fully utilize high performance hardware.

• The proper implementation of key kernel computations can, and usually does, depend on both the machine architecture and the problem. It is not always possible to provide a single kernel that is optimal for all input conditions within a problem class.

• It is not reasonable to assume that all, or even most, key computations will be efficiently handled by compilers (even if problem characteristics are available at compile time).

In the next section, the ramifications of these facts are explored.

ACTIVE VECTORIZATION OF SCIENTIFIC SOFTWARE

Returning briefly to the example of matrix multiply, it was observed that of the three methods A, B, C, each has its merits on appropriate hardware. Method A is superior on virtual-memory scalar machines. C is best on the CRAY-1. On the CRAY X-MP, with its three paths to memory and liberal chaining conditions, all three methods can achieve the same asymptotic rate, which approaches the theoretical maximum for that hardware. In fact, for the X-MP the preferred method is a function of startup time alone. The more complex the computation, the more surprising the examples tend to be. If we examine two algorithms for convolution on the CRAY-1, we find that asymptotic performance can be most deceiving. If FILTERG (provided by CRAY Research in SCILIB) is compared to HSFILT (provided by BCS in CRAYPACK), striking differences are observed. FILTERG runs at 140 MFLOPS. HSFILT runs only at 60 MFLOPS. Nevertheless, HSFILT performs almost nine times faster on convolution of a 2-D grid of dimension 10,000 by 4,000. This is an example of improved performance through superior algorithm (and data structure) choice for a given architecture and a given problem.

These examples have served to illustrate the impact of relatively small changes in architecture on elementary computations. It would be a rather ambitious project to characterize the "space" of computation as being "spanned" by a "basis" of key kernel computations. A macroscopic project of this kind has not, to our knowledge, been attempted. Yet quite often this process is occurring "in-the-small." For example, the following process occurs frequently in practice. A large program is to be moved to a vector computer. The underlying algorithms are examined and reviewed for their appropriateness for target vector computer. In some cases, alternate solution techniques are implemented. Their performance is often fine-tuned by optimally coding the basic key kernel computations. This process might be called "passive" vectorization for it occurs after the fact. That is, after the vector machine is chosen and after the specific application is slated to be moved to the new architecture.

It is time, in our judgment, that the software community begin approaching this new hardware technology in a more "active" manner. That is, approach large application areas, by industry or problem type, and examine the impact of parallel computation before a specific detailed architecture design is chosen, thus removing the near-term conversion pressure and perhaps short-sighted approach that a constrained conversion process can bring. The same aspects of conversion would be addressed but with an attitude that provokes innovation. To lay out a definitive plan for active vectorization is, in our judgment, a worthy research project in the scientific software discipline and requires a thoughtful decomposition of scientific software. We offer here a platform for discussion. The process should include the following steps:

- Review the overall model. Identify model simplifications and approximations and explore the appropriateness of these simplifications in view of future technology (e.g., memory size, computational power).

- Review known algorithms for vectorizability and explore alternate algorithm choices for a given model. This type of process would build on current numerical analysis research in parallel computing.

- Substructure each algorithm into computational kernels and appropriate alternative kernels that exploit parallelism.

- Examine and classify memory access requirements of the data structures imposed by various algorithms and kernels.

- Examine the vectorization ratio (i.e., the percentage of the entire application that could directly employ long vector operations) of major application codes as they are restructured, not only as they exist currently.

The first four steps describe a process of decomposing and application into a computational hierarchy: the model, algorithm, key kernels, and data structures. At each successive level, architecturally-dependent alternatives are to be defined. Improving the vectorization ratio is more of an "objective function" for specific hardware implementation.

The specific benefits of this active approach are hard to quantify, but it is likely that software developers, software users, and hardware manufacturers will all gain by the process. Benefits that we foresee include:

- Multimachine software design. The reviewed model will be defined in terms of several numerical algorithms and their underlying computations. When specific architecture characteristics are defined, the specific machine implementation can proceed by mapping the proper algorithms and underlying kernels to the architecture at hand.

- Usage portable programs and usage portable algorithms can often result.

- More intelligent evaluation of new hardware designs by users. This is due to the fact that the best potential vector design is available or, at least, the major design issues are identified prior to the evaluation.

- Characterization of software requirements to give hardware designers of scientific processors clearer objectives.

- The potential definition of a relatively small but repeated set of key computational kernels that pervade scientific computation.

- The identification, before actual hardware availability, of application models that new hardware designs make feasible and that more closely solve the "real problem." Currently, computer capacity is not adequate to solve some very "real" models. Instead a problem is solved that is feasible but only approximates the real problem. The impact of new hardware should be assessed by its potential impact on the "real" problem!

- New communication between users and producers of hardware.

- New research directions in numerical analysis, hardware development, and software development can proceed from a more systematized body of knowledge.

RECOMMENDATIONS AND CONCLUSION

This discussion has not provided iron-clad solutions but, rather, has attempted to define a problem. As new computer designs exploit parallelism in computation, an increasing impact on software design will be felt. With MIMD architecture, the parallelism invades the instruction stream itself. The impact can be felt even higher in the computational hierarchy of an application than on SIMD architecture. In the MIMD setting, attempts to resolve questions of efficiency within the domain of a higher level language like FORTRAN are likely to be fruitless. We have observed that even on SIMD machines, seemingly subtle architecture differences can impact algorithm choice in a manner that higher level languages cannot totally address. Certainly, algorithms and possibly the models themselves will become computer-dependent. It is our hope that an order can be put to this process with a more "active" approach to vectorization. Perhaps the formation of an international committee, group, or society is required whose purpose is to be the focal point for a "hierarchical vector software taxonomy" of scientific applications by industry or discipline.

ACKNOWLEDGMENT

The author would like to acknowledge the following colleagues at Boeing Computer Services whose technical contributions and work formed the basis of this presentation: Drs. Ben Dembart, David S. Dodson, A. M. Erisman and John G. Lewis.

REFERENCES

1. Hockney, R.W., and C.R. Jesshope. Parallel Computers, Adam Hilger Ltd., Bristol, England, 1981.
2. Neves, K.W. "The Vector Computer Challenge: A Mathematical Survey of Vector and Array Processors," Proceedings of EPRI Parallel Processing Conference, Dallas, October 1980.
3. Bunch, J.R., J.J. Dongarra, C.B. Moler, and G.W. Stewart. LINPACK User's Guide, Siam Publications, Philadelphia, 1979.
4. Dembart, B. and K.W. Neves, "Sparse Triangular Factorization on Vector Computers," Exploring Applications of Parallel Processing, Electric Power Research Institute, EL-566-QR, 57-103, Palo Alto, 1977.
5. Neves, K.W. "Mathematical Libraries for Vector Computers," Computer Physics Communications, 26, 303-310, 1982.

THE SOLUTION OF SPARSE LINEAR EQUATIONS ON THE CRAY-1

Iain S. Duff
Computer Science and Systems Division,
Atomic Energy Research Establishment,
Harwell, Oxon OX11 0RA, England.

General codes for the solution of sets of sparse linear equations by direct methods employ indirect addressing in the inner loop. Since these loops will not vectorize on the CRAY-1, we consider algorithms which use direct addressing in the crucial loops. We examine the effect of switching to full code when the reduced matrix becomes sufficiently dense and discuss the design of frontal and multifrontal codes which use direct addressing throughout. We illustrate our remarks with runs of sparse codes from the Harwell Subroutine Library on the CRAY-1 at Harwell.

1. Introduction

Vector processors are having a profound influence on large scale scientific computing. Not only are much larger problems being solved but more realistic models in real time applications such as weather forecasting can be used and a whole range of parametric studies are now feasible. Indeed, a single run of an oil reservoir simulation has reputedly paid for the cost (around $10 million) of a CRAY-1 (Cray, 1981) by indicating a procedure for greater oil recovery.

At the kernel of most large scale scientific applications lies the solution of linear equations. It is this area on which we concentrate. In particular, we discuss the solution of large sparse sets of linear equations using recently developed techniques which perform well on machines capable of vectorization. The techniques we consider are direct methods based on Gaussian elimination and are not specialized to matrices from a particular application area.

It is easy to reap the benefits of vectorization when solving systems where the coefficient matrix is full. When the matrix is sparse, however, the innermost loop generally involves at least one level of indirect addressing which inhibits vectorization. We discuss this more fully in section 2 and, in the remainder of this paper, consider techniques for solving general sparse equations which avoid indirect addressing in the innermost loops.

In section 3, we discuss software which contains code for both full and sparse innermost loops. The use of these hybrid codes and their performance on the CRAY-1 is studied. We describe in section 4 our frontal code, MA32, which uses full matrix code in its innermost loop

NATO ASI Series, Vol. F7
High-Speed Computation. Edited by J. S. Kowalik
© Springer-Verlag Berlin Heidelberg 1984

and, in the following section, discuss attempts to achieve optimal performance in that loop. One of our algorithms involves optimization over both innermost and next to innermost loops. In the concluding section, we consider extensions of the frontal technique and reflect upon the influence of vector processors on computational science.

Although our computational experience is based on the CRAY-1 at Harwell, the techniques we consider are not specifically geared to the architecture of that computer and will perform well on any machine which processes vectors efficiently. It is only in section 5 that we concentrate specifically on the CRAY-1.

2.   The innermost loop in sparse codes

The principal problem with the vectorization of a general purpose code for sparse matrices lies in the use of indirect addressing in the innermost loop. Typically this is of the form

$$
\left.\begin{array}{ll}
& \text{DO 10 JJ = J1,J2} \\
& \text{J = ICN(JJ)} \\
& \text{W(J) = W(J) + AMULT * A(JJ)} \\
\text{10} & \text{CONTINUE}
\end{array}\right\} \qquad (2.1)
$$

and is often referred to as a sparse SAXPY, borrowing the terminology of the BLAS (Lawson et al (1979)).

One approach to enhancing the performance of a sparse code on a vector processor is to tackle loop (2.1) directly. This can be done by using a GATHER operation of the form

$$
B(I) = W(ICN(I)), \quad I = J1,J2
$$

followed by a vectorizable inner loop

```
      DO 10 JJ = J1,J2
      B(JJ) = B(JJ) + AMULT * A(JJ)
   10    CONTINUE
```

followed by a SCATTER of the form

$$
W(ICN(I)) = B(I) \quad I = J1,J2 \quad .
$$

Since assembly coded routines or microcode for implementing GATHER and SCATTER are likely to remain a standard feature of vector processors (these are basic instructions on the Cyber 205), this approach has the merit of comparative portability. It is important to note that the value of (J2-J1+1) is often very small (around 5 to 10 typically) and so the advantage of using basic instructions can be masked by the start up time.

For a particular machine, it may be more profitable to code the whole of loop (2.1) in assembler language. This is the approach adopted by Dodson (1981) in Boeing Computer Services Library CRAYPACK. In Table 2.1 we show the relative times and asymptotic rates for loop (2.1) on the CRAY-1, using the CRAY-1 Fortran Compiler (CFT-Version 1.09), using the sparse SAXPY from CRAYPACK, and using GATHER/SCATTER where the GATHER was performed within a vectorizable loop of the form

```
        DO 10 JJ = J1,J2
        B(I) = GATHR(LOCW+ICN(JJ)) + AMULT * A(JJ)
10      CONTINUE
```

where LOCW is the starting address of array W and the vector function GATHR was written by David Dent of the European Centre for Medium Range Weather Forecasts (ECMWF) in Reading, Berkshire. B(I) was then SCATTERed to W using the CRAY-1 SCILIB routine SCATTER.

	Time for vector length of 10 (microseconds)	Asymptotic speed (microseconds) (vector length n)	Asymptotic Megaflop rate
CFT	6.1	.55n	3.6
CFT and GATHR/SCATTER	8.5	.29n	7.0
CRAYPACK	3.6	.16n	12.4

Table 2.1 Vectorization of sparse SAXPY on the CRAY-1

Dodson (1981) has used the CRAYPACK routine to replace the inner loop of a general code for sparse symmetric equations (SPARSPAK, George et al, 1980) and reports on an overall Megaflop rate of about 3 Megaflops, the degradation from the value in Table 2.1 being caused by the considerable amount of non-vectorized fixed point overhead in such a code.

Although we have concentrated on the SAXPY operation in the foregoing, Gaussian elimination can be implemented using inner (scalar or dot) products as in compact elimination. Conventional folklore suggests that the scalar product

```
        DO 10 I=1,N
        S = S+X(I)*Y(I)                          (2.2)
  10    CONTINUE
```

called SDOT in BLAS terminology, is not easily vectorizable but, on the
CRAY-1, a recursive vector sum instruction enables the CAL coded CRAY-1
SCILIB routine SDOT to attain an asymptotic rate of 74 Megaflops.
Generally, sparse codes do not use an inner-product formulation because
of the difficulties in implementing it efficiently even on scalar
computers. A sparse SDOT is, however, often used in the solution of
equations subsequent to the matrix factorization and some solution
schemes in SPARSPAK, for example one-way dissection and the refined
quotient tree ordering, use sparse SDOT in inner loops. Dodson (1981)
has coded a sparse SDOT in CAL and has used this CRAYPACK routine to
replace loops in SPARSPAK. The asymptotic rate of the CRAYPACK sparse
SDOT is 16.3 Megaflops and an overall rate of nearly 6 Megaflops has been
recorded for the appropriate modified SPARSPAK routines.

While the efforts of Dodson and others in coding sparse SAXPY's and
sparse SDOT's is very valuable and can significantly improve the
performance of existing sparse codes on the CRAY-1 with little subsequent
effort, we prefer an approach where efficient performance is achieved
through algorithm redesign. There are two main reasons for our
preference. We believe that greater machine independence can be achieved
by our approach. Additionally, although achieving a Megaflop rate on the
CRAY-1 of over 16 for an inner loop employing direct addressing is no
mean performance, we will indicate in this paper that far higher rates
can be attained if indirect addressing can be avoided altogether.

Another approach to the solution of sparse sets of equations on
vector processors is to recognise the replication of structures within
the sparse matrix (for example, Calahan, 1982) which is a common feature
of systems from partial differential equations. This approach can be
difficult to implement and can lose efficiency when numerical stability
considerations force a different choice of pivots in each replicated
structure. Of course, when the matrix entries are themselves block
matrices (usually of order 3 to 5) advantage can be taken of the vector
architecture since each single operation in the earlier loops is now an
operation involving short vectors. Both these techniques require a
certain regularity in the structure and, to some extent, in the numerical
values. In this study we are, however, interested in methods for a wider

class of underlying structures.

A suggestion of Calahan (1982) for general sparse codes is to take advantage of the fact that usually several operations in sparse Gaussian elimination are independent and so it is possible to fill the registers with several operands and perform operations on them effectively in parallel. It is easy, for example, to organise a nested dissected ordering to split a problem into independent subproblems. Again there are some difficulties in pivoting when using this approach but the most severe drawback lies in storing and manipulating the operator information required to implement this scheme. Calahan (1982) estimates that .75 of a 64 bit word is required for each floating point operation and, as we shall indicate in section 4, we commonly encounter problems with well over 100 million operations. For small problems, however, the Megaflop rate of 12-16 is attractive.

We wish to develop software which not only is applicable to a wide range of problems but also will perform well on non-vectorizing computers. The techniques which we discuss in the following sections all make use of the fact that code employing direct addressing in the solution of full linear systems can be easily vectorized. For example, Jordan (1979) reports rates of 100-125 Megaflops for the solution of sets of equations with 100-300 variables on the CRAY-1 and, since then, even higher rates have been recorded (for example, Saunders and Guest, 1982). In the remainder of this paper we discuss three codes for the solution of sparse sets of linear equations which for most or all of the inner loop operations replace the sparse SAXPY of (2.1) with a direct SAXPY of the form

$$
\left.
\begin{array}{l}
K = 1 \\
DO\ 10\ J=J1,J2 \\
W(K) = W(K) + AMULT\ *\ A(J) \\
K = K+1 \\
10\quad CONTINUE
\end{array}
\right\} \tag{2.3}
$$

The maximum Megaflop rate for this loop on the CRAY-1 is about 50 Megaflops and it is by combining sequences of these that the high rates of the Jordan codes can be attained. We will discuss the vectorization of this inner loop on the CRAY-1 in more detail in section 5.

3.   Hybrid full and sparse codes

Even if the original matrix is quite sparse the non-zeros
created by the Gaussian elimination operation

$$a_{ij} := a_{ij} - a_{ik} [a_{kk}]^{-1} a_{kj} \qquad (3.1)$$

where a_{ik}, a_{kk}, a_{kj} are all non-zeros and a_{ij} was originally zero, cause
the remaining active or reduced matrix to become increasingly dense. We
illustrate this in Table 3.1 where we show the density of the reduced
matrix when it has a particular order. We see that, in the final stages
of the decomposition, the reduced matrix is full and so code for Gaussian
elimination on full matrices could be employed. Even on a scalar machine
this would be advantageous since not only would the removal of indirect
addressing speed up the innermost loop but also all the considerable
amount of data manipulation present in a general sparse code could be
avoided.

Order Non-zeros	147 2441	1176 18552	199 701	292 2208	130 1282	541 4285
Order of reduced matrix						
200	–	.32	–	.04	–	.13
150	–	.44	.03	.08	–	.26
100	.20	.68	.05	.18	.10	.42
50	.53	1.0	.15	.50	.23	.75
20	1.0	1.0	.80	1.0	.72	1.0
10	1.0	1.0	1.0	1.0	1.0	1.0

Table 3.1 Density of reduced matrix in Gaussian elimination

The idea of switching to code for full matrices towards the end of
sparse Gaussian elimination is not new. Gustavson incorporated it in the
DMOOP routine of the IBM package SLMATH (IBM, 1976) and Munksgaard (1980)
employed a switch to full code in his code MA31 in the Harwell Subroutine
Library. Both of these codes, however, only use full code in the initial
decomposition (which we call ANALYZE-FACTOR) and use indirect addressing
throughout both in subsequent decompositions on matrices of the same
sparsity pattern (FACTOR.. actually such an entry does not exist in MA31)
and in the solution of systems using the factorized matrix (SOLVE).
Additionally, in DMOOP alterations to the source code are needed if it
is desired to switch to full code before the reduced matrix is 100%
dense. We will see that significant further gains can be obtained by
allowing a switch at lower densities. We have examined the effect of

switching to full code in DMOOP (Duff, 1979) on a scalar machine (IBM 370/168) and have found that gains of up to 30% in the ANALYZE-FACTOR times can be achieved (if we switch when the reduced matrix is 50% dense) although the times are in general much slower than for more recent sparse codes. The MA31 code which solves symmetric positive definite systems was studied in this context by Duff (1982) who examined the performance at different switch over densities both on the IBM 3033 and the CRAY-1 and found that savings of 30% and up to 50% respectively could be obtained (at switch over densities of around 50% and 20% dense respectively). We refer the reader to the two aforementioned publications for further details on these experiments.

We have recently incorporated a switch to full code in the ANALYZE-FACTOR, FACTOR, and SOLVE phases of Harwell Subroutine MA28 for the solution of unsymmetric sparse linear equations (Duff, 1977). We present the results of running this code on some test problems (see Duff and Reid, 1979, for a description of these) in Table 3.2.

Order	147	1176	199	292	130	541
Non-zeros	2441	18552	701	2208	1282	4285
Time for ANALYZE-FACTOR						
No switch	.724	4.143	.105	.459	.160	1.207
1.0	.611	4.281	.103	.454	.157	1.180
0.8	.501	2.772	.095	.445	.158	1.160
0.6	.466	2.872	.102	.416	.145	1.137
0.4	.467	3.373	.098	.428	.152	1.175
Time for FACTOR						
No switch	.158	1.046	.019	.094	.035	.231
1.0	.141	1.074	.019	.089	.028	.234
0.8	.155	.896	.022	.091	.028	.232
0.6	.196	1.169	.021	.098	.026	.247
0.4	.285	2.188	.023	.155	.033	.342
Time for SOLVE						
No switch	.010	.049	.004	.012	.003	.027
1.0	.012	.048	.004	.012	.003	.027
0.8	.010	.049	.006	.013	.004	.027
0.6	.012	.054	.005	.012	.003	.027
0.4	.014	.066	.005	.015	.004	.029

Table 3.2   Times (in seconds) for runs of MA28 on the IBM 3033. The density of reduced matrix at which the switch to full code is made is shown in the left hand column.

These runs were performed on the IBM 3033 and we can see that, while gains of over 30% can be achieved in the ANALYZE-FACTOR entry, switching to full code provides at most a marginal benefit in the other entries. If, however, we perform the same runs on the CRAY-1 we obtain, as we see from the results in Table 3.3, a somewhat different picture. As in our

previous experiments with MA31, the benefits of the switch to full code
are evident at much lower densities of the reduced matrix. However, the
savings can now be over 70% in ANALYZE-FACTOR and savings of nearly 50%
can be obtained in FACTOR. Although the gains in SOLVE are not so
substantial there are instances when over 40% savings are attained.

Order Non-zeros	147 2441	1176 18552	199 701	292 2208	130 1282	541 4285
Time for ANALYZE-FACTOR						
No switch	.427	2.585	.0613	.276	.1078	.749
1.0	.365	2.610	.0601	.278	.1047	.739
0.8	.277	1.541	.0569	.250	.1006	.723
0.6	.207	1.429	.0545	.228	.0992	.696
0.4	.153	1.055	.0523	.201	.0972	.657
0.2	.114	.806	.0489	.169	.0899	.587
0.05	.132	1.025	.0645	.252	.0900	.810
Time for FACTOR						
No switch	.073	.529	.0087	.0417	.0179	.105
1.0	.058	.526	.0083	.0408	.0150	.101
0.8	.047	.304	.0080	.0379	.0138	.098
0.6	.042	.292	.0079	.0366	.0134	.097
0.4	.042	.283	.0080	.0375	.0133	.097
0.2	.052	.331	.0094	.0501	.0157	.149
0.05	.093	.618	.0330	.1745	.0653	.514
Time for SOLVE						
No switch	.0050	.0230	.0024	.0057	.0018	.0127
1.0	.0044	.0230	.0024	.0057	.0018	.0124
0.8	.0038	.0193	.0023	.0055	.0017	.0122
0.6	.0035	.0189	.0023	.0053	.0017	.0121
0.4	.0032	.0178	.0023	.0052	.0017	.0117
0.2	.0030	.0170	.0024	.0051	.0018	.0111
0.05	.0027	.0186	.0031	.0061	.0023	.0129

Table 3.3   Times (in seconds) for runs of MA28 on the CRAY-1.
The density of reduced matrix at which the switch to
full code is made is shown in the left-hand column.

The differences between the results in Table 3.2 and 3.3 are not
unexpected. Indeed, if the full matrix code were written in CAL rather
than Fortran the gains would be even greater and faster times would occur
at even lower densities of the reduced matrix.

Naturally, when we switch to full code before the reduced matrix is
completely full we will normally require more storage for the entries in
the factors since some zeros will now be held explicitly. This increase
in the number of entries held in the factors is indicated in Table 3.4.
At first glance, this may appear to be the penalty we pay for our gains

due to vectorization. However, in addition to avoiding indirect
addressing when using full code, we do not need to store integer indexing
information on the non-zeros. When this saving is taken into account we
see that, far from needing more storage, the total storage is less until
the switch over density becomes very low. Indeed, in most cases, the
switch over density can be set for fastest ANALYZE-FACTOR times with only
very little extra storage required.

Order Non-zeros	147 2441	1176 18552	199 701	292 2208	130 1282	541 4285
Number entries in factors						
No switch) 1.0)	5669	21177	1464	5215	1331	12571
0.8	6055	22858	1499	5323	1371	12701
0.6	6734	26554	1576	5695	1481	13301
0.4	8454	37048	1733	7171	1869	15237
0.2	12497	51338	2492	11640	3709	28965
0.05	21609	86326	9674	35260	16900	78251
Total storage						
No switch	11338	42354	2928	10430	2662	25142
1.0	9972	42293	2787	10264	2496	24469
0.8	9304	37255	2712	9865	2421	24249
0.6	9246	39655	2714	9872	2481	24301
0.4	10187	46874	2793	10745	2780	22301
0.2	13333	58158	3387	14258	4396	36029
0.05	21612	91430	10135	36298	16903	81976

Table 3.4 Storage requirements in CRAY-1 words after switch over
to full code at densities of reduced matrix shown in
the left-hand column.

4. The use of a frontal method

A common algorithm which avoids indirect addressing in the inner
loop is the variable band or profile scheme (Jennings, 1966). This is a
generalization of a band matrix approach which permits the first non-zero
in each row of the matrix to be a varying distance from the diagonal.
All entries between the first non-zero and the diagonal are stored and
operated upon and so it is possible to use direct addressing in the
innermost loops. Matrices of a suitable form for profile elimination
arise with some simple orderings of discretizations of partial
differential equations (for example, the reverse Cuthill McKee ordering)
and the SPARSPAK package (George et al, 1980) has an option for
implementing this ordering. Dodson (1981) has CAL coded the inner loops
and reports overall Megaflop rates of nearly 7 for the decomposition and
over 9 for the subsequent solution of equations. The full asymptotic
rate of direct SAXPY is not achieved because of the non-vectorizable data

manipulation in the code and the short length of the vectors processed in the innermost loops. It is possible that a complete redesign of the algorithm could yield higher rates but we prefer to concentrate on the frontal approach which we now describe and which can be viewed as a generalization of the variable band technique.

Although the frontal method, as designed and coded by Duff (1981) for the MA32 package in the Harwell Subroutine Library, can be used to solve any set of unsymmetric linear equations, we will briefly describe the approach in terms of finite element problems. In a finite element problem the matrix A is a sum

$$A = \sum_{\ell} B^{(\ell)} \qquad (4.1)$$

where each $B^{(\ell)}$ has non-zeros in only a few rows and columns and corresponds to contributions to the matrix from finite element ℓ. It is normal to hold $B^{(\ell)}$ in packed form as a small full matrix together with an indexing vector to identify where the non-zeros belong in A. The basic "assembly" operation when forming A is thus of the form

$$a_{ij} := a_{ij} + b_{ij} . \qquad (4.2)$$

If we examine the basic step in Gaussian elimination (3.1), viz.

$$a_{ij} := a_{ij} - a_{ik} [a_{kk}]^{-1} a_{kj} \qquad (4.3)$$

it is evident that it can be performed before all assemblies (4.2) are completed, provided only that the terms in the triple product in (4.3) have been fully summed (otherwise we will be subtracting the wrong quantity). In a frontal code the elements are assembled one by one and each variable can be eliminated whenever its row and column is fully summed, that is after its last occurrence in a $B^{(\ell)}$. This permits all intermediate working to be performed in a full matrix whose size increases when a variable appears for the first time and decreases when one is eliminated. The order of elimination is determined from the order of the assembly. If the elements are ordered systematically from one end of the region to the other, then the active variables form a front that moves along it. For this reason the full matrix in which all arithmetic is performed is called the frontal matrix. For symmetric positive definite matrices (for example, the code of Irons, 1970), all variables may be eliminated as soon as they are fully summed. For more general systems (for example, the unsymmetric frontal code of Hood, 1976) some form of pivoting is required to ensure numerical stability. In the MA32 code each pivot $a_{\ell k}$ is required to satisfy a threshold criterion of the form

$$|a_{\ell k}| \geqslant u.\max_i |a_{ik}|$$

for some preset threshold u in the range (0,1]. If no such pivot can be found in the fully-summed rows and columns, then the elimination is delayed so that the front is temporarily bigger than it would otherwise have been.

For non-element problems, the rows (equations) are "assembled" one at a time and a variable becomed fully summed whenever there are no further equations in which it appears (Duff, 1981). It is this entry which is the generalization of variable band methods discussed earlier.

For the purpose of this present study, the main feature of the frontal method that is of interest is the fact that all pivoting and elimination operations are performed within a full submatrix and so direct addressing can be used in the innermost loop.

The frontal code, MA32, has recently been used on the CRAY-1 by Andrew Cliffe of the Theoretical Physics Division at Harwell in the solution of nonlinear partial differential equations arising in fluid flow. He used a finite-element method based on a Galerkin formulation of the velocity-pressure version of the Navier-Stokes equations. We show some results from Cliffe et al (1983) in Table 4.1 where the elements were nine-node isoparametric quadrilaterals with biquadratic interpolation for the velocities and piecewise linear interpolation for the pressure. The only difference between the runs in columns three and four is that a CRAY-1 Assembler Language inner loop was used for the runs in column 4. We have augmented these results by runs on two artificial problems. The first (column 5) is a grid of ten-node rectangular elements with nodes at corners, midpoints and centroid and with five variables at each node. The second (column 6) is a finite-difference problem arising from the five-point discretization of the Laplacian operator on a rectangular grid. For the flow problems, which were modelling flow over a backward facing step, the upper and lower grid sizes refer to the element grid before and after the step respectively.

Dimensions of grid of elements or equations	5×5 15×10	20×24 60×36	20×20 60×40		16×16	64×64
Order (degrees of freedom)	7942	29506	31282		5445	4096
Maximum front size	94	159	175		195	65
Total time in seconds for solution (including back substitution)	6.01	46.0	56.5	42.9	12.58	3.55
Time in innermost loop (in seconds)	2.36	24.8	31.9	16.9	7.63	1.49
Number operations in inner loop (in millions)	62	745	980		238	33
Inner loop megaflops	26	30	31	58	31	22
Total megaflops	10	16	17	23	91	9

Table 4.1   Performance of frontal code on the CRAY-1

In all the runs in Table 4.1, except column 4, the innermost
loop of the frontal code was a direct SAXPY coded in Fortran and
vectorized by the CFT compiler (version 1.09). We discuss coding this
loop in CAL in the next section.

The two artificial cases have been run on the CRAY-1 with
vectorization inhibited and the times for the element and the equation
input were 59.6 and 9.8 seconds respectively. Thus the overall increase
in speed due to the vectorizing capability of the CRAY-1 was 4.7 and 2.8
with the inner loop running over 7 and 5 times faster on the element and
equation problem respectively.

In addition to using direct code in the innermost loop, the frontal
method can be used to solve very large problems on both scalar and vector
machines by virtue of the fact that only the frontal matrix need be held
in core. The size required for this frontal matrix for the problems we
have just considered is given in Table 4.1. Now, although the overall
times include the CPU costs of writing the factors to auxiliary storage
and reading them during back substitution, an additional charge is made
by the CRAY-1 accounting algorithm for I/O since the job remains in
central memory during the actual I/O operation. Minimization of this
overhead is a separate study in its own right and some initial attempts
at this are discussed by Duff and Reid (1981a) and Duff (1983).

In the next section we describe some of our current thoughts on
optimizing the inner loop on the CRAY-1 and discuss some of the
implications of this.

5.   Tuning the frontal code for the CRAY-1

As we discussed in the previous section, the innermost loop of the frontal code is a direct SAXPY. We show in Table 5.1, the Megaflop rate for a range of implementations of this basic loop on the CRAY-1. In this table, the relative costs of start up times are reflected in the performance at different vector lengths.

Vector length	Fortran CFT version 1.09	Cray SCILIB	Boeing CRAYPACK	Multiple SAXPY
20	17.7	11.3	16.7	32.5
30	21.2	15.0	21.4	43.2
50	25.4	20.4	27.8	55.2
100	29.7	28.0	35.7	58.6
150	31.5	31.9	39.5	59.5
200	32.4	34.3	41.7	59.9
300	33.4	37.1	44.1	62.8
Asymptotic	35.7	44.4	50.0	66.4

Table 5.1   Megaflop rates for different implementations of direct SAXPY and for a multiple SAXPY.

In the frontal code at each elimination stage we perform a sequence of direct SAXPYs corresponding to eliminations by the pivot row on all other rows of the frontal matrix. Since the SAXPY operation

$$\underline{x} := \underline{x} + \alpha \underline{y} \qquad\qquad (5.1)$$

requires two memory loads and one store for each pair of floating point operations, the optimal rate is limited by memory accesses and is bounded by 50 Megaflops when the multiplication and addition are chained with one of the loads. Thus, very little further improvement can be obtained over the figures in columns 2-4 of Table 5.1 which fall a long way short of the full potential of the CRAY-1.

However, higher rates can be obtained by observing that, at each elimination stage in the frontal code, a sequence of direct SAXPYs corresponding to eliminations by the pivot row on all other rows of the frontal matrix is performed. The sequence can be represented by several SAXPYs of the form (5.1) where the vector $\underline{x}$ and the scalar α change but $\underline{y}$ (which represents the pivot row) remains constant. Thus, if we can keep $\underline{y}$ in the vector registers throughout the sequence of SAXPYs we need only one load and one store for each two floating point operations, yielding a maximum asymptotic rate of nearly 80 megaflops. The CAL code, written by Alistair Mills of CRAY Research (UK) Ltd, in column 5 of Table 5.1 implements this idea. A call to this multiple-SAXPY CAL routine replaces both the innermost and next-to-innermost loops in our frontal code.

Although further optimization is possible, it is clearly faster than the maximum rate for a single SAXPY.

It is possible to do even better. In any realistic problem, there are several fully-summed rows and columns in the frontal matrix at each stage. If just two elimination steps can be combined, then our inner loop can run at well over 100 Megaflops. This is done by loading the two pivotal rows into the vector registers and chaining the load of the first non-pivotal row with the floating point operations from the first pivotal row. The SAXPY operations from the second pivotal row are then chained and the second non-pivotal row is simultaneously loaded from memory. The operations of the two pivot rows on this second non-pivotal row are then overlapped with the store of the first non-pivotal row and the load of the third non-pivotal row respectively. We continue in this way always keeping both arithmetic pipes busy, and so achieve optimal performance. A prototype CAL code implementing this runs at over 90 Megaflops and it is hoped to improve this further.

Although the prospect of a fairly general sparse code whose inner loop runs at well over 100 Megaflops on the CRAY-1 may raise one's pulse rate considerably, a small caveat is in order. If we look in Table 5.2 at the ratio of inner loop time to total time for the 16x16 element example of Table 4.1 on the IBM 3081K and the CRAY-1 (using CFT), the values are .86, .60 respectively reflecting the fact that the inner-loop time is reduced much more than the rest of the code through vectorization. Thus, if we speed up the inner loop even

	CPU time (seconds)		% time in inner loop	% time selecting pivots
	Total	inner loop		
3081K	119	102	86	9
CFT	12.6	7.6	60	9
CAL	7.5	3.7	49	16
"NEW ALG CAL"	5.8	2.0	35	21
Optimize pivot selection	4.7	2.0	43	1.5

Table 5.2   Effect of vectorization on 16x16 example

more, this ratio will decrease further until the computation time in the inner loop ceases to be dominant. This is a common phenomenon of vectorization and is witnessed by the ratio of inner loop to total time reducing to .35 when CAL is used. Indeed, if we can get the inner-loop running at 130 megaflops the overall Megaflop rate for our five problems in Table 4.1 is only increased from 10→15, 16→28, 17→30, 19→35 and 9→14 respectively. A corollary of this is that originally non-dominant parts of the code may now be significant. This is seen dramatically in the last column where the pivoting time which was negligible on the IBM now uses 21% of the CPU time. It is relatively easy to vectorize this part of the code and the overall savings in CPU time are not far short of 20% as is shown in row 5 of the table.

Another important lesson from these results is that, although it is conceivable that the compiler could be smart enough to perform optimization to the level of CAL (the third row in Table 5.2) further substantial gains can be attained by algorithmic redesign quite outwith the scope of any present day compilers.

6.   Extensions and Conclusions

The frontal code, discussed in sections 4 and 5, will become less efficient if variables remain in the front for long without becoming fully assembled. However, we can view the frontal matrix at any stage as one of the $B^{(\ell)}$ of equation (4.1), albeit in general of larger size than the original elements. If we allow ourselves to store the frontal matrix, to continue our computation assembling other elements and eliminating fully-summed variables, and to reassemble previously stored frontal matrices we can avoid the overhead of retaining variables in the front and performing operations on them at each step. We call this class of methods multifrontal since, during the computation, several previous frontal matrices might be held in store. Duff and Reid (1982b,1983) show how to implement this method efficiently using a simple stack to hold any stored frontal matrices and have developed codes MA27 and MA37 in the Harwell Subroutine Library, for the numerically stable solution of sparse indefinite and unsymmetric systems respectively.

Since this multifrontal method also uses only direct addressing in the inner loop we would expect it to perform well on vector processors. The results, however, are a little disappointing with gains of only about twice the difference in scalar speeds between the CRAY-1 and the IBM 3081K. The reason is that there is much more fixed point overhead in the multifrontal codes than the frontal one. Indeed the inner loop of MA37 on the IBM 3081K accounts for less than 50% the total time on most of our test examples.

An important but often understressed effect of vector processors on computational science can be seen if we consider in more detail the problem in column 2 of Table 4.1 which had about 30,000 variables. The total data was over 8 Megawords and so much I/O had to be performed. The solution of the nonlinear system required 2.5 Gigaflops and the overall time on the CRAY-1 (including I/O) was about 4 minutes. Although the IBM 3081K cannot match the asymptotic speed of the CRAY-1, it has efficient integer arithmetic and is a better balanced machine with respect to I/O.

The overall time for the same problem on the IBM 3081K was thus a creditable 24 minutes. The turn-around time on the two machines was, however, 12 minutes and (effectively) 24 hours respectively. Since this was one run in a long simulation study where each run was preceded by an interpretation of the previous one the effect was dramatic. The total simulation could not be contemplated on the IBM (estimated time 2 months) but was completed on the CRAY-1 in 2 days. Admittedly such comparisons depend on computer management policy but it is this kind of experience more than inner-loop Megaflops which establishes the benefit of vector processors in computational science.

In this paper, we have shown that it is possible to design algorithms for the direct solution of sparse linear equations which use direct addressing in their innermost loops and will thus perform well on vector processors. The algorithms we have discussed also perform well on scalar machines and make no particular demands on the structure of the coefficient matrix. We have illustrated the performance of our algorithms on the CRAY-1 and have indicated how special coding can be used to obtain high computational speeds.

References

Calahan, D.A. (1982). Vectorized direct solvers for 2-D grids. Proc. 6th Symposium on Reservoir Simulation, New Orleans, Feb. 1-2, 1982. Paper SPE 10522.

Cliffe, K.A., Jones, I.P., Porter, J.D., Thompson, C.P. and Wilkes, N.S. (1983). Laminar flow over a backward facing step: numerical solutions for a test problem. Harwell Report CSS 142.

CRAY (1981). User News. Cray Channels 3 (2), p.20, Cray Research Inc.

Dodson, D. (1981). Preliminary timing study for the CRAYPACK library. Boeing Computer Services Memorandum G4550-CM-39.

Duff, I.S. (1977). MA28 - a set of Fortran subroutines for sparse unsymmetric linear equations. AERE Report R.8730, HMSO, London.

Duff, I.S. (1979). Practical comparisons of codes for the solution of sparse linear systems. In Sparse Matrix Proceedings 1978. I.S. Duff and G.W. Stewart (editors). SIAM Press, pp.107-134.

Duff, I.S. (1981). MA32 - A package for solving sparse unsymmetric systems using the frontal method. AERE Report R.10079, HMSO, London.

Duff, I.S. (1982). Full matrix techniques in sparse Gaussian elimination. In Numerical Analysis. Proceedings, Dundee 1981. G.A. Watson (Ed.), Springer-Verlag. pp.71-84.

Duff, I.S. (1983). Enhancements to the MA32 package for solving sparse unsymmetric systems. AERE Report R.11009, HMSO, London.

Duff. I.S. and Reid, J.K. (1979). Performance evaluation of codes for sparse matrix problems. In Performance Evaluation of Numerical Software. L. Fosdick (Ed.), North Holland, pp.121-135.

Duff, I.S. and Reid, J.K. (1982a). Experience of sparse matrix codes on the CRAY-1. Computer Physics Communications 26, pp.293-302.

Duff, I.S. and Reid, J.K. (1982b). The multifrontal solution of indefinite sparse symmetric linear systems. AERE Report CSS 122. To appear in ACM Trans. Math. Softw.

Duff, I.S. and Reid, J.K. (1983). The multifrontal solution of unsymmetric sets of linear equations. AERE Report CSS 133.

George, A., Liu, J. and Ng, E. (1980). User Guide for SPARSPAK: Waterloo Sparse Linear Equations Package. Research Report CS-78-30 (Revised Jan. 1980). Department of Computer Science, University of Waterloo.

Hood, P. (1976). Frontal solution program for unsymmetric matrices. Int. J. Numer. Meth. Engng. 10, pp.379-399.

IBM (1976). IBM System/360 and System/370 IBM 1130 and IBM 1800 Subroutine Library - Mathematics. User's Guide. Program Product 5736-XM7. IBM Catalogue #SH12-5300-1.

Irons, B.M. (1970). A frontal solution program for finite element analysis. Int. J. Numer. Meth. Engng. 2, pp.5-32.

Jennings, A. (1966). A compact storage scheme for the solution of symmetric linear simultaneous equations. Comput. J. 9, pp.281-285.

Jordan, T.L. (1979). A performance evaluation of linear algebra software in parallel architectures. In Performance Evaluation of Numerical Software. L. Fosdick (Ed.). North-Holland, pp.59-76.

Lawson, C.L., Hanson, R.J., Kincaid, D.R. and Krogh, F.T. (1979). Basic linear algebra subprograms for Fortran usage. ACM Trans. Math. Softw. 5, pp.308-323.

Munksgaard, N. (1980). Solving sparse symmetric sets of linear equations by preconditioned conjugate gradients. ACM Trans. Math. Softw. 6, p.206-219.

Saunders, V.R. and Guest, M.F. (1982). Applications of the CRAY-1 for quantum chemistry calculations. Computer Physics Communications 26, pp.389-395.

On Two Numerical Algorithms for Multiprocessors [*]

A. Sameh
Department of Computer Science
University of Illinois at Urbana-Champaign

1. Introduction

In this paper we present multiprocessor algorithms for solving two important problems. The first problem concerns solving large banded positive definite linear systems such as those that arise from the numerical solution of two-point boundary value problems via the finite-element method. The second problem is that of approximating few of the smallest (or largest) eigenvalues and the corresponding eigenvectors of large sparse generalized eigenvalue problems $Ax = \lambda Bx$, where A and B are symmetric and sparse with B being positive definite.

Both algorithms are designed so as to minimize interprocessor communication, hence reducing synchronization penalties. Each algorithm consists of several stages with the most time-consuming stages consisting of independent tasks (one task per processor) that can be performed with no interprocessor communication.

Higher speedup may be achieved in each algorithm if each of these independent tasks can be performed on a tightly coupled cluster of processors. These clusters are, in turn, interconnected via a global switch.

* This work is supported in part by the National Science Foundation under grant US NSF MCS 81-17010.

2. Block-tridiagonal systems

Block tridiagonal linear systems of equations arise in many applications in engineering and mathematical physics. In many important situations these systems are symmetric positive definite. Let the system under consideration be given by

$$Ax = f \, , \tag{2.1}$$

where $A = [B_{j-1}^T, A_j, B_j]$ is of order $n = \gamma m$, $\gamma \gg 1$, and B_j, A_j are each of order m. Further, we assume that the system (2.1) arises from the numerical treatment of a boundary-value problem via the finite element method. In other words A and f may be generated whenever needed. We wish to solve this system on a multiprocessor consisting of p processors, where we assume that $q = n/p$ is an integer. If the system (2.1) is partitioned into p block-rows, then the i-th of which, $1 \leq i \leq p$, is of the form

$$[(O, E_i), T_i, (G_i, O)] \, , \tag{2.2}$$

or

$$
\begin{array}{ccccc}
B_{\alpha-1}^T & A_\alpha & B_\alpha & & 0 \\
0 & B_\alpha^T & A_{\alpha+1} & B_{\alpha+1} & 0 \\
\cdot & & \cdot & \cdot & \cdot \\
0 & & & B_{i\upsilon-1} & A_{i\upsilon} & B_{i\upsilon}
\end{array}
$$

where $\alpha = (i-1)\upsilon + 1$, with υ being the integer q/m. Note that $B_0 = B_\gamma = 0$. The algorithm we propose here, see [SaKu78] and [LaSa83], consists of the following stages.

Stage 1:

Each processor $1 \leq i \leq p$, generates the $m \times m$ matrices A_k and B_{k-1}, $k = (i-1)\nu + 1, \ldots, i\nu$ as well as the corresponding part of the right-hand side f_i.

Stage 2:

Using the Cholesky factorization of each matrix T_i, solve in each processor i the linear systems

$$T_i U_i = E_i, \ T_i V_i = G_i , \quad T_i g_i = f_i \tag{2.3}$$

at a cost of $O(m^2 n/p)$ arithmetic operations. Now we have the linear system

$$Cx = g$$

where C is a block-tridiagonal matrix of the form

$$C = [(O, U_i), I_q, (V_i, O)] . \tag{2.4}$$

Stage 3:

Solve the independent system which consists of the $(p-1)$ pairs of the m equations above and m equations below each partitioning line in (2.4). We denote this banded system of order $2m(p-1)$ by

$$Wy = h , \tag{2.5}$$

where W is of the form

$$
\begin{array}{cccc}
I & P_1 & 0 & O \\
Q_2 & I & 0 & R_2 \\
S_3 & 0 & I & P_3 & 0 & 0 \\
& & Q_4 & I & 0 & R_4 \\
& & S_5 & 0 & I & P_5 \\
& & & Q_6 & I & \ddots \\
& & & & & I & P_{k-3} & 0 & 0 \\
& & & & & Q_{k-2} & I & 0 & R_{k-2} \\
& & & & & S_{k-1} & 0 & I & P_{k-1} \\
& & & & & & & Q_k & I
\end{array}
$$

(2.6)

in which $k = 2(p-1)$. Note that the first m rows of (2.5) are contained in processor 1, processor i, $2 \leq i \leq p-1$, contains rows $(2i-3)m+1, (2i-3)m+2,..., (2i-1)m$, and the last m rows are contained in processor p.

The cost of solving this reduced system depends on how these processors are interconnected:

(1) If these processors are linearly connected, then the system (2.5) is solved sequentially. The matrix P_1 and the corresponding part of the right-hand side h_1 are transmitted from processor 1 to processor 2 where the first block in (2.6) is reduced to the upper triangular form using Gaussian elimination without pivoting. This is possible since it can be shown that all the eigenvalues of W are positive. Once P_3 and the corresponding part of the right-hand side are updated, they are transmitted to processor 3,... and so on. Finally, (2.6) is reduced to the upper triangular form

$$\begin{array}{ccccc} I & P_1 & 0 \\ & H_2 & 0 & R_2 \\ & & I & \hat{P}_3 & 0 \\ & & & H_4 & 0 & R_4 \\ & & & & I & \hat{P}_5 \\ & & & & & H_6 \\ & & & \cdot \\ & & \cdot & & \cdot & & 0 \\ & & & \cdot & & & 0 & R_{k-2} \\ & & & & \cdot & & & I & \hat{P}_{k-1} \\ & & & & & & & & H_k \end{array} \qquad (2.7)$$

where each H_j is upper triangular. This system may be solved sequentially by transmitting data in the opposite direction, from processor p towards processor 1. The solution vector y yields $2m(p-1)$ components of x, the solution of (2.1), in positions $jq-m+1,..., jq+m-1, jq+m$ for $j = 1, 2,..., p-1$. The cost of this option is $O(m^3 p)$ time steps.

(2) On the other extreme, if these p processors have access to a global memory via a reasonably powerful interconnection network with a broadcasting facility, then the reduced system (2.6) may be solved at a lower cost using the following algorithm.

(a) Solve in each processor i, $1 \leq i \leq p-1$, the linear systems

$$\begin{vmatrix} I_m & P_{2i-1} \\ Q_{2i} & I_m \end{vmatrix} \begin{vmatrix} Y_{2i-1}^{(1)} & Z_{2i-1}^{(1)} & h_{2i-1}^{(1)} \\ Y_{2i}^{(1)} & Z_{2i}^{(1)} & h_{2i}^{(1)} \end{vmatrix} = \begin{vmatrix} S_{2i-1} & 0 & h_{2i-1} \\ 0 & R_{2i} & h_{2i} \end{vmatrix}, \qquad (2.8)$$

where $h^T = (h_1^T, h_2^T, \ldots, h_{2(p-1)}^T)$ is the right-hand side in (2.5), and P_j, Q_j are as given in (2.6). For $p = 9$, the system is now of the form,

$$
\begin{array}{cccc|cc}
I & 0 & 0 & Z_1^{(1)} & & \\
0 & I & 0 & Z_2^{(1)} & & \\
Y_3^{(1)} & 0 & I & 0 & 0 & Z_3^{(1)} \\
Y_4^{(1)} & 0 & 0 & I & 0 & Z_4^{(1)} \\
 & Y_5^{(4)} & 0 & & I & 0 \\
 & Y_6^{(1)} & 0 & & 0 & I \\
\end{array}
$$

$$
\begin{array}{cccc|ccc}
I & 0 & 0 & Z_{11}^{(1)} & & & \\
0 & I & 0 & Z_{12}^{(1)} & & & \\
Y_{13}^{(1)} & 0 & I & 0 & 0 & Z_{13}^{(1)} \\
Y_{14}^{(1)} & 0 & 0 & I & 0 & Z_{14}^{(1)} \\
 & Y_{15}^{(1)} & 0 & & I & 0 \\
 & Y_{16}^{(1)} & 0 & & 0 & I \\
\end{array}
$$

Figure 1

(b) For the sake of illustration let $p-1 = 2^\theta$. Now, for $j = 2, 3,..., \theta$ we perform the following steps:

(i) In each processor i, $1 \leq i \leq 2^{\theta-j+1}$, solve the linear systems

$$
\begin{vmatrix} I_m & Z_{\sigma(i)}^{(j-1)} \\ Y_{3+\sigma(i)} & I_m \end{vmatrix}
\begin{vmatrix} Y_{\sigma(i)}^{(j)} & Z_{\sigma(i)}^{(j)} & h_{\sigma(i)}^{(j)} \\ Y_{3+\sigma(i)}^{(j)} & Z_{3+\sigma(i)}^{(j)} & h_{3+\sigma(i)}^{(j)} \end{vmatrix} =
$$
$$
\begin{vmatrix} Y_{\sigma(i)}^{(j-1)} & 0 & h_{\sigma(i)}^{(j-1)} \\ 0 & Z_{3+\sigma(i)}^{(j-1)} & h_{3+\sigma(i)}^{(j-1)} \end{vmatrix},
\tag{2.9}
$$

where $\sigma(i) = (2i-1)2^{(j-1)} - 1$, $Y_l^{(j)} = 0$ for $l < 1+2^{(j-1)}$, and $Z_l^{(j)} = 0$ for $l > 2^{(\theta+1)} - 2^{(j-1)}$.

(ii) Retrieve the rest of the $m \times m$ matrices $Y_\nu^{(j)}$ and $Z_\nu^{(j)}$ as well as the updated portions of the right-hand sides $h_\nu^{(j)}$. For

$i = 1, 2,..., 2^{\theta-j+1}$, obtain

$$Z_{\nu(i)}^{(j)} = - Z_{\nu(i)}^{(j-1)} Z_{3+\sigma(i)}^{(j)} , \qquad (2.10a)$$

$$Y_{\nu(i)}^{(j)} = Y_{\nu(i)}^{(j-1)} - Z_{\nu(i)}^{(j-1)} Y_{3+\sigma(i)}^{(j)} , \qquad (2.10b)$$

$$h_{\nu(i)}^{(j)} = h_{\nu(i)}^{(j-1)} - Z_{\nu(i)}^{(j-1)} h_{3+\sigma(i)}^{(j)} , \qquad (2.10c)$$

where $\nu(i) = (i-1)2^j + 1,..., (2i-1)2^{j-1}$ with $\nu(i) \neq \sigma(i)$, and

$$Z_{\eta(i)}^{(j)} = Z_{\eta(i)}^{(j-1)} - Y_{\eta(i)}^{(j-1)} Z_{\sigma(i)}^{(j)} , \qquad (2.11a)$$

$$Y_{\eta(i)}^{(j)} = - Y_{\eta(i)}^{(j-1)} Y_{\sigma(i)}^{(j)} , \qquad (2.11b)$$

$$h_{\eta(i)}^{(j)} = h_{\eta(i)}^{(j-1)} - Y_{\eta(i)}^{(j-1)} h_{\sigma(i)}^{(j)} , \qquad (2.11c)$$

where $\eta(i) = \nu(i) + 2^{j-1}$ with $\eta(i) \neq 3+\sigma(i)$. Y_l, Z_l, and h_l, in equations (2.10) and (2.11), are evaluated using one processor for each matrix multiplication.

Figure 2 shows the form of the matrix of coefficients of the reduced system for $j = 3$, for the case where $p = 9$.

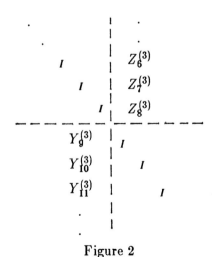

Figure 2

(c) Solve the linear system

$$
\begin{vmatrix} I_m & Z_{p-2}^{(\theta)} \\ Y_{p+1}^{(\theta)} & I_m \end{vmatrix} \begin{vmatrix} h_{p-2}^{(\theta+1)} \\ h_{p+1}^{(\theta+1)} \end{vmatrix} = \begin{vmatrix} h_{p-2}^{(\theta)} \\ h_{p+1}^{(\theta)} \end{vmatrix} \tag{2.12}
$$

in one processor, where $y_{p-2} = h_{p-2}^{(\theta+1)}$ and $y_{p+1} = h_{p+1}^{(\theta+1)}$ and retrieve the rest of the solution of (2.5):

$$
\begin{aligned}
y_i &= h_i^{(\theta+1)} = h_i^{(\theta)} - Z_i^{(\theta)} h_{p+1}^{(\theta+1)} , & 1 \le i \le p-3 , \quad i = p-1 , \\
y_i &= h_i^{(\theta+1)} = h_i^{(\theta)} - Y_i^{(\theta)} h_{p-2}^{(\theta+1)} , & i = p , \quad p+2 \le i \le 2p-2 ,
\end{aligned} \tag{2.13}
$$

using as many processors as possible, one processor for each matrix-vector multiplication.

The bottleneck in this algorithm is clear from (2.10), (2.11), and (2.13); several matrices are to be multiplied by the same matrix or vector. Consider, for example, the case of obtaining $Z_\nu^{(3)}$ for $p = 9$. From (2.10a) and (2.11a) we see that $Z_1^{(2)}$, $Z_2^{(2)}$, and $Z_4^{(2)}$ are to be multiplied by $Z_6^{(3)}$, while $Y_5^{(2)}$, $Y_7^{(2)}$, and $Y_8^{(2)}$ are to be multiplied by $Z_3^{(3)}$. Assigning one processor to each matrix multiplication and assuming that m is not too small, it is possible to overlap the time consumed by broadcasting by that of the arithmetic. If the two $m \times m$ matrices to be multiplied are $A = [a_1, a_2, \ldots, a_m]$ and $B = [b_1, b_2, \ldots, b_m]$ where $b_j^T = (\beta_{1j}, \ldots, \beta_{mj})$, then the j-th column of the product $C = AB = [c_1, c_2, \ldots, c_m]$ is given by $c_j = Ab_j = \sum_{i=1}^m \beta_{ij} a_i$. Hence, each broadcast of β_{ij} correspond to approximately $2m$ arithmetic operations. Consequently the cost of this option is $O(m^3 \log_2 p)$ time steps.

Stage 4:

Once the solution of (2.5) is obtained, the remaining components of solution
of (2.1) are obtained via perfect parallelism. In each processor $1 \leq i \leq p$ the
remaining $q-2m$ components of the subvector x_i, of order q, are retrieved using
the fact that

$$x_i = g_i - U_i y_{2i-3} - V_i y_{2i} .$$

This stage consumes, therefore, $O(mn/p)$ time steps.

The total cost of this algorithm clearly depends on the relationship between
m, n, and p, as well as the architecture of the machine.

I.   If the number of processors p is much smaller than n, the above algorithm
      consumes time proportional to $m^2 n/p$. Further, provided that the matrix
      of coefficients of (2.1) can be generated in the p processors, the processors
      need only be connected linearly. The algorithm achieves maximum speedup
      when p is proportional to $\sqrt{n/m}$.

II.   If p is proportional to n/m, then provided that these p processors are
      tightly coupled via an interconnection network allowing broadcasts, option 2
      of stage 3 becomes viable leading to an algorithm for solving (2.1) in time
      proportional to $m^3 \log_2 n$. This scheme may be regarded, in this case, as an
      alternative to block-cyclic reduction [Hell76].

Finally, we would like to point out that the systems (2.3) may be solved
using the preconditioned conjugate gradient algorithm, [MeVo77] and [CoGO76].
This can be more economical especially if $q = n/p$ is large and the matrices T_i

in (2.3), $1 \le i \le p$, are sparse within the band. The cost of the algorithm can be further reduced if we have $p = O(\sqrt{n/m})$ clusters of processors with each cluster consisting of $(2m+1)$ processors. Each processor handling one system of (2.3) using the sequential conjugate gradient algorithm with a preconditioning strategy.

3. The sparse generalized eigenvalue problem

The problem of computing a few of the smallest (or largest) eigenvalues and eigenvectors of the large, sparse, generalized eigenvalue problem

$$Ax = \lambda Bx , \qquad (3.1)$$

where A and B are symmetric matrices of large order n, with B being positive definite, arise in many important applications [BaWi73], [Grub78], and [Fisc82]. We present a new method: "trace minimization", [SaWi82] and [Gole82], which is suitable for multiprocessors for handling this problem. This method is competitive with the Lanczos algorithm, [Parl80], for solving (3.1), especially when the matrices A and B are so large and sparse with a sparsity pattern such that the Cholesky factor of either matrix has to be contained in auxiliary storage.

The main idea behind our algorithm, [SaWi82], depends on the following observation:

Let $\mathbf{Y}$ be the set of all $n \times p$, $p < n$, matrices Y for which $Y^T B Y = I_p$. Then

$$\min_{Y \epsilon \mathbf{Y}} tr(Y^T A Y) = \sum_{i=1}^{p} \lambda_i , \qquad (3.2)$$

where $tr(A) = \sum_{i=1}^{n} \alpha_{ii}$ denotes the trace of A, and

$\lambda_1 \leq \lambda_2 \leq \cdots \leq \lambda_p < \lambda_{p+1} \leq \cdots \leq \lambda_n$ are the eigenvalues of (A,B).

Let Y_k be an $n \times p$ matrix approximating the p eigenvectors corresponding to the smallest p eigenvalues of (3.1), i.e.

$$Y_k^T A Y_k = \Sigma_k = diag(\sigma_1^{(k)}, \ldots, \sigma_p^{(k)}), \qquad (3.3a)$$

and

$$Y_k^T B Y_k = I_p . \qquad (3.3b)$$

Now, choose an $n \times p$ correction matrix Δ_k and a $p \times p$ scaling matrix S_k to construct the new iterate

$$Y_{k+1} = (Y_k - \Delta_k)S_k \qquad (3.4)$$

so that

$$Y_{k+1}^T A Y_{k+1} = \Sigma_{k+1} = diag(\sigma_1^{(k+1)}, \ldots, \sigma_p^{(k+1)}), \qquad (3.5a)$$

$$Y_{k+1}^T B Y_{k+1} = I_p , \qquad (3.5b)$$

and

$$tr(Y_{k+1}^T A Y_{k+1}) < tr(Y_k^T A Y_k) . \qquad (3.5c)$$

The most time-consuming part of this algorithm is the choice of Δ_k which ensures that (3.5c) holds. Several choices are possible, we present here the one resulting from the following constrained optimization problem

$$minimize \ tr(Y_k - \Delta_k)^T A(Y_k - \Delta_k)$$
$$subject \ Y_k^T B \Delta_k = 0 . \qquad (3.6)$$

Without loss of generality we assume that A is positive definite, for if A is indefinite, (3.1) is replaced by

$$(A - \eta B)x = (\lambda - \eta)Bx ,$$

where η is chosen so that $(A - \eta B)$ is positive definite, i.e., $\eta < \lambda_1 < 0$. For a positive definite A then, (3.6) is reduced to the p problems:

$$minimize \ (y_j^{(k)} - d_j^{(k)})^T \ A(y_j^{(k)} - d_j^{(k)})$$

$$subject \ Y_k^T B d_j^{(k)} = 0, \quad for 1 \leq j \leq p \ , \tag{3.7}$$

where $y_j^{(k)} = Y_k e_j$ and $d_j^{(k)} = \Delta_k \ e_j$, in which e_j is the j-th column of I_n. Let the orthogonal factorization of BY_k be given by $Q_k R_k$, where Q_k is an $n \times p$ matrix with orthonormal columns and R_k an upper triangular matrix of order p. Also, let $\tilde{Q}_k$ be an $n \times (n-p)$ matrix with orthonormal columns such that $[Q_k, \tilde{Q}_k]$ is an orthogonal matrix. Now, the problems in (3.7) are equivalent to solving the p independent positive definite linear systems

$$(\tilde{Q}_k^T A \tilde{Q}_k) g_j^{(k)} = \tilde{Q}_k^T A y_j^{(k)} \ , \quad i \leq j \leq p \ , \tag{3.8}$$

where $d_j^{(k)} = \tilde{Q}_k g_j^{(k)}$.

Dropping all sub- and superscripts from (3.8), and using the conjugate gradient algorithm starting with the initial iterate for g to be zero, we can obtain estimates for $(y-d)$ directly. The C.G. scheme for (3.8) is therefore given by:

(i) <u>initialization</u>

$z_0 = y \ ,$

$r_0 = (I-P)Az_0 \ , \quad where \ P = (I-QQ^T) \ ,$
and

$p_0 = r_0$

(ii) <u>for $i = 0, 1, 2,...$</u>

$z_{i+1} = z_i - \alpha_i p_i \ ,$

$\alpha_i = r_i^T r_i / p_i^T A p_i \ ,$

$$r_{i+1} = r_i - \alpha_i (I-P) A p_i \,, \tag{3.9}$$

$$p_{i+1} = r_{i+1} + \beta_i p_i \,,$$

$$\beta_i = r_{i+1}^T r_{i+1} / r_i^T r_i \,.$$

The C.G. algorithm is terminated once a measure of the error in z_i falls below the corresponding measure of the error in the eigenvector y. It can be shown [SaWi82] that for the j-th system the C.G. iteration (3.9) may be terminated after m steps when

$$\alpha_m \, || \, r_m \, ||_2^2 \le (\sigma_j / \sigma_{p+1})^2 \, (\alpha_0 || \, r_0 || \, |_2^2) \,, \tag{3.10}$$

where σ_i is the current estimate of λ_i.

This globally convergent algorithm may be summarized as follows:

Stage 1 (Initialization)

Choose an $n \times s$ matrix Y such that Y is of rank s. Here s is slightly more than p, the number of desired eigen pairs. Usually $s \ge p+1$.

Stage 2 (B-orthonormalization)

Obtain $\hat{Y}$ in the space spanned by Y such that $\hat{Y}^T B \hat{Y} = I_s$. This is done via a generalization of the Gram-Schmidt process [Luen69].

Stage 3 (Forming a section)

Obtain the spectral decomposition $\hat{Y}^T A \hat{Y} = U \Sigma U^T$. Now, $\tilde{Y} = \hat{Y} U$ yields the section

$$\tilde{Y}^T A \tilde{Y} = \Sigma \text{ ,and } \tilde{Y}^T B \tilde{Y} = I_s \,.$$

Here, $\Sigma = diag(\sigma_1, \sigma_2, \ldots, \sigma_s)$.

Stage 4 (Convergence)

Accept $(\sigma_j, \tilde{y}_j)$ as an eigen pair if $\max_{1 \le j \le p} ||A\tilde{y}_j - \sigma_j B\tilde{y}_j||_1$ is below a specified tolerance.

Stage 5 (Factorization)

Obtain the orthogonal factorization $B\tilde{Y} = QR$.

Stage 6 (Updating)

Solve the s independent positive definite systems in (3.8) using the C.G. algorithm. The j-th C.G. process is terminated when the stopping criterion (3.10) is satisfied. The s resulting solution vectors form the columns of the new matrix Y; go to stage 2.

This trace minimization technique, which has a linear rate of convergence, can be improved tremendously if it is applied to the s eigenvalue problems

$$(A - \nu_j B)x_j = (\lambda_j - \nu_j)Bx_j, \quad 1 \le j \le s.$$

Here, ν_j is a suitable shift chosen from the Ritz values σ_j, $1 \le j \le s$, obtained in stage 3. In this case, stages 1 through 5 remain unchanged. In stage 6, however, we solve the s linear systems in (3.8), via the C.G. process, with the matrix A in the j-th system replaced by $(A - \nu_j B)$. An appropriate strategy for choosing these shifts is necessary to maintain global convergence and to ultimately achieve cubic convergence, see section 3 in [SaWi82]. If we shift the j-th problem by the Ritz value σ_j too late, we needlessly take several passes of stages 1-6 at the slower linear rate of convergence when a cubic rate of convergence is possible. On the other hand, if we shift the j-th problem by σ_j

too soon, global convergence is lost; this is heralded by a nondescent step in the C.G. process in stage 5.

The algorithm is suitable for multiprocessors. Let us assume that we have a ring of s linearly connected processors with each having enough local memory to contain few vectors each of order n. Further, we assume that each processor can simultaneously perform an arithmetic operation, receive a floating-point number from an immediate neighbor, and send a previously computed number to the other immediate neighbor.

Making the crucial, and not unreasonable, assumption that the elements of A and B can be generated whenever needed, the most time-consuming part of the algorithm (stage 6) is performed with perfect speedup. Stages 2 to 5, however, require interprocessor communication.

The spectral decomposition, in stage 3, of $\hat{Y}^T A \hat{Y}$ is handled via the one-sided Jacobi method, [Luk80], which is suitable for implementation on our linearly connected set of processors, [Same82]. Also, an organization of the orthogonal factorization of $B\tilde{Y}$ on the above ring is given in [Same82]. A related algorithm, that of the Gram-Schmidt B-orthogonalization of the columns of Y, stage 2, i.e., the factorization $Y = \hat{Y}R$ where $\hat{Y}^T B \hat{Y} = I_s$ with $R = [\rho_{ij}]$ being an upper triangular matrix of order s, is given by:

$$Y = [y_1^{(1)}, \ldots, y_s^{(1)}],$$
For $i = 1, 2, \ldots, s$

$$\rho_{ii} = (y_i^{(i)^T} B y_i^{(i)})^{1/2}$$

$$\hat{y}_i = y_i^{(i)}/\rho_{ii}$$

For $j = i+1,..., s$

$$\rho_{ij} = \hat{y}_i^T B y_j^{(i)}$$

$$y_j^{(i+1)} = y_j^{(i)} - \rho_{ij}\hat{y}_i$$

The above Gram-Schmidt scheme is performed by pipelining across the processors of our ring and is completed in $O(sn)$ time steps plus the time required for s multiplications of an n-vector by the matrix B.

Different algorithm organizations of stages 2, 3, 5 and 6 are necessary for higher speedup if we have a CEDAR-like architecture [GKLS83] consisting of s clusters, and where the matrices A and B are contained in the global memory.

The choice algorithm for solving (3.1) on a sequential machine is that due to Lanczos [Parl80]. In each step of the Lanczos algorithm we need to solve accurately a system of linear equations of the form $Bu = h$. This high accuracy is necessary to assure that the Lanczos vectors in steps $j-1$, j, and $j+1$ are B-orthonormal. Further, linear independence among the Lanczos vectors, until convergence to the extreme eigenvalues of (3.1), should be maintained in order to avoid spurious eigenvalues and to minimize the number of the Lanczos steps. This is achieved either by selective orthogonalization [Parl80] or periodic reorthogonalization [Grca81]. Both strategies may require auxiliary storage for large problems leading to an I/O bound algorithm on multiprocessors. While a comprehensive comparison between the trace minimization and the Lanczos algorithms must await actual experiments on multiprocessors of different architectures, we suspect that our trace minimization scheme is to be preferred for multiprocessors with limited interconnection networks and for exceedingly large problems.

References

[BaWi73]   K. Bathe and E. Wilson, Solution methods for eigenvalue problems in structural mechanics, *Intl. J. Num. Meth. Eng. 6*, 213-226.

[CoGO76]   P. Concus, G. Golub, D. O'Leary, A generalized conjugate gradient method for the numerical solution of elliptic partial differential equations, in *Proc. Sparse Matrix Computation*, ed. J. Bunch and D. Rose, Academic Press, 1976.

[Fisc82]   C. Fischer, Approximate solution of Schrodinger's equation for atoms, in *Numerical Integration of Differential Equations and Large Linear Systems*, ed. J. Hinze, *Lecture Notes in Mathematics 968*, Springer-Verlag, 1982, 71-81.

[GKLS83]   D. Gajski, D. Kuck, D. Lawrie, A. Sameh, Plan for the construction of a large scale muiltiprocessor, Department of Computer Science (Cedar Doc. No. 3), University of Illinois at Urbana-Champaign, February 1983.

[Gole82]   A. Golebiewski, Variational pseudo-gradient method for determination of m first eigenstates of a large real symmetric matrix, in *Numerical Integration of Differential Equations and Large Linear Systems*, J. Hinze, ed., *Lecture Notes in Mathematics 968*, Springer-Verlag, 1982, 370-383.

[Grca81]   J. Grcar, Analysis of the Lanczos algorithm and of the approximation problem in Richardson's method, Ph.D. thesis, Department of Computer Science, University of Illinois at Urbana-Champaign, 1981.

[Grub78]   A. Gruber, Finite hybrid elements to compute the ideal magnetohydrodynamic spectrum of an axisymmetric plasma, *J. Comp. Physics 26*, 1978, 379-389.

[Hell76]   D. Heller, Some aspects of the cyclic reduction algorithm for block tridiagonal linear systems, *SIAM J. Num. Anal. 13*, 1976, 484-496.

[LaSa83]   D. Lawrie and A. Sameh, The computation and communication complexity of a parallel banded system solver, submitted for publication, 1983.

[Luen69]   D. Luenberger, *Optimization by Vector Space Methods*, J. Wiley, 1969.

[Luk80]   F. Luk, Computing the singular-value decomposition on the Illiac IV, *ACM Trans. Math. Software 6*, 1980, 524-539.

[MeVo77]   J. Meijerink and H. van der Vorst, An iterative solution method for linear systems of which the coefficients matrix is a symmetric M-matrix, *Math. Comp. 31*, 1977, 148-162.

[Parl80]   B. Parlett, *The Symmetric Eigenvalue Problem*, Prentice-Hall, 1980.

[SaKu78]   A. Sameh and D. Kuck, On stable parallel linear system solvers, *J. ACM 25*, 1978, 81-91.

[Same82]   A. Sameh, Solving the linear least squares problem on a linear array of processors, *Proc. Purdue Workshop on Algorithmically Specialized Computer Organization*, W. Lafayette, Indiana, September 1982, Academic Press (to appear).

[SaWi82]   A. Sameh and J. Wisniewski, A trace minimization algorithm for the generalized eigenvalue problem, *SIAM J. Num. Anal. 19*, 1982, 1243-1259.

A PARALLEL FIRST-ORDER METHOD FOR PARABOLIC

PARTIAL DIFFERENTIAL EQUATIONS

Garry Rodrigue
Lawrence Livermore National Laboratory
Livermore, California 94550

1. Introduction

In this paper, it is shown how computing architectures have affected the
direction of research in deriving numerical time - differencing schemes for
parabolic partial differential equations. In particular, the problem of solving
the two-dimensional diffusion equation is considered. The equation of interest is
given by

$$\frac{\partial \phi}{\partial t} = \nabla \cdot \kappa (x,y) \nabla \phi$$

$$\phi (x,y,0) = \phi_0 (x,y)$$

(1.1)

over a finite time interval $0 \leq t \leq \tau$. ϕ is defined on a bounded convex
region R and satisfies a mixed Dirichlet and Newmann boundary condition.
Numerical solutions are constructed by superimposing a lattice of points on R and
approximating the diffusion operator $\nabla \cdot \kappa \nabla \phi$ in such a way that the value of
ϕ at each node of the lattice is a function of its values at its immediate
neighboring nodes, cf. [1], [2]. A system of linear ordinary differential
equations

$$\frac{d\bar{\phi}(t)}{dt} = A \bar{\phi} (t) + \bar{f}$$

$$\bar{\phi} (0) = \bar{\phi}_0$$

(1.2)

is generated where the vector $\bar{\phi}(t)$ has as its components the numerical

NATO ASI Series, Vol. F7
High-Speed Computation. Edited by J. S. Kowalik
© Springer-Verlag Berlin Heidelberg 1984

approximations to $\phi(t)$ on the lattice. $\bar{f}$ is a constant vector originating from the boundary conditions of (1.1). Since $\nabla \cdot \kappa \nabla \phi$ is symmetric in the Hilbert space L_2 (R) and $\kappa > 0$, the matrix A is symmetric and negative-definite. The solution to (1.2) is

$$\bar{\phi}(t) = \exp (tA) [\bar{\phi}_0 + A^{-1} \bar{f}] - A^{-1} \bar{f} . \tag{1.3}$$

and numerical methods for solving (1.2) are constructed by approximating the operator exp (τA) by another operator E(τA) to yield, [3],

$$\psi(\tau) = E(\tau A) [\bar{\phi}_0 + A^{-1} \bar{f}] - A^{-1} \bar{f} . \tag{1.4}$$

E(τA) is said to be accurate up to order p if

$$\tau^{-1} \| [E(\tau A) - \exp(\tau A)] \bar{\phi} \tau \| = 0 (\tau^p) , p > 0 \tag{1.5}$$

and stable if

$$\| E (\tau A) \| \leq 1 . \tag{1.6}$$

Formally, if $t_0 = 0 < t_1 < t_2 < .. < t_{m-1} < t_m = \tau$ and $\Delta t_i = t_{i+1} - t_i$, then

$$E(\tau A) = \prod_{i=1}^{m} R_i (\Delta t_i A) \tag{1.7}$$

where $R_i (z)$ is a rational polynomial,

$$R_i(z) = [D_i(z)]^{-1} N_i(z) \tag{1.8}$$

where $D_i(z)$, $N_i(z)$ are polynomials of a scalar z,cf. [3]. A sufficient
condition for (1.6) is

$$\| R_i(\Delta t_i A)\| \le 1 \ , \ i = 1, \dots , m. \tag{1.9}$$

$N_i(\Delta t_i A)$ is called the explicit part of R_i and $D_i(\Delta t_i A)$ the
implicit part.

2. Explicit Calculations

If the ordering of the components of $\bar{\phi}(t)$ correspond to a natural numbering
of the grid (i.e., the grid points are numbered from left to right, bottom to
top), then the matrix A takes the form, [1],

$$A = \begin{bmatrix} a_{11} & a_{12} & 0 & \cdots\cdots & 0 & a_{1k} & a_{1,k+1} & \\ a_{12} & a_{22} & a_{23} & & & a_{2k} & a_{2,k+1} & a_{2,k+2} \\ & \ddots & \ddots & \ddots & & & \ddots & \ddots & \ddots \\ a_{1k} & a_{2k} & & & & & & \\ a_{1,k+1} & a_{2,k+1} & a_{3,k+1} & & & & \\ & a_{2,k+2} & \ddots & \ddots & & \\ & & \ddots & \ddots & \\ & & & \end{bmatrix} \tag{2.1}$$

The main computational task in an explicit calculation is a matrix-vector
multiplication. The algorithm used for this calculation depends on the
hierarchical structure of the computer and calculational capabilities of the basic

processing units. The hierarchical structure defines how the matrix A is to be "blocked". That is,

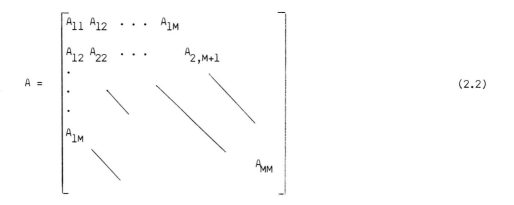

$$A = \begin{bmatrix} A_{11} & A_{12} & \cdots & A_{1M} \\ A_{12} & A_{22} & \cdots & & A_{2,M+1} \\ \vdots & & & & \\ \vdots & & & & \\ \vdots & & & & \\ A_{1M} & & & & \\ & & & & A_{MM} \end{bmatrix} \qquad (2.2)$$

where the A_{ij} are sub-matrices and the operation Ax is done with "column" algorithms, cf. [4]. The size of each hierarchical level determines the coarseness of the blocks. A multi-level hierarchy may require further sub-blocking of the A_{ij} matrices. To pipeline the algorithm requires the expression of A in terms of diagonal sums, [5]. That is, if $A_{\pm k}$ is the matrix whose only non-zero elements are $A_{i,i\pm k}$, then the operations $A_{\pm k}^- x$ is given by

$$\begin{bmatrix} A_{k,1} & x_1 \\ A_{k,2} & x_2 \\ & \cdot \\ & \cdot \\ A_{M,M-k} & x_k \end{bmatrix} \qquad \text{or} \qquad \begin{bmatrix} A_{1,k} & x_k \\ A_{2,k} & x_{k+1} \\ & \cdot \\ & \cdot \\ A_{M,k} & x_{k+M} \end{bmatrix}$$

Hence, a pilelineable algorithm is given by

$$Ax = \sum_{k=-M}^{M} A_k x .$$

3. Implicit Calculations

Implicit calculations involve the solution of a system $[\sum_{i=0}^{s} \alpha_i A^i] x = b$.
For simplicity, assume the system is of the for $Tx = [I - \Delta tA] x = b$. Then, T
has the same structure as (2.1). If sufficient memory and speed are available,
then the implicit equations are solved by direct methods. Direct methods are
based on elimination techniques and can be subdivided into three basic processes:

The Decomposition: Construct a sequence of matrices Q_i and orthogonal
matrices S_i, $i = 1, . . , k$ and calculate

$$[\prod_{t=1}^{k} Q_i] T [\prod_{t=1}^{k} S_i] = U ; \tag{3.1}$$

The Forward Substitution: Calculate

$$[\prod_{t=1}^{k} Q_i] b = \tilde{b} ; \tag{3.2}$$

The Backward Substitution: Solve

$$U [\prod_{i=1}^{k} S_i^t] x = \tilde{b} .$$

For implicit calculations, the choice of algorithm depends not only on the
hierarchical structure of the computer and the computational capabilities of the
individual processing units, but also on the communication efficiency between the
hierarchical levels. The hierarchy determines the data-structure blocks of T as
in (2.2), whereas, the communication efficiency determines the Q_i and S_i
matrices. The capabilities of the processing units determines the algorithm for
carrying out the appropriate matrix multiplications.

Once the appropriate block structure of T is determined, the matrices Q_i
and S_i are constructed so as to be either elimination, permutation, or scaling

matrices. These are referred to collectively as elementary transformation
matrices. If Q_i is an elimination matrix, then $S_i = I$ and if Q_i is a
permutation or a scaling matrix, then $S_i = Q_i^t$, cf. [4]. Elimination matrices are
defined so that pre-multiplication by them results in the introduction of zeroes
in pre-specified entries of the product. Formally, $Q = I - E$ so that if the
(i,j) block of the product QG is to be zeroed, then the (i,j) block of E is
$[G_{ij} \ G_{ii}^{-1}]$. Also, it is necessary that the diagonal blocks of E are zero, cf. [4].
The position that the zeroes are to be placed depends on two factors: the
rapidity of the computational hardware to get the blocks G_{ij} and G_{ii}^{-1} together in
order to form their appropriate calculations and the anticipation of the next
pre-multiplication by a Q_i matrix, see [6], [7], [8] for examples.

The algorithm for performing the multiplication of an elimination matrix
against another matrix G depends not only on the computing architecture but on the
sparsity pattern of the matrix G. A row or column algorithm is used when the
non-zero blocks of E appear in a row or column respectively, cf. [4]. A diagonal
algorithm is used when

$$Q_i = \sum_{k=-m}^{m} Q_k$$

so that

$$QG = \sum_{k=\ell}^{-\ell} F_k \qquad \text{where} \qquad F_k = \sum_{i+j=k} Q_i \ G_j .$$

$Q_i \ G_j$ is given by the elementwise multiplication of two vectors, cf [5]. Note
that all three algorithms can be pipelined; however, the gains achieved from
pipelining can be slight if the pertinent non-zero column, row, or diagonal of Q
is sparse.

Scaling matrices take on the same form as elimination matrices and are
introduced to reduce the condition number of the calculation. Permutation
matrices are used to rearrange data either between or within the specific
hierarchical levels. As architectures become more complex, the application of
permutation matrices will occupy more of the overall computation time for the

matrix inversion process (3.1) - (3.3). For systems of the form (2.1), the permutations involved are patterned and can be exploited by the architecture, see [9], [10]. An important feature of any efficient elimination algorithms of the form (3.1) - (3.3) is the appropriate choice of permutation matrices and is heavily dependent on the particular data transfer rates of the architecture. It is for this reason that algorithms are difficult to design when firm transfer speeds have not been established.

Ideal algorithms (3.1) - (3.3) are those that minimize the number of multiplications by the elementary transformation matrices. Iterative methods for solving Tx = b are generated by defining an elimination process (3.2) - (3.3) with the difference that the solution $\tilde{x}^{(k)}$ of (3.3) provides a vector that is used to define a k-th iterative approximation, $x^{(k)}$, to the exact solution x. In this way the number of elementary transformations can be as small as desired with caveat that the number of iterations increases if too few or ill-chosen transformations are used, cf. [3], [11].

4. Explicit vs. Implicit vs. Hybrid Schemes

Because of the recursiveness in the algorithm for solving implicit equations, explicit methods seem to be the obvious choice. However, if one considers the simple 2-dimensional heat diffusion equation $\partial \phi / \partial t = \Delta \phi$ on $[0,1] \times [0,1]$ and uses the 5-point central difference approximation to generate the equation (1.2), then on a 100 x 100 lattice,

$$E(1 \cdot A) = \prod_{i=1}^{4000} (I + \Delta t \, A)$$

where Δt = .00025 for stability. Consequently, even though explicit methods are highly parallel, it is not difficult to generate a problem that renders them computationally impractical.

However, since matrix-vector multiplication is a highly parallel operation, time differencing schemes that make use of this fact are desirable. This leads to the question as to whether explicit, implicit, and iterative methods can be combined so as to provide parallel time-differencing schemes. To see how this idea can be implemented, let us consider the numerical solution of the simple 1-dimensional heat equation

$$\frac{\partial u}{\partial t} = \frac{\partial^2 u}{\partial x^2} \quad , \qquad 0 < x < \pi , \qquad 0 < t < \tau ,$$

with boundary conditions $u(0) = u(\pi) = 0$, $u(x,0) = f(x)$, where $f(x)$ has a convergent Fourier series. Then the solution operator is given by

$$u(x, t + \Delta t) = S(t + \Delta t, t) \, u(x, t)$$

$$= \sum_{r=1}^{\infty} a_r \, e^{-r^2(t+\Delta t)} \, e^{irx}$$

Consider the first order explicit Euler method on

$$0 = x_0 < x_1 < \ldots < x_{N+1} = \pi , \quad \Delta x = x_{i+1} - x_i , \quad \Delta x = \pi/n+1 .$$

In its discrete form

$$u_i^{n+1} = u_i^n + \frac{\Delta t}{\Delta x^2} \, (u_{i-1}^n - 2u_i^n + u_{i+1}^n)$$

Let

$$\bar{u}(x,t + \Delta t) = u(x,t) + \frac{\Delta t}{\Delta x^2} \, (u(x - \Delta x,t) - 2u(x,t) + u(x+\Delta x,t))$$

$$= C_1 \, (\Delta t, \, \Delta x) \, u(x,t)$$

Theorem 4.1, [12]

The local truncation error is given by

$$\frac{[C_1(\Delta t, \Delta x) - S(t+\Delta t, t)] \, u \, (x,t)}{\Delta t} = O(\Delta t) + O(\Delta x^2)$$

and stability is assured if $\Delta t \leq \Delta x^2 / 2$.

Let us consider the implicit Euler method

$$(I - \Delta t A) \, \bar{u}^{n+1} = \bar{u}^n \, .$$

If Jacobi's method is used to solve the implicit equations, then the iteration is as follows:

$$(I - \Delta t \, A_0) \, \bar{u}^{n^{(k+1)}} = \Delta t \, N \bar{u}^{n^{(k)}} + \bar{u}^n,$$

$$I - \Delta t A = I - \Delta t A_0 - \Delta t N, \quad A_0 = \text{diagonal } (A) \tag{4.1}$$

$$\bar{u}^{n^{(0)}} = \bar{u}^n \, .$$

Since the splitting (4.1) is regular, $\bar{u}^{n^{(k)}} \to \bar{u}^{n+1}$ as $k \to \infty$. Now consider the time-differencing method

$$(I - \Delta t A_0) \, \bar{u}^{n^{(k+1)}} = \Delta t N \bar{u}^{n^{(k)}} + \bar{u}^n \, ,$$

$$\bar{u}^{n+1} = \bar{u}^{n^{(s)}}$$

where s is a fixed integer and A_0, N, $\bar{u}^{n^{(0)}}$ are as before. Then

$$\bar{u}^{n+1} = C_2 (s, \Delta t, \Delta x) \bar{u}^n$$

Theorem 4.2

For the transition operation $C_2(1, \Delta t, \Delta x)$, the local truncation error is

$$\sum_{r=1}^{\infty} a_r e^{-r^2 t} e^{irx} r^2 [(\frac{2 \Delta t / \Delta x^2}{1 + 2\Delta t/\Delta x^2}) + O(\Delta t) + O(\Delta x^2)]$$

Proof:

Let $\alpha = 2\Delta t/\Delta x^2$ and $\xi_r = (1+\alpha)^{-1} (1+\alpha \cos r\Delta x)$. Then $C_2 \bar{u} = \sum_{r=1}^{\infty} a_r e^{-r^2 t} e^{irx} \xi_r$

Further,

$$\xi_r = \frac{1+\alpha(1-r^2\Delta x^2/2 + r^4\Delta x^4/24 + O(\Delta x^8))}{(1+\alpha)}$$

$$= 1 - \frac{\Delta t r^2}{(1+\alpha)} + \frac{1}{12} (\frac{r^4 \Delta t \Delta x^2}{1+\alpha}) + O(\Delta t \Delta x^4)$$

Since $e^{-r^2 \Delta t} = 1 - r^2\Delta t + r^4 \Delta t^2/2 + O(\Delta t^3)$,

$$e^{-r^2 \Delta t} - \xi_r = r^2\Delta t [\frac{\alpha}{1+\alpha}] + r^4\Delta t [\frac{\Delta t}{2} - \frac{1}{12} (\frac{\Delta x^2}{1+\alpha}) + \ldots]$$

and the result follows.

Let us now consider a slight variation of the method given by (4.1):

$$(I - \Delta t A_0) \bar{u}^{n(k+1)} = \Delta t N \bar{u}^{n(k)} + \bar{u}^n,$$

$$\bar{u}^{n+1} = \bar{u}^{n(s)}, \qquad\qquad (4.2)$$

$$\bar{u}^{n(0)} = (I + \Delta t A) \bar{u}^n.$$

That is, the initial guess for the iteration is provided by an explicit Euler operation on the previous solution $\bar{u}^n$. Then

$$\bar{u}^{n+1} = C_3 (s, \Delta t, \Delta x) \bar{u}^n$$

Theorem 4.3

For the transition operation $C_3(1, \Delta t, \Delta x)$, the local truncation error is given by

$$\sum_{r=1}^{\infty} a_r e^{-r^2 t} e^{irx} [\tfrac{1}{2} r^4 (\tfrac{4-3\alpha}{1+\alpha}) \Delta t + O(\Delta x^2)] = O(\Delta t) + O(\Delta x^2) , \qquad \alpha = 2\Delta t/\Delta x^2$$

Proof:

Let $\beta_r = \cos r\Delta x$. Then, dropping the subscript r on β,

$$C_3\bar{u} = \sum_{r=1}^{\infty} a_r e^{-r^2 t} e^{irx} [\tfrac{1+\alpha\beta + (\alpha^2/2) (\cos 2r\Delta x - 2\beta+1)}{(1+\alpha)}]$$

Then,

$$\tfrac{1+\alpha\beta}{1+\alpha} = [1 - \tfrac{\Delta t r^2}{1+\alpha} + \tfrac{1}{12} (\tfrac{r^4 \Delta t \Delta x^2}{1+\alpha}) + O(\Delta t \Delta x^4)]$$

and

$$\tfrac{\cos(2r\Delta x) - 2\beta+1}{1+\alpha} = \tfrac{-r^2\Delta x^2 + (7/12) r^4 \Delta x^4 + O(\Delta x^8)}{(1+\alpha)}$$

Hence,

$$C_3\bar{u} = \sum_{r=1}^{\infty} a_r e^{-r^2 t} e^{irx} [1 - r^2\Delta t + (\tfrac{7}{6}) (\tfrac{r^4 \Delta t^2}{1+\alpha}) + O(\Delta t \Delta x^2)]$$

Since $e^{-r^2 \Delta t} = 1 - r^2\Delta t + r^4 \Delta t^2/2 + O(\Delta t^3)$, the result follows.

Theorem 4.3 states that only one iteration is necessary to achieve $O(\Delta t)$ accuracy when an explicit Euler operation is applied to the previously computed solution $\bar{u}^n$. Hence, we see that because of the rapid rate of execution of the matrix-vector multiplication opeation on parallel architectures, the opportunity of devising new time-differencing schemes that take advantage of this fact now becomes practical. Experimentation with more powerful iterative methods such as Gauss-Siedel,[13] and Incomplete Factorization is ongoing and will be reported in a future paper.

5. Computational Results

Problem 1: The problem $\partial u/\partial t = \partial^2 u/\partial x^2$ is solved on the interval $0 \le x \le 1$ with boundary conditions $u(0) = u(1) = 0$ and initial condition $u(x,0) = \sin(\pi x)$. The exact solution is $u(x,t) = e^{-t} \sin(\pi x)$. Method I is described by (4.1) and Method II is described by (4.2) where in both methods $s = 1$. The local truncation error from both methods are compared for $\Delta t = .0025$ and $\Delta x = .05$.

In this case, the local truncation error is given by $(\Delta t)^{-1} \| \bar{u}(x, n\Delta t) - \bar{u}^n \|_\infty$.

Problem 2: The two-dimensional problem $\partial u/\partial t = \partial^2 u/\partial x^2 + \partial^2 u/\partial y^2$ was solved on $[0,\pi] \times [0,\pi]$ with $u = 0$ on the boundary and initial condition $u(x,y,0) = \sin(x)\sin(y)$. The exact solution is given by $u(x,t) = e^{-2t}\sin(x)\sin(y)$. A central difference spatial approximation, [11], is used with $\Delta x = \Delta y = \pi/26$ to generate the standard 5-point Laplacian matrix. As before the local truncation error of Methods I and II are compared in Table II with $\Delta t = .005$.

In both of the above applications, the stability bounds were computationally determined in which case stability was assured if for

Problem 1: $\Delta t/\Delta x^2 \le 1.5$

Problem 2: $\Delta t/(\Delta x^2 + \Delta y^2) \le .25$.

Table I

n	I	II
1	6.47	1.96×10^{-2}
2	10.57	3.83×10^{-2}
3	14.52	5.61×10^{-2}
4	18.32	7.29×10^{-2}
5	21.97	8.80×10^{-2}
6	25.48	1.09×10^{-1}
7	28.84	1.18×10^{-1}
8	32.07	1.32×10^{-1}
9	35.17	1.45×10^{-1}
10	38.14	1.57×10^{-1}

Table II

n	I	II
1	1.66×10^{-2}	1.28×10^{-5}
2	2.60×10^{-2}	9.49×10^{-5}
3	3.54×10^{-2}	1.75×10^{-4}
4	4.45×10^{-2}	2.54×10^{-4}
5	5.35×10^{-2}	3.31×10^{-4}
6	6.23×10^{-2}	4.07×10^{-4}
7	7.09×10^{-2}	4.81×10^{-4}
8	7.94×10^{-2}	5.53×10^{-4}
9	8.78×10^{-2}	6.25×10^{-4}
10	9.60×10^{-2}	6.94×10^{-4}

6. Acknowledgements

The author would like to thank Jeff Scroggs for carrying out the calculations and the Applied Mathematical Sciences Division of the Office of Basic Energy Sciences for support. This work was performed under the auspices of the United States Departmednt of Energy at Lawrence Livermore National Laboratory under Contract No. W-7405-ENG-48.

7. References

1. G. Rodrigue, C. Hendrickson, M. Pratt, "An Implicit Numerical Solution of the Two-Dimensional Diffusion Equation and Vectorization Experiments", Parallel Computations, Academic Press, 1982.
2. D. Kershaw, "Differencing of the Diffusion Equation in Lagrangian Hydrodynamic Codes", LLNL Report, UCRL-82747, May 1979.
3. R. Varga, Matrix Iterative Analysis, Prentice-Hall, 1962.
4. G. Stewart, Introduction to Matrix Computations, Academic Press, 1973.
5. N. Madsen, G. Rodrigue, J. Karush, "Matrix Multiplication by Diagonals on a Vector/Parallel Processor", J. of Info. Proc. Letters, Vol. 5, No. 2, June 1976.
6. J. Kowalik, R. Lind, S. Kumar, "Design and Performance of Algorithms for MIMD Parallel Computers", this book.
7. E. Reiter, G. Rodrigue, "An Incomplete Cholesky Factorization by a Matrix Partition Algorithm", Proceedings of Conference on Elliptic Problem Solvers, Academic Press.
8. D. Lawrie, A. Sameh, "The Computation and Communication Complexity of a Parallel Banded System Solver", personal communication.
9. G. Rodrigue, D. Wolitzer, "Preconditioning by Incomplete Block Cyclic Reduction" to be published Math. of Comp.
10. J. Ehrel, A. Lichnewsky, F. Thomasset, "Parallelism in Finite Element Computation", Proceedings of IBM Symposium on Vector Computers and Scientific Computation, Rome, 1982.
11. L. Hageman, D. Young, Applied Iterative Methods, Academic Press, 1981.
12. R. Richtmeyer, K. Morton, Difference Methods for Initial Value Problems, Interscience, 1957.
13. M. Berger, J. Oliger, G. Rodrigue, "Predictor-Corrector Methods for the Solution of Time-Dependent Prabolic Problem on Parallel Processors", Proc. Conf. Elliptic PDE Methods, Academic Press, 1980.

SOME VECTOR AND PARALLEL IMPLEMENTATIONS FOR PRECONDITIONED CONJUGATE GRADIENT ALGORITHMS

A. LICHNEWSKY

Université de Paris-Sud
91405 ORSAY, France

Paper presented to the NATO Advanced Research Workshop on HIGH-SPEED COMPUTATIONS, 20-22 June 1983, Julich, F.R.G.

ABSTRACT

We consider the adaptation of the Preconditioned Conjugate Gradient to several Parallel and Vector Architectures. Some variants based mostly on renumbering techniques are considered, as well as their effectiveness to exploit various architectures. We give some results concerning the numerical properties of these techniques.

INTRODUCTION

This paper will describe some adaptations of the Preconditioned Conjugate Gradient Method for parallel and vector architectures. Our first aim has been to test various alternatives which allow to use so their desirable convergence properties. We will thus show that some parallelisation heuristics do permit to increase the amount of available and exploitable parallelism.

Our second aim has been to look in more details to variants suitable for MIMD-multiprocessors as well as for vector machines. We shall give some results about the applicability of our technique to various confi- gurations. Since we consider the case of a general sparse method on a general 2D or 3D domain, these models show the influence of the overall domain complexity on the speed-up which is obtained. Concerning the MIMD approach, we will mainly give the results of evaluations by simple models, although we have some experimental results for bi-processors which may become useful on machines similar to the Cray-XMP.

Since most of the Conjugate Gradient algorithm consists of matrix multiplications, vector combinations and scalar products which can be performed efficiently on parallel architectures, we need only consider the resolution of the linear system which arises because of the precon- ditioning operator, and over which we have some control. Our technique

is based on renumberings of the unknown, while imposing a sparsity
structure on the linear system. Using a graph partitionning algorithm,
with small separators, we exhibit weakly connected subdomains suitable
for multi-processor implementations. Turning over to coloring techniques,
variants give vector type parallelism with increased vector lengths.
The adaptations we propose for multi-vector-processors combine the two
heuristics, which have arisen so far, in a quite unified setting. The
new coloring technique of Wei-Pei Tang & R. Schreiber [1983] is a
further step in this direction, although little seems presently known
of the optimal renumbering technique.

The efficiency of the Preconditionned Conjugate Gradients and its
adaptation to vector processors has been the result of many studies
which include J.A. Meijerink & H. A. Van Der Vorst [1977, 1981] ,
Dubois, Greenbaum & G. Rodrigue [1979] , G. Rodrigue & D. Wolitzer
[1982], G. Meurant [1983], Concus, G. Golub & G. Meurant [1982],
O. Johnson, Michelli & G. Paul [1982], R. Schreiber & Wei-Pai Tang
[1983]. Our approach has evolved from A. Lichnewsky [1981, 1982].

1.   The Conjugate Gradient Method with Incomplete Choleski Precondi
      tionning.

Let a be a symmetric definite positive matrix of order n and b a
prescribed vector ; we are looking for the solution of the linear
system :

(1) $A \; x = b$

In order to increase the convergence rate of the C.G. method one applies
it to the equivalent system :

(1-bis) $L^{-1} A \; (L^{T})^{-1} \; x = L^{-1} \; b$

where L is lower triangular. Further criteria for L selection are its
ease of representation, inversion and also the new rate of convergence,
which is closely related to the spectral properties of the matrix
(similar to (1-bis)'s) :

(2) $B = (L^{T})^{-1} \; L^{-1} \; A$

Among the properties of B's spectrum that are related to the overall
efficiency of the method are such things as "Eigenvalue Grouping"
(see O. Axelsson [1976], P. Concus, G. Golub & G. Meurant [1982]) and
this   suggests the following choice :

(3)   Compute L and its transpose using the equation

$$L L^T = A + R$$

where the residual matrix R is not actually computed and has to satisfy some constraints. Also in the actual computations a "square root" free variant is usually adopted.

The heuristic can be summarized as follows : if R = 0 then B will actually be the identity matrix which will cause the Conjugate Gradient to return the result after the first iteration. However this would require much more computations, because of fill-in, than the method we are constructing. Since we are not looking for an exact inverse of A, we will impose further constraints on L, which will help make it easy to represent and invert.

To describe the structural constraints on L, it is useful to associate to a symmetric matrix A its labelled undirected graph : G(A) =(V(A), E(A)). The vertex set V(A) consists of n elements V(A) = $\{v(1), v(2),...,,v(n)\}$ and the edge set E(A) describes the sparsity structure of A in the following way :

(4) $\{v(i), v(j)\} \in$ E(A) $\Longleftrightarrow$ A(i,j) $\neq$ 0

The incomplete Choleski factorisation may now be constructed :

-- first the graph G(L+L^T) is determined a priori, we will note it G(IC). This choice can be quite arbitrary but G(IC) will usually be much smaller than the perfect elimination graph of A, which will in effect limit the amount of fill-in we are willing to admit. A typical choice is G(IC) = G(A) ; the choice of graphs with more edges does improve the convergence rate of the algorithm and is discussed in J. A. Meijerink & H.A. Van Der Vorst [1981].

-- the set of constraints is now :
a) the only non zeroes in L can be those compatible with G(IC)
b) impose R(i,j) = 0 if $\{x(i), x(j)\} \in$ E(IC)

This construction is possible for M-matrices or diagonally dominant matrices ; for more general positive definite systems, the shifting method of Manteuffel [1978] can be used.

The algorithm can be written as follows :

```
Incomplete-Choleski-Conjugate-gradient(u0 : vector) : vector ;

     Const  A : sparse-matrix
            L : triangular-sparse-matrix ;

var     u,s,r,d : vector ;
⌠First Gradient Step⌡
```

$$u := u0 \; ; \; s := Au-b \; ; \; r = (L^T)^{-1} L^{-1} s \; ; \; d := -r \; ;$$
$$\eta := <s,r> \; ;$$

```
⌠Loop until u meets the desired accuracy⌡
repeat
  begin
```

$$r := A\,d \; ; \qquad\qquad \lambda := \eta \; / < d,r > ;$$
$$u := u + \lambda d \; ; \qquad s := s + \lambda r \; ;$$
$$r := (L^T)^{-1} L^{-1} s \; ;$$
$$\zeta := <r,s> \; ;$$
$$\gamma := \zeta/\eta \; ; \qquad\qquad \eta := \zeta ;$$
$$d := -r + \gamma d \; ;$$

```
  end
```

until $(\zeta<\varepsilon)$ ⌠this is a convenient norm of the residual s⌡

return (u)   ⌠the result⌡

```
end.
```

Fig. 1

This makes apparent that the main difficulty with respect of the exploitation of parallel architectures comes from the resolution of the triangular systems. However one must keep in mind that the matrix L can be selected quite arbitrarily.

2. Using Separators to Increase Parallelism

We will now introduce a "Subdomain Approach" for the sole purpose of obtaining some parallelism by decoupling, to some extent, the unknowns in the linear systems we have to solve. Our systematic tool will thus be separation results on graphs. Since we are not taking care of fill-in, which was simply suppressed by assumption, we shall not need the sophisticated techniques of A. George, Lipton & R.E. Tarjan [1979], Gilbert [1980], Gentleman.

DEFINITION : "Separator"

Let   V,E   be a graph. The subset S   V separates G into V1 and V2
if and only if :

    a) V can be partitionned into V1, V2 and S

    b) no vertex in V1 is adjacent to a vertex in V2

DEFINITION : "f(.)-separation".

 class S of graphs has the f(.)-separation property if :

    a) S is closed for taking subgraphs : subgraphs of elements of S
       are in S.

    b) There exists constants α, β with $0.5 \leq \alpha < 1$ and $\beta > 0$ such
       that if G   S, then G can be separated into V1 and V2 with :

(5) $|V1| \leq \alpha |V|$; $|V2| \leq \alpha |V|$;

          $|S| \leq \beta \; f(|V|)$

Where $|G|$ stands for the number of vertices in the graph G.

    In two dimensions, many finite element matrices have graphs with
$\sqrt{(.)}$-separation properties, as shown by Lipton & Tarjan [1979] . In
three dimensions (.)   - separation properties are known for very
restrictive classes of graphs. These results give us worst case evaluations for most general meshes in 2D, as well as for matrices which
come from other fields of application. In many practical situations,
the problem has natural subdomains of interest which we can make use of,
and usually separators are much smaller than these estimates imply.

    The new numbering of the unknowns we introduce is equivalent to a
labelling of the vertices v(i) in V(GI) and V(A). We will note v(i)
the vertex with original label i and $\Pi(i) = \Pi (v(i))$ its new label,
thus defining a permutation of the unknowns :

(6)   P : i ---→ $\Pi(i)$ which transforms A into $A' = P \; A \; P^T$

In order to obtain some parallelism, we define Π recursively. Starting
from dissection level 0 and the graph G(IC) we use the separation
property to separate V-G(IC) into V1 and V2 using separator S. This
step leads to the requirement :

(7) $\Pi(V1)$ < $\Pi(V2)$ < $\Pi(S)$

We then proceed by applying the same procedure at first level on V1 and V2, thus obtaining two sets of relations of the same form. After ν levels of dissections we end up with 2^ν disjoints subgraphs and 2 separators which can be ordered according to their level. Roughly speaking, we have thus introduced 2^ν subproblems which can be solved in parallel in the resolution of the linear systems : they correspond to blocks indexed by subdomains. The blocks corresponding to separators do have to be processed serially, one level at a time : this part of the algorithm has less parallelism and embodies the more "fully coupled" part of the preconditionner. It is also important to remark that the numbering is not fully specified inside the subdomains themselves and within separators : adapted numbering can still be used to optimize within these blocks to achieve further goals. In our experiments, we have used this fact to vectorise within subdomains, the coloring techniques of Schreiber [1983] could also be used to increase vector length inside subdomains.

---

(8)   Example of Block Structure obtained with 2 levels of Dissection

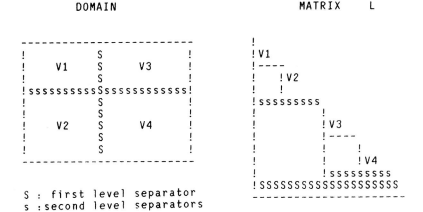

Fig. 2

349

3. Performance evaluation of the subdomain technique

The first check that can be made is that this process did not degrade significantly the convergence rate of the ICCG method, when compared to the natural ordering of unknowns. (Fig. 3 - 4). This relative insensitivity of the ICCG to the ordering of unknowns has been confirmed since our experiments [Lic 1981, ELT 1982] by [WPS 82], where orders that introduce systematic decoupling of unknowns are studied. The latter results show increases in the number of iterations for the Poisson's equation of 24 % for Red-Black reordering and 15 % for a 4-color reordering.

The next step is to analyze the possible speedup that this gives. To do so we have made a simple analysis, taking into account parameters like communication times between processors, and also geometric parameters which describe quantitalitatively how well a given finite element domain lends itself to partitionning.

In this model we have taken the number of processors equal to the number of subdomains we have separated. This is obviously not the best strategy in the presence of many subdomains of widely varying size that might arise if the whole graph cannot be partitionned efficiently. This may explain the very pessimistic estimates in this case, while creating more subdomains and allocating the tasks so as to minimize the processor waiting times might be practical and more efficient. In view of the sensitivity to the geometric properties of the discretized domain we think that improved procedures for partitionning in practical cases will be of interest. For configurations of highly repetitive use ad-hoc and manually adjusted numberings might prove very valuable.

Another set of parameters which appear in the model pertains to interprocessor communication times. By setting the relative values of communication start-up times (which includes synchronization) and data transfer speed we model various system configuration ranging from local memory to shared memory. It must be noted that the only data that need to be transmitted, apart from partial sums in scalar products and the like, are portions of vectors whose indices run on "separator" subgraphs. This is very different from the technique of [WTR1983] where parallelism (vector length, to be more specific) is increased at the expense of going through the data as many times as there are colors in the retained coloring. (5 colors for general planar graphs, since 4 colorings are to costly to construct).

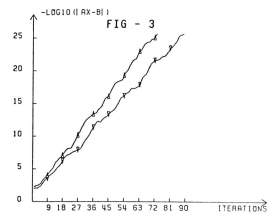

FIG - 3

INFLUENCE OF RENUMBERING ON THE CONVERGENCE RATE FOR THE
POISSON EQUATION , WITH DIRICHLET BOUNDARY DATA ON SQUARE
Q1 Finite Elements. Number of Unknowns = 961 .

Δ   Level 0   : Original numbering
∇   Level 2   : Renumbering twice thus giving 16 'subdomains'

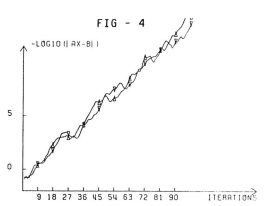

FIG - 4

WITH NEUMANN BOUNDARY DATA ON SQUARE , number of unknowns= 1089

Δ   Level 0   : Original numbering

∇   Level 2   : Renumbered twice, giving 16 'subdomains'.

The following parameters appear on figures 5 - 7.

Alpha, beta, gamma : Are the constants appearing in the graph separation
definition. We have taken f(.) = (,)** gamma
For 2D we have given results for the square and
the worst case for which the matrix graph is still
planar.
For 3D we have given the results for the cube and
some rather well behaved graphs, since we do not
know a general worst case bound.

K : Number of nonzeros per matrix line, is another
characteristic of the finite element method.

Trini : Time taken to initialize any interprocessor data
transfer. (Relative to floating-point op).

Trvit : Time taken to transfer 1 floating-point datum.

N : Number of unknowns.

The comparison between the set of illustrated parameters and real
configurations is left for the reader. Howewer we think that the case
with Trini = 100 may prove quite close to the performance of Cray-XMP,
the data being kept in shared memory and Trinit representing the synchronisation cost using the fastest primitives proposed in [CRI 1983]. A
more general remark is that our technique is effective for rather large
problems (N > 10000) running on a relatively low number of processors
(2-16). The geometrical properties of the matrix graph or finite element
domain also has a major influence on the overall performance.

4. Towards Multi-Vector Processors : vectorizing on subdomains

The vectorisation of the I.C.C.G. algorithm, has been studied by
many authors [RW 1982], [SWT 1983], [VDV 1983] , [CGM1982] & [Meu 1983].
In our experiments, the use of an odd-even by lines or slices numbering
on the whole domain has proved competitive and suffices to give adequate
vector length on the Cray-1 and the Cray-XMP [ELT 1982], [Lic 1982]
(Algorithms VECGIC-2D & VECGIC-3D). The work of Schreiber yields longer
vector length and may prove most useful on the CDC-Cyber-205.

Table 1 gives some performance data, along with some of the published
results of [Meu 1983]. All times are in seconds, for Fortran programs,
the compilers used being CRT 1.09 and X.11. Processor effectiveness can

be estimated from the MFLOPS ratings which appear between slashes.

All the tests in table 1 are with Dirichlet boundary conditions on the unit square, the differential operator being either the Laplace operator (constant coefficients) or the varying coefficients operator :

$$a(y) \; \frac{\partial^2}{\partial x^2} \; + \; \frac{\partial^2}{\partial y^2} \qquad \text{where } a(y) = \begin{array}{l} 1 \quad\;\; \text{when } y \leqslant 0.5 \\ 10000 \;\; \text{when } y > 0.5 \end{array}$$

FIG-5

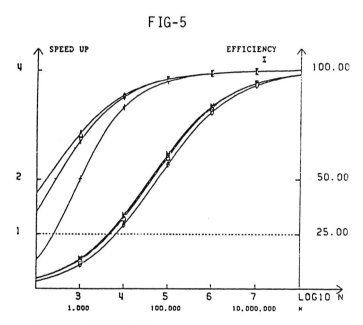

2 D MESH, 4 PROCESSORS

SPEED UP FOR VARIOUS DOMAINS & TRANSFER RATIOS
(THEORETICAL MODEL)

	NU	ALPHA	BETA	GAMMA	K	TRINI	TRVIT
△	2	0.50	1.00	0.50	5	0.0	0.0
▽	2	0.50	1.00	0.50	5	10.0	0.3
+	2	0.50	1.00	0.50	5	100.0	1.0
X	2	0.50	15.50	0.50	5	0.0	0.0
▯	2	0.50	15.50	0.50	5	10.0	0.3
◇	2	0.50	15.50	0.50	5	100.0	1.0

FIG-6

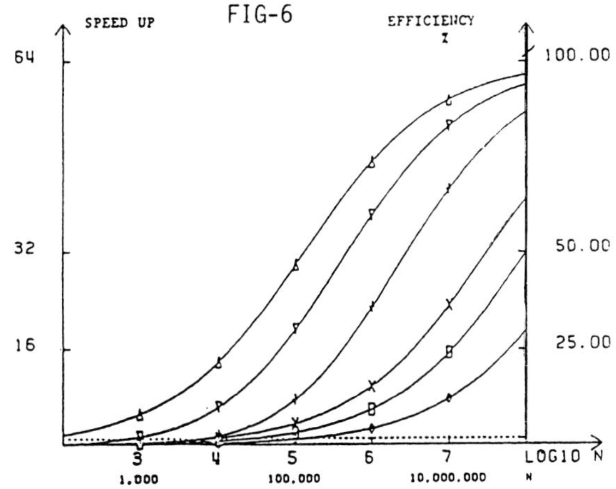

2 D MESH, 64 PROCESSORS

SPEED UP FOR VARIOUS DOMAINS & TRANSFER RATIOS
(THEORETICAL MODEL)

	NU	ALPHA	BETA	GAMMA	K	TRINI	TRVIT
Δ	6	0.50	1.00	0.50	5	0.0	0.0
∇	6	0.50	1.00	0.50	5	10.0	0.3
+	6	0.50	1.00	0.50	5	100.0	1.0
X	6	0.50	15.50	0.50	5	0.0	0.0
⊡	6	0.50	15.50	[illegible].50	5	10.0	0.3
◊	6	0.50	15.50	0.50	5	100.0	1.0

FIG-7

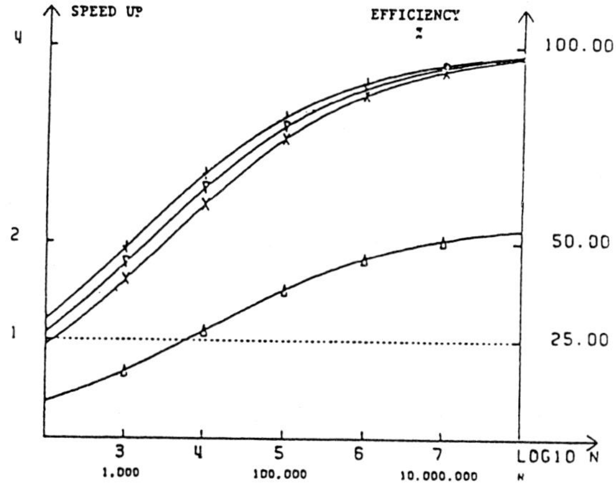

3 D MESHES, 4 PROCESSORS

SPEED UP FOR VARIOUS DOMAINS (Theoretical model)

TRANSFERS : SHARED MEMORY

	NU	ALPHA	BETA	GAMMA	K	TRINI	TRVIT
Δ	2	0.67	3.00	0.66	7	0.0	0.0
∇	2	0.50	1.00	0.66	7	0.0	0.0
+	2	0.50	0.85	0.66	7	0.0	0.0
X	2	0.50	1.00	0.66	40	0.0	0.0

		Constant Coefficients			Varying coefficients			
N	DECREASE Residue	# ITERS	CPU Cray-1		DECREASE Residue	# ITERS	CPU Cray-1	CPU XMP
40					7.0E-13	51	0.11 /25/	0.06 /46/
50	1.0E-6	34	0.096		1.0E-12	60	0.17 /29/	
	1.0E-12	65	0.23					
60					1.6E-12	73	0.27 /33/	0.13 /69/
120	0.8E-6	88	1.00		8.6E-12	114	1.29 /43/	0.54 /102/
	1.5E-11	114	1.29					

Center: TIMINGS FOR VECGIC - 2D

TABLE 1 - 1

TIMINGS FOR BLOCK ORIENTED INCOMPLETE METHODS
(Taken from Meurant [Meu1983])

METHOD	AUTHOR	N	# ITERS	DECREASE residue	CPU-Cray-1 /MFLOPS/
IC (1,1)	[MVV1977]	50	35	1.0E-6	0.172 /15/
INV(1)	[CGM1982]	50	15	1.0E-6	0.135 /9/
IC(1,1)VDV	[VDV1983]	50	35	1.0E-6	0.110 /29/
VECGIC-2D (added for comparison[+])	[ELT1982]	50	34	1.0E-6	0.096 /29/
INVV1(1)	[Meu1983]	50	31	1.0E-6	0.089 /30/
INVV3(1)	[Meu1983]	50	16	1.0E-6	0.064 /31/

TABLE 1 - 2

[+] Measured with different R.H.S. , tests in same case under way but not available yet.

Table 2 gives similar results for the 3D problem in the cube.

	Constant Coefficients			Varying coefficients, Random RHS			
MESH	DECREASE Residue	# ITERS	CPU Cray-1	DECREASE Residue	# ITERS	CPU Cray-1	CPU XMP
20*20*20	2.0E-13	41	0.42 /30/	2.0E-13	34	0.36 /30/	
30*30*30	2.4E-13	58	1.47 /39/	2.5E-13	48	1.28 /39/	0.49 /103/
10*50*50	1.05E-12	46	1.09 /37/				

TABLE 2

5. Towards Multi-Vector Processors : an experiment with 2 processors

The above results indicate that this type of "Subdomain Renumbering" approach might be a good candidate for Multi-Vector-Processors which are being designed at present times. The estimate we have shown above in Fig. 5-7 give some indication of what can be expected, but many causes of inefficiency may have been overlooked in such a simple model. Some parameters, like the cost of task switching, lock setting and event forwarding by the operating system, are not under our control. In order to get some feedback on these issues, we devised a simple dual-processor experiment that we have run on a CII-HB/DPS-68 under Multics O.S. at INRIA, and that we hope to run eventually on the Cray-XMP. As for the Multi-Tasking environment we have implemented a full emulation of CRI 1983 , however slight modifications were necessary to run under Multics (discussed in Erhel 1983).

The test problem we used is : Solve Poisson's equation with Dirichlet boundary condition on a square, which is cut into 2 subdomains by a thin separator. We have specialised a process by subdomain, and stored all matrix data pertaining to subdomains in storage local to that process. The vector data have been stored in shared storage. This is summarized in the figure 8.

The result are summarized in Table 3, for the processor usage consideration and in Figure 9 for the numerical properties of this version of the algorithm. The given times are in second and refer to virtual CPU times for both Multics processes, and elapsed (Wall) time.

The number of exchanged messages give the actual number of messages that were sent through the Multics Interprocess Channel mechanism and that were not dealt with by faster TEST-AND-SET instructions. This should give an indication of the number of times a process actually had to wait for completion of the other, keeping in mind that the synchronisation pattern is independent of mesh size. Its decrease as the problem size increases is due to better task balance (smaller relative separator size), and to the smaller cost of synchronisation primitives relative to task size.

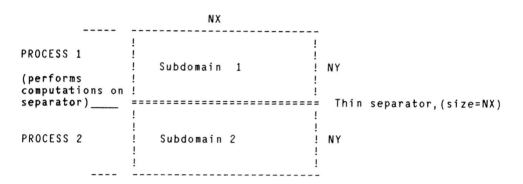

FIG - 8

MEASURED EXECUTION TIMES ON CII-HB:68/ Multics								
MESH NX*NY	# ITER	CPU proc 1	CPU proc 2	WALL time	SPEEDUP	YIELD %	EXCHANGED MESSAGES	
51*51	100	235	206	264	1.67	83 %	620	
71*71	100	456	400	510	1.68	84 %	575	
81*81	100	590	519	618	1.79	90 %	550	

TABLE   3

FIG - 9

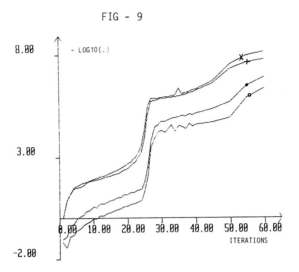

CONVERGENCE RATES FOR 2 SUBDOMAINS.POISSON's EQUATION   WITH
DIRICHLET BOUNDARY CONDITIONS. (NX = 51, NY = 51)

+ L^∞ NORM OF ERROR   o L^∞ NORM OF RESIDUAL
X L^2 NORM OF ERROR   • L^2 NORM OF RESIDUAL

CONCLUSION

We have presented an adaptation of fast numerical algorithms, that are quite implicit, to the parallel processing environment. To get usable performance comparisons, tradeoffs have to be made between the purely numerical behaviour (Number of iterations,..) and suitability to existent processor classes (Parallelism, access to operands, synchronisation mechanisms ...). Our results are coherent with those of [RW 1982], [CGM 1982], [Meu 1983] & [VDV 1983] and indicate that implicit techniques can benefit from parallel architectures and give good overall performance.

Further work in the direction of application to industrial finite element meshes [Erh 1983 b], and adaptation to SIMD - processors with Omega network interconnexion [Jal 1983] seem promising.

ACKNOWLEDGEMENT

The author thanks F. Thomasset and J. Erhel for their help with the numerical implementation and experiments.

REFERENCES

O. Axelsson [Ax 1976]
    "Solution of linear systems of equations : iterative methods", in Sparse Matrix Techniques, V.A. Barker Ed, Springer.

P. Concus, G. Golub & G. Meurant [CGM 1982]
    "Block preconditionning for the conjugate gradient method", rep LBL-14856, Stanford University, Stanford CA.

Cray Research Inc. [CRI 1983],
    "Proposed Multi-tasking Facility for CFT"

P.F. Dubois, A. Greenbaum & G. Rodrigue [DGR 1979]
    "Approximating the inverse of a matrix for use in iterative algorithms on vector processors", Computing, 22, pp 257-268.

J. Erhel [Erh 1983]
    "CREM : User's manual", Tech. Rep. INRIA, n° 25, May 1983.

J. Erhel [Erh 1983 b]
    "Parallelisation d'un algorithme de gradient conjugue preconditionne" Rapp. Rech. INRIA, n° 189, February 1983.

J. Erhel, A. Lichnewsky & F. Thomasset [ELT 1982]
    "Parallelism in finite element computation", Proc. IBM Symp. on Vector Computers & Sc. Comp., Rome.

W.M. Gentleman [Gen 1981]
   "Design of Numerical Algorithms for Parallel Processing",
   C.R.E.S.T. course, Bergamo.

J.A. George [Geo 1977]
   "Solution of linear systems of equations : direct methods for
   finite element problems", in Sparse Matrix Techniques, V.A. Barker
   Ed, Springer.

J.R. Gilbert [Gil 1980]
   "Graph separator theorems and sparse gaussian elimination",
   Ph. D. Thesis, Stanford.

W. Jalby [Jal 1983]
   These de 3ème cycle, Université de Paris Sud, Orsay.

O. G. Johnson, C.A. Michelli & G. Paul [JMP 1982]
   "Polynomial preconditionning for conjugate gradient calculation"
   Tech. Rep., IBM T.J. Watson Res. Cent., Yorktown Heights, NY.

A. Lichnewsky [Lic 1981]
   "Sur la résolution de systèmes linéaires issus de la méthode des
   éléments finis par une machine multiprocesseurs", Rapp. Rech.
   #119, INRIA.

A. Lichnewsky [Lic 1982]
   "Solving some linear systems arising in finite element methods
   on parallel processors" SIAM Natl. Meeting, Stanford.

R.J. Lipton & R.E. Tarjan [LT 1979]
   "A separation theorem for planar graphs", SIAM J. on Appl. Math.
   36, pp. 177-189.

T.A. Manteuffel [Man 1978]
   "The shifted incomplete Choleski factorization", SAND/78/8226,
   Sandia Lab., Albuquerque, NM.

J.A. Meijerink & H.A. Van Der Vorst [MVV 1977]
   "An iterative solution method for linear systems of which the
   coefficient matrix is a symmetric M-matrix", Math. Comp., v31,
   pp 148-162

J.A. Meijerink & H.A. Van Der Vorst [MVV 1981]
   "Guidelines for the usage of incomplete decompositions in solving
   sets of linear equations as they occur in practical problems",
   J. of Comp. Phys., v. 44, pp. 134-155.

G. Meurant [Meu 1983]
   "Vector preconditionning for the conjugate gradient method", to
   appear

R. Schreiber & Wei-Pei Tang [SWT 1983]
   "Vectorizing the conjugate gradient method", to appear.

G. Rodrigue & D. Wolitzer [RW 1982]
   "Preconditionning by Incomplete block cyclic reduction",
   Res. Rep. UCID-19502, L.L.N.L, Livermore, CA.

H.A. Van Der Vorst [VDV 1983]
   "On the vectorisation of some simple ICCG methods", in 1st Internat.
   Coll. on Vector and Parallel Comp. in Sc. Appl., Afcet Gamni -
   Isina, Paris.

DATA PROCESSING IN HIGH ENERGY PHYSICS

AND VECTOR PROCESSING COMPUTERS

T. Bloch[*] and D. Lellouch[**]
Centre de Calcul Vectoriel pour la Recherche
Ecole Polytechnique

91128 Palaiseau, France

I. INTRODUCTION

The data handling done in high energy physics in order to extract the results from the large volumes of data collected in typical experiments is a very large consumer of computing capacity. Throughout the 1960's and the first half of the 1970's the large high energy physics laboratories in Europe and in the United States were amongst the very first customers of the largest available mainframes : about 10 % of the CDC 6600's, IBM/360-91's, CDC 7600's and IBM/360-195's went to the computer centres of these places and others where data handling for large accelerator experiments played an important role.

More than 70 vector processing computers have now been installed and many fields of applications have been tried on such computers as the ILLIAC IV, the TI ASC, the CDC STAR-100 and more recently on the CRAY-1, the CDC Cyber 205, the ICL DAP and the CRAY X-MP. But nobody has used these computers in any significant way to process results from high energy physics experiments. This paper attempts to analyse the reasons for this situation in order to see if it is likely to change over the next few years.

Little real work has been done so far to look at the posssible vectorisation of the large codes in this field, but the motivation to apply vector processing computers in high energy physics data handling may be increasing as the gap between the scalar performance and the vector performance offered by large computers available on the market widens.

II. THE GROWTH OF COMPUTING DEMAND.

The computing performed in high energy physics today is dominated, for at least 75 % of the total load, by the processing of events : collisions of particles in magnetic fields as registered by very sophisticated detector apparatus (figure 1). The computing time required for the analysis of an experiment is dependent on parameters such

[*]CERN, DD, CH-1211 GENEVE 23
[**]Laboratoire de Physique Nucléaire des Hautes Energies, Ecole Polytechnique

Figure 1 : The UA2 detector giving a feeling for the complexity of a modern high energy physics experiment.

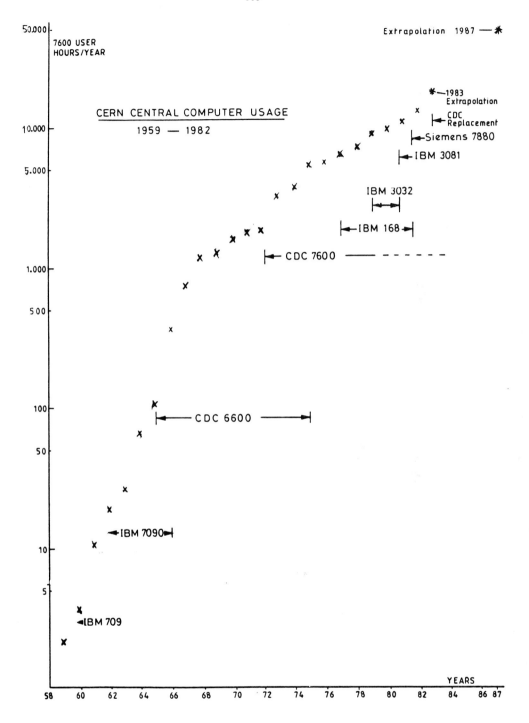

Figure 2 : Total CPU Usage at CERN since 1958

as the complexity and the number of events generated by the beam, noticed by the detectors and registered by the data collecting computers. The off-line computing consists of the processing of these discrete events which are recorded by the million in large experiments and which may contain up to one hundred thousand bytes of information each.

In order to analyse the growth of the off-line computing requirements of high energy physics we have plotted the CERN central computer usage from 1959 to 1982 (figure 2). This graph shows that there was a global increase by a factor 2 every 2 years up to 1968 and then a considerable slowdown -to a doubling every 4 years or so. We can see at least three reasons for this rather dramatic slowdown in growth rate :

- a policy decision that the off-line computing requirements of CERN-based experimental physics should be distributed around Europe based on a rule of one third at CERN and two thirds in the collaborating institutes in the member states ;

- the impact of changes in experimental techniques : less and less bubble chamber pictures and more and more minicomputer capacity installed on-line for immediate data selection ("filtering") in the electronic detector experiments ;

- the volume of data collected in electronic detector experiments is limited by electronics, beam intensity and, in the final analysis the speed of the magnetic tape -and these physical parameters do not keep doubling every two years.

Today C.E.R.N., the European Organization for Nuclear Research, fairly consistently supports a third of the total off-line computing load generated by 2500 high energy physicists in 12 member states.

With the more modest rate of progression of demand since 1968 it has not been unduly difficult to find reasonable "classical" solutions (doubling up of computers, replacement of old hardware with new) to the problems of computing capacity at C.E.R.N. The distribution of computing has also required investments on such items as interactive access and networks : at C.E.R.N. a medium speed network (CERNET) links together almost one hundred computers and links to computers in France, England and Italy contribute to making international collaboration in high energy physics more effective.

III. A SUMMARY OF THE MAIN CHARACTERISTICS OF THE PROGRAMS

Major high energy physics experiments require considerable resources and several years to prepare. They then spend several years collecting data and analysing it. Recent very large experiments at C.E.R.N., UA1 and UA2, which earlier this year discovered the W boson and the Z° are conducted by collaborations between tens of institutes and upwards of one hundred physicists. Such experiments are pushing the state of the art physically and organizationally to get the data detectors working and the on-line electronics and computers organized. The off-line data handling problems are considerable, as well, involving between 100 000 and 200 000 lines of FORTRAN code in the various programs which analyse the thousands of tapes which will be written during the experiments.

These programs contain hundreds of subroutines and a few tens of physicists, typically, contribute on a part time basis to write them and to execute them on various large computers (CDC, IBM, UNIVAC) all over Europe. Strict standards on the FORTRAN employed, the tapes and data structures and the memory management are imposed since these programs have to execute efficiently on computers with and without virtual memories, with various word lengths and without any international standards as far as regards control statements, floating point data representation and FORTRAN extensions in the I/O area. The C.E.R.N. library of subroutines as well as elaborate rules for the structuring of data, both in the computer and on the external media, exist and help to make this feasible. For a more complete discussion of all these aspects of computing in high energy physics, including the use of graphics and on-line event selection please refer to ref. 1 and 2. A recent workshop (ref. 3) was entirely devoted to a survey of present methods employed in software development within high energy physics and in other fields in an attempt to determine the necessary actions for the future data processing programs which will be used by the very large collaborations around LEP, the new Large Electron-Positron colliding beam accelerator being constructed at C.E.R.N. for the late 1980's.

Although not much linked with the main subject of this paper one cannot write about High Energy Physics data handling today without mentioning the effort which goes into the building of simplified S/370 "emulators" using bit-slice technology. These "emulators" have a (micro-) instruction set which allows them to execute the machine language programs generated by the standard IBM FORTRAN compiler after they have been passed through a translator program. They are much simplified compared to a real S/370, in particular as far as concerns I/O, cost very little to build and have started to contribute in a non-trivial way to the on-line capacity. So far, this approach has not had any significant impact on the total data processing capacity available for off-line processing, although about 40 of these engines, each of the capacity of about one third of an IBM/370-168, are in operation now and projects for the next generation -3 times the capacity- exist amongst such laboratories as S.L.A.C., C.E.R.N. and D.E.S.Y. (ref. 4).

IV. TECHNICAL PROBLEMS IN USING VECTOR PROCESSING COMPUTERS

In the big experiments mentioned earlier the interesting events contain tens of particle trajectories coming out from the collision point in all directions. These trajectories must be reconstituted as exactly as possible in three-dimensional space on the basis of the information from the detectors so that the properties of the outgoing particles (mass, momentum, charge) can be determined based on the detailed knowledge of the magnetic field. The data in each event is, in a complex case, more than 100 000 bytes (see figure 3) and the processing time is approximately ten seconds per event on a 3081K processor (half the "dyadic" one). In later, less time consuming phases of the processing chain, detailed statistical analysis of the relevant parameters of interesting events (i.e. those which are recognized to contain the particles which are being studied) take place. The programs which do the pattern recognition and the trajectory/magnetic field calculations have to concern themselves with much variability in the data presented and much imperfection and calibration problems in detectors which may contain hundreds of thousands of electronic channels triggered by nanosecond coincidence logic. These programs have loops, of course, but they have many more IF tests than loops.

Early benchmarks on vector processing computers confirm this qualitative image. Late in 1980, a benchmark of the CRAY-1 showed that it only performed at an average of about twice the CDC 7600 on the "standard" set of ten large codes used by C.E.R.N. for benchmaking new computers ; small improvements (a few man weeks of effort altogether) brought the average well above two but many of the improvements also speeded up the same programs on the CDC 7600. It was not easy to improve further as no particular sections of code dominated the execution time by then.

These results were confirmed in 1982 when the CRAY-1/M and the CRAY X-MP were benchmarked.

V. TWO CASE STUDIES

Monte Carlo

Monte Carlo methods are widely employed for the simulation of the apparatus response to "a priori" known events. One can distinguish between two general types of Monte Carlo :

  i) single detector simulation,
  ii) global apparatus simulation.

Single detector simulation is mainly of interest before the construction of the apparatus and for the analysis of tests. The FORTRAN programs use the geometrical physical parameters describing the detector as input data. The particles for which the detector is designed are then randomly generated around a typical distribution of momentum, impact angles, etc.

This kind of program usually includes code to deal with the following two problems :

  - trajectory tracking through magnetic fields : vectorizing these parts of the

EVENT 2958. 1279. 69576

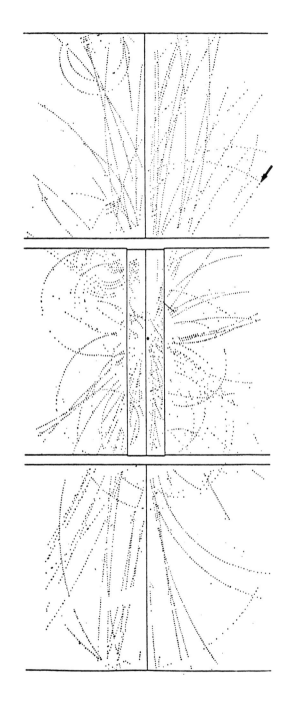

Figure 3 : A 65 particle tracks UA1 event containing a high transverse energy electron indicative of the decay of a W boson (arrow).

code may require GATHER-type operations since fields are often tabulated
rather than parametrized ;

- "cascade" generation : a particle "cascades" if its interaction with the
matter the detector is constitued of gives rise to "daughter" particles. The
multiplicity (i.e. total number of particles) of such events may reach numbers
as large as 100 000. The intrinsic tree-structure of the events is a difficult
challenge to vectorization but it might be possible to achieve reasonable
performance with more appropriate data management.

Global apparatus simulation is a "simplified" generalisation of the Monte Carlo for
individual detectors. It can be looked upon as an integration over a domain whose
bounds cannot be analytically defined. It consists of the generation of the physi-
cals events corresponding to the processes physicists are interested in. Product
particles are them followed through each part of the apparatus. These programs are
run in order to determine the acceptance curves of the apparatus (i.e. number of
detected events/number of actual events as a function of the different physical
parameters) but sophisticated versions can even produce pseudo "raw data tapes" -
These tapes are used for monitoring the efficiency and stability of the reconstruc-
tion and analysis programs.

Can a global Monte Carlo be vectorized ? The answer obviously depends on the complexity of the apparatus and of the topology (number of secondaries) of the studied
events. Such an attempt, involving rewriting of the program structure, is currently
being carried out for an experiment (NA-10).

Theoretical physics

Normally, purely theoretical calculations at C.E.R.N. have represented about 5 % of
the total load of the computer centre although a particular project in 1973 (g-2
calculations) brought it higher for one year. Very recently, however, Quantum
Chromo Dynamics lattice gauge calculations have become of considerable interest and
a joint effort between physicists and expert programmers has resulted, early in
1982, in a program which executed very fast indeed on the CRAY-1.

A description of this effort may be of interest (private communication by H. Lipps
and R. Petronzio) :

"The problem under investigation is to simulate the behaviour of a small cube of
matter, about 10^{-13} cm in length, according to the theory of quantum chromodynamics and thus derive basic properties (such as the masses) of a whole range of
elementary particles. In our model, matter is represented by 1000 points in
space over a period of 20 time steps ; i.e. a four-dimensional lattice of 20'000
points in all. The forces between neighbouring points are described by unitary
matrices in order three. Once these forces have been established (by means of a
Monte Carlo calculation that constitutes the first step in our calculation),
twelve complex state variables for each point of the lattice are determined by a

set of 12 times 20'000 (= 240'000) complex linear equations. This set of equations, which is sparse, must be solved for twelve sets of right-hand sides, thus resulting in nearly six million words of results. Their computation by means of an iterative (relaxation) process represents the second step of our calculation.

Given the number of equations and the number of non-zero elements of the coefficient matrix, our program requires in excess of 1.6 million words of main storage. It might be run on a machine with only one million words of main memory through the use of some buffering scheme, but only at a CPU efficiency of probably less than 20 percent !

The Monte Carlo calculation required for step 1 requires 25 minutes at present. This is about 13 times the speed of the program we had for the 7600. Using some more effort on program optimization, we expect to reduce the execution time of this program to below 15 minutes.

It is not, however, enough to solve the afore-mentioned problem just once. Firstly, for a given configuration of forces in the cube of matter, as obtained from the Monte Carlo calculation, our set of equations depends also on a linear parameter (called kappa). One wants to know how the solutions of the linear system depend on kappa.

To estimate the true dimension of the computing problem on hand, however, one must remember that the configuration of forces in the lattice, as established at the first step of the calculations, is not unique, but just one random sample of many possible states of the little cube of matter. To obtain quantities that are meaningful in particle physics, such as the mass of the pion, it is necessary to solve the problem not only for one sample configuration of forces in the cube, but for many ; i.e. for a number of cases that is statistically meaningful –50 at a guess.

The state variables computed at step 2 of the calculation for one single sample cube nearly fill a reel of magnetic tape recorded at 6250 bits per inch. This then forms the raw data for answers to a variety of questions that are of interest to particle physicists. To answer any of these questions, a suitable analysis program is required that condenses the raw data accordingly by computing different functions of time at 20 points each and that from these values may be derived the masses of different elementary particles. This gain has allowed the tackling of calculations which would otherwise have been out of reach and the first results have now been published from these calculations : the theoretical mass of the rho-particle (ref. 6)."

Similar types of calculations could become of considerable importance in the future and certainly require the performance of vector processing computers to be carried out on a realistic scale.

VI. THE FUTURE

Whether high energy physics event processing will, eventually, use vector processing computers depends on the answer to the following questions :

1. Will there be sufficient economic motivation (difficulties in finding enough computing capacity on scalar machines) ?

2. Will it become easier organizationally to use vector processing computers (Portability, style of development) ?

3. To what extent will it be possible, technically, to "vectorize" the programs ?

These questions will take several years to answer as the industry offerings in vector processing computers evolve and as the vision of the next generation of high energy physics experiments, in particular around LEP, gets clearer.

The economic motivation

It is expected that the complexity of events generated by LEP from 1988 onwards will be such that the total computing requirements of experiments will increase by a factor three or four over those of today's active experiments. It is not clear whether these requirements can be met economically with conventional computers -but it is not excluded neither.

Organization

The portability constraints listed earlier may well become less of a hindrance to the vectorization of the codes than they are today. The increased need for LEP experiments to process the data fast in order to obtain the new results quickly could well have a centralizing effect on the data processing requirements and thus make it possible to optimize the codes more for specific types of computers. FORTRAN will also soon have standard vector constructs and several "normal" large computers will have hardware incorporated to support these constructs efficiently. This evolution will allow vector processing to enter the field more easily -as opposed to the situation today where it is necessary to invest a considerable amount of effort in converting the codes.

Technically

There is no doubt that the type of data processing typical of particle physics is particularly resistent to attempts at vectorization. Algorithms used in the pattern recognition part could perhaps benefit from image processing techniques developed in other fields although the density and contrast of the tracks pose some new problems. The overall organization of the processing chains may also have to be changed if vectorisation is to succeed, in particular with respect to the structuring of the data.

An isolated attempt to look for "horizontal parallelism" also has to be mentioned here : the processing of several events in parallel (cf. ref. 5). In a simple test case it was possible to vectorize significantly by this "lock step" approach at a cost of a factor two or three in total computing requirements and at a considerable expense of effort throughout the whole program —including the rewriting of basic FORTRAN library routines such as ARCTAN in order to make the code invariant ; i.e. execute the same instructions independently of the arguments submitted. It seems doubtful though, that this approach could be applied to the more complex situations normally prevailing. The coexistence of vector processing and scalar computers in High Energy Physics will probably persist for a long time and this sort of extreme approach is not satisfactory in such an environment.

Another, perhaps more logical, approach would be to explore the application of MIMD techniques thus taking advantage of the inherent independency of each event and avoiding the problem of the considerable data dependency in the actual processing. A small array of computers of a few MIPS each might be a very cost effective solution within reach, even commercially, over the next few years.

VII. CONCLUSIONS

High Energy Physics programs are not easy to vectorize but the spectacular experience recently made with theoretical calculations in this field may now encourage experimenters to look more closely at their future computing requirements and the possibilities to benefit from the substantial price/performance increases which properly exploited vector processing computers offer. The construction of a new accelerator in Europe, LEP, for the late 1980's is well suited to encourage such a study now.

REFERENCES

1. P. Zanella, CERN preprint DD/83/6, March 1983.

2. R.K. Bock, CERN preprint EP RB/el., 23 February 1983.

3. Proceedings of the Workshop on Software in High-Energy Physics, CERN Geneva, Switzerland, 4-6 October, 1982, CERN Yellow Report 82-12, November 1982.

4. P.F. Kunz, M. Gravina, G. Oxoby, Q. Trang, A. Fucci, D. Jacobs, B. Martin and K.M. Storr, CERN preprint DD/83/3, March 1983.

5. V. Zacharov, CERN preprint DD/82/1, January 1982.

6. H. Lipps, Martinelli, R. Petronzio, F. Rapuano, CERN preprint TH3542, April 1983.

A METHODOLOGY FOR EXPLOITING PARALLELISM

IN THE FINITE ELEMENT PROCESS

Loyce M. Adams
Robert G. Voigt

ICASE, NASA Langley Research Center
Hampton, Virginia 23665

1.   Introduction

The   finite   element   method   is   an   important   technique   for
constructing approximate solutions to boundary value problems.   Very
briefly,

(1)   the region of interest is subdivided into elements,

(2)   basis   functions   which   span   the   subspace   in   which   the
        approximate solution is assumed to lie are chosen,

(3)   the   contribution   of   the   elements   is   determined   by
        integrating the basis functions over each of the elements,

(4)   the contributions of all of the elements are assembled into
        a single system,

$$Kx = f, \qquad\qquad (1.1)$$

(5)   the system is solved for the approximate solution.

A complete description of the process may be found in a number of
references from the finite element literature such as Strang & Fix
[1973].

Traditionally, the bulk of the computational work is contained in
steps (3) and (5) and researchers have tried many techniques in order
to reduce the required computational time.   Some of these have
involved   improvements   in   numerical   algorithms   and   the   underlying
software systems.

A particular example which will be discussed in the next section
is that of substructuring or matrix partitioning, see for example
Noor, Kamel and Fulton [1978].   Another example is the FEARS project
begun at the University of Maryland, Zave and Rheinboldt [1979].   This

NATO ASI Series, Vol. F7
High-Speed Computation. Edited by J. S. Kowalik
© Springer-Verlag Berlin Heidelberg 1984

latter effort attempts to improve the efficiency of the solution process for two dimensional problems by utilizing adaptive grids.

FEARS also uses another technique for improving performance that is becoming increasingly popular, namely, parallel computation. In its simplest form, parallel computation means that relevant computations within the solution process of a single problem are performed simultaneously. In the FEARS project the parallelism is achieved by creating tasks for both the assembly and the solution process which may be executed on independent processors with a modest amount of communication, Zave and Cole [1983]. This suggests a computer organization of the multiple-instruction-multiple-data, MIMD, type in the classification of Flynn [1966].

Another MIMD computer concept under investigation for finite element analysis is the Finite Element Machine at the NASA Langley Research Center, Jordan [1978]. Ultimately, the system will contain 36 16-bit microprocessors with each processor connected to its eight nearest neighbors in a plane and connected to every other processor via a global communications bus. To date, this system has been used primarily to investigate the parallel assembly of (1.1) followed by its solution using iterative methods, Adams [1982].

The purpose of this paper is to provide a discussion of the parallelism available in the finite element process applied to three dimensional structural analysis problems. We use a top down methodology that allows the specification of the necessary environments required to exploit and analyze this parallelism. In particular, following a discussion of substructuring in Section 2, various types of parallelism are considered and the difficulties and opportunities of exploiting them are discussed in Section 3.

At this point many researchers would introduce a section on computer architecture and discuss the implementation details of a particular solution method. We will take a different tack.

We believe that it is essential to provide environments in which scientists can study the different issues that relate to the overall system. For example, calculating the stresses on the wing of an aircraft or investigating the inter-processor communication required by a numerical algorithm are both important in determining the eventual architecture. A methodology for developing the environments, the "virtual machine concept", is introduced in Pratt, et al., [1983] and we will rely heavily on concepts given there for the discussion in Section 4.

375

In Section 5, we develop a numerical analyst's virtual machine; in Section 6 we introduce an example 3-dimensional problem; and in Section 7 we discuss the example in light of the virtual machine. Finally, the benefits of this approach are discussed in Section 8.

2. Substructuring

The method of substructuring in structural analysis is based on dividing a large structure or region into pieces. In particular, if one is interested in displacements of a structure based on some external forces, the displacements for the interfaces of these pieces are determined first. This information may then be used to determine the values of the unknowns within each piece or substructure, see Noor, Kamel and Fulton [1978].

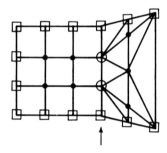

Figure 1.   Example Structure

We will now make these ideas more precise by using Figure 1 as an example. The squares represent boundary points of the structure while the solid dots are interior points. The line segments indicate dependencies between points by defining the individual finite elements. Thus part 1 of the figure consists of rectangular elements that might represent plates and part 2 consists of triangular elements that might also be plates or some other element such as beams. There is a natural interface between the two parts of the structure indicated by the arrow. A structural engineer might use this interface to separate the structure into two "substructures". Note that these substructures are connected by only four points: two boundary points and two interface points indicated by circles.   The circled points also become boundaries of the two substructures.

Now assuming that the elements are fixed and the basis functions are chosen, the individual element contributions to the overall problem are determined.   These may be assembled into a global stiffness matrix once the ordering of the points is determined.   The interior points of each substructure are numbered completely before considering the next substructure. Then the boundary and interface are numbered. A substructure, j, therefore yields a matrix of the form

$$\begin{bmatrix} K_{ii}^{(j)} & K_{ib}^{(j)} \\ K_{bi}^{(j)} & K_{bb}^{(j)} \end{bmatrix}$$

where $K_{ii}^{(j)}$ represents the contribution from the interior points, $K_{bb}^{(j)}$ represents the contribution from the boundary and interface points, which for simplicity we will refer to as boundary points, and $K_{ib}^{(j)}$ and $K_{bi}^{(j)}$ represents the dependencies or connections between interior points and boundary points.

In general one obtains a global stiffness matrix,

$$\begin{bmatrix} K_{ii}^{(1)} & & & & K_{ib}^{(1)} \\ & K_{ii}^{(2)} & & & K_{ib}^{(2)} \\ & & \ddots & & \vdots \\ & & & K_{ii}^{(I)} & K_{ib}^{(I)} \\ K_{bi}^{(1)} & K_{bi}^{(2)} & \cdots & K_{bi}^{(I)} & K_{bb} \end{bmatrix}$$

where for the example in Figure 1, I = 2. The K_{bb} matrix represents the contributions of all $K_{bb}^{(j)}$ in the global numbering system.

If the structure is under some force and we are interested in the displacements we obtain a matrix equation (1.1) where

$$X = (x_i^{(1)}, \ldots, x_i^{(I)}, x_b)^T \text{ and } f = (f_i^{(1)}, \ldots, f_i^{(I)}, f_b)^T$$

with x_i, f_i, and x_b, f_b representing the displacements and external forces at the internal and boundary points respectively.

For our purposes the most important feature of this matrix is that the $K_{ii}^{(j)}$ are decoupled. This suggests a block elimination scheme for factoring the matrix K because the $K_{ii}^{(j)}$ may themselves be factored in parallel. Thus, substructuring can be viewed as a technique for decoupling the global stiffness matrix in order to introduce parallelism in the solution process.

The solution process then requires the following steps:

1) For all $j = 1, \ldots, I$ form $K_{ii}^{(j)} = L_j U_j$;

2) For all $j = 1, \ldots, I$

Form $\left(K_{ii}^{(j)}\right)^{-1} K_{ib}^{(j)}$ and $\left(K_{ii}^{(j)}\right)^{-1} f_i^{(j)}$ by solving

$$L_j U_j (M_j) = K_{ib}^{(j)}$$
and
$$L_j U_j (q_j) = f_i^{(j)}$$

Form $\bar{K}_{bb}^{(j)} = K_{bb}^{(j)} - K_{bi}^{(j)} M_j$

$$\bar{f}_b^{(j)} = f_b^{(j)} - K_{bi}^{(j)} q_j$$

3) Form $\bar{K}_{bb} = \sum_j \bar{K}_{bb}^{(j)}$

$$\bar{f}_b = \sum_j \bar{f}_b^{(j)}$$

where the $\sum_j$ denotes the addition of the substructure boundary

contributions into the proper location in the global matrices.

4) Form $\bar{K}_{bb} = L_b U_b$ and solve $L_b U_b x_b = \bar{f}_b$

5) For all $j = 1, 2 \ldots, I$ solve $L_j U_j x_i^{(j)} = - K_{ib}^{(j)} x_b^{(j)} + f_i^{(j)}$

Algorithm 1. Solution via Substructuring

It is worth noting some distinguishing characteristics of the above process:

a) Steps 1), 2), and 5) exhibit natural parallelism requiring no cooperation among procesors.

b) The matrices $K_{ii}^{(j)}$ are banded but in general do not have the same size or structure.

c) Step 3) produces fill in the matrix $\bar{K}_{bb}$ and must be done with care in a parallel computing environment since it may change existing, or introduce new, non zeroes in $\bar{K}_{bb}$.

d) The matrix $\bar{K}_{bb}$ is banded.

Item b) points out the difficulty in using this solution technique on a vector computer if one were to try to vectorize across the substructures or $K_{ii}^{(j)}$. The diversity of the $K_{ii}^{(j)}$ suggests a collection of asynchronous processors.

The activity described in c) can require multiple modifications to the same location in K_{bb}. This would occur, for example, in the structure given in Figure 1 for all nodes on the line indicated by the arrow. In general, it occurs for all nodes on the common boundary of two or more substructures. This will be discussed further in the next section.

In Section 5 we will discuss a specific example which will provide insight into the size and form of the block matrices in (2.1). We will also compare the substructuring approach with a different ordering of the nodes which yields a single banded matrix K for which the bandwidth is small.

3. Parallelism in Substructuring

In this section, we discuss the parallelism that is inherent in the substructuring procedure outlined in section 2.

We begin by focusing on the creation of the matrices of (2.1). These matrices can be generated simultaneously for all substructures by independent tasks. The tasks must be of the MIMD type since the substructures normally will contain different types of elements as shown in Figure 1, and hence will require different operations during the elemental integrations. Only when each substructure is identical can we achieve parallelism by vectorizing across the substructures. Each substructure may be composed of many elements, and integrations over these elements may also be carried out asynchronously; in essence, an element may be considered as the smallest possible substructure.

It is the diversity of substructures and elements that make the assembly process unattractive for vector computers such as the Cyber 200 or Cray 1, or SIMD arrays. In both types of computer systems one needs to perform the same arithmatic operations on a group of operands or vectors. This is generally not possible either within a substructure or across substructures.

During the solution process, several operations may be performed asynchronously across the substructures. First, the matrix factorization in Step 1 of the algorithm of Section 2 will parallelize across all j. Then the formation of the new matrices indicated in Step 2 may also be done in parallel for all j. In addition, within a given substructure, we have the flexibility to assume that the operations in step 2 may be performed in a sequential manner, if we have limited available parallelism or alternatively, we may choose to exploit the parallelism in any one or all of the following:

(1) the solution of the systems

$$K_{ii}^{(j)} M_i^{(j)} = K_{ib} \text{ and } K_{ii}^{(j)} q_i^{(j)} = f_i^{(j)}$$

depending on the particular form of $K_{ii}^{(j)}$, followed by

(2) the parallel multiplication of the matrices

$$C = K_{bi}^{(j)} M_i^{(j)}, \quad d = K_{bi}^{(j)} q_i^{(j)} \text{ and finally}$$

(3) the matrix and vector subtractions $K_{bb}^{(j)} - C$ and $f_b^{(j)} - d$.

Second, the formation of the $\overline{K}_{bb}$ in Step 3 of the algorithm can be done in parallel phases as follows: If all substructures are "colored" such that any two substructures that share a common interface node are different colors, it is clear that all substructures of the same color will not have contributions to the same location in the matrix K_{bb} and therefore may be assembled simultaneously without memory contention, (Berger, et. al., [1982]). The creation of K_{bb} may then be achieved in c parallel phases where c is the number of colors.

So far, the parallelism in the formation of the matrices $\overline{K}_{bb}$ and $\overline{f}_b$ for the solution for the boundary nodes has been described. We now turn to what appears to be the sequential part of the algorithm, namely the solution of $\overline{K}_{bb} x_b = \overline{f}_b$ in Step 4.

As with the operations in Step 2, the characteristics of the matrix $\overline{K}_{bb}$ must be known to extract all the parallelism. However, some observataions can be made now and will be made more precise for an example problem in Section 5. First, $\overline{K}_{bb}$ will be of size q x q where q is the total number of boundary nodes in the structure; furthermore, q will generally be an order of magnitude smaller than the number of interior nodes. The fill-in that occurs in $\overline{K}_{bb}$ will only be between the interface nodes of a given substructure. Hence for most structures, the matrix $\overline{K}_{bb}$ will be sparse and can be ordered as a banded matrix with as small a bandwidth, β, as possible. If $\overline{K}_{bb}$ is of size q x q, the system $\overline{K}_{bb}x_b = \overline{f}_b$ can be solved by factorization in q steps using β tasks. These tasks, however, do not have the completely asynchronous nature of the substructure tasks described earlier since they must cooperate during the decomposition of $\overline{K}_{bb}$. These techniques for solving this system will be described in detail in Section 5 for a particular example.

The operations in Step 5 are again completely asynchronous and may be done in parallel across the substructures. This provides the solution for the interior nodes once the solution for the boundary nodes for the substructure has been obtained. As was pointed out earlier, if we have limited parallelism, the operations may be done sequentially for a given substructure. To describe all the parallelism in the step, we must know the form of $K_{ii}^{(j)}$ and $K_{ib}^{(j)}$. This is problem dependent and also varies across the substructures.

At this point, the parallelism in the substructuring technique has been described, but many questions must be answered before an efficient overall environment for specifying and extracting this parallelism can be determined. In the next section, we give the methodology that will help us begin to answer these questions and in Section 5 we demonstrate this methodology with an example problem.

4. The Virtual Machine Concept

It is often tempting to take the description of the parallelism in a given solution process, like that described in Section 3, and propose a computer hardware organization to support its implementation. We believe that decisions about hardware should not be made until the user environment and the several levels of software required to effectively implement the finite element process have been carefully studied. This top-down approach to design, or virtual machine concept, is described in Pratt, et al. [1983] and will be briefly discussed below.

Each class of computer user would like to view the machine that runs his problems in different ways. To date we have considered the following four levels:

> User's Virtual Machine. The perspective of a structural engineer may be that of a workstation that allows him to store the description of his structural models, to use applications packages to analyze the models, and finally to display the results.

Researcher's Virtual Machine. The numerical analyst or research user may view his machine in terms of a high-level language (like Fortran) that allows him to specify the data structures, operations and their sequences, and the parallelism in the linear algebra necessary to implement efficiently a structural engineer's application.

Systems Programmer's Virtual Machine. By specifying the tasks, their scheduling, communication between them, and the storage representation of the data, the system programmer's virtual machine that implements the high level language can be defined.

Hardware Virtual Machine. The last level of virtual machine which implements the system programmer's low level language may be the hardware itself. ("Virtual" because it may be implemented by micro programs on yet lower level hardware.)

By formally specifying the data objects, operations on these data objects, control mechanisms, and storage management techniques of each virtual machine, a detailed hardware/software design can be obtained that specifies the function of each level as well as its implementations on the next lower level. Our research uses the methods of H-graph semantics, Pratt [1981], for making this formal specification. Simulations can then be used to test the feasibility and efficiency of the overall system before commitment to hardware is made.

In the next section, we will give some insight into this approach by showing how the numerical analyst's virtual machine can be designed (not formally specified) using Algorithm 1 for the substructuring technique of the last section.

5. A Numerical Analyst's Virtual Machine

In this section we introduce the data objects, the operations on those data objects, and the sequence controls required to define the virtual machine for Algorithm 1 of Section 3. The data objects are listed in Table 1. We have also included the storage required by these data objects for a particular example to be introduced in Section 7. The variables t, a, etc. in Table 1 are parameters of that example. The data object T_j is a table of integers needed for an operation explained later and the data object $\bar{K}$ is a matrix that will be discussed later.

DATA OBJECT	TYPE	SIZE	STORAGE
$K_{ii}^{(j)}(L_j U_j)$	Banded Sym. Matrix Band: $6t^2+t+12$	$6t^3 \times 6t^3$	$72t^5$ (after fill)
$K_{ib}^{(j)}$	Sparse-Blocked Matrix	$6t^3 \times 6(a^3-t^3)$	$1944t^2$
$\bar{K}_{bb}^{(j)}$	Dense Matrix	$6(a^3-t^3) \times 6(a^3-t^3)$	$36(a^3-t^3)^2$
$\bar{K}_{bb}$	Banded Sym. Matrix Band: $6n^2+6s$	$q \times q$ $q = \Theta(n^2 d)$	$36n^4 d$ (after fill)
M_j	Dense Matrix	$6t^3 \times 6(a^3-t^3)$	$36t^3(a^3-t^3)$
$Q_j, F_b^{(j)}$	Dense Vectors	$6t^3 \times 1$	$18t^3$
$X_b, \bar{F}_b$	Dense Vectors	$q \times 1$	$12(n^3-d^3t^3)$
T_j	Dense Integer Matrix	$6(a^3-t^3) \times 2$	$12(a^3-t^3)$ integers
$\bar{K}$	Banded Sym. Matrix Band: $6n^2+6n+12$	$N \times N$	$36n^5$

Table 1. Data Objects and their required storage in terms of floating point numbers for the example of section 7.

The second step in describing the numerical analyst's virtual machine is to list the operations that must occur on these data objects. At this point, we make the assumption that the operations within a given substructure, that is a particular j in steps 1), 2), and 5), will be done sequentially. As mentioned in Section 3, more parallelism can be obtained within a given substructure by exploiting available matrix operations, but for simplicity we do not consider that here. On the other hand, we assume that factorization and solution with $\bar{K}_{bb}$ in Step 4) will be done in parallel. This will be described in detail later. The necessary operations are summarized below.

OPERATION	on	DATA OBJECT	creates	DATA OBJECT
Sequential Decompose		Symmetric Banded Matrix		
Sequential Forward Solve		Lower Triangular Banded System		
Sequential Backward Solve		Upper Triangular Banded System		Dense Vector
Replace/Add (Matrix)		Dense Matrix/Banded Sym Matrix		
Replace/Add (Vector)		Dense Vector/Dense Vector		
Parallel Decompose		Symmetric Banded Matrix		
Parallel Forward Solve		Lower Triangular Banded System		Dense Vector
Parallel Backward Solve		Upper Triangular Banded System		Dense Vector
Select		Dense Vector		Dense Vector

Table 2. OPERATIONS ON DATA OBJECTS

Sequence of Operations

A control mechanism appropriate to specify the sequence of operations in Algorithm 1 is the FORALL statement which has the form

```
FORALL J in SET DO
        BEGIN
        STATEMENT 1
            .
            .
        STATEMENT n
        END
    STATEMENT n + 1
```

STATEMENTS 1, ...,n will be executed for each J simultaneously, to the extent possible, and STATEMENT n + 1 will not be executed until all instances of J are completed.

The meaning of the operations in Table 2 will now be explained. The first three are the standard operations associated with the Cholesky solution technique. The replace/add operation of any dense matrix A into a symmetric banded matrix B where both are visualized as being organized by rows and columns requires the following steps:

(1) A lookup in table T_j (of Table 1) to find the subscripts i´ and j´ corresponding to the subscripts i and j of a_{ij}.

(2) Adding a_{ij} to the value of b_{ij} and replacing this sum into b_{ij}. Note that if B were organized by bands, a

similar lookup would be required where i´ would be the band number and j´ the element within the i´th band. The select operation must involve a similar table lookup, for instance, to extract a substructure's boundary values $X_b^{(j)}$ from X_b.

At this point a high level version of the numerical analyst's virtual machine has been sketched; however, it is likely that a researcher might want to study some or all of the operations in Table 2 in further detail. To demonstrate how this might be done we will focus on the "Parallel Decompose" operation. The approach we will discuss involves the generation of parallel tasks, and we will address the question of how the tasks must communicate and synchronize with each other. This begins to raise issues at the level of the system programmer's virtual machine and even at the level of the actual hardware. We will leave a detailed discussion of these levels along with a comparison of other techiques for implementing the "Parallel Decompose" for a future paper.

If the symmetric N x N matrix K has bandwidth β. the basic algorithm consists of N-1 steps. At step i, β tasks numbered i..i + β - 1 simultaneously operate on the β rows, one task per row, directly below the pivot row i, updating the components of K. To perform step i, each of the β tasks must have access to the $(\beta + 1)$ coefficients of the pivot row. In addition, task j must have access to row j + 1 of K and this row will be called task j's computation row. Furthermore, after step i is completed task i terminates, and task j continues to operate on the same computation row for j - i more steps at which time row j + 1 will become the pivot row and task j will terminate. This description is not correct from step N - β to step N, but this special case will be ignored here.

The following issues must be considered:
(1) How and when are the tasks created and destroyed. In particular, do the same β tasks move through the array K, or does array K move through these tasks, or are new tasks created and old ones destroyed from step to step?
(2) Does the creator (parent) task also perform any operations on the pivot row or is a $(\beta+1)$st task required to do this? Which approach leads to less communication?
(3) How do these tasks get access to the pivot row and their current computation row?

We will not attempt to answer all of these questions here, but
rather we will discuss one approach in which a parent task is in
control of the process. The parent task "owns" the array K, and
initiates β subtasks with the data for their computation row and
then executes the following repeatedly:

- perform any necessary operations on the pivot row,
- "broadcast" the pivot row to these tasks,
- initiate a new task for the last row in the next step,
- wait for the first subtask to complete and send back its
  completed computation row (the new pivot row),
- broadcast this row to the β tasks.

The β subtasks on a given step are more passive. In general,
they execute the following β times

- receive a pivot row from the parent,
- perform computation on their computation row using this pivot
  row
- wait until the next pivot row is received.

After β pivot rows are used, the subtask sends the parent a
terminate signal and also the values of its computation row which will
become the new pivot row. Note that only one subtask can be sending
the parent task the new pivot row at a given time. This approach
requires addition of the operations given in Table 3 to our virtual
machine:

OPERATION	EFFECT
INITIATE	Initiates a task with a Dense Vector as initial data.
SEND	Sends a Dense Vector to a particular task.
RECEIVE	Receives a Dense Vector from a particular task
BROADCAST	Sends a dense vector to a given set of tasks.

TABLE 3.   OPERATIONS FOR PARALLEL DECOMPOSE

Now, the implementation of this approach in the virtual machine we
have designed to this point is given below in Algorithm 2. The
authors are indebted to Piyush Mehrotra for developing Table 3 and
Algorithm 2.

```
PROCEDURE PARENT:
      K: symmetric banded matrix (N, 6n² + 6n + 12)
```

K: symmetric banded matrix $(N, 6n^2 + 6n + 12)$

```
      BEGIN
      FORALL i in 1.. β  DO
                  BEGIN
                        INITIATE SUBTASK (i) WITH ROW (i + 1) OF K;
                  END;
            FOR i in 1.. N - 1 DO
                  BEGIN
                  -- DO NECESSARY COMPUTATIONS ON ROW (i) OF K
                  BROADCAST ROW (i) OF K TO ALL SUBTASKS;
                  INITIATE SUBTASK (i + β ) WITH ROW  (i + β + 1) of K;
                  RECEIVE ROW (i + 1) OF K FROM SUBTASK (i);
                  END;
END;


TASK SUBTASK (id, V);
V:  dense vector  (β + 1);                    (*computation row*)
PIVOT-ROW:  dense vector  (β + 1);

BEGIN
            FOR i in 1..  β DO
                  BEGIN
                  RECEIVE PIVOT-ROW from PARENT;
                  --COMPUTE ON PIVOT-ROW AND V
                  END;
            SEND V TO PARENT:
END;
```

ALGORITHM 2. PARALLEL DECOMPOSE

Algorithm 2 requires three communications per step; namely, the parent must receive the next pivot row, broadcast it to the β subtasks, and the subtasks must receive this pivot row before computation can begin. Hence, the required communication is $O(3N)$ where we are assuming these three types of communication cost the same amount and the unit of cost is that required to communicate $\beta + 1$ elements. Clearly, a system that requires time largely independent of β for this communication is desired.

This now completes the discussion of the numerical analyst's virtual machine. In the next section we introduce a three dimensional example, and in Section 7 we analyze the example in light of the virtual machine.

6. Three Dimensional Example

In this section we introduce a model structure with which to study the substructuring process as given in Algorithm 1. The model is an n-cube composed of d^3 individual a-cubes. The reader interested in the details of the model structure or of the matrices which are introduced later should refer to Adams and Voigt [1983].

We consider each a-cube to be a substructure composed of finite elements. The exact type of finite element(s) is not important to our analysis, nor is the exact form of the partial differential equation; instead, we focus on the connectivity of the nodes which determines the structure of the matrices and data objects of Sections 3 and 5. In particular, we assume that each node in an a-cube is connected to its eight nearest neighbor nodes in its x-y plane as well as its nine nearest neighbors in x-y planes directly above and below.

To determine the structure and sizes of the data objects in Table 1, we assume there are 6 equations at each node (for example 3 displacements and 3 rotations) and set

$$N = 6n^3 \qquad x = 6(a^3 - t^3)$$
$$t = a - 2 \qquad q = 6n^3 - 6d^3t^3$$
$$y = 6t^3 \qquad s = (d+1)\ (2n - (d + 1)).$$

Furthermore, we assume that all interior nodes of a given a-cube are numbered left to right, front to back in a given horizontal plane with planes considered bottom to top. After all a-cubes are numbered, the remaining boundary points are numbered the same way by considering them to be on horizontal planes. Then, each $K_{ii}^{(j)}$ is a $6t^3$ x $6t^3$ block tridiagonal matrix.

Similarily, each $K_{ib}^{(j)}$ matrix is a $6t^3$ x $6(a^3 - t^3)$ matrix representing the connectivity of the t interior planes to the a planes containing boundary points. For simplicity we assume $K_{ib}^{(j)} = (K_{bi}^{(j)})^T$. Note that in general because of varying elements and connectivity, the sub-matrices forming $K_{ii}^{(j)}$ and $K_{ib}^{(j)}$ have neither the same numerical values nor the same zero, non-zero structure.

Each $K_{bb}^{(j)}$ is a $6(a^3 - t^3)$ x $6(a^3 \pm t^3)$ block tridiagonal matrix representing the connectivity of the boundary nodes on the a planes to each other. However, during the process of eliminating $K_{bi}^{(j)}$ in Step 2 this matrix fills and for our purposes we assume that it becomes dense.

Lastly, of particular note, $\overline{K}_{bb}$ is a q x q block tridiagonal matrix. This matrix provides the connectivity of the boundary nodes to each other on all n planes after the fill-in from Step 3. The bandwidth of $\overline{K}_{bb}$ is $6n^2 + 6s$ and we assume storage is required within the entire band due to the fill-in caused in Step 3 and the subsequent factorization in Step 5. The storage requirements are summarized in Table 1 where for simplicity we include only the highest order term.

If we order the nodes of the original n-cube left to right, front to back, bottom to top with no substructuring the resulting matrix, denoted by $\overline{K}$ in Table 1, is N x N and will be discussed later. Since $t = O(n/d)$, as n becomes large, the maximum storage required for Algorithm 1 is either $O\left(72 \left(\frac{n}{d}\right)^5\right)$ or $O(36n^4 d)$ depending on the value d. Nevertheless, this storage will be less than that for $\overline{K}$, $O(36n^5)$, whenever $d < O(n)$. Note that we do not specify how this data is to be stored or what kind of memory system is provided since these decisions should be made at a lower level of the virtual machine. Our purpose here is simply to provide the magnitude and form of the data.

7. Analysis of the Example

We now summarize the amount of parallel arithmetic and communication, and the required number of tasks for the substructuring technique of Algorithm 1 (using Algorithm 2 for the solution of $\overline{K}_{bb} x_b = f_b$) and for the traditional band solver (also using Algorithm 2). We then give conditions for when one technique might be preferred over the other.

Table 4 summarizes this information where a denotes the amount of arithmetic in units of floating point multiplication/addition pairs, c denotes the number of times a bandwidth of numbers are communicated, and t represents the number of tasks.

The number of sequential operations for either method is $O(n^7)$.

METHOD	FACTOR $K_{ii}^{(j)}$	FILL-IN $\overline{K}_{bb}^{(j)}$	FACTOR $\overline{K}_{bb}$	TOTAL
Substr.	a: $108\dfrac{n^7}{d^7}$	a: $(36)^2\dfrac{n^7}{d^7}$	a: $108n^4 d$	a: $(36)^2 \dfrac{n^7}{d^7}$ if $d<n^{3/8}$ $108\,n^4 d$ otherwise
	c: 0	c: 0	c: $54n^2 d$	c: $54n^2 d$
	t: d^3	t: d^3	t: $6n^2 + 12nd$	t: $\Theta(6n^2 + 6s, d^3)$
Banded			a: $36n^5$	a: $36n^5$
			c: $18n^3$	c: $18n^3$
			t: $6n^2 + 6n + 12$	t: $6n^2 + 6n + 12$

Table 4. OPERATION COUNTS

For simplicity, we have omitted the time required for the forward and backward substitutions. If they are done in parallel, both the arithmetic and communication complexities are less than that of the factorizations. However, for a complete design these must be considered since the type of communication required is slightly different than that for factorization and would add more operations to the virtual machine.

Now, if we let

C_a = cost of one floating point multiply/add

C_c = cost of broadcasting or receiving $\beta + 1$ floating point numbers,

the total amount of work, W_s and W_b required by the substructuring and banded methods respectively, is

$$W_s = C_a (36)^2 \frac{n^7}{d^7} + C_c (54) n^2 d \quad \text{if} \quad d < n^{3/8}$$

$$C_a (108) n^4 d + C_c (54) n^2 d \quad \text{otherwise} \qquad (5.1)$$

$$W_b = C_a (36) n^5 + C_c (18) n^3$$

First, observe from (5.1) that the substructuring technique requires less communication than the banded solver if $d < n/3$. Second, the arithmetic for substructuring is also less than that of the banded solver whenever d is in the following approximate range.

$$(36)^{1/7} n^{2/7} < d < n^{3/8} \qquad (5.2)$$

or

$$n^{3/8} < d < n/3 \qquad (5.3)$$

The inequality (5.2) can be satisfied only for $n > 280$, and if $n = 280$ the underlying problem contains 132 million equations. Since problems of such size are beyond serious consideration at this time, we will focus on the second inequality. Note that when d satisfies (5.3) the arithmetic and communication work increases linearly with d; thus the optimal operation count occurs for the smallest d greater than $n^{3/8}$.

Inequality (5.3) can be interpreted as meaning that d must be at least $O(n^{2/7})$ so that the parallelism at the substructure level overcomes the sequential operations within a given substructure, but on the other hand, d can not be more than $O(n/3)$ so that the work of putting the substructures together (solving $\overline{K}_{bb} x_b = f_b$) is not too large. Note that in the limit as $d \rightarrow n$, the substructuring technique requires three times more arithmetic and 3 times more communication than does the band solver. This is due to the extra fill-in in the matrix $\overline{K}_{bb}$ that results from the substructure ordering.

Of course $\overline{K}_{bb}$ could be ordered in a variety of ways in order to decouple it and to introduce more parallelism. For example, the red/black ordering could be applied to the x-y boundary planes. However, an argument similar to the one above indicates that this approach will introduce more work as $d \rightarrow n$. A possible important advantage is that fewer tasks may be required. For example, the red/black ordering requires $O(24nd)$ tasks rather than the $O(6n^2 + 12nd)$ tasks reported in Table 4 for the banded ordering.

In summary, the substructuring and banded solver techniques have been programmed using the data objects, operations, and sequence control mechanisms of our virtual machine. If the implementation of this virtual machine on the other levels of virtual machine is "free" we can make the statements below:
(1) For the range of d in (5.3), the substructuring technique is more promising than the banded solver technique.

(2) For both techniques, as long as $C_a > \dfrac{C_c}{2n^2}$, the amount of time

for arithmetic exceeds that for communication.

We realize that this analysis must be expanded to include costs of the lower levels of machine before the best method is really determined. Here, we have only attempted to give a flavor of the design process.

Acknowledgement

This paper is a preliminary report on the activities of a group of researchers and would not have been possible without the contributions of all the group, which includes, in addition to the authors, Merrell Patrick of Duke University, Terrence Pratt of the University of Virginia and Piyush Mehrotra and John Van Rosendale of ICASE. The group has benefitted immeasurably from discussions with Robert Fulton and Olaf Storaasli of the Structures and Dynamics Division of the NASA Langley Research Center, Ahmed Noor of George Washington University and Tom Crockett and Judson Knott of the Finite Element Machine project at the NASA Langley Research Center.

References

(1) Adams, Loyce, [1982], "Iterative Algorithms for Large Sparse Linear Systems on Parallel Computers," NASA Contractor Report No. 166027. Also published as a Ph.D. Thesis in the Department of Applied Mathematics and Computer Science at the University of Virginia, Charlottesville, VA in 1983.

(2) Adams, Loyce and Robert G. Voigt, [1983] "A Methodology for Exploiting Parallelism in the Finite Element Process." ICASE Report No. 83-33, 29 pages.

(3) Berger, Ph., P. Brouaye and J. C. Syre, [1982], "A Mesh Coloring Method for Efficient MIMD Processing in Finite Element Problems," Proceedings of the 1982 International Conference on Parallel Processing, IEEE Catalog No. 82CH 1794-7, pp. 41-46.

(4) Flynn, Michael, [1966], "Very High-Speed Computing Systems," Proceedings IEEE, vol. 54, pp. 1901-1909.

(5) George, Alan and Joseph Liu, [1981], "Computer Solution of Large Sparse Positive Definite Systems," Prentice Hall, Englewood Cliffs, NJ.

(6) Jordan, Harry, [1978], "A Special Purpose Architecture for Finite Element Analysis," Proceedings of the 1978 International Conference on Parallel Processing, IEEE Catalog No. 78CH1321-9C, pp. 263-266.

(7) Noor, Ahmed, Hussein Kamel and Robert Fulton, [1978], "Substructuring Techniques - Status and Projections," Computers and Structures, vol. 8, pp. 621-632.

(8) Pratt, Terrance, [1981], "H-Graph Semantics," Department of Applied Mathematics and Computer Science Reports Nos. 81-15 and 81-16, University of Virginia, Charlottesville, VA.

(9) Pratt, Terrance, Loyce Adams, Piyush Mehrotra, Merrell Patrick, John Van Rosendale and Robert Voigt, [1983], "The FEM-2 Design Method," Proceedings of the 1983 International Conference on Parallel Processing, Bellaire, MI, to be published by IEEE Computer Society.

(10) Strang, G. and George Fix, [1973], "An Analysis of the Finite Element Method," Prentice-Hall, Englewood Cliffs, NJ.

(11) Zave, Pamela and George Cole, Jr., [1983] "A Quantitative Evaluation of the Feasibility of, and Suitable Hardware Architecture for, an Adaptive, Parallel Finite Element System," ACM Trans. Math Software, to appear.

(12) Zave, Pamela and Werner Rheinboldt, [1979], "Design of an Adaptive, Parallel Finite-Element System," ACM Trans. on Math. Software vol. 5, pp. 1-17.

Support for this research was provided by NASA Contract Numbers NAS1-17070 and NAS1-17130.

ICASE

Mail Stop 132C

NASA Langley Research Center

Hampton, VA 23665

THE EVOLUTION OF MSC/NASTRAN AND THE SUPERCOMPUTER

FOR ENHANCED PERFORMANCE

J. F. Gloudeman, C. W. Hennrich and J. C. Hodge
The MacNeal-Schwendler Corporation
815 Colorado Boulevard
Los Angeles, California 90041

SUMMARY

The primary purpose of this paper is to present the expected and actual development efforts and resulting performance of MSC/NASTRAN on a CRAY-1 supercomputer. First the primary types of matrix equations typically solved in the analysis of large, complex structures are briefly described. Then the size and general architecture of MSC/NASTRAN are discussed, followed by a brief overview of typical computational sequences.

The architecture and performance of the CRAY computer are then discussed from the viewpoint of MSC/NASTRAN's particular requirements. The efforts to adapt MSC/NASTRAN to both the standard CRAY operating system (COS) and Lawrence Livermore National Laboratory's CTSS operating system are presented along with some observations on their respective performance.

Based on experiences to date, the challenges and opportunities offered by vector processing are addressed. Included is the rationale for deactivating the vector processor depending on the nature of particular matrix operations. Performance figures are given for both typical element generation and matrix operations.

Finally, some observations are made about the strengths and weaknesses of the CRAY versions of MSC/NASTRAN. The expected benefits of announced improvements are discussed and additional areas in need of attention are identified.

THE METHODOLOGY OF MSC/NASTRAN

MSC/NASTRAN is a large-scale general purpose digital computer program which solves a wide variety of engineering analysis problems by the Finite Element Method (FEM). The program capabilities include static and dynamic structural analysis (linear and nonlinear), heat transfer, acoustics, electromagnetism and other types of field problems. It is used worldwide by large and small companies in such diverse fields as automotive, aerospace, civil engineering, shipbuilding, offshore oil, industrial equipment, chemical engineering, biomedical research, optics and

NATO ASI Series, Vol. F7
High-Speed Computation. Edited by J. S. Kowalik
© Springer-Verlag Berlin Heidelberg 1984

government research. FEM technology is the most widely accepted approach for engineering analysis, thanks both to its flexibility and proven uses.

The MSC/NASTRAN source code consists of more than 480,000 statements, of which approximately 98% are in FORTRAN. These statements are organized into approximately 4,000 subroutines which in turn comprise nearly 200 modules. Its modular design has many advantages, including ease of incorporating new features and capabilities, portability, quality assurance, optimization in handling large problems, the timely detection and resolution of user difficulties, extensive life cycle and wide applicability. MSC/NASTRAN is used to solve a wide variety of problem types. Linear static analysis is presented here due to its heavy use and because it is a prerequisite to other usage such as dynamic analysis. In addition, the challenge of solving problems in linear static analysis allows for a rather straightforward presentation on the challenges and opportunities available in vectorizing supercomputers.

The fundamental matrix equation for linear static analysis is:

$$[K]\{U\} = \{P\} \quad (1)$$

where:

[K]   is the <u>stiffness matrix</u> generated from input data provided by the user.

{U}   is the vector of unknown <u>displacement</u> components at grid points and is the fundamental output vector in static analysis.

{P}   is a vector of <u>loads</u> applied to grid points and is generated from input data provided by the user.

The computations required to generate [K] and {P} and to subsequently solve for {U} are most substantial, especially for large-sized problems having complex geometries. For example, the analysis of an automobile or an airplane could lead to a very sparse stiffness matrix (e.g. a matrix 90% whose elements have zero value) having more than 50,000 degrees-of-freedom. Because of the random patterns of non-zero elements, automated substructuring methods and efficient algorithms are essential to optimally use main and secondary storage and the CPU.

The finite element approach enables an analyst to represent a distributed physical problem by a discrete number of idealized finite elements that are interconnected at a finite number of grid points. The extensive library of finite elements in MSC/NASTRAN enables the analyst to solve problems ranging from relatively simple truss structures to the most complicated thick-walled shell structures. More than 40 pre-formatted solution sequences are available to the user which allow relatively sophisticated problems to be solved with a minimum of manual effort. A higher-order language, DMAP (Direct Matrix Abstraction Programming) allows the user to write tailor-made solution sequences by manipulating the data files and functional modules. Solving problems with nonlinear material behavior can significantly increase the resources used during problem solution due to required iterative solution techniques. Additionally, increased attention given to computerized design optimization techniques which, because they tend to be iterative in nature, place further demands on computer hardware resources. MSC's recently released Design Sensitivity capability represents an important step in design optimization.

BASIC FEATURES OF THE CRAY SUPERCOMPUTER

Early publications by the manufacturer, and by an independent observer, indicated excellent computational power of the CRAY. (1) (2). Expected performance levels have been met for selected problems. (3).

The CRAY's 64-bit word length lends itself to floating point operations for large problem solving. This is complemented by the one to four million word main memory; the fast CPU with a 12.5 nsec clock period; the 12 full-duplex channels; the 5 sets of registers; the 12 fully segmented functional units; and the 2 to 48 DD-29 storage units which provide the speed and size to cope with MSC/NASTRAN's demands for at least 250 million words of disk space at rates of 550,000 words per second.

The data and instruction movement along parallel paths serves to minimize resource contention. Chaining increases the rate of certain vector computations. The vector processor looked most attractive for matrix operations involving moderate to long vectors, whether contiguous or noncontiguous. (4). It was anticipated that vector processor "start-up costs" would require careful trade-off study to help establish criteria for processor selection. Fortunately, the critical matrix operations (e.g. decomposition, forward/backward substitution, multiply/add, eigenvalue extraction, etc) are well isolated in MSC/NASTRAN which limited such studies to those portions of the code offering the highest payoff. An additional strong point is the good scalar performance of the CRAY, a weakness in many other vector-oriented machines. (5).

Since MSC/NASTRAN fully exploits and taxes the capabilities of mature systems, hardware and software problems were expected during the adaptation effort.

Previous experience with other adaptation efforts at MSC had taught us that Compilers, Loaders and other operating system software prove to be inadequate to handle a program of the magnitude and variety of MSC/NASTRAN. There was concern that the Circular I/O routines could be implemented in MSC/NASTRAN in such a way as to provide for sufficient overlapping of CPU and I/O processing. It was expected that the front-end host interface would present problems.

The task of converting MSC/NASTRAN to the CRAY (COS version) was initiated in November 1979. A limited version was available in November 1980. Full system operation was achieved in April 1981. This initial effort is discussed below.

REVIEW OF INITIAL ADAPTATION EFFORT

The initial estimate of the adaptation of MSC/NASTRAN to the CRAY under COS was approximately 3 man-years of effort over a period of one year. (1). The tasks required to accomplish the adaptation were defined as follows: conversion of machine-independent code; conversion of machine-dependent code; development of a Linkage Editor/Loader; development of a maintenance system; system integration, test and quality assurance; and documentation.

The machine-independent source code, comprising more than 400,000 FORTRAN statements, was expected to account for approximately 5% of the total conversion effort. In the initial pass through the Compiler all but 5 routines were successfully compiled. Unfortunately, Compiler difficulties requiring substantial corrective action were exposed later in the project when the object code produced by the compiler was tested.

The machine-dependent source conversion was envisioned to represent approximately 1/5 of the total project effort. This involved developing assembly language and computer-dependent FORTRAN routines totaling approximately 10,000 statements. Every effort was made to utilize FORTRAN rather than CRAY-1 assembly language. The machine-dependent source includes GINO, the input/output package for MSC/NASTRAN. The matrix condensation and expansion routines, and the routines involved in the matrix operations on large matrices or vectors.

A unique Linkage Editor/Loader had to be developed due to limitations in the COS Relocatable Loader. This task was expected to require somewhat less than 1/5 of the total conversion effort. MSC/NASTRAN consists of 15 individual programs called links. The links are designed to use minimal main memory during program execution. The COS Relocatable Loader was inadequate because it calls for a definition of the total overlay structure at the time of compilation rather than at link time and is limited to single entry points for segments which limits downward calls. Also included in this effort was the development of a loader routine to load segments and links and a boot-strap routine to be loaded by the CRAY-1 loader to initiate execution of MSC/NASTRAN.

The development of a maintenance system was envisioned as less than 1/6 of the total task. New utilities and procedures had to be developed to aid in transferring the program from MSC's in-house computer and to aid in compiling, linking, and testing the resulting system.

The testing of MSC/NASTRAN was estimated to represent approximately 1/3 of the total effort. The initial plan involved 350 test cases of varying sizes which were designed to both validate the code and assist in the operational fine-tuning. Particular targets in the validation process are the basic matrix operations, the fixed solution sequences, and elements in the MSC/NASTRAN Library.

Documentation was expected to account for approximately 5% of the total effort. The machine-dependent documentation for installation and usage of the program is in Section 7 of the MSC/NASTRAN Application Manual. (6). This includes computer resource estimates and the procedures for interfacing with the operating system. Descriptions of unique operations and subroutines were also planned for the MSC/NASTRAN Programmers Manual. (6) (7).

The actual effort proved reasonably close to these estimates. There were modest overruns especially to cope with Compiler difficulties and to improve performance both in the computational and input/output portions.

BASIC PERFORMANCE CHARACTERISTICS

Before discussing performance, a few precautionary words are necessary. MSC tries to be even-handed in dealing with hardware manufacturers and, as a matter of company policy, does not publish performance evaluations comparing computers from different vendors. Hence, the CRAY-1 performance figures are given here relative to a baseline high-speed scalar processor. Timing information for various computers is published (6) and performance charts are presented from time to time but their interpretation is left to the individual. (6) (9).

Performance in structural analysis is often based on the number of degrees-of-freedom, but this can be misleading because of peculiarities in geometry and topology. Three dimensional structures can be expected to consume more computer resources than two dimensional problems. Simple geometric shapes are likely to be computed and analyzed faster and cheaper than complex geometric shapes. Internal renumbering schemes can realign the non-zero elements to reduce the costs of computation. Since a large stiffness matrix usually exceeds the limits of main

398

memory, highly effective input/output and logical routines are needed to assure optimal performance.

Performance is further affected by the availability and exploitation of key computer resources including main memory and peripheral storage. Benchmark tests can be manipulated even for medium sized problems by changing selected input and control values (e.g. resources available), that do not affect computational results.

Table 1 shows the CPU time in seconds to generate an element of the stiffness matrix for the more frequently used elements including: one-dimensional line elements (1D); two-dimensional (2D) triangles for both 3-node and 6-node elements and 4- and 8-noded two-dimensional quadrilateral elements; three- dimensional solid (3D) pentagons (6 nodes) and bricks (8 nodes). As shown by the ratios, the speed improvements of the CRAY over the baseline computer ranges from 5% to 35%. The time required to generate the stiffness matrix is often relatively small compared to the total CPU time, so the ratios shown are not useful measures of total CPU performance. They are presented here to indicate the relative speeds in a scalar processing mode.

Table 1 - Stiffness Matrix Generation Time

| ELEMENT TYPE | Ti (seconds per element) | | B-C |
	CRAY (C)	BASELINE (B)	B
ROD (1D)	.003	.004	.25
BEAM (1D)	.007	.010	.30
TRIA3 (2D)	.007	.009	.22
TRIA6 (2D)	.060	.072	.17
QUAD4 (2D)	.013	.016	.19
QUAD8 (2D)	.124	.130	.05
PENTA (6N, 3D)	.013	.020	.35
HEXA (8N, 3D)	.025	.034	.26

Table 2 lists the ratios of CPU times (C/B = CRAY/BASELINE) for symmetric decomposition of the stiffness matrix for different size problems measured in the number of Degrees of Freedom (No. DOF) for 2D problems and for 3D problems. This metric was chosen because of the relatively dominant role of decomposition for very large problems.

Table 2

No. DOF	C/B (2D)	C/B (3D)
1,000	0.92	0.38
2,000	0.68	0.28
5,000	0.48	0.21
10,000	0.38	0.18
20,000	0.30	0.16
50,000	0.24	0.14
100,000	0.20	0.13
∞	0.125	0.125

RECENT HARDWARE EFFECTS ON PERFORMANCE

Since completing the initial adaptation of MSC/NASTRAN to the CRAY-1 in April 1981, MSC has actively sought to improve performance, both through code modification and use of new CRAY developments. This section highlights some of the exciting enhancements that are available to users of MSC/NASTRAN on current and future CRAY systems.

CRAY now offers three series of computers: The CRAY-1/S, the CRAY X-MP, and the new CRAY-1/M.

The CRAY-1/S was the immediate successor to the CRAY-1. While it has the same CPU as the CRAY-1, the CRAY-1/S offered expanded memory (up to 4 million words) and enhanced I/O options. The CRAY X-MP features two identical processors, each having more power than the single CPU CRAY-1/S. The CRAY-1/M is similar to the CRAY-1/S but utilizes MOS-memory technology to achieve superior price/performance.

These new systems are downward compatible for software developed for the CRAY-1; hence MSC/NASTRAN executes successfully on this hardware. Tests indicate that the CPU performance for the 1/S is the same, the X-MP about 1/3 better, and the 1/M slightly less than the results presented in the above tables for the CRAY-1.

Future developments on the 1/M should bring its performance up to that of the CRAY-1/S.

Cray's response to the I/O performance problem is the introduction of new high speed, high capacity, secondary storage devices. The CRAY-1/S and the CRAY X-MP systems feature an I/O Subsystem. The I/O Subsystem connects to the CRAY mainframe and provides up to eight million 64-bit words of Buffer Memory. Cray Research has also introduced the Solid-state Storage Device (SSD), a secondary storage device with up to 32 million 64-bit words of MOS-technology memory. This device connects to the CRAY-1/S across an 850 Mbyte/sec. channel and to the CRAY X-MP across a 10 Gigabit/sec channel.

Initial benchmark tests with MSC/NASTRAN have provided exciting results with combinations of these new I/O devices. As presented in (2), improvements of up to 23 to 1 in I/O performance have been realized.

THE CTSS/CRAY VERSION OF MSC/NASTRAN

In March 1982, MSC initiated a project to adapt the COS version of MSC/NASTRAN to the CTSS Operating System which is utilized on the CRAY-1 at the National Magnetic Fusion Energy Computer Center (NMFECC) at the Lawrence Livermore Laboratories. This project was completed in October 1982.

The NMFECC provides an extensive nationwide computer network which services 48 sites with approximately 2,000 users. These magnetic fusion researchers utilize the network to share information, codes, and data in addition to computer power. The user sites include Los Alamos Scientific Lab., Oak Ridge National Lab., Princeton Plasma Physics Lab., and General Atomic Co. (10).

The heart of the NMFECC network consists of three computers: a CDC 7600 and two CRAY-1's. The CRAY mainframes use the CTSS Operating System. CTSS is an interactive operating system developed at the Lawrence Livermore Laboratory for the CRAY-1 computers. The only common code between COS and CTSS is the FORTRAN Compiler and math library routines (8).

Initial discussions between MSC and NMFECC concerning the possibility of adapting MSC/NASTRAN to CTSS revealed mutual interest and potential benefits. The NMFECC management pledged the assistance of their technical staff in planning and implementing the necessary changes to effect the adaptation. From MSC's standpoint, not only was there interest in satisfying the engineering analysis requirements of the current network users, but there was considerable interest in CTSS. CTSS appeared to be a powerful and flexible operating system. All of the required facilities to operate MSC/NASTRAN effectively were available in CTSS in FORTRAN.

Among the features which impressed MSC were the Librarian, the interactive debugger and the hierarchical data storage system. All of these facilities were integrated into one system by a job control system, scoring high marks for user friendliness. MSC also noted the wide spread expectation that CTSS will be more widely used in the future than at present.

THE CTSS ADAPTATION EFFORT

The adaptation of MSC/NASTRAN to CTSS was initially estimated to take 1 1/2 man years of effort. The task breakdown and proportion of time for each task was expected to be the same as the COS adaptation except that the CTSS Segment Loader would be utilized rather than developing a Linkage Editor/Loader. It was anticipated that the project would cost only 1/2 of the COS adaptation effort for the following reasons:

1. CTSS uses the COS FORTRAN Compiler, which had achieved much better reliability since the COS adaptation.

2. The user friendliness of CTSS.

3. The close working relationship of the MSC and CTSS staff.

4. The program development aids of CTSS, especially the interactive debugger.

5. The use of the CTSS Segment Loader.

The only negative factor expected to affect the project was the communication hook-up between MSC and NMFECC. All direct communication was at 1200 baud, which required mailing hard copy print during the quality assurance test phase of the project.

The actual effort took only 10 man months. The primary reasons that the adaptation took less manpower than expected were the amount and quality of assistance from the NMFECC technical staff and the reduction of the amount of dependent code in MSC/NASTRAN. This latter factor will benefit future adaptation efforts at MSC.

PERFORMANCE OF THE CTSS VERSION OF MSC/NASTRAN

Since CTSS uses the COS Compiler and math library routines, the CPU performance of MSC/NASTRAN under CTSS was expected to be essentially the same as under COS. This has proven to be the case. In fact, the differences average less than 5%. While it is more difficult to evaluate the I/O performance, the two systems do not appear to vary significantly from one another.

CONCLUSIONS

In terms of the project goals, the adaptation of MSC/NASTRAN for the CRAY-1 was successful. The initial COS adaptation was somewhat more difficult than expected, primarily due to Compiler reliability. Performance testing indicated reasonably good performance for large problems. A few problem areas were exposed, such as inefficient handling of integer arithmetic by the Compiler and slow I/O access relative to vector processing speeds. These problems are being alleviated by utilizing hardware and software enhancements currently in progress at Cray Research, Inc.

REFERENCES

1. "The Adaptation of MSC/NASTRAN to a Supercomputer" by J. F. Gloudeman and J. C. Hodge, presented at the 10th IMACS World Congress on Systems Simulation and Scientific Computation, August 8 - 13, 1982, in Montreal, Canada.

2. "CRAY Supercomputers and Finite Element Analysis", Finite Element News, Issue No. 5, October 1982.

3. Ingrid Y. Bucher & James W. Moore, "Comparative Performance Evaluation of Two Supercomputers" submitted to Computer Measurement Group XII Meeting, New Orleans, Louisiana, December 1 - 4, 1981.

4. Dr. Myron Ginsberg, "Some Observations on Supercomputer Computational Environments" presented at the Tenth IMACS World Congress on System Simulation and Scientific Computation, Montreal, Canada, August 8 - 13, 1982.

5. R. N. Hockney, "Characterization of Parallel Computers" presented at the Tenth IMACS World Congress on System Simulation and Scientific Computation, Montreal, Canada, August 8 - 13, 1982.

6. MSC/NASTRAN Application Manual.

7. MSC/NASTRAN Programmers Manual.

8. Kirby W. Fong, "The National MFE Computer Center CRAY Time Sharing System", Lawrence Livermore Laboratories Report No. UCRL-88569, Preprint Submitted to Software Practice and Experience (1983).

9. The MacNeal-Schwendler Corporation's User's Conference held in Pasadena, California, March 19 - 20, 1981.

10. The Buffer, Newsletter of the National Magnetic Fusion Energy Computer Center, Volume 6, Number 9, September 1982.

FAST FOURIER TRANSFORMS ON THE CYBER 205

Clive Temperton
Meteorological Office
Bracknell, Berkshire, U.K.

1. Introduction

The Fast Fourier Transform (FFT) is one of the most widely used algorithms in computational physics. In a recent paper $/11/$, the author presented a unified derivation of the algorithm and its many variants, and outlined some of its uses in the field of numerical weather prediction. The specialization of the algorithm to the real/half-complex case was described in $/12/$.

The increasing use of vector machines for large-scale scientific computation has had considerable impact on the development of numerical algorithms, including the FFT. A detailed study of the implementation of FFT's on the Cray-1 was presented in $/10/$; Swarztrauber $/9/$ has described the problem of vectorizing the FFT in more general terms, but with particular reference to the Cray-1. Wang $/14/$ also considered the problem in a rather general way. Implementation on the CDC STAR-100 has been described by Korn and Lambiotte $/7/$ and Fornberg $/3/$.

In this paper we consider the vectorization of the FFT algorithm on the CDC Cyber 205, a machine which is a direct descendant of the STAR-100. Section 2 outlines some relevant features of the 205, and in particular some important ways in which it differs from the Cray-1. In Sections 3 and 4, various ways of vectorizing the complex radix-2 algorithm are studied. Section 5 summarizes the relationship between the vectorization schemes developed here for the Cyber 205 and those developed in $/10/$ for the Cray-1. Section 6 describes a package for multiple mixed-radix real/half-complex transforms developed for a numerical weather prediction model on the Cyber 205 at the U.K. Meteorological Office $/3/$, and compares its performance with that of a similar package developed for use on the Cray-1 at ECMWF. Conclusions are presented in Section 7.

2. The Cyber 205

For a detailed description of the architecture and technology of the Cyber 205 (and other vector machines), a very useful reference is the book by Hockney and Jesshope $/6/$. From the point of view of implementing the FFT algorithm, there are several important differences between the Cyber 205 and the Cray-1.

First, the definition of a vector is different. On the Cyber 205 the elements of a vector must be stored contiguously in memory, while on the Cray-1 they can be separated by any constant increment.

Second, all arithmetic on the Cyber 205 is memory-to-memory, in contrast to the register-to-register arithmetic on the Cray-1. (Operands in Cray-1 arithmetic must first be loaded from memory, and results stored; temporary results can be held in the vector registers, and the memory transfers can take place in parallel with the

NATO ASI Series, Vol. F7
High-Speed Computation. Edited by J. S. Kowalik
© Springer-Verlag Berlin Heidelberg 1984

arithmetic).

For 64-bit arithmetic, the maximum possible computation rate (expressed in millions of floating-point operations per second, or megaflops) is similar on the two machines: up to 100 megaflops on the (two-pipe) Cyber 205 and 75 megaflops on the Cray-1 for additions or multiplications, or 200 and 150 megaflops respectively for triadic operations of the form $\underset{\sim}{a} = b * (\underset{\sim}{c} + \underset{\sim}{d})$ or $\underset{\sim}{a} = b * \underset{\sim}{c} + \underset{\sim}{d}$. Here one of the operands must be a scalar on the Cyber 205, but all three may be vectors on the Cray-1. The Cyber 205 also has provision for 32-bit floating-point arithmetic, which can proceed at up to twice these rates, i.e. up to 400 megaflops for triadic operations.

On any vector machine, the time taken for a vector instruction can be expressed as $T = a + bN$, where a is a start-up time, b is the arithmetic rate and N is the length of the vector. An important difference between the Cray-1 and the Cyber 205 is in the start-up time a; it is less than 10 machine cycles on the Cray-1, but typically 50 cycles on the Cyber 205. (A machine cycle is 12.5 ns on the Cray-1, 20 ns on the Cyber 205). An instructive way of looking at the effect of the vector start-up time is to consider Hockney's parameter $n_{\frac{1}{2}}$ [6], the vector length required to achieve half the maximum performance. The value of $n_{\frac{1}{2}}$ is around 10 for the Cray-1 while on the two-pipe Cyber 205 it is approximately 100 for 64-bit arithmetic (150 for triadic operations) and 200 for 32-bit arithmetic (300 for triadic operations). On the Cray-1 the maximum speed is reached for a vector length of 64, while on the Cyber 205 the efficiency continues to increase up to a maximum allowable vector length of 64K-1.

To compensate for the restriction to contiguously stored vectors on the Cyber 205, several means are provided for the efficient rearrangement of data in memory. Two such operations are the merge and gather/scatter instructions. If two vectors $\underset{\sim}{A}$ and $\underset{\sim}{B}$ are merged using a bit string consisting of a pattern of n 1's followed by n 0's, repeated as often as required, then the result vector contains the first n elements of $\underset{\sim}{A}$, followed by the first n elements of $\underset{\sim}{B}$, then the next n elements of $\underset{\sim}{A}$, and so on. (In fact, this regularity is not necessary; the bit string can be completely random). The merge instruction has a start-up time of about 50 cycles, and then delivers 2 64-bit results or 4 32-bit results per cycle (i.e., the same result rate as for addition or multiplication).

The gather and scatter instructions are equivalent to the Fortran statements $A(I)=B(INDEX(I))$ and $A(INDEX(I))=B(I)$.

3. Vectorization of the radix-2 algorithm

Let us assume that we need to compute M simultaneous transforms, each of length N. On the Cray-1, provided that M is quite modest (roughly $M > \sqrt{N}$), the most effective solution is simply to do the transforms in parallel, with a constant vector length of M [10]. The details of the FFT indexing structure then become irrelevant from the point of view of vectorization. The data to be transformed can be stored as rows or columns of a two-dimensional array; provided that memory bank conflicts are avoided, either choice is equally efficient. (This is particularly convenient for a two-dimensional transform).

On the Cyber 205, because of the restriction to contiguously stored vectors, the data to be transformed must be stored as <u>columns</u> of a (row-wise indexed) two-dimensional array; in other words, the transforms must be interleaved. A constant vector length of M can then be achieved in exactly the same way as on the Cray-1. Unless M is very large (of order at least several hundred), this will not be very efficient, because of the large value of $n_\frac{1}{2}$. Fortunately, interleaving the transforms allows us to take advantage of the degree to which a single transform is vectorizable. If an operation in the single transform can be done with a vector length n, then the same operation in the case of M interleaved transforms can be done with a vector length Mn. For notational convenience we can therefore consider the vectorization of a single transform.

Suppose that the factors of N have been stored in an array IFAX(1) to IFAX(NFAX) and that a complex array of trigonometric function values has been defined by

TRIGS(K+1) = exp(2iKπ /N), $0 \leq K \leq N-1$.

The data to be transformed is in an array A, and a work array C is provided. Each array acts alternately as input or output for successive stages of the algorithm. The decimation-in-frequency form can be expressed by the following simple program:

```
C     DECIMATION IN FREQUENCY
      COMPLEX A(N),C(N),TRIGS(N)
      INTEGER IFAX(NFAX)
      LA=1
      DO 10 I=1,NFAX
      IFAC=IFAX(I)
      CALL PASS(A,C,TRIGS,IFAC,LA,N)
C     /now reverse roles of A and C/
      LA=LA*IFAC
10    CONTINUE
      STOP
      END
```

Use of the decimation-in-time variant will change the details of the following discussion, but will not affect the conclusions.

At the risk of reinforcing the myth that only the radix-2 version of the FFT is worth considering, we will use this simple case as an example of the indexing structure in the subroutine PASS. The following corresponds to the "self-sorting" [11] or "Stockham" version of the algorithm:

```
C     SELF-SORTING, DECIMATION IN FREQUENCY FOR IFAC=2
      SUBROUTINE PASS(A,C,TRIGS,IFAC,LA,N)
      COMPLEX A(N),C(N),TRIGS(N)
C
```

```
      MU=N/IFAC
      IA=1; IB=MU+1; JA=1; JB=LA+1
      I=Ø; J=Ø; JUMP=(IFAC-1)*LA
      DO 2Ø K=1,MU,LA
      DO 1Ø L=1,LA
      C(JA+J)=A(IA+I)+A(IB+I)
      C(JB+J)=TRIGS(K)*(A(IA+I)-A(IB+I))
      I=I+1
      J=J+1
   1Ø CONTINUE
      J=J+JUMP
   2Ø CONTINUE
      RETURN
      END
```

Clearly the innermost (DO 1Ø) loop is vectorizable, with an increment of 1 between the elements of each vector. There are four vectors, with starting addresses A(IA),A(IB),C(JA),C(JB) (each of these is of course a _complex_ vector, corresponding to two real vectors). The trigonometric function value TRIGS(K) is a scalar within the loop. The vector length is LA, which is 1 during the first pass, and (in the radix-2 case) doubles at each successive pass. In the multiple case the vector length is M during the first pass, increasing to $MN/2$ by the last pass. Apart from the fact that it uses decimation in frequency rather than in time, this is the multiple Stockham algorithm as implemented by Korn and Lambiotte [7].

Pease [8] developed a version of the FFT algorithm with a different indexing structure; unlike the self-sorting algorithm, it delivers the results in scrambled (bit-reversed) order. The outer structure is the same as for the algorithm described above, but the subroutine PASS becomes simpler:

```
C     PEASE, DECIMATION IN FREQUENCY FOR IFAC=2
      SUBROUTINE PASS(A,C,TRIGS,IFAC,LA,N)
      COMPLEX A(N),C(N),TRIGS(N)
      MU=N/IFAC
      IA=1; IB=MU+1; JA=1; JB=2
      I=Ø; J=Ø
      DO 1Ø K=1,MU
      C(JA+J)=A(IA+I)+A(IB+I)
      C(JB+J)=TRIGS(K)*(A(IA+I)-A(IB+I))
      I=I+1
      J=J+2
   1Ø CONTINUE
      RETURN
      END
```

In this case a __different__ TRIGS array is required for each pass. The two vectors
A(IA+I), A(IB+I) still have increments of 1, but C(JA+J) and C(JB+J) now have increments of 2. On the Cray-1 they are nevertheless valid vectors, and as shown in $\angle 10\angle$
this is the best way to vectorize a single transform on the Cray-1 if the final
unscrambling step is not counted as part of the cost of the transform. (In some
applications it can be dispensed with). However, on the Cyber 205 C(JA+J) and C(JB+J)
are not valid vectors. The remedy is to modify the inner loop as follows:

```
      DO 1Ø K=1,MU
      C(IA+I)=A(IA+I)+A(IB+I)
      C(IB+I)=TRIGS(K)*(A(IA+I)-A(IB+I))
      I=I+1
   1Ø CONTINUE
```

and to follow it by a permutation step. It is easy to see that the required vector
of length N can be assembled by alternately picking successive elements from the
vectors of length N/2 starting at C(IA) and C(IB), so the merge instruction can be
used. In the multiple case, the Pease algorithm can be carried out with vector
lengths of NM/2 for the arithmetic loop and MN for the merge instruction. This
corresponds to the implementation described by Korn and Lambiotte $\angle 7\angle$ and Wang
$\angle 14\angle$.

As mentioned above, the disadvantage of the Pease algorithm is that the results
appear in scrambled order; considerable effort is devoted in $\angle 7\angle$ and $\angle 14\angle$ to
the vectorization of the unscrambling step. A little thought shows that the modified
code given above can equally well be used to implement the Stockham algorithm. As
in the case of the Pease algorithm vectorized for the Cyber 205, a different TRIGS
array is required for each pass. In this case we also need a different bit string
in each pass for the merge step; the required result vector consists of LA elements
from C(IA), then LA elements from C(IB), then the next LA elements from C(IA), and
so on. Again the vector length in the multiple case is MN/2 for the arithmetic loop
and MN for the merge instruction. This corresponds to the implementation of the
Stockham algorithm described by Fornberg $\angle 4\angle$ and Wang $\angle 14\angle$.

We have just shown that the Stockham (self-sorting) algorithm can be vectorized
as efficiently as the Pease algorithm; since the Stockham algorithm also eliminates
the unscrambling step, there is no need to consider the Pease algorithm further.
The question which remains to be resolved concerns the relative advantages of the
two distinct ways of implementing the Stockham algorithm: the original scheme with
shorter vectors, or the modified scheme which has longer vectors but requires a
merge operation after each pass. In the next section, these two schemes will be
analysed and compared.

4. Analysis of schemes for the radix-2 Stockham algorithm

Let us denote by Scheme C the first procedure described above, using a nested
loop with shorter vectors, and by Scheme D the second procedure using a single loop

followed by a merge operation. It is immediately clear that Scheme C is much more economical in terms of the storage of trigonometric function tables; since TRIGS(K) is a _scalar_ within the inner loop, only $N/2$ complex (N real) values are required for the whole algorithm. In Scheme D, TRIGS(K) is a _vector_ within the loop, and so an array of MN real values is required for each pass, where M is the number of transforms being performed together. Moreover, since a different TRIGS array is required for each pass (except the last, where TRIGS(K)=1 for all K and the multiplication can be omitted), a total of $MN(\log_2 N-1)$ trigonometric values must be stored if none of them are to be recalculated and the array is to be reusable. In the following analysis, it is (perhaps rather generously) assumed that enough storage is available for Scheme D to be implemented in this way.

The fact that TRIGS(K) is a scalar in Scheme C but a vector in Scheme D also has important consequences in terms of the amount of vector arithmetic required. The Scheme D loop requires 2 complex additions and 1 complex multiplication, a total of 6 real vector additions and 4 real vector multiplications. In Scheme C, each of these multiplications can be linked with an addition using triadic operations. In terms of real arithmetic, the complex statement

$$C(JB+J)=TRIGS(K)*(A(IA+I)-A(IB+I))$$

would normally be written in the form

$$\underset{\sim}{c}' = \underset{\sim}{a}_0 - \underset{\sim}{a}_1$$

$$\underset{\sim}{d}' = \underset{\sim}{b}_0 - \underset{\sim}{b}_1$$

$$\underset{\sim}{c} = \cos\theta * \underset{\sim}{c}' - \sin\theta * \underset{\sim}{d}'$$

$$\underset{\sim}{d} = \sin\theta * \underset{\sim}{c}' + \cos\theta * \underset{\sim}{d}'$$

where $\underset{\sim}{c} + i\underset{\sim}{d}$ corresponds to $C(JB+J)$, $\cos\theta + i\sin\theta$ to TRIGS(K), $\underset{\sim}{a}_0 + i\underset{\sim}{b}_0$ to $A(IA+I)$, and $\underset{\sim}{a}_1 + i\underset{\sim}{b}_1$ to $A(IB+I)$.

This sequence can be rewritten as four triadic operations:

$$\underset{\sim}{c}'' = \cos\theta * \left(\underset{\sim}{a}_0 - \underset{\sim}{a}_1\right)$$

$$\underset{\sim}{d}'' = \cos\theta * \left(\underset{\sim}{b}_0 - \underset{\sim}{b}_1\right)$$

$$\underset{\sim}{c} = \underset{\sim}{c}'' - \tan\theta * \underset{\sim}{d}''$$

$$\underset{\sim}{d} = \tan\theta * \underset{\sim}{c}'' + \underset{\sim}{d}''$$

The only snag here is that $\tan\theta$ may be infinite; to minimize round-off error, if $|\tan\theta| > 1$ the sequence can be rewritten using $\sin\theta$ and $\cot\theta$. The inner loop of Scheme C can thus be implemented in 2 real vector additions and 4 triadic operations.

We will now examine the time required by each scheme for a single pass. We assume that the real and imaginary parts of the complex numbers are stored in separate arrays; the number of vector start-ups could be reduced slightly by re-arranging the data, but this will not greatly affect the following analysis.

In Scheme C, the inner loop is performed $N/(2*LA)$ times. For K=1, TRIGS(K)=1 and the multiplication can be omitted; the loop simply contains 4 real vector additions. For K > 1, the loop contains 2 real vector additions and 4 triads.

Assuming start-up times of 50 cycles for an addition and 75 cycles for a triad, the total time spent in vector start-ups is

$$200(N/LA - 1) \text{ cycles}$$

The additional time spent on arithmetic (for M simultaneous transforms) is

$$M (3N/2 - LA) \text{ cycles}$$

including the saving during the first pass through the inner loop.

In Scheme D, there are 10 real arithmetic operations of vector length $MN/2$, and two merges of length MN (one each for the real and imaginary parts). We can in fact omit the redundant complex multiplications as in Scheme C, so the vector length is reduced to $M*(N/2-LA)$ for 6 of the arithmetic operations. The time spent in vector start-ups is 600 cycles, and the time spent on arithmetic and merges is

$$M(7N/2 - 3*LA) \text{ cycles}$$

Thus Scheme C will be faster than Scheme D if

$$200N/LA < 800+2M(N-LA)$$

i.e. if

$$M > 100(\frac{1}{LA} - \frac{3}{N-LA}) \quad.$$

Scheme C is at the greatest disadvantage during the first pass, when $LA=1$ and the vector length is only M; the above analysis shows that Scheme C will still be faster for M 100. During the penultimate pass, when $LA=N/4$, Scheme C will always be faster. During the last pass, both schemes are equivalent since the complex multiplications are all redundant, and no merge operation is required in Scheme D.

In Table 1, we present measured times for $N=64$ and $M=16$, 64 and 256, for each stage of the transform. The time taken by Scheme C decreases rapidly with successive passes (especially for small M), as the vector length increases and the number of start-ups is reduced. The corresponding time taken by Scheme D decreases slowly, the only saving being the smaller number of complex multiplications required at each stage. Eventually, Scheme C becomes faster than Scheme D; for $M=256$ this is true throughout. The results of the above analysis are thus confirmed.

The analysis can be extended to compare the use of Schemes C and D to compute the whole transform. We use the relationships

$$\sum \frac{1}{LA} = 2 - \frac{2}{N} , \quad \sum LA = N-1$$

where the sums are taken over the $\log_2 N$ passes. The savings during the last pass are also taken into account.

Scheme C takes a total of $400N - 200(\log_2 N+2)$ cycles for vector start-ups, and $1.5MN \log_2 N-M(N-1)$ cycles for arithmetic. Scheme D takes $600 \log_2 N-400$ cycles for vector start-ups, and $3.5MN \log_2 N-M(4N-3)$ cycles for arithmetic and merges. Overall, Scheme C is faster if

$$M > (400N-800 \log_2 N)/(2N \log_2 N-3N+2)$$

For example if $N=64$, Scheme C is faster for $M \geq 36$; if $N=256$, Scheme C is faster for $M \geq 29$.

Notice also that if M is large enough, the contribution of the vector start-ups

Table 1: Times in μs for each stage of a set of M complex transforms of length
N = 64 = 2^6

| | M=16 | | M=64 | | M=256 | |
LA	C	D	C	D	C	D
1	414	99	492	311	858	1160
2	222	97	314	307	672	1144
4	132	96	220	299	572	1114
8	86	92	172	284	505	1052
16	59	84	136	253	441	929
32	38	38	100	100	346	346

Table 2: Total times in μs for M complex transforms of length N=64=2^6

M	C	D	D+C
16	951	506	475
32	1102	854	755
84	1434	1554	1246
128	2084	2950	2061
256	3394	5745	3394

can be ignored. In the limit, Scheme C is more than twice as fast as Scheme D.

On the Cray-1, the fastest way to compute a single transform (with input and output correctly ordered) is to use one vectorization scheme initially, and to switch to a different scheme during the later stages of the transform $\boxed{10\,}$. The same is true here; we can use Scheme D initially, and switch to Scheme C as LA increases. Table 2 presents the total time for M transforms of length N=64 using Schemes C, D and the combined scheme in which the fastest method is used at each stage. For M=16 the switch is made halfway through the process (i.e. after 3 passes), while for M=256 the fastest method is to use Scheme C throughout.

The analysis presented in this Section can easily be extended to the case of 32-bit arithmetic; the time spent on vector start-ups is the same as for 64-bit arithmetic, while the time spent on arithmetic is halved. For a single pass, Scheme C will be faster than Scheme D if

$$M > 200(\frac{1}{LA} - \frac{3}{N-LA})$$

Thus for the first pass (LA=1), Scheme C will be faster for M > 200. For the penultimate pass (LA=N/4) Scheme C will always be faster.

For the whole transform, Scheme C will be faster if

$$M > (400N-800 \log_2 N)/(N \log_2 N - 1.5N + 1)$$

i.e. the break-even value of M is doubled over that for 64-bit arithmetic. It remains true in 32-bit arithmetic that Scheme C is asymptotically more than twice as fast as Scheme D.

The subroutine PASS given in Section 3 can be generalized $\angle 11\angle$ to factors other than 2, and the vectorization schemes described above can be extended to the general case. Details for the radix-4 transform were given in $\angle 13\angle$.

5. Relationship between Cray-1 and Cyber 205 vectorization schemes

In $\angle 10\angle$, two distinct vectorization schemes, A and B, were developed for computing a single transform on Cray-1. The best approach was found to consist of a combination in which one or two passes were carried out using Scheme B, and the remainder using Scheme A. For M simultaneous transforms, a simple vectorization scheme was developed in which the transforms were done in parallel. It was found that only a very modest value of M was needed to make this the fastest approach.

On the Cyber 205, with its much larger value of $n_{\frac{1}{2}}$ $\angle 6\angle$, computing a single transform of length N via the FFT would necessarily be slow and inefficient unless N was very large indeed. In this paper we have developed two schemes, C and D, for the vectorization of M simultaneous transforms. Both of these schemes may be regarded as extensions to the multiple case of the Cray-1 Scheme A.

Unfortunately there is no corresponding multiple analogue on the Cyber 205 of the Cray-1 Scheme B, which might be used to increase the vector length during the early stages of the transform. Scheme B is developed by turning the nested loop structure of subroutine PASS inside-out, and it works on the Cray-1 despite the fact that the elements of the resulting vectors are no longer contiguously stored. The only way to implement this scheme on the Cyber 205 would be to shuffle the data before and after each pass, and the results of the previous sections suggest that this would not be worthwhile.

One disadvantage of using the self-sorting variant of the FFT to compute M simultaneous transforms of length N is that a work space of length MN is required. On the Cray-1 this should rarely be a problem, since there is nothing to be gained by increasing M beyond 64; nevertheless, as pointed out in $\angle 10\angle$, it is possible to eliminate the work space (at the expense of extra memory references) by using the Cooley-Tukey $\angle 2\angle$ or Gentleman-Sande $\angle 5\angle$ variants of the FFT algorithm. On the Cyber 205 we really want to use as large a value of M as possible in order to maximize the vector length, and the availability of work space is more likely to be a problem. As in the self-sorting case, the FFT variants of $\angle 2\angle$ and $\angle 5\angle$ could be implemented with a vector length M*LA, but unfortunately on the Cyber 205 this would still require a similar amount of work space. The reason lies in the memory-to-memory arithmetic; while on the Cray-1 temporary results can be held in the vector registers, on the Cyber 205 extra memory must be provided for them, and it is not difficult to see that if a vector length of M*LA is to be achieved then work space of order MN must be provided, and we might as well have used the self-sorting variant in the first place. Thus it seems that eliminating the work space on the Cray-1 is possible but rarely necessary, while on the Cyber 205 it is highly desirable but impossible.

6. A real transform package

In this section we report on a multiple real FFT package implemented on the Cyber 205 for the operational numerical weather prediction model at the U.K. Meteorological Office $\sqrt{3\_7}$. From a mathematical point of view, the package is identical to that described in $\sqrt{12\_7}$, which was implemented on a Cray-1. The transform length is restricted to values of the form $N=2^p 3^q 5^r$. In order to decrease the operation count, there is scope for grouping the factors together, so that in addition to the factors 2, 3 and 5 there are sections of coding for factors 4, 6 and 8. As in $\sqrt{12\_7}$, the algorithm for a real/half-complex transform of the form

$$x_j = \sum_{k=0}^{N-1} c_k \exp(2ijk\pi/N) \tag{1}$$

or its inverse

$$c_k = \frac{1}{N} \sum_{j=0}^{N-1} x_j \exp(-2ijk\pi/N) \tag{2}$$

where the x_j's are real and the c_k's satisfy $c_{N-k} = c_k^*$, is derived by pruning out redundant operations from the corresponding full complex transform of length N. A saving of 20% or so in the operation count is thereby obtained over the more conventional techniques described in $\sqrt{1\_7}$.

The approach to vectorizing the complex transform denoted by Scheme C in preceding sections translates directly to the specialized real-half-complex transform algorithm. The entire transform can be carried out using an array of trigonometric function values of length N. All complex multiplications can be implemented using triadic operations. The vector length is in general LA*M, though in fact since it is convenient in this algorithm to interleave real and imaginary parts of complex numbers in blocks of length LA*M $\sqrt{12\_7}$, it is frequently possible to handle real and imaginary parts together, thus doubling the vector length.

Scheme D could also be translated to this case, though the more complicated structure of the real/half-complex transform algorithm would cause considerable difficulty and loss of efficiency. As in the complex case, enormous arrays of trigonometric function values and bit strings would be required. It is clear from the analysis of the previous sections that Scheme D would only be competitive for a rather small number of simultaneous transforms, and this approach was not pursued.

The real FFT package for the Cyber 205 was first written in straightforward vector Fortran, and subsequently translated into "special call" format using Q8 calls for all vector instructions and descriptor manipulations. This gave some speed advantage at short vector lengths, but the main reason was to permit the use of 32-bit arithmetic before a suitable compiler became available. The timing information presented here refers to the special call version, and to the forward transform, Eq. (1). The inverse transform, Eq. (2), runs slightly slower because of some multiplications which could not readily be linked with additions in this case.

Comparative figures are given for the FFT package described in $\angle$12$\angle$ and run on the Cray-1, using the simple multiple vectorization scheme with a vector length of M. It should be noted that the Cray-1 package was written in CAL (Cray Assembly Language), and runs about twice as fast as a corresponding vectorized Fortran version. 32-bit arithmetic is not available on Cray-1.

Table 3 presents the time per real transform (in microseconds) for three values of N, and for four values of M, the number of transforms being performed together. Results for N=180, 192 and 200 are shown to demonstrate that the choice of N is not as critical as is sometimes thought for efficiency of the FFT. Values of M=16, 64, 256 and 1024 are shown to demonstrate the increasing efficiency of long vectors on the Cyber 205 in contrast to the Cray-1 where there is no advantage in increasing the vector length beyond 64.

Table 3: Time per real transform in μs

N	M	Cyber 205 (64-bit)	Cyber 205 (32-bit)	Cray-1 (64-bit)
180 (5×6^2)	16	87	78	36
	64	35	26	26
	256	22	13	26
	1024	18	10	26
192 ($4 \times 6 \times 8$)	16	81	72	36
	64	33	24	25
	256	21	12	25
	1024	18	9	25
200 ($5^2 \times 8$)	16	98	88	41
	64	40	30	30
	256	25	15	30
	1024	21	11	30

Notice that 32-bit arithmetic is asymptotically twice as fast as 64-bit arithmetic on the Cyber 205, but because the start-up times for each vector operation (and other overheads) remain the same, many transforms must be performed together before this ratio is approached.

Table 4. Megaflop rates for real FFT packages

N	M	Cyber 205 (64-bit)	Cyber 205 (32-bit)	Cray-1 (64-bit)
180 (5×6^2)	16	32	35	74
	64	80	106	104
	256	129	214	104
	1024	152	277	104
192 $(4 \times 6 \times 8)$	16	32	35	71
	64	78	105	100
	256	124	207	100
	1024	145	274	100
200 $(5^2 \times 8)$	16	34	37	79
	64	83	111	109
	256	132	220	109
	1024	155	293	109

Comparing times on the Cyber 205 with those on the Cray-1, at M=16 the Cray-1 is markedly faster. At N=64, 32-bit arithmetic on the Cyber matches 64-bit arithmetic on the Cray. At M=256, 64-bit arithmetic on the Cyber beats that on the Cray, while at M=1024 32-bit arithmetic on the Cyber is almost three times as fast as 64-bit arithmetic on the Cray.

It is also of interest to compare the performance achieved in terms of megaflops. As detailed in Section 2, for a computation in which there are as many multiplications as additions (and assuming on the Cyber 205 that they can all be linked), the machine architectures impose maximum limits on the Cray-1 of about 150 megaflops, and on the (two-pipe) Cyber 205 of 200 megaflops for 64-bit arithmetic, or 400 megaflops for 32-bit arithmetic. For computations in which the mix of additions and multiplications is in the ratio 2:1, the corresponding limits are about 110, 150 and 300 megaflops respectively. Table 4 shows that these limits are very nearly achieved in the FFT packages, but that many transforms must be performed together on the Cyber 205 before maximum performance is approached.

7. Conclusions

In this paper we have shown that the multiple Stockham (self-sorting) FFT algorithm can be implemented on the Cyber 205 as efficiently as the multiple Pease algorithm, and is preferable since it eliminates the need for reordering the data. There are two ways to implement the Stockham algorithm, denoted here by Schemes C and D. Scheme D is faster for a small number of transforms and during the early stages of the algorithm, but requires a large amount of storage for trigonometric function values. Scheme C requires only N such values, and is asymptotically about twice as fast as Scheme D.

Timing results were presented for a multiple real transform package based on Scheme C, and compared with corresponding results for the Cray-1. In 64-bit arithmetic, the Cyber 205 is faster than the Cray-1 if more than about 200 transforms can be performed in parallel. 32-bit arithmetic on the Cyber 205 is faster than 64-bit arithmetic on the Cray-1 for more than 64 simultaneous transforms.

From a theoretical point of view, the Cray-1 and Cyber 205 may be considered equivalent since both are pipelined vector computers. However, comparing the results of this paper with those of $\lfloor 10\rfloor$, and considering the different approaches found to be appropriate in each case, it is clear that in some respects the two machines are quite dissimilar in practice. Important differences arise not just because of the different value of the parameter $n_{\frac{1}{2}}$, as discussed by Hockney and Jesshope $\lfloor 6\rfloor$, but also because of the difference between memory-to-memory and register-to-register arithmetic, and because of the different definitions of a vector on the two machines.

References

$\lfloor 1\rfloor$ J. W. COOLEY, P.A.W. LEWIS & P.D. WELCH, The Fast Fourier Transform algorithm: programming considerations in the calculation of sine, cosine and Laplace transforms, J. Sound Vib. 12 (1970), 315-337.

$\lfloor 2\rfloor$ J.W. COOLEY & J.W. TUKEY, An algorithm for the machine calculation of complex Fourier series, Math. Comp. 19 (1965), 297-301.

$\lfloor 3\rfloor$ M.J.P. CULLEN, Current progress and prospects in numerical techniques for weather prediction models, J. Comp. Phys. 50 (1983), 1-37.

$\lfloor 4\rfloor$ B. FORNBERG, A vector implementation of the Fast Fourier Transform algorithm, Math. Comp. 36 (1981), 189-191.

$\lfloor 5\rfloor$ W.M. GENTLEMAN & G. SANDE, Fast Fourier Transforms - for fun and profit, Proc. AFIPS Joint Computer Conference 29 (1966), 563-578.

$\lfloor 6\rfloor$ R.W. HOCKNEY & C.R. JESSHOPE, "Parallel Computers", Adam Hilger Ltd., Bristol, U.K., 1981.

$\lfloor 7\rfloor$ D.G. KORN & J.J. LAMBIOTTE, Computing the Fast Fourier Transform on a vector computer, Math. Comp. 33 (1979), 977-992.

$\lfloor 8\rfloor$ M.C. PEASE, An adaptation of the Fast Fourier Transform for parallel processing, J.ACM 15 (1968), 252-264.

$\lfloor 9\rfloor$ P.N. SWARZTRAUBER, Vectorizing the FFT's, in "Parallel Computations" (ed. G. Rodrigue), Academic Press, 1982.

$\lfloor 10\rfloor$ C. TEMPERTON, Fast Fourier Transforms and Poisson-solvers on Cray-1, in "Supercomputers" (ed. R. W. Hockney and C. R. Jesshope), Infotech State of the Art Report, Infotech International Ltd., Maidenhead, U.K., 1979.

$\lfloor 11\rfloor$ C. TEMPERTON, Self-sorting mixed-radix Fast Fourier Transforms, to appear in J. Comp. Phys.

$\lfloor 12\rfloor$ C. TEMPERTON, Fast mixed-radix Real Fourier Transforms, to appear in J. Comp. Phys.

$\lfloor 13\rfloor$ C. TEMPERTON, Fast Fourier Transforms on the Cyber 205, Met O 11 Tech. Note No 170, Meteorological Office, 1983.

[14] H. H. WANG, On vectorizing the Fast Fourier Transform, BIT 20 (1980), 233–243.

PLASMA SIMULATION AND FUSION CALCULATION

B. L. Buzbee*

Computing Division
Los Alamos National Laboratory
Los Alamos, New Mexico

ABSTRACT

Particle-in-cell (PIC) models are widely used in fusion studies associated with energy research. They are also used in certain fluid dynamical studies. Parallel computation is relevant to them because

1. PIC models are not amenable to a lot of vectorization--about 50% of the total computation can be vectorized in the average model;

2. the volume of data processed by PIC models typically necessitates use of secondary storage with an attendant requirement for high-speed I/O; and

3. PIC models exist today whose implementation requires a computer 10 to 100 times faster than the Cray-1.

This paper discusses parallel formulation of PIC models for master/slave architectures and ring architectures. Because interprocessor communication can be a decisive factor in the overall efficiency of a parallel system, we show how to divide these models into large granules that can be executed in parallel with relatively little need for communication. We also report measurements of speedup obtained from experiments on the UNIVAC 1100/84 and the Denelcor HEP.

PARTICLE-IN-CELL MODELS

We discuss particle-in-cell (PIC) models in the context of studying the behavior of plasmas in the presence of force fields [7]. We assume a two-dimensional region that has been discretized with N cells per side for a total of N^2 cells in the region. The discretization is illustrated in Fig. 1. The approach is to randomly distribute particles over the two-dimensional region and then study their movement as a function of time and forces acting on them. Typically, the average number of particles per cell will be $O(N)$ and particle information includes position, velocity, charge, etc. Thus, the total particle information will be $O(N^3)$. In its simplest form, the plasma simulation proceeds as follows:

1. "Integrate" over particles to obtain a charge distribution at cell centers (a cell center is denoted by "X" in Fig. 1).

2. Solve a Poisson equation for the potential at cell centers.

3. Interpolate the potential onto particles for a small interval of time Δt; i.e., apply force to the particles for a small time interval, recomputing their positions, velocities, etc.

---

*This work was supported in part by the Applied Mathematical Sciences Program, Office of Basic Energy Sciences of the US Department of Energy and the Air Force Office of Scientific Research.

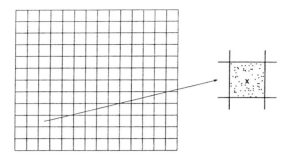

Fig. 1. Relationship of region, mesh, and particles.

Step 2 requires $O(N^2)$ operations. Steps 1 and 3 require $O(N^3)$ operations and thus dominate the overall computational process. Generally, the particle information is stored in a large array and there is no correlation between particle position in that array and particle position in the rectangle. Thus, Step 1 is a many-to-one mapping of random elements from the list onto a cell center. Conversely, Step 3 is a one-to-many mapping of information at the cell center onto random elements of the particle list. These mappings from and to random elements in a list generally preclude efficient vector implementation. In general, only about 50% of the total operations in a PIC model are subject to efficient vector implementation. Of course, to achieve the highest level of performance from a vector processor, one needs to vectorize 90% or more of the total work in a computation [9]. Further, some PIC simulations used within the fusion energy research community require a computer that is about 100 times faster than the Cray-1 to successfully model phenomena of interest [4]. This need for higher performance combined with difficulties in implementing PIC efficiently on vector processors motivates our interest in asynchronous parallel (MIMD) formulations of them.

PIC ON A MASTER/SLAVE CONFIGURATION

Assume that we have an MIMD processor with a master/slave control schema as illustrated in Fig. 2. In practice a single processor may execute the function of both the master and one of the slaves, but for purposes of discussion we assume that they are distinct. The key to achieving efficient parallel implementation of PIC on a master/slave configuration is to divide the particles equally among the slaves and to keep all particle-related information within the slaves. Assuming that the master has the total charge distribution in its memory, the computational procedure is as follows:

Step 2B.   Master solves potential equation and broadcasts potential ($O(N^2)$) to each slave.
Step 3.   Each slave applies the potential for Δt (moves its particles).
Step 1A.   Each slave integrates over its particles to obtain their contribution to total charge distribution at cell centers.
Step 1B.   Each slave ships its charge distribution ($O(N^2)$) to the master.
Step 2A.   Master sums charge distribution from slaves.

Note that in this approach the "particle pushing" ($O(N^3)$) portion of the computation is shared equally among the slaves. The amount of computation done by the master is $O(N^2)$ and the amount of interprocessor communication is $O(N^2)$. Further, the potential calculation is amenable to parallel implementation [2], but because the particle pushing dominates the overall calculation, we will not concern ourselves with parallel processing the potential calculation.

The key to efficient parallel implementation of PIC on a master/slave configuration lies in dividing particles equally among the slaves irrespective of particle position in the region. This was not our first approach in attempting to parallel process PIC. Rather, our initial approachs considered dividing the region into subregions and having a processor assigned to particles in each of the subregions. Such an approach produces a number of complications. For example, at the end of each time step some particles will migrate to their neighboring subregion. Thus, there must be an "exchange" of particles between processors at each time step. This exchange will necessitate garbage collection within the particle list of a given processor and, should the particles eventually concentrate in a small region, a single processor will do most of the computation while the others sit idle. To rectify such a situation, the region must be resubdivided, particles reallocated, etc. The computational cost of such processes is significant.

A similar phenomenon seems to occur in the parallel solution of elliptic equations. Again, the natural approach is to subdivide the region and to assign a processor to a subregion. It is extremely difficult to do this in a fashion that will yield a net gain in computational efficiency [1]. The point is that efficient implementation involves techniques that are somewhat counter-intuitive.

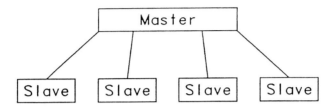

Fig. 2. Master/slave communication geometry for four processors.

PARALLEL PROCESSING PIC ON A RING CONFIGURATION

PIC can also be efficiently implemented on an MIMD machine with a ring control/communication organization. For purposes of discussion we assume a four-element ring with communication from left to right as indicated in Fig. 3. The key to success in this environment is again to divide particles equally among the processors but, in addition, have processors do a significant amount of redundant computation. Assuming that each processor has the total charge distribution at cell centers in its memory, the computational process is as follows:

Step 2. Each processor solves the potential equation.
Step 3. Each processor moves its particles.
Step 1A. Each processor integrates over its particles to obtain their contribution to the total charge distribution.
Step 1B. For $1 = 1, 2, 3, 4$: pass partial charge distribution to neighbor; add the one received to "accumulating charge distribution."

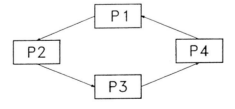

Fig. 3. A four-element ring configuration.

ESTIMATING PERFORMANCE OF THE MASTER/SLAVE IMPLEMENTATION

The key issue in parallel processing is speedup as a function of the number of processors used. We define speedup as

$$S_p = \frac{execution\ time\ using\ one\ processor}{execution\ time\ using\ p\ processors}$$

To estimate performance of the master/slave formulation, we use a model of parallel computation introduced by Ware [8]. We normalize the execution time using one processor to unity.

Let
  p = number of processors,
and
  α = percent of parallel processable work.

Assume at any instant that either all p processors are operating or only one processor is operating; then

$$S_p = \frac{1}{(1-\alpha) + \dfrac{\alpha}{p}}\ .$$

Also

$$\frac{dS_p}{d\alpha}\bigg|_{\alpha=1} = p^2 - p\ .$$

Figure 4 shows the Ware model of speedup as a function of α for a 4-processor, an 8-processor, and a 16-processor system, respectively. The quadratic behavior of the derivative is dramatic and results in low speedup for α less than 0.9. Consequently to achieve significant speedup, we must have highly parallel algorithms. Therein lies the challenge in research in parallel processing. In 1970 Minsky [6] conjectured that average speedup in parallel processing would go like $\log p$. Indeed, if only 60% or 70% of the total computation is implemented in parallel, then he will be correct. However, for the master/slave implementation of PIC, recall that we are parallel processing the $O(N^3)$ component of the calculation and sequentially processing the $O(N^2)$ component. Thus, we have the possibility of achieving relatively high efficiency, at least on systems with a few processors.

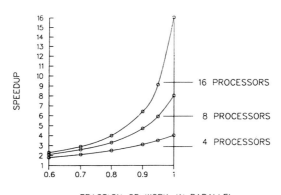

Fig. 4. Ware's model of speedup for 4, 8, and 16 processors.

Those who have experience with vector processors will note a striking similarity between the Ware curves and models of vector performance where the abscissa is the percent of total vectorizable computation. This is because the assumption of the Ware model implies a two-state machine, that is, in one state only one processor works and in the other state all p processors work. A vector processor can also be viewed as a two-state machine. In one state it is a relatively slow general purpose machine, and in the other state it is capable of high performance on vector operations. Thus, Fig. 4 also gives the performance of vector processors where p is the relative performance of the vector and scalar states.

To estimate S_p for PIC in the master/slave environment, let

$$T = \textit{Total Operation Count}$$

$$= \underset{\substack{\uparrow \\ \text{Poisson} \\ \text{Solve}}}{C_1 N^2 \log N} + \underset{\substack{\uparrow \\ \text{Mesh} \\ \text{Transmission}}}{C_{2p} N^2} + \underset{\substack{\uparrow \\ \text{Particle} \\ \text{"Push"}}}{C_3 K N^2}$$

and

$$\alpha = \frac{particle\ push\ operations}{T}$$

$$= \cfrac{1}{1 + \cfrac{C_1 \log N + C_2 p}{C_3 K}}$$

$$\cong 1 \text{ if } C_1 \log N + C_2 p \ll C_3 K ,$$

where K = average number of particles/cell.

If we further assume that each of the processors has performance comparable to the Cray-1, then

$$C_1 = 0.300 \ \mu s/\text{cell},$$

$$C_2 = 0.075 \ \mu s/\text{cell, and}$$

$$C_3 = 5.500 \ \mu s/\text{particle}.$$

Assume

$$N = K = 128;$$

then

p	α	Sp
4	0.99	~ 3.8
8	0.99	~ 7.5
16	0.99	~13.9

COMPUTATIONAL EXPERIMENTS

Because of the p^2 behavior in the slope of S_p as α approaches 1, the only way to be sure of how well a parallel implementation will work is to implement it and measure speedup experimentally. In other words, small perturbations in seemingly insignificant areas of the computation may, in fact, lead to large perturbations in overall performance. Thus, to confirm our analysis, we have implemented variants of the master/slave configuration of PIC on two parallel processing devices--the UNIVAC 1100/84 and the Denelcor Heterogeneous Element Processor (HEP).

The UNIVAC 1100/84 is a commercially available system whose typical use is to process four independent job streams. With the help of UNIVAC personnel, and a bit of ingenuity, Los Alamos personnel have devised ways to control all four processors in this machine and use them to process a single PIC model [5]. Speedup measurements as a function of p are given in Table I. These results compare favorably with our estimates and reflect the fact that indeed we have successfully parallel processed a large percentage of the total computation.

Table I. Speedup Measurements for a Master/Slave Implementation		
Equipment	p	Speedup
UNIVAC 1100/84	2	1.80
	3	2.43
	4	3.04
Denelcor HEP		6.0

Recently, a PIC model was implemented on HEP. HEP is designed to do task switching on each instruction. The architecture of a single processor is reminiscent of the CDC-6000 series Peripheral Processor System. There is an eight-slot barrel with a task assigned to each of the slots, and the processor examines the slots sequentially, executing a single instruction from eight concurrent processes. Most instructions in the machine require about eight cycles for execution. Thus, loosely speaking, a single processor is analogous to an eight-processor parallel system. Los Alamos personnel have implemented a PIC model on HEP, first as a single-process and then as a multiple-process calculation. The ratio of the associated execution time is given in Table I. Again reflecting the fact that a large percentage of the total computation is being done in parallel.

CONCLUSION

High-performance computer systems involving several vector processors that can operate in parallel have already been announced [3]. Realizing the highest levels of performance of a parallel system requires that a large percentage of the total computation be done in parallel. In the case of PIC models we were able to realize high parallelization, and thus good performance, by partitioning particles among processors. Consequently, parallel implementation of "off the shelf" PIC models is likely to be easier than their implementation on a vector processor.

ACKNOWLEDGMENTS

I am endebted to Ingrid Bucher, Paul Frederickson, Robert Hiromoto, and Jim Moore, all of the Los Alamos National Laboratory, for the experimental results discussed herein.

REFERENCES

[1] D. Boley "Vectorization of Some Block Relaxation Techniques, Some Numerical Experiments," *Proceedings of the 1978 LASL Workshop on Vector and Parallel Processors.* Los Alamos National Laboratory report LA-7491-C (1978).

[2] B. L. Buzbee, "A Fast Poisson Solver Amenable to Parallel Implementation." *IEEE Trans. on Computers,* Vol. C-22, No. 8 pp. 793-796 (August 1973).

[3] Datamation, "Seymour Leaves Cray," pp. 52-59 (January 1980).

[4] D. Forslund, "Large Scale Simulation Requirements for Inertial Fusion," presented at the conference on High Speed Computing, Gleneden Beach, Oregon, 1981.

[5] R. Hiromoto, "Results of Parallel Processing a Large Scientific Problem on a Commercially Available Multiple-Processor Computer System," Los Alamos National Laboratory report LA-UR-82-862 (1982).

[6] M. Minsky, "Form and Content in Computer Science," ACM Lecture, JACM 17, pp. 197-215, 1970.

[7] R. L. Morse, C. W. Nielson, "One-, Two-, and Three-Dimensional Numerical Simulation of Two Beam Plasmas," *Phys. Rev. Letters* 23, 1087 (1969).

[8] W. Ware, "The Ultimate Computer," *IEEE Spect,* pp. 89-91 (March, 1973).

[9] W. J. Worlton, "A Philosophy of Supercomputing," *Computerworld,* (October 1981).

MOLECULAR DYNAMICS ON CRAY, CYBER AND DAP

H.J.C. Berendsen, W.F. van Gunsteren and J.P.M. Postma
Laboratory of Physical Chemistry
University of Groningen
Nijenborgh 16
9747 AG GRONINGEN
The Netherlands

1. INTRODUCTION

A rapidly growing application of high-speed computation is the simulation of the statistical and dynamic behaviour of complex molecular systems (1). While the theoretical treatment of solids can benefit from simplification due to symmetry and gases are relatively simple because of the low dimensionality of intermolecular interactions, disordered condensed phases and complex molecular systems are inherently complicated. Such systems include liquids, even of simple molecules, liquid mixtures and solutions, polymers and biological macromolecules, and aggregates of even higher complexity. Typically the number of atoms to be treated is in the range of thousands or ten thousands and the number of interacting neighbours of each atom is of the order hundred. Detailed quantum-mechanical treatments of such systems are completely out of reach, whatever improvement in computer performance may be conceivable.

The purpose of simulations of molecular systems is to understand and predict the behaviour (structure and dynamics) of a complex system of interacting particles on the basis of basic interactions between the particles. The shape of these basic interactions can be either derived from ab-initio quantum mechanical calculations (requiring high-speed computation themselves) or from empirical or semi-empirical considerations. In most cases the approximation that the total potential energy can be written as a sum of pair interactions is valid, although it may be essential to employ effective pair potentials that describe the average pair interaction in the condensed phase rather than the interaction between isolated particles.

If we are interested in properties of molecular systems in their electronic ground state, and temperatures are not very low, the application of classical mechanics is generally sufficient. In some cases, when light atoms as hydrogen are involved or when high vibrational frequencies occur, quantum corrections will be required. In their simplest form, quantum corrections can be made a posteriori on the computed properties, or else they may be applied in the form of a modification of the potential energy functions; no severe complications are involved in that case.

NATO ASI Series, Vol. F7
High-Speed Computation. Edited by J. S. Kowalik
© Springer-Verlag Berlin Heidelberg 1984

On the other hand, when dynamical trajectories have to be based on quantum-mechanical principles, the simulations rapidly become prohibitively difficult.

Two basic methods of simulation are common practice (2): monte carlo (MC) and molecular dynamics (MD). In MC a representative statistical ensemble of configurations of the molecular system is generated. A new configuration is generated by a random move of one or more particles followed by acceptance or rejection based on the energy change in the system. Typically, for a system of several hundred particles, a million single-particle moves are required for a sufficiently accurate statistical ensemble. Only static equilibrium properties can be derived by this method. In MD a dynamic trajectory of the system is generated by solving Newton's equation of motion, where the forces are spatial derivatives of the potential energy function. While the computational effort of MD is comparable with or only slightly larger than MC, the generated trajectories give dynamic information in addition to the static information obtainable by MC. Therefore in most cases MD will be preferred and we will now concentrate on the latter method.

2. MOLECULAR DYNAMICS OF MOLECULAR SYSTEMS

Consider the simulation of liquid water, H_2O, as a simple example of MD. The simplest possible and still fairly accurate interaction model (3) consists of three point charges on the positions of both hydrogen atoms (+q) and oxygen atom (-2q). In addition to Coulomb interactions between charges of molecular pairs, oxygen atoms interact with a Lennard-Jones potential of the form $-(A/r)^6 + (B/r)^{12}$. Thus any interacting pair of molecules interacts through 9 charge pairs and one Lennard-Jones pair. The long-range character of coulombic interaction requires that pairs within a distance of 0.8 to 0.9 nm are taken into account, which amounts to roughly 100 pair interactions per molecule. To avoid boundary effects, the molecules are placed in a cubic box, which is repeated in a cubic lattice. The size of the box must exceed twice the interaction radius to avoid artefacts as a result of the artificial periodic molecules in the simulation, although for some properties much larger systems are required. Thus, for a system size of 200 particles, there are 20,000 molecular pairs of which 10,000 are within interactive range. Per dynamic step the forces on each atom are calculated, which requires the computation of 300,000 force components. Typically, Newton's equations are solved in steps of 10^{-15}s, while evaluation of physical properties of the ensemble requires a trajectory simulated over 10^{-11}s. Thus one simulation requires 10^4 steps and the evaluation of 3×10^9 force components. The time consuming part of the computation is the force evaluation FORCE; updating coordinates and velocities per step is trivial even if complicated algorithms are used.

When the molecular model is rigid, the molecule is constrained to keep its geometry constant during the simulation (4). Using cartesian coordinates, this is accomplished by a special coordinate resetting procedure, called SHAKE (5) that ensures that constraints are conserved as required by the equations of motion. The CP time required for SHAKE is small compared with FORCE. In the next section tests of the performance of several computers including CRAY-1, CYBER 205 and ICL-DAP on water MD are reported.

The simulation of water, as described above, requires about 2 s per step or about 5 hours on a conventional high speed computer (CDC 7600), and about $\frac{1}{2}$ hour on a supercomputer. This is a reasonable effort, allowing effective research on liquids of small molecules and simple solutions. Matters are quite different when more complicated molecular systems are being studied, such as polymers and proteins or nucleic acids in an aqueous environment. In order to simulate a small protein in aqueous solution, several thousand water molecules are required to surround a macromolecule consisting of some thousand atoms of many different types. It is clear that the evaluation of forces is much more complex, because each different atom pair requires separate parameters, while bond angles and dihedral angles (rotation around bonds) correspond to completely different terms in the potential energy. But more serious is the fact that motions of sections of macromolecules are much slower than motions in liquid water, while fast components exist as well. The time range of interest now extends into the nanosecond region requiring 10^5 dynamic steps. With a CP time per step close to a minute (CDC 7600), the available computer time will be the limiting factor. As is described in the next section, vectorization of complex protein MD programs is not as effective as in the simpler water case and even on supercomputers the required CP time per simulation runs into tens of hours.

It is not difficult to envisage molecular systems of high biological or chemical interest that will require many orders of magnitude more CP time if the straightforward "brute force" MD methods are used. Table 1 gives some modest examples.

Many processes in chemistry (such as reactions) involve crossing of an energy barrier: a physically infrequent event for which brute force simulations would be very inefficient. In other cases the number of degrees of freedom involved in the system is so enormous that brute force simulation is prohibitive. The simulation of such processes requires different techniques that are now being developed and tested for practical application. The most promising development is the neglect of the detailed behaviour of less important degrees of freedom, approximating the forces they would exert on the relevant degrees of freedom by stochastic forces (13). Potentials are modified to potentials of mean force with respect to the less important degrees of freedom. These stochastic dynamics (SD) methods can also be used to simulate barrier-crossing events (14). The progress in such new methods is rapid and promises perspective for extensive future application of simulation methods in chemical and biological problems.

TABLE 1 Computer effort in dynamic simulations

year	ref	system (example)	degrees of freedom	number of steps	CP hours on supercomputer *) (approx.)
1960	6	monoatomic liquids (liquid argon)	750	5000	0.05
1971	7	molecular liquids (water, $C\,Cl_4$)	2500	10^4	1
1974	8	molten salts ($K\,Cl$)	750	5.10^3	1
1975	9	small polymers (decane)	1000	10^4	1
1978	10	protein in vacuum (BPTI)	1500	2.10^4	4
1980	11	membranes (2 x 64 decane)	4000	10^4	4
1982	12	protein in water (BPTI)	12000	2.10^4	30
future		surfaces, nucleic acids, large polymers, micelles, liquid crystals, organic systems	10^4	10^6 10^7	10^3 10^4
		reactions	10^4-10^5	10^9-10^{12}	10^7-10^8
		macromolecular complexes	10^5	10^{10}	10^8
		protein folding	10^4	10^{12}	10^9

*) CRAY or CYBER 205, assuming "brute force" dynamics.

429

3. SUPERCOMPUTERS FOR MOLECULAR DYNAMICS

In principle algorithms for MD can be adapted for use on vector or matrix processors, but often the programs need to be redesigned from the start if best use of the vectorcapabilities is to be made. We have performed tests on various machines using a program for water dynamics with the following user-oriented guiding principles:

a. Redesign to permit vectorizability (or "matrizability" for the DAP) is allowed

b. Programs are to be written in Fortran and not in assembler code

c. Machine-dependent Fortran-callable routines are allowed in CP-intensive routines. These principles are a compromise between machine-independent design and maximal attainable speed, while retaining some degree of portability.

It turns out that vectorizability can be obtained for both CRAY and CYBER 205 by the same general principles:

a. avoid any decisions within inner loops,

b. if possible, organise data structures such that the operands of vector operations are contiguously stored,

c. avoid indexed array operations.

Actually, the second requirement can be relaxed for the CRAY if equal spacing of operands is possible. For the CYBER 205, the possibility of logical vector operations using bitvectors also relaxes the requirement of contiguous storage. The specific use of these machine-dependent features is less desirable where it influences the program structure on a high organisational level, because portability and the possibilities for program exchange between scientists using different machines is then significantly reduced. The use of machine dependent routines at a low organisational level is not so objectionable, because adaptation for a different machine is then more transparent and much easier to implement. For the scientist-user it would be desirable if the architecture of future vector machines and internationally agreed vector-extensions to Fortran (or other high-level languages) would concurrently develop along the same lines, limiting machine dependent peculiarities to the low organisational level of coding.

For the ICL-DAP implications of machine architecture for programming are entirely different. CRAY or CYBER-vectorisable programs may not be suitable for the DAP at all. The principal reasons are the matrix-oriented SIMD architecture of the DAP, the single bit structure of the processing elements (e.g. allowing very effective logical masking operations, but very ineffective high-accuracy arithmetic) and the availability of shift operations in two dimensions. Portability, even partially on the high organisational level only, of efficient DAP-oriented programs to vector-oriented machines, is an illusion.

At the high organisational level of a MD program, the most important choice is the method of selecting interacting neighbours. There are three types of methods:

a. all possible pairs are tested for a distance criterion at every step and forces calculated if the criterion is satisfied.

b. all possible pairs are tested for a distance criterion and a neighbour list is constructed every so many steps; at every step forces are calculated on the basis of the neighbour list,

c. neighbours are found every step on the basis of grid techniques: the coordinates of a particle determine directly the grid cell in which the particle occurs, while particles within one cell are connected by a linked list.

Which method is to be preferred depends on the size of the simulated system as well as on the characteristics of the computer. We shall return to this in Section 6.

4. TESTS ON CYBER 205, CRAY 1 AND CONVENTIONAL COMPUTERS

Our original MD water program, being designed for sequential machines, was of the type where all pairs were tested at every step. The number of water molecules is 216, the number of potential neighbours 23220 and the number of relevant neighbours about 10000. The decision whether a pair shall be considered for force computation is made in the inner loop over all pairs and for this reason the program can not vectorize. Therefore the program was modified to employ a neighbour list. The process of constructing the neighbour list is not easily vectorisable, but it is a simple procedure that has to be carried out only once in about 10 steps. Using the neighbour list directly in the vector operations of force calculation implies the undesirable use of indexed arrays. Therefore the data (coordinates) of relevant pairs were simply copied such that arbitrarily long vectors for force calculations were contiguously stored. The resulting force calculation now easily vectorizes on both CRAY or CYBER 205, but at the expense of some overhead for constructing the neighbour list and copying the data.

When testing the programs on various machines the first remarkable observation was that the vectorizable version was slightly faster on the sequential CYBER 170 machine, despite the extra memory mapping, than the sequential version. This is due to the size of the program stack in the Cyber 170, making do-loops less efficient if the number of decisionless operations is small.

Table 2 gives CP timings for various machines for the nonvectorisable routine NBRL that constructs the neighbour list, the reasonably vectorisable FORCE routine, the well-vectorisable SHAKE routine and the total DYNAMIC STEP. In the column "overhead" all activities in the dynamic step except the force calculation and SHAKE

TABLE 2   CP-Times of Water Dynamics Program (ms)

	NBRL	FORCE	+ SHAKE	+ Overhead (% of FORCE)	= DYNAMIC STEP
CYBER 205, Minneapolis*	116	148	7.2	39%	213
CYBER 203, Minneapolis	117	416	30	17%	515
CRAY 1, Daresbury	64	205	12.5	11%	240
CDC 7600, London	242	1681	160	2.9%	1890
CYBER 170/760, Groningen	304	2330	180	5.2%	2630
CYBER 170/750, Amsterdam	415	3300	250	4.5%	3700
AMDAHL V7, Orsay	525	4522	349	4.4%	5069
AMDAHL V7B, Leiden	732	5900	417	4.5%	6580
IBM 370/168, Orsay	792	6540	423	4.5%	7256
IBM 370/158, Nijmegen	4770	30700	2380	8.9%	35800

* Two-pipe machine, 64 bit word length
  All machines: 60 or 64 bit precision
  CYBERS: Fortran IV, Opt = 2 compiler
  IBM, AMDAHL: FORTX AUTODOUBLE
  Vector length used: 256

TABLE 3   Relative CP Times

	NBRL	SHAKE	DYN.STEP
CYBER 205	2.6	25	12
CYBER 203	2.6	6	5
CRAY 1	4.7	14	11
CDC 7600	1.3	1.1	1.4
CYBER 170/760	1	1	1
CYBER 170/750	0.73	0.72	0.71
AMDAHL V7	0.58	0.52	0.52
AMDAHL V7B	0.42	0.43	0.40
IBM 370/168	0.38	0.43	0.36
IBM 370/158	0.064	0.076	0.073

NBRL is not vectorisable, SHAKE is well-vectorisable,
DYN.STEP is overall

are given as a percentage of FORCE. It should be noted that both for CYBER 205
and CRAY special Fortran callable vector routines were incorporated.

For the sake of clarity, relative timings are given in Table 3 for a typical
non-vectorisable routine, a typical vectorisable one, and the overall performance.

The results of those tests show the known fact that the CRAY has a faster scalar
processor than the CYBER 205 (which is identical in scalar processing to the
CYBER 203). On the other hand, for well-vectorisable routines using long vectors,
the CYBER 205 is clearly faster than the CRAY. This applies for the 64 bit word
length; if half-precision words (32 bit) can be used, the CYBER will be still faster
by a factor of two. For the overall performance on the water MD program, the two
supercomputers are comparable; they are about 10x faster than a CYBER 170/760
or 30x faster than an IBM 370/168. It is clear that the overhead for
non-vectorisable parts in the programs is larger for vector machines than for
sequential machines, but for the CYBER this effect is much more severe than for
the CRAY.

The influence of vector length was tested by varying the number of neighbour
pairs of which the coordinates were copied into contiguous arrays, between 64 and
1024. For the CRAY 1 a length of 64 is already optimal and longer vectors give no
further improvement. On the CYBER 205, however, vector length is far more
critical and a factor of almost 2 can be gained in the vectorisable parts when
vectors are increased from 64 to 1024.

Hockney (15) has introduced the notion of half-performance length $n_{\frac{1}{2}}$ as the
vector length at which the performance is degraded to 50% of the infinite length
vector performance. Using diadic operations written in Fortran, the CYBER 205
appears to have a half-performance length of about 100. For larger, not completely
vectorisable programs, the half-performance length is reduced. Figure 1 shows the
CP times for the DYNAMIC STEP and for FORCE as a function of the inverse
vector length. The measured points follow the equation

$$t_n = t_\infty (1 + n_{\frac{1}{2}}/n)$$

$t_{\frac{1}{2}}$ is about 50 for FORCE and only 36 for the overall dynamic step.

The conclusion is that the more effort is put into vectorisation, the more critical
the non-vectorisable overhead becomes and the more important it is to work with
long vectors. The latter is much more important for the CYBER 205 than for the
CRAY.

CP TIME (ms)

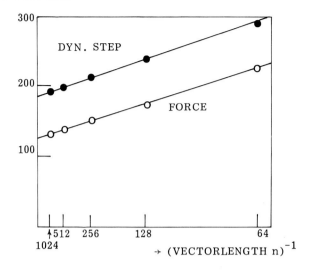

Fig. 1. CYBER 205 CP times using various vector lengths.

5. TESTS ON THE ICL-DAP

The architecture of the ICL-DAP calls for a completely different handling of neighbour pairs than the neighbour list method used for the CRAY and CYBER 205. The pair calculations should be carried out simultaneously by as many processors as possible. With the help of Dr. S. MacQueen of ICL the following method was chosen to produce the neighbour list and compute the forces.

First envisage the DAP as a large machine, not limited to 64 x 64 processors. For the actual computation a large two-dimensional array can be broken up into 64 x 64 blocks. The coordinates for all 216 particles are stored in the first column of 216 length and subsequently "broadcast" over 216 rows (see fig. 2). The memory now contains 216 copies of all coordinates. The same procedure is then followed with rows and columns interchanged. Thus the coordinates of all pairs (i,j) are stored in the array location (i,j). Next a logical mask is produced that indicates which pairs are within the cut-off range. This mask of 216 x 216 (requiring 16 blocks of the 64 x 64 DAP) is in fact the neighbour list. Force calculation is done under control of this logical mask. The efficiency is increased by first compressing the relevant pairs (using the logical mask) into fewer blocks and expanding the results again. The timings for the production of the neighbour list and for the calculation of the forces are compared with CYBER 205 and CRAY in Table 4.

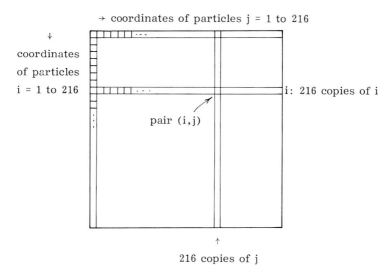

coordinates of particles j = 1 to 216

↓ coordinates of particles i = 1 to 216

pair (i,j)

i: 216 copies of i

216 copies of j

Fig. 2.   Construction of neighbour list in DAP

TABLE 4   DAP timings (ms)

CP time (ms)	NBRL	Force
DAP	26	595 (5)*
		682 (6)*
CYBER 205	116	148
CRAY	64	205

*The member in parentheses is the number of blocks into which the neighbour pairs are compressed. This is not always the same.

The conclusion is that the neighbour list construction is very efficient on the DAP, in contrast to the vector computers. The computation of the forces is roughly 3x slower on the DAP than on CYBER or CRAY. We note that the DAP was used in 32 bit floating point arithmetic. In 64 bit the DAP would be much slower, while optimal matching of arithmetic type and accuracy (which was not attempted) could increase the efficiency even further.

It is clear that DAP timings cannot easily be compared to CYBER 205 or CRAY and comparisons will be very dependent on the problem at hand and the effort put into programming. For the programmer who is used to sequential programming and new to vector and matrix architecture, the DAP requires an initial effort of at least an order of magnitude more than the CRAY or CYBER. It also seems that the DAP is a very cost-effective machine for certain classes of problems, but unsuitable for other classes of problems that cannot be formulated in terms of massive identical parallel processing of different data.

6. MD OF BIOLOGICAL MACROMOLECULES

Molecular Dynamics simulations of large complex macromolecules such as proteins and nucleic acids differ from simulations of simple liquids in the complexity of the potential energy functions. The force field now consists of different terms describing covalent bond interactions, bond-angle interactions, torsional angle contributions and non-bonded (Van der Waals and Coulomb) interactions. The latter interactions are different for all pairs of different types of atoms and the number of different parameters used may amount to several hundred. This requires extensive table look-up operations and specific exclusions of certain types of pairs. Both operations are likely to spoil easy vectorisability of the programs.

We made tests for several large proteins and DNA molecular complexes on a CRAY-1 computer, comparing CP time with the Cyber 170/760 in Groningen (16). As the size of the simulated systems increases, the neighbour list method for selecting interacting non-bonded atom pairs requires increasing amounts of memory. In the Cyber 170/760 with its limited storage, the neighbour list method can only be used for small systems of a few thousand degrees of freedom. Larger systems can be handled adequately by grid methods, but these methods we find to be less effective (by a factor of 1.5) than neighbour list methods. Hence comparing a 1 M word CRAY with the Cyber 170/760 is not straightforward in those cases where the CRAY allows the use of a more effective neighbour search technique.

Vectorisability can not be carried out to the same extent as in the case of the water program. The non-vectorized sequential program was twice as fast on the CRAY than on the Cyber 760; simple general-purpose vectorisation did not yield more than another factor of two. Thus a gain of only 4x was obtained, compared to 10x for a simple molecular liquid. Recent experience, however, has shown that by partly programming in Cray Assembler Language and meticulous vectorisation, another factor of 3 can be gained (16).

In Table 5 a few preliminary results are given for three representative systems.

In two of these the neighbour list method could not be used on the Cyber 760 and CRAY neighbour list results can only be compared with grid techniques used on the Cyber 760.

TABLE 5 Biological macromolecules

Case[a]	degrees of freedom	number in neighbour list	time per step (s)[b]	
			neighbour list [c]	grid method [d]
A	1737	24000	0.63 (2.94)	2.20 (4.70)
B	6450	97000	3.89 (−)	8.78 (23.4)
C	10314	226000	11.8 (−)	20.1 (41.6)

[a] A: protein molecule BPTI (basic pancreatic trypsin inhibitor) in vacuum, 567 atoms + 4 internal water molecules

B: DNA-protein complex (DNA-Cro)

C: 4 protein molecules (BPTI) + 390 water molecules in crystal (periodic)

[b] CRAY-1 times (Cyber 760 times)

[c] CRAY times after vectorisation of main routines.

[d] CRAY routines for grid method were not optimized.

In case A and B isolated molecules are considered, while in case C a periodic system was simulated. The CRAY routines were most optimized for the isolated molecules using a neighbour list. In those cases a factor of 6 to 7 was obtained compared to the Cyber 760 using the grid method. In the periodic system (case C), the optimization was not carried out to the same extent and another 30% gain may be expected. The CRAY time of 11.8 s in case C includes 7.9 s of neighbourlist construction. Since the neighbour list is only made once in, say, 10 steps, the effective time per step is about 4.7 s, which is better than 8x faster than the Cyber 760 time using the grid method.

In conclusion we can say that for complex molecules a factor of 4 can be easily obtained, but with more effort in vectorization and making use of the best neighbour search method, a factor of 14 can be reached.

7. FUTURE OF M.D.

Molecular dynamics of complex molecules is just in its initial stage of development. Even with present-day supercomputers the effort needed to simulate a biologically relevant system over a time in which the processes of interest occur runs into several hundred hours of CP time for a single experiment. Future development of computer power into the 10 Gflop range will make relevant applications possible with methods presently available. Future developments of the methods will undoubtedly provide improvements by another two or three orders of magnitude in the time scale of simulated processes.

Applications of medical and industrial pharmaceutical interest that are closest to realisation are in the field of drug and enzyme design. The detailed molecular action of substrates and inhibitors on enzymes can be simulated and used to design specific drugs in those cases where the structure of the receptor site is known. The effects of modifications of the structure of enzymes can be simulated; such modifications can be inserted by genetic engineering techniques on an industrial scale. The use of molecular dynamics simulations to aid these developments may be quite realistic when the technology of high-speed computation combined with methodological developments will give us just the few orders of magnitude improvement that are needed for full scale applications.

ACKNOWLEDGEMENTS

The authors are grateful to Drs. P. van der Ploeg, J.P. Hollenberg (Groningen), F. Colonna, D. Perahia (Orsay), Grabowsky (CDC), S. MacQueen (ICL), Haneef, D. Fincham (London) and many collaborators of various computer centers for their help in vectorizing and running programs. Financial aid was obtained from the Netherlands Organisation for Pure Research (ZWO), the Dutch Computerboard (CRIVA), the "Werkgroep Supercomputers" of the Netherlands Ministery of Education and Science and the Centre Européen de Calcul Atomique et Moléculaire (CECAM). We thank Dr. C. Moser of CECAM for his continued interest and support.

REFERENCES

1. W.F. van Gunsteren and H.J.C. Berendsen, Trans. Biochem. Soc., 600th Meeting, Oxford 10 (1982) 301

2. B.J. Berne, Statistical Mechanics, part B: Time dependent processes. Plenum Press, New York, 1977

438

3. H.J.C. Berendsen, J.P.M. Postma, W.F. van Gunsteren and J. Hermans, in "Intermolecular Forces", ed. B. Pullman, p 331, Reidel Publ. Cy. Dordrecht 1981

4. H.J.C. Berendsen and W.F. van Gunsteren, in Proc. NATO Advanced Study Institute on Superionic Conductors, Odense 1980, Plenum Press, N.Y. 1983

5. J.P. Ryckaert, G. Ciccotti and H.J.C. Berendsen, J. Comput. Phys. 23 (1977) 327

6. A. Rahman, Phys. Rev. 136A (1964) 405

7. A. Rahman and F.J. Stillinger, J. Chem. Phys. 55 (1971) 3336

8. M.J.L. Sangster and M. Dixon, Adv. Phys. 25 (1976) 247

9. J.P. Ryckaert and A. Bellemans, Chem. Phys. Lett. 30 (1975) 123

10. J.A. McCammon, B.R. Gelin and M. Karplus, Nature (London) 267 (1977) 585

11. P. van der Ploeg and H.J.C. Berendsen, J. Chem. Phys. 76 (1982) 3271; Mol. Phys. 49 (1983) 233

12. W.F. van Gunsteren, H.J.C. Berendsen, J. Hermans, W.G.J. Hol and J.P.M. Postma, Proc. Natl. Acad. Sci. (USA) 80 (1983) 4315

13. W.F. van Gunsteren and H.J.C. Berendsen, Mol. Phys. 45 (1982) 637

14. W.F. van Gunsteren, H.J.C. Berendsen and J.A.C. Rullmann, Mol. Phys. 44 (1981) 69

15. R.W. Hockney, Computer Phys. Comm. 26 (1982) 285

16. W.F. van Gunsteren, H.J.C. Berendsen, F. Colonna, J.P. Hollenberg, D. Lellouch and D. Perahia, to be published

Names and Address of Participants.

T. Axelrod
Livermore National Laboratory
P. O. Box 808
Livermore, California 94550 USA

F. R. Bailey
NASA Ames Research Center
Moffett Field, California 94035 USA

H. J. C. Berendsen
Laboratory of Physical Chemistry
Nijenborgh 16
University of Groningen
9747 AG Groningen, NETHERLANDS

H. Beyer
Kernforschungsanlage, Postfach 1913
D-5170 Julich
FEDERAL REPUBLIC OF GERMANY

T. Bloch
Direction des Laboratories
Ecole Polytechique
91128 Pailaiseau Cedex, FRANCE

B. L. Buzbee
Los Alamos National Laboratory
P. O. Box 1663
Los Alamos, New Mexico 87545 USA

S. Chen
CRAY Research Company
Chippewa Falls, Wisconsin 54729 USA

I. S. Duff
AERE Harwell
Oxfordshire, OX11 ORA ENGLAND

H. Ehlich
University of Bochum
Bochum, FEDERAL REPUBLIC OF GERMANY

D. W. Fox
Department of the Air Force
AFSC
Bolling AFB, DC 20332 USA

D. D. Gajski
Department of Computer Science
University of Illinois
1304 West Springfield Avenue
Urbana, Illinois 61801-2987 USA

Wolfgang Gentzsch
DFVLR.AVA
Bunenstrasse 10
3400 Gottingen
FEDERAL REPUBLIC OF GERMANY

H. Gietl
DFG, University of Munchen
Munchen
FEDERAL REPUBLIC OF GERMANY

Joe F. Gloudeman
MacNeal-Schwendler Corporation
815 West Colorado Boulevard
Los Angeles, California 90041 USA

J.-Fr. Hake
Kernfoschungsanlage, Postfach 1913
D-5170 Julich
FEDERAL REPUBLIC OF GERMANY

W. Handler
Informatik, Martenstrasse 3
University of Erlangen
8520 Erlangen
FEDERAL REPUBLIC OF GERMANY

Ulrich Herzog
Informatik, Martenstrasse 3
University of Erlangen
8520 Erlangen
FEDERAL REPUBLIC OF GERMANY

F. Hertweck
MPI
Garching
FEDERAL REPUBLIC OF GERMANY

R. W. Hockney
Department of Computer Science
University of Reading
Whiteknights Park
Reading RG6 2AX ENGLAND

F. Hossfeld
Kernforschungsanlage
Postfach 1913
D-5170 Julich
FEDERAL REPUBLIC OF GERMANY

440

Names and Address of Participants

D. A. H. Jacobs
Central Electricity
Leatherhead, ENGLAND

C. R. Jesshope
Department of Electronics
University of Southampton
Southampton SO9 5NH ENGLAND

G. R. Joubert
Nederlandse Philipsbedrijven B.V.
ISA-ISC-TIS/CARD, Building SAQ2
5600 MD Eindhoven NETHERLANDS

Mike J. Kascic
Control Data Corporation
4105 North Lexington Avenue
Arden Hills, Minnesota 55112 USA

Janusz S. Kowalik
Boeing Computer Services, ATAD
P. O. Box 24346
Seattle, Washington 98124 USA

B. Krahl-Urban
Kernforschungsanlage, Postfach 1913
D-5170 Julich
FEDERAL REPUBLIC OF GERMANY

J. Lenfant
IRISA
Campus de Beaulieu
35042 Rennes Cedex, FRANCE

A. Lichnewsky
Universite de Paris-Sud Et Centre
National de la Recherche Scientifique
Laboratoire D'Analyze Numerique
Batiment 425
91405 Orsay Cedex, FRANCE

Freerk Lootsma
Department of Mathematics
Delft University of Technology
2628 Delft, Julianalaan 132
NETHERLANDS

G. A. Michael
Livermore National Laboratory
P. O. Box 808
Livermore, California 94550 USA

H. Mierendorff
GMD
Bonn, FEDERAL REPUBLIC OF GERMANY

K. Miura
Project Manager, Supercomputer Planning
Mainframe Division
Fujitsu Ltd.
1015 Kamikodanaka Nakahara-ku
Kawasaki 211 JAPAN

D. W. Mizell
Department of the Navy, ONR
Western Regional Office
1030 East Green Street
Pasadena, California 91106 USA

J. J. Modi
DAP Support Unit, Computing Center
Queen Mary College
University of London
Mile End Road
London E1 4NS ENGLAND

Tohru Moto-oka
Department of Electrical Engineering
University of Tokyo
7-3-1 Hongo, Bunkyo-ku
Tokyo 113 JAPAN

Kenneth W. Neves
Boeing Company
ETA Division, M.S. 9C-01
565 Andover Park West
Tukwila, Washington 98188 USA

W. Oed
Kernforschungsanlage, Postfach 1913
D-5170 Julich
FEDERAL REPUBLIC OF GERMANY

Names and Address of Participants

Dennis Parkinson
DAP Support Unit, Computer Center
Queen Mary College
University of London
Mile End Road
London E1 4NS ENGLAND

S. F. Reddaway
International Computers Ltd.
Cavendish Road
Stevenage
Herts. SG1 2DY ENGLAND

K. D. Reinartz
Martenstrasse 3
University of Erlangen
8520 Erlangen
FEDERAL REPUBLIC OF GERMANY

Garry H. Rodrigue
Livermore National Laboratory
P. O. Box 808
Livermore, California 94550 USA

W. Ronsch
University of Braunschweig
Braunschweig
FEDERAL REPUBLIC OF GERMANY

Ahmed Sameh
Department of Computer Science
University of Illinois at Urbana
1304 West Springfield Avenue
Urbana, Illinois 61801-2987 USA

W. Schonauer
University of Karlsruhe
Karlsruhe
FEDERAL REPUBLIC OF GERMANY

O. Skovgaard
Laboratory of Applied
Mathematical Physics
The Technical University of Denmark
DK-2800 Lyngby DENMARK

Burton Smith
Denelcor, Inc.
P. O. Box 31500
Aurora, Colorado 80041 USA

G. M. Sokol
Chief, Communication Engineering and
Computer Science Branch
Department of the Army
U.S. Army Research, Development and
Standardization, Group (UK), Box 65
FPO, New York 09615 USA

Clive Temperton
UK Meteorological Office,
London Road, Bracknell
Berkshire RG12 2SZ ENGLAND

Stanislaw Ulam
1122 Old Santa Fe Trail
Santa Fe, New Mexico 87501 USA

Robert G. Voigt
Institute for Computer Applications in
in Science and Engineering
NASA Langley Research Center
Hampton, Virginia 23665 USA

Hugh F. Walsh
IBM Corporation
Dept. B79, Building 915
P. O. Box 390
Poughkeepsie, New York 12603 USA

P. Weidner
Kernforschungsanlage
D-5170 Julich, Postfach 1913
FEDERAL REPUBLIC OF GERMANY

Kenneth Wilson
Department of Physics
Cornell University
Ithaca, New York 14853 USA

NATO ASI Series

Series F: Computer and Systems Sciences

Springer-Verlag
Berlin
Heidelberg
New York
Tokyo

No. 1

Issues in Acoustic Signal – Image Processing and Recognition

Editor: **C.H.Chen**
Published in cooperation with NATO Scientific Affairs Division
1983. VIII, 333 pages. ISBN 3-540-12192-7

Contents: Overview. – Pattern Recognition Processing. – Artificial Intelligence Approach. – Issues in Array Processing and Target Motion Analysis. – Underwater Channel Characterization. – Issues in Seismic Signal Processing. – Image Processing. – Report of Discussion Session on Unresolved Issues and Future Directions. – List of Participants.

This volume of the NATO ASI series is primarily concerned with underwater acoustic signal processing and seismic signal analysis, with a major effort made to link these topics with pattern recognition, image processing and artificial intelligence. The approach of artificial intelligence to acoustic signal analysis is completely new, as is the pattern recognition method to target motion analysis.

No. 2

Image Sequence Processing and Dynamic Scene Analysis

Editor:**T.S.Huang**
Published in cooperation with NATO Scientific Affairs Division
1983. IX, 749 pages. ISBN 3-540-11997-3

Contents: Overview. – Image Sequence Coding. – Scene Analysis and Industrial Applications. – Biomedical Applications.– Subject Index.

This volume contains the proceedings of a NATO Advanced Study Institute held 21 June – 2 July 1982 in Braunlage/Harz, Federal Republic of Germany, which was devoted to the rapidly emerging field of analyzing time-varying scenes and imagery. Twelve invited papers and twenty-six contributory papers cover a wide spectrum of topics which fall into three overlapping categories: displacement and motion estimation; pattern recognition and artificial intelligence techniques in dynamic scene analysis; and applications to diverse problems, including television bandwidth compression, target tracking, cloud pattern analysis, cell motion analysis and description, and analysis of heart wall motion for medical diagnosis. About half of the invited papers are tutorial overviews, while the rest – along with the contributory papers – describe the most recent progress in research. Together, they represent an invaluable reference tool for scientists and engineers working in time-varying imagery analysis and related areas, and perhaps the best single source of information for researchers just starting in the field.

NATO ASI Series

Series F: Computer and Systems Sciences

Springer-Verlag
Berlin
Heidelberg
New York
Tokyo